Rules without Rights

Transformations in Governance

Transformations in Governance is a major new academic book series from Oxford University Press. It is designed to accommodate the impressive growth of research in comparative politics, international relations, public policy, federalism, and environmental and urban studies concerned with the dispersion of authority from central states to supranational institutions, subnational governments, and public–private networks. It brings together work that advances our understanding of the organization, causes, and consequences of multilevel and complex governance. The series is selective, containing annually a small number of books of exceptionally high quality by leading and emerging scholars.

The series is edited by Liesbet Hooghe and Gary Marks of the University of North Carolina, Chapel Hill, and Walter Mattli of the University of Oxford.

Rules without Rights

Land, Labor, and Private Authority
in the Global Economy

Tim Bartley

OXFORD
UNIVERSITY PRESS

OXFORD
UNIVERSITY PRESS

Great Clarendon Street, Oxford, OX2 6DP,
United Kingdom

Oxford University Press is a department of the University of Oxford.
It furthers the University's objective of excellence in research, scholarship,
and education by publishing worldwide. Oxford is a registered trade mark of
Oxford University Press in the UK and in certain other countries

First Edition published in 2018

Impression: 1

Published in the United States of America by Oxford University Press
198 Madison Avenue, New York, NY 10016, United States of America

British Library Cataloguing in Publication Data

Data available

Library of Congress Control Number: 2017954180

ISBN 978-0-19-879433-2

Printed and bound by
CPI Group (UK) Ltd, Croydon, CR0 4YY

Acknowledgments

It took a tremendous amount of help from scholars, practitioners, colleagues, and friends to produce this study of land and labor in Indonesia and China. A number of scholars helped me build the contacts necessary to begin the research. These include: Ethan Michelson, Teri Caraway, Errol Meidinger, Pam Jagger, Ben Cashore, Ho-fung Hung, Ching Kwan Lee, Eli Friedman, Pun Ngai, David Sonnenfeld, Michael Stone, Kathleen Buckingham, and many others who have provided tips along the way.

In the field, a handful of people were especially important in helping me get my bearings and further build my contacts. Peter Sprang generously shared his insights, contacts, and invitations, as well as cold beers in Jakarta and Bali. Hari Nugroho graciously introduced me to both Indonesian sociology and several key individuals. Jeff Ballinger provided useful documents and contacts—and I was happy to return the favor by delivering a motorcycle lock to a friend of his in Jakarta. Ellen Friedman was helping to organize a joint labor research center in Guangzhou (with Katie Quan and He Gaochao) when I arrived; her warm welcome and the center's initial workshop proved extremely helpful. At Sun Yat-sen University, Wang Jin was an extraordinarily warm office neighbor who also shared stories over meals, introduced me to the area, and helped me secure the much-needed business cards. In Beijing, Yi Han welcomed me on several occasions and helped arrange access to valuable data on factories in Guangdong province.

I am especially indebted to the practitioners I interviewed. Many went out of their way to have long conversations, direct me to useful reports, and connect me with others. They cannot be named here, but they have been indispensable to this project. I suspect that some will disagree with the message of the book while others will appreciate it, but I hope that they will at least feel that I have gotten the specifics right and understood the practical challenges of their work.

My main research assistant in China, Wang Zhuo, intrepidly arranged and interpreted interviews, translated documents, and interviewed garment workers with help from Shu Binbin. In Indonesia, Endang Rokhani followed up on the details of several cases, while also sharing insights from her own work. I had the pleasure of collaborating with Niklas Egels-Zandén on some of the

Acknowledgments

research in Indonesia, and his students later conducted supplemental interviews that fleshed out our understanding of particular cases. James Davis at
the American Center for International Labor Solidarity in Jakarta facilitated
access to their survey data, though this does not necessarily imply an endorsement of my analyses or conclusions. I also owe a huge debt of gratitude to
Doug Kincaid, Siqi Han, James Conran, Enying Zheng, and Wenyuan Jin for
their valuable work on data coding, management, and/or analysis. Jaime
Kucinskas and Joe DiGrazia also provided helpful research assistance early in
the project.

The Department of Sociology at Sun Yat-sen University was an ideal base in
Guangzhou. I thank Cai He and Wang Ning for facilitating my visit. I also had
the pleasure of visiting the Center for International Forestry Research (CIFOR)
in Bogor, where I learned a huge amount in two short stays. I was lucky to be a
visiting scholar at MIT and the Max Planck Institute for the Study of Societies
at other points in the research and writing process. The Max Planck Institute
was a wonderful place to put the final touches on the manuscript, and I was
able to incorporate some of the feedback from my lectures there.

The project could not have gotten off the ground without the plethora of
ideas and support from my colleagues at Indiana University, and it could not
have been completed without the time, resources, and supportive colleagues
and graduate students at Ohio State University.

Christi Smith, Graeme Auld, Ethan Michelson, Lu Zhang, Mark Dallas, and
Jonathan Zeitlin generously commented on various parts of the manuscript.
Conversations with Matt Amengual, Jennifer Bair, Stephanie Barrientos, Tim
Büthe, Bruce Carruthers, Salo Coslovsky, Greg Distelhorst, Marie-Laure Djelic,
Tim Hallett, Sebastian Koos, Bill Liddle, Richard Locke, Olga Malets, John
F. McCarthy, Gerry McDermott, Christine Overdevest, Sigrid Quack, Amy
Quark, Andrew Schrank, Gay Seidman, and Susan Silbey also helped me to
think through key issues at various points in the project.

I also benefitted from the feedback of audiences at the University of
Manchester's Global Development Institute, Université Paris-Dauphine, Ohio
State University, the Max Planck Institute for the Study of Societies, MIT,
University of Michigan, McGill, Stanford, New York University, Boston Uni-
versity, University of Amsterdam, Emory University, and University of Illinois,
as well as workshops held at Duke, York University (for the Transnational
Business Governance Interactions project), the University of Mannheim, the
Ruhr-University Bochum, the Freie Universität Berlin, Brown, Georgetown,
and in Tokyo (for the Corporate Social Responsibility in a Globalizing World
project). Being involved in the Social Science Research Council's "Governing
Global Production" group (which I co-directed with Layna Mosley) and the
journal *Regulation & Governance* (which I co-edited with David Levi-Faur,
Cristie Ford, and Walter Mattli) have rubbed off in innumerable ways. Various

pieces of the book were presented at the annual conferences of the International Studies Association, American Sociological Association, and Society for the Advancement of Socio-Economics. The initial research was supported by a small grant from the American Sociological Association/National Science Foundation Fund for the Advancement of the Discipline.

My editor at Oxford University Press, Dominic Byatt, has been extraordinarily supportive—and patient as I pulled the pieces of the manuscript together. The reviewers enlisted by the press provided astute suggestions that helped to strengthen the analyses and appeal of the book. I thank Walter Mattli for initially inviting me to the "Transformations in Governance" series and providing sage advice about the structure and organization of the final manuscript. I also thank Sue Ferentinos for her expert assistance in cleaning up the footnotes and bibliography and Paula Douglass for preparing the index.

More than anyone else, I thank Christi Smith, whose love and deep insight have allowed this book to come to fruition. This book has been a long journey, and a more fluent travel companion could not exist. I treasure our life together, and I dedicate this book to you and our son Victor, who has now managed to get a book dedication from each of us in his first two years of life.

Table of Contents

List of Figures

List of Tables

List of Tables

1

Transnational Standards and Empty Spaces

The teak plantations of Java, established by Dutch colonial authorities and taken over by the Indonesian state, were to become a model of sustainability and social responsibility. In 1990, the US-based Rainforest Alliance made the pioneering move of certifying them as such, granting its approval to the state forestry company, Perum Perhutani, and giving furniture manufacturers and their buyers in Europe and North America an alternative to timber harvested through the clear-cutting and burning of forests. Perum Perhutani's agroforestry practices had been designed to sustain the land, and by allowing residents to engage in small-scale farming, the company was said to be "oriented towards the social and economic needs of local communities".[1]

But as this project expanded into a global system for certifying "well-managed forests" under the auspices of the Forest Stewardship Council, the situation at Perum Perhutani worsened. Javanese forests had long been managed through what Nancy Peluso has called a "custodial-paramilitary approach", and by 2001, violent clashes between Perhutani's armed guards and Javanese villagers could no longer be ignored.[2] Citing intractable problems, the Rainforest Alliance suspended Perhutani's certificates. The company's attempts to get re-certified dragged on, as auditors grappled with the killing of another villager and the danger of the Forest Stewardship Council's name being used for "greenwashing". Several Perhutani forests were eventually re-certified, after the company disarmed forest guards and introduced a new production-sharing program. But villagers continued to have little control over land, and certification could hardly wipe away the fact that, as one practitioner noted, Perhutani "has a history—[as] a company that's killed a lot of illegal loggers".[3]

In a different setting, similar forms of scrutiny, recognition, and reform were being applied to labor standards. The world's largest manufacturer of athletic

---

[1] Donovan 2001.   [2] Peluso 1992.   [3] Interview with NGO representative, 9/21/2010.

footwear, Yue Yuen, churns out hundreds of millions of shoes per year for Nike, Adidas, and Reebok among others, combining low prices and high quality with what a sympathetic portrait of Nike called "management by terror and browbeating".[4] Anti-sweatshop campaigns in the mid-1990s made this highly visible, revealing, for instance, a factory in Vietnam where workers were forced to run laps until many fainted in the sweltering sun.[5] Footwear brands and the Fair Labor Association began sending auditors to assess compliance with their codes of conduct. At Yue Yuen's massive factory-dormitory complex in south China, managers initially responded by falsifying records and coaching workers to give "correct" answers, but with continued scrutiny, factory managers began making reforms. They replaced toxic adhesives with safer alternatives, for instance, and replaced "terror and browbeating" with "emotion management" assistance for supervisors and "counselling rooms" for aggrieved workers.

In 2014, more than a decade into Yue Yuen's apparent moral turn, protests at its complex in south China quickly spiraled into the largest strike in China's recent history, halting production by more than 40,000 workers for ten days.[6] The company, workers discovered, had not been making its legally required contributions to the social insurance fund. Some strikers also began to demand their own representation, a strong departure from the practice of the state-controlled All-China Federation of Trade Unions (ACFTU)—and a demand that led some activists to be detained by police. Yue Yuen had received accolades in the "beyond compliance" world of corporate social responsibility, but it had not attained basic legal compliance.

In these examples, we see fragments of an increasingly prominent model of transnational governance, as well as hints of its contexts and limits. The model makes global supply chains into infrastructures for the flow of rules— that is, standards for sustainability, fairness, human rights, and safety. It imposes some degree of regulation on factories, forests, and farms around the world by relying not on governments, the traditional arbiters of rules and rights, but rather on the reputational investments of transnational corporations, the moral authority of international non-governmental organizations (NGOs), and the assessment capacities of auditing and certification bodies.

For large brands and retailers—from Nike, Apple, and H&M to Ikea, Nestlé, and The Home Depot—adopting rules for suppliers is a way to respond to activists' "naming and shaming" campaigns, to build a reputation for sustainability and responsibility, and to appeal to socially responsible investment funds and

---

[4] Katz 1994:157.

[5] Vietnam Labor Watch 1997; Herbert 1997. The factory was owned by Yue Yuen's parent company, Pou Chen.

[6] Committee for a Workers' International 2014; Borromeo 2014.

conscientious consumers. This was once novel, but by 2014, every one of the world's twenty-five most valuable brands had rules pertaining to labor conditions and/or environmental management in their supply chains.[7] Some call for compliance with rules established by multi-stakeholder initiatives where NGOs have a seat at the table, such as the Forest Stewardship Council, Social Accountability International, and Roundtable on Sustainable Palm Oil.[8] NGOs such as WWF and Oxfam have committed to "market transformation" projects that both push and partner with companies, while certification and testing firms such as SGS and Bureau Veritas have seen their businesses triple in size as they have taken the "audit society" global.[9] Taken together, the result is a form of "transnational private regulation" that has become essential not only for labor and environmental standards in global industries, but also for financial flows, product quality, and food safety.[10]

This is the sort of governance that is often posited but rarely examined closely in theoretical accounts of globalization and transnationalism. In Saskia Sassen's (2006) account, there has been a historic reconfiguration of territory, authority, and rights. These three domains were bundled together under the guise of the nation-state system, but they are being unbundled in various ways by global commerce, migration, and new forms of regulation. Tracing histories of trade, finance, and citizenship, she highlights the rise of private, de-territorialized forms of authority and a de-nationalized state that has "incorporate[ed] the global project of its own shrinking role".[11] "The new privatized institutional order for governing the corporate global economy has governance capabilities and a type of specialized and partial normative authority," she argues. It springs in part from the actions of states, but it rejects *"raison d'État"* as the "master normativity of modern times".[12]

Others point to a master trend of global standardization. A vast "world of standards" has emerged in tandem with the global economy, generating both the technical standardization needed for global business and a formalized expression of moral order.[13] While critical political economy scholars see this as a project to solidify the dominance of transnational corporations and

---

[7] This is based on searching the websites of the twenty-five most valuable brands as ranked by Interbrand in 2014. Google initially lacked such standards, but once it became involved in hardware manufacturing, it developed a "responsible manufacturing" code. Even brands primarily in business-to-business markets, such as Oracle and SAP, have supply chain standards.

[8] See Cashore, Auld, and Newsom 2004; Auld 2014; Vogel 2005; Ponte 2014.

[9] This is based on Compustat Global data on employees and revenues. From 1999 to 2014, SGS went from approximately 31,000 to 84,000 employees and 1.4 to 4.8 billion Euros in revenues. Bureau Veritas went from approximately 17,000 to 66,000 employees and 1.3 to 4.2 billion Euros in revenues from 2003 to 2014.

[10] Cafaggi 2012; Scott 2012; Havinga 2006; Büthe and Mattli 2011; Porter 2014.

[11] Sassen 2006:231. For earlier statements see Jessop 1997 and the literature collected in Cutler, Haufler, and Porter 1999 and Hall and Biersteker 2002.

[12] Sassen 2006:412.   [13] Brunsson and Jacobsson 2000.

professionalized NGOs from the global North, neo-institutionalists such as John Meyer and colleagues in the "world society" school see the same trends as reflecting a vision of scientific progress and individual rights that has gained tremendous legitimacy throughout the world.[14] They have argued that global norms about the environment and human rights are "surprisingly consensual" and have spread less through coercion than through governments'—and now corporations'—attempts to legitimate themselves.[15]

Transnational private regulation fits easily into these frames. It is a de-territorialized form of authority, whose backers hope it can transcend the limits of territorial nation states. It emerged, as we will see, as governments offloaded regulation to the private sector to promote a neoliberal model of governance, and it generally accepts rather than challenges the power of northern transnational corporations and NGOs. Trends toward standardization and homogenization have made formalized auditing, accreditation, certification, and "multi-stakeholder" representation common across fields centered on sustainability, labor, and human rights.

But sweeping accounts of authority and standardization do little to explain what these rules accomplish. From "10,000 feet up", one can see only blurry structures—that is, broad contours of rule-making, legitimation, and convergence. But one cannot see how managers of firms targeted by these rules respond, how auditors judge compliance, or how workers or residents complicate or seek to co-opt corporate responsibility and sustainability agendas. As seen in the case of Yue Yuen, some practices may be more open to reform than others. And as the Perum Perhutani case suggests, de-territorialized authority may struggle with territory on the ground. Nor can a distant and sweeping account explain why private regulation seems to be stronger in some fields and locations than in others. As we will see, sustainability and labor standards are similar in form but divergent in performance. And ironically, high standards may be proving easier to implement in more repressive environments.

To understand the prospects for sustainable development and decent work in the global economy, we must dispense with the seductive idea that rules for corporate responsibility and sustainability can somehow bypass or transcend existing forms of domestic governance. This book will ask how private rules are shaped by domestic governance at the point of implementation, what reforms tend to follow, and why some rules have proven more meaningful

---

[14] Banerjee 2008; Rodríguez-Garavito and Santos 2005; Meyer, Boli, Thomas, and Ramirez 1997.

[15] Meyer, Boli, Thomas, and Ramirez 1997; Meyer, Pope, and Isaacson 2015. Other neo-institutionalists have highlighted more circumscribed and contentious fields of transnational governance, but still with an emphasis on formalization and legitimation on the global stage. Djelic and Sahlin-Andersson (2006b) argue that "models and blueprints spread around the world and generate partial homogenization of governance forms and activities across sectors, levels and territorial boundaries" (p. 18), but "fields of transnational governance are also battlefields" (p. 23).

than others. It is true, as Göran Ahrne and colleagues write, that "the space for standard-based organizations is ... great at the global level, where they do not have to compete with state rules and state agencies."[16] But the implementation of standards always occurs in particular places. Seeing corruption, weak institutions, and low rule of law, many scholars of transnational governance have portrayed poor and middle-income countries as little more than "empty spaces" to be filled by globalizing norms.[17] They are severe "regulatory voids" and "areas of limited statehood" into which transnational rules may bring some semblance of order.[18] Partially as a result, attention has largely been focused elsewhere—on agenda-setting by international NGOs, the adoption of standards by transnational corporations, the design of voluntary initiatives, and the legitimacy of private authority as a form of global governance.

If theorists downplay the places of implementation, many corporate social responsibility and sustainability projects seem to actively *deny* them. They are animated by the idea that pushing standards through supply chains can transform markets by, in effect, pulling factories, forests, and farms out of their local contexts and up to global best practices. I call this the "hope of transcendence". It rests on one hand on a view of local socio-political contexts as backwards, repressive, and incapable of effective regulation and on the other hand on a view of global markets as extricating firms from their local contexts. Thus, a forest, factory, or farm can be brought up to global best practices, regardless of where it is located, if only its buyers demand it. "100 companies control 25% of the trade of all 15 of the most significant commodities on the planet," said WWF's Jason Clay, explaining the group's "market transformation" approach. "300–500 companies control 70% or more of the trade ... If we work with those, if we change those companies and the way they do business, *then the rest will happen automatically*."[19] When the UN released its Guiding Principles on Business and Human Rights in 2011, it echoed this idea in a different way, giving governments the duty to "protect" human rights but charging transnational corporations with the responsibility to "respect" human rights as "a global standard of expected conduct for all business enterprises wherever they operate ... independently of States' abilities and/or willingness to fulfil their own human rights obligations."[20]

---

[16] Ahrne, Brunsson, and Garsten 2000:66.

[17] See, for instance, Abbott and Snidal 2009b, Sabel et al. 2000, and Meyer et al. 1997, as discussed further below.

[18] Börzel and Risse 2010; Risse 2013; Thauer 2014; Braithwaite 2006.

[19] Jason Clay, "How Big Brands Can Help Save Biodiversity" TED Talk, August 2010, https://www.ted.com/talks/jason_clay_how_big_brands_can_save_biodiversity/transcript?language=en, accessed November 20, 2015. Emphasis added.

[20] United Nations Office of the High Commissioner on Human Rights 2011:13. Even the standard definition of corporate social responsibility as "beyond compliance" activity imagines a kind of rising above, while dismissing compliance with national law as an insufficient baseline.

Through a comparative look at land and labor in Indonesia and China, this book suggests that the hope of transcendence is misplaced. Rather than a rising tide of standards and a declining significance of place, we will see that the imprints of transnational structures, while not trivial, are colored by domestic circumstances. The book will trace assurances of sustainable and responsible global business to a range of sites—including the endangered and contested forests of Indonesian Borneo (Kalimantan), the rapidly expanding timber plantations of southwestern China, the export processing zones and industrial districts of greater Jakarta, and the apparel and footwear factories that made south China the "factory to the world". It is here that managers make or resist reforms and auditors construct compliance. We will see a variety of actors, including indigenous rights activists and insurgent labor unions, who have sought to make seemingly symbolic corporate commitments more real in their consequences. Indonesia and China are important locations for both fair labor and sustainable forestry projects, but the difference in their political regimes—since democratization in Indonesia—provides a chance to examine how the same forms of transnational governance operate in different domestic contexts. We will see that private rules have traveled far and wide through global supply chains, but they have been channeled, constrained, and even reconfigured by domestic governance, sometimes in perverse ways.

Based on interviews, documentary evidence, and some quantitative analyses, the case studies at the core of the book shed rare light on the concrete implications of private rules and the contexts of implementation. They reveal—and attempt to resolve—several specific puzzles. Why, for instance, were so few forests in Indonesia certified despite the pioneering certification of Perum Perhutani and ongoing controversies over deforestation? And why did Forest Stewardship Council certification grow quickly, albeit shakily, under the heavy hand of the state in China? How have factories in China been constructed as complying with "freedom of association" rules in codes of conduct and SA8000 factory certification standard, while the burgeoning trade union movement in Indonesia struggled to use these codes as leverage?

Despite variation across locations and industries, private rules for land and labor have mostly failed to produce meaningful forms of sustainability and fairness. The rules that flow through global supply chains are more than empty "myth and ceremony" but much less than a transformation of capitalism, or even a reliable impetus for improvement. Through contextualized portraits of private rules in practice, we will see why private rules have so often failed—not only, I will argue, because of the widely acknowledged problems of voluntarism, evasion, and "checklist" auditing, but because of the "hope of transcendence" itself.

More broadly, this book develops a *critical, contextual, and substantive theory of transnational governance*—that is, a theory that clarifies the accomplishments and failures of private rules, the ways in which they intersect with domestic governance, and their fit with different industries and issues. The theory provides an alternative to sweeping gazes and empty spaces in studies of globalization and transnationalism, provides testable propositions about political authority beyond the nation-state, and crystalizes emerging insights about corporate responsibility and sustainability. Like research on the "translation" of global standards, the theory acknowledges that global norms are altered as they travel to different locations, but it seeks to specify precisely *how* this works for private rules.[21] In tune with theories of political and organizational "fields", this account reveals an array of actors vying for the power to control loosely structured arenas, but against formalistic and content-free tendencies in organizational theory, I will argue that the *substance* of a reform project matters.[22] Finally, this account extends the growing body of research on corporate social responsibility, sustainability, and human rights standards, but it seeks to make sense of implementation *across* different industries and issues rather than being limited to one.[23] This chapter introduces the topic, and the next chapter develops the theoretical account, including propositions about the content of rules, their modal consequences, and their ability to reshape territory, authority, and rights.

Retailers to the Rescue: The Rise of Transnational Private Regulation

Private regulation refers to a structure of oversight in which non-state actors—whether for-profit companies, non-profit organizations, or a mix of the two—adopt and to some degree enforce rules for other organizations, such as their suppliers or clients. This can be called *transnational* private regulation if any of this activity operates across national borders. This includes arrangements in which retailers and brands set standards for their global supply chains—whether pertaining to product safety, sustainability, or labor conditions—as well as initiatives that certify or otherwise recognize companies that are complying with a given set of rules, assuming this occurs in more than one country. In traditional forms of self-regulation, companies cooperate to create standards and oversight for their own conduct, usually through "soft" norms that gain force through informal discussions, structured comparisons, and a growing sense that these organizations inhabit a "community of fate".[24]

---

[21] See Merry 2006; Halliday and Carruthers 2009; Quack 2007.
[22] See Fligstein and McAdam 2012; Rao, Morrill, and Zald 2000.
[23] See, for instance, Seidman 2007 and Locke 2013 on labor, or Cashore, Auld, and Newsom 2004, Potoski and Prakash 2006b, and Ponte 2014 on environment and sustainability.
[24] Rees 1994; Gunningham and Grabosky 1998.

Private regulatory rules, in contrast, are intended to apply to *other* organizations and—perhaps as a result—are often specific, "hard" rules rather than broad norms.[25]

Private regulation is not entirely new. In the early twentieth century, certification by the Underwriters' Laboratory, created by American insurers, became a widespread assurance of electrical safety.[26] Around the same time, the National Consumers' League "White Label" program was certifying garments "made under clean and healthful conditions", melding concern for workers' rights with xenophobic fears of "diseased" tenement sweatshops.[27] The reliability of "kosher" food designations was greatly increased by a private regulatory system that took shape in the 1960s.[28] And by the 1970s, organic agriculture was evolving from a movement to a market, with certification bodies charged with enforcing standards.[29]

The globalizing economy of the 1980s and 1990s greatly expanded the scope and scale of private regulation. For one, there was an explosion of standards intended to harmonize national differences in accounting, quality grading, and technical specifications, including those issued by the International Organization for Standardization (ISO). Global commerce created a demand for standards, while the capacities of competing national constituencies determined whose standards got globalized.[30] In addition, exposés of exploitation and environmental degradation inspired numerous projects to improve conditions in global industries. Only a handful existed in the mid-1990s, as organic and Fair Trade certification were growing, ISO was expanding into environmental management with the ISO 14001 standard, and Rugmark was certifying carpets as made without child labor. A decade later, there were dozens of initiatives working to certify sustainable forests, fisheries, or farms; to improve working conditions in apparel, footwear, toy, electronics, and home furnishings factories; or to protect human rights in oil and mineral extraction areas.[31] One study found twenty-two initiatives focused on sustainable agriculture alone.[32] A seemingly endless array of new initiatives has continued to emerge, focused on electronic waste, environmental degradation and child labor in cocoa production, and pollution and forced labor in the shrimp industry, to name just a few.[33]

---

[25] This is not to imply that private regulation is necessarily strict; to the contrary, one can have relatively permissive rules and/or lax enforcement and still have a system of private regulation, so long as there are some demands being made of targets.

[26] Cheit 1990.   [27] Sklar 1998; Wolfe 1975.   [28] Lytton 2013.

[29] Guthman 2004.

[30] Büthe and Mattli 2011; Quark 2013; Murphy and Yates 2009.

[31] For an overview, see Vogel 2005; RESOLVE 2012; Bartley, Koos, Samel, Setrini, and Summers 2015.

[32] Fransen, Schalk, and Auld 2016.

[33] See Renckens 2015; Barrientos 2016; Bush, Belton, Hall, Vandergeest, Murray, Ponte, Oosterveer, Islam, Mol, and Hatanaka 2013.

Considering the fields that are central to this study, from its founding in 1993 until 2001, Forest Stewardship Council (FSC) certification grew to cover 292 forest management enterprises on 22 million hectares of land, amounting to roughly 1 percent of all forest land worldwide that was designated for production or multiple use.[34] By 2012, more than 160 million hectares, or approximately 7.5 percent of eligible land, had been certified to the FSC's standards.[35] The Home Depot, B&Q/Kingfisher, Ikea, and French furniture retailer Maisons du Monde were promoting FSC certification in their supply chains, as were the Office Depot, Staples, Kimberly-Clark, and other paper retailers and manufacturers, sometimes in response to "market campaigns" waged by environmental NGOs.[36] Other companies adopted timber sourcing policies with preferences for certification by a competing initiative, the Programme for the Endorsement of Forest Certification (PEFC), an umbrella group of "homegrown" initiatives spawned by industry associations, landowners, and sometimes governments.[37] This group had certified roughly 11 percent of eligible land by 2012.

In the case of labor standards, starting with just eight factories in 1998, certification to Social Accountability International's SA8000 standard reached more than 100 facilities by early 2002.[38] Ten years later, there were more than 3,000 SA8000-certified facilities, employing roughly 1.8 million people, and by 2014, this had grown to more than 2 million people, amounting to roughly 0.5 percent to 1 percent of the total workforce in global production networks.[39] American and European companies, such as The Gap, Timberland, Disney, Tchibo, and the Otto Group, were among those encouraging SA8000 certification in their supply chains. Other brands, including Nike, Adidas, Liz Claiborne, and H&M, had thrown their weight behind the auditing and capacity-building projects of the Fair Labor Association. The UK-based Ethical Trading Initiative took a similar approach, albeit with more support from NGOs and unions. Industry associations spawned additional programs, such

---

[34] FSC certification list, March 31, 2001; Food and Agriculture Organization (FAO) 2006.

[35] Forest Stewardship Council, "Global FSC certificates: type and distribution," September 2012, https://ic.fsc.org/preview.facts-and-figures-september-2012.a-1038.pdf; Food and Agriculture Organization (FAO) 2010.

[36] Auld 2014.

[37] These included the Sustainable Forestry Initiative in the US, the Canadian Standards Association's sustainable forestry standard, PEFC affiliates in Germany and Sweden, the Malaysian Timber Certification Scheme, and the Brazilian Forest Certification Programme (CERFLOR). The history and trajectory of the Indonesian program, Lembaga Ekolabel Indonesia, differs in important ways, as described in Chapter 3.

[38] SA8000 Certified Facilities as of March 2002, http://web.archive.org/web/20020409033551/http://www.cepaa.org/certification.htm.

[39] Corporate Register 2012; SA8000 Certified Facilities as of June 30, 2014. The ILO (2015) estimates that roughly 453 million people work in global production networks, but only around 203 million of them are engaged in the final assembly of products, which is where certification is most likely.

as the Business Social Compliance Initiative in Europe and the Worldwide Responsible Apparel Production program in the US. Meanwhile, the NGO-sponsored Fair Wear Foundation and Worker Rights Consortium developed small but important presences in particular market niches. This was a crowded, fragmented field, but one in which some degree of rule-making and oversight of suppliers had become nearly ubiquitous.[40]

Markets, states, and civil society in the rise of transnational private regulation

The rise of transnational private regulation cannot be credited solely to the globalization of capitalism. Indeed, it is possible for a globalized economy to be governed in a variety of ways by territorially bound governments and seemingly gridlocked international organizations.[41] But a confluence of changes in markets, civil society, and states has led to a remarkable shift, in which retailers, brands, and their NGO partners and watchdogs are taking on roles that have more often been the domain of states—such as guaranteeing rights, protecting natural resources, and ensuring safety.

First, markets became increasingly contentious as the branding and market-control strategies of corporations met the "naming and shaming" strategies of social movements. "Branding" infused corporate images with mythologies, from the empowerment narratives of Nike to the communitarian ethos of Starbucks to the smooth creativity of Apple.[42] By one estimate, the value of corporations' intangible assets, including their brand images, increased from roughly 17 percent to 80 percent of total market value from 1975 to 2005.[43] In the retail sector, mega-retailers and "big box" stores captured a growing share of the market, as seen in the rise of Wal-Mart, Target, and Best Buy in the US or Carrefour, Decathlon, and B&Q/Kingfisher in Europe. In addition, the rise of "shareholder value" theories of corporate governance made executives especially sensitive to their images with investors, including increasingly demanding institutional investors.[44]

None of these trends were lost on activist groups, which developed media-savvy campaigns highlighting large, high-profile companies' links to environmental degradation, labor exploitation, or human rights abuses.[45] Greenpeace and Amnesty International exposed Shell's role in the degradation of land and

---

[40] Fransen 2011; Fransen and Conzelmann 2015; O'Rourke 2003.
[41] See Vogel 1995; Vogel and Kagan 2004; Mosley 2011; Hafner-Burton 2009.
[42] Klein 1999; Fitzsimons, Chartrand, and Fitzsimons 2008.
[43] Lindemann 2009.   [44] Davis 2009.
[45] Schurman 2004; Schurman and Munro 2009; King and Pearce 2010; Soule 2009; Bartley and Child 2014.

violence against indigenous people in Nigeria, for instance.[46] The Rainforest Action Network campaigned against Burger King's use of "rainforest beef", The Home Depot's destruction of old growth forests, and Victoria's Secret's use of paper from endangered forests for its catalogs.[47] The National Labor Committee and other anti-sweatshop groups mobilized media attention to the exploitative supply chains of Disney, The Gap, Nike, and many others.[48] When first thrust into the spotlight, retailers and brands often denied or deflected responsibility. "The pictures you showed me mean nothing to me," the CEO of Wal-Mart infamously said on national television in 1992, when confronted with images of children in Bangladesh producing shirts for the company.[49] But as scrutiny mounted, sometimes affecting sales or stock prices, companies began to accept at least partial responsibility for improving conditions in their supply chains.[50] Usually this meant adopting rules, auditing compliance, and/or supporting external monitoring or certification initiatives. Even some companies that had not been directly targeted began to adopt codes of conduct or promote third-party certification.[51]

Second, the structure of many industries changed, putting well-known corporations at the helm of global production networks.[52] The "supply chain revolution" of the 1980s and 1990s remade the global economy. As traditional manufacturers shed their factories to rely on sourcing from independent suppliers, other firms, such as Nike, were "born global", with design and marketing machines but no factories of their own. Mega-retailers from Wal-Mart to Ikea, built their dominance by nimbly managing orders and pushing down suppliers' prices. Integrated multinational corporations such as General Electric and Unilever survived but often evolved to look more like these new networked transnational corporations, which coordinate

---

[46] Holzer 2007. [47] Conroy 2007; Sasser, Prakash, Cashore, and Auld 2006.
[48] Bartley and Child 2014; Krupat 1997; Brooks 2007; Bair and Palpacuer 2012; Fransen and Burgoon 2015. Similarly, anti-GMO activists leveraged the market power of retailers such as Marks & Spencer and Tesco in the UK, while they struggled in the more fragmented retail market in the US (Schurman and Munro 2009).
[49] Quoted in Benoit and Dorries 1996.
[50] Spar and LaMure 2003; King and Soule 2007; Bartley and Child 2011.
[51] Bartley 2005; Conroy 2007.
[52] Some have described this structure of production under the heading of "global value chains" or "global commodity chains." I will use the term "global production networks" (GPNs) throughout, due to its intuitive appeal and this tradition's enduring attention to the territorial embeddedness of transnational production (Coe, Dicken, and Hess 2008; Henderson, Dicken, Hess, Coe, and Yeung 2002). The term "global commodity chain" has a history of use in sociology (Hopkins and Wallerstein 1986; Gereffi and Korzeniewicz 1994), but this work has gradually merged with work on "global value chains" (GVCs) emanating from business, economics, and political economy research (see Gereffi, Humphrey and Sturgeon 2005). Debates between the GVC and GPN traditions have mostly been matters of emphasis. Both describe the same phenomena and see "upgrading" of firms' capacities as the path to economic development. The GVC tradition is more sensitive to how technical requisites and transaction costs shape the structure of production, while the GPN tradition is more attentive to social movements' and labor unions' attempts to shape production processes.

production processes that they do not own. By the 2000s, global production networks had become essential to the production of apparel, footwear, home furnishings, food, toys, electronics, and automobiles, and a growing presence in service industries as well.[53] By one estimate, roughly one fifth of workers worldwide now work in global production networks, making either final products or "intermediates" for export.[54]

Global production networks connected well-known brands and retailers to numerous sites of exploitation and environmental degradation, while also putting them in the position of being quasi-regulators of the production process, not just participants in it. Integrated multinationals had been called to task for unethical dealings and links to repressive regimes in the past.[55] But global production networks allowed transnational corporations to "source" from countries where large capital investments would have been risky. Meanwhile, development policies in many poor and middle-income countries prioritized export-oriented production and integration into global supply chains, even if firms had to enter into precarious or exploitative relationships to do so. Although the relationship between "lead firms" and their suppliers varies, activists pointed out that large corporations in affluent countries routinely exercise power over the design of products, the materials used, and the prices paid to suppliers—so perhaps they should be expected to set labor and environmental standards as well.

A third contributing factor was that governments offloaded regulation to the private sector in various ways, partly reflecting neoliberal ideas about the power of markets to solve social problems. In the US and UK, the Clinton and Blair administrations sought to "reinvent government" by promoting voluntary programs, private sector partnerships, and corporate social responsibility initiatives.[56] Among other initiatives, they convened groups of companies, NGOs, and unions to create labor codes of conduct and auditing systems, spawning the Apparel Industry Partnership/Fair Labor Association in the US and Ethical Trading Initiative in the UK.

In addition to promoting a neoliberal model of governance, in which states take a "steering" rather than "rowing" role, governments were constrained by the free trade rules they had signed onto by joining the World Trade Organization (WTO) and its predecessor, the General Agreement on Tariffs and Trade (GATT). GATT and WTO rules restrict regulations that create discriminatory non-tariff barriers to trade. They do not preclude all import restrictions, as a growing body of research on WTO-compliant environment and safety

---

[53] Gereffi, Humphrey, and Sturgeon 2005; Yeung and Coe 2015; Henderson, Dicken, Hess, Coe, and Yeung 2002; Borrus and Zysman 1997; Gibbon, Bair, and Ponte 2008.
[54] International Labour Organization 2015.   [55] See Vogel 1978; Sikkink 1986.
[56] Moon 2004; Kinderman 2012; Fiorino 2009; Bartley 2005; O'Rourke 2003; Esbenshade 2004.

standards has pointed out, but they have raised the threshold for and style of government action.[57] Because GATT and WTO rules do not apply directly to private actors, though, reform projects have increasingly been channeled to the private sector.[58] In one clear instance of this, in the early 1990s, the Austrian government had to revise its initial response to campaigns against tropical deforestation. It had passed laws requiring the labeling of tropical timber and increasing import tariffs. As it became clear that these would be challenged as discriminatory trade barriers under the GATT, the government rescinded the laws—and then donated roughly $1.2 million to a private sector solution, the emerging Forest Stewardship Council.[59]

In addition, a number of reformers became disillusioned with both governments and inter-governmental organizations, which they viewed as either unwilling or incapable of passing stringent rules for global industries. International environmental NGOs, for instance, had been pushing for a binding forest convention at the 1992 UN Conference on Environment and Development (the "Earth Summit"). When this proposal fell through, as had a call for inter-governmental action through the International Tropical Timber Organization, environmental NGOs turned increasingly to the private sector.[60] This was especially true of WWF, which helped found the Forest Stewardship Council and then went on to spread the certification model to a number of other industries. Similarly, labor and human rights NGOs pointed to the failed efforts to add a "social clause" to the GATT, the WTO's decision not to address labor rights, and the International Labour Organization's lack of enforcement power when arguing that private regulation and consumer pressure could serve as "an additional weapon in the arsenal for human rights."[61]

Few reformers have given up entirely on governments and inter-governmental organizations, but many have embraced the possibilities for transnational corporations to push standards through their supply chains, whether as a second-best solution when policy windows are closed or as a more "direct" way of reforming markets. Notably, calling "retailers to the rescue" is not limited to global problems that outstrip the capacities of national governments. Retailers have been pressured, and in some cases have accepted the responsibility, to regulate hazards to consumer health,

---

[57] DeSombre and Barkin 2002; Chorev 2012; Neumayer 2004; Shaffer 2001; Kysar 2004.

[58] Bernstein and Cashore 2004; Bernstein and Hannah 2008; Shaffer 2015.

[59] Varangis, Crossley, and Braga 1995; Elliott 2000; phone interview with NGO representative, 9/2/02; interview with certification initiative representative, Oaxaca, 7/25/02.

[60] Gale 1998; Dudley, Jeanrenaud, and Sullivan 1995; Cashore 2002.

[61] Interview with NGO representative, Santa Cruz, 8/22/02. See Posner and Nolan 2003; Compa 2008; Varley 1998. The International Labor Rights Fund, for instance, was central to the call for a social clause in the GATT and later became a partial, if tentative, supporter of private regulation. See Collingsworth, Goold, and Harvey 1994.

including toxic phthalates in cosmetics and flooring.[62] This kind of private regulation has been especially prominent in the US, where governmental regulation of hazardous substances lags behind the EU.[63]

To what extent has transnational private regulation made a difference? Most of what is known about this comes from studies of a single industry or issue. Studies of food safety, for instance, have revealed the power of large supermarkets to push standards onto farms and food processing companies around the world.[64] ISO technical standards have clearly facilitated the globalization of production and trade, and global financial markets have come to rely to a surprising extent on private standards supplied by the International Swaps and Derivatives Association.[65] Emerging evidence is revealing various implications of labor codes, sustainability certification, and human rights norms. The consequences of transnational private regulation as a general form, though, remain difficult to specify.

A Cross-field, Cross-national Approach

Comparisons can reveal parallels that would be missed by studying a single issue or location, as well as details and differences that are obscured by more distant and sweeping theories. Rather than zooming from "10,000 feet up" down to highly particular ethnographic sites—as Michael Burawoy's (1998) "extended case method" and Anna Tsing's (2005) "ethnography of global connection" would do—this book seeks to hover at something like "1,000 feet up" both empirically and theoretically.[66] The goal is to be close enough to see how transnational rules are put into practice but still able to compare across fields and countries. Like other comparative case study research, I will draw on a wide range of data sources to construct detailed narrative case studies, highlighting key events, processes, and patterns.[67] I will then use the commonalities and divergences across the cases, in combination with insights from existing research, to develop the theoretical account. At root, my research centers on a comparison of transnational fields concerned with land and labor as put into practice in a democratic and an authoritarian country.

---

[62] See the Mind the Store Campaign, developed by consumer health and environmental organizations.

[63] Vogel 2012.

[64] Havinga 2006; Hatanaka, Bain, and Busch 2005.

[65] Murphy and Yates 2009; Porter 2014; Riles 2009.

[66] Burawoy 1998; Tsing 2005. See Salzinger 2003, Gille 2016, and Miraftab 2015 for provocative examples of global ethnography.

[67] See Evans 1995; Halliday and Carruthers 2009; Dezalay and Garth 2010b for examples.

Land and labor

Land and labor, as theorized by Karl Polanyi, are "fictitious commodities" that cannot be fully subjugated to the dictates of the market without unleashing backlashes that seek to re-embed them in society.[68] For sociologists, this perspective has most often been applied to labor, where it resonates with the Marxist argument that labor is a "special commodity" because the product and the seller are inseparable. By either account, as the growth of capitalism expands the market for wage-labor, one finds various attempts to protect workers from pure market forces, via labor law, unions, and welfare states.[69] With the expansion of global capitalism comes the expansion of labor unrest, as well as various attempts to de-commodify across borders, including cross-border solidarity campaigns and calls for global labor standards.[70]

While sociologists have paid more attention to this Polanyian "double movement" for labor, land also has qualities that make it impossible to fully commodify.[71] Land and the people who inhabit it are logically separable, but the importance of land to livelihoods and collective identities makes it practically difficult to do so. Fully commodifying land may require expelling those who inhabit it, as the growing body of research on dispossession shows.[72] In addition, as Derek Hall (2013) argues, the melding of territory with national sovereignty since the nineteenth century, and especially since the decline of colonialism, limits the extent to which land is treated as an ordinary commodity.

There are also ecological processes that prevent land from functioning as a pure commodity. In Polanyi's words, if the natural environment were fully subordinated to the dictates of the market "nature would be reduced to its elements, neighborhoods and landscapes defiled, rivers polluted, ... and the power to produce food and raw materials destroyed."[73] Perhaps most importantly, exploitation of a particular piece of land—whether from mono-cropping, careless harvesting, or use of fertilizers and pesticides that disrupt the ecosystem—can degrade its future productive capacity and spill over to other parcels through erosion, damaged water supplies, invasive species, or declining biodiversity.[74]

In the twentieth century, the re-embedding of land and labor revolved around state policy and national social movements, but in the twenty-first

---

[68] Polanyi 1944.   [69] See Western 1998.
[70] Silver 2003; Evans 2010.   [71] See Kaup 2015.
[72] Levien 2013; White, Borras Jr, Hall, Scoones, and Wolford 2012. Levien argues that while commodification of labor is ongoing and subject to covert resistance, commodification of land "poses a sudden, exogenous and irreversible threat to people's livelihoods, homes, and ways of life" (p. 362) and breeds overt resistance.
[73] Polanyi 1944: 73.
[74] For relevant but varied analyses of this sort, see Vayda and Walters 1999; Bunker 1990; Putz, Blate, Redford, Fimbel, and Robinson 2001.

century, reformers are often seeking to enforce rules across borders—and looking to the private sector to do so. The certification of sustainable forest management in the timber, paper, and furniture industries provides one important case. As a field, forest certification has been widely studied and imitated, becoming "one of the most innovative and startling institutional designs of the past 50 years."[75] But its implications at the forest level, especially in poor and middle-income countries, are often a mystery.

Private labor standards in the apparel and footwear industry emerged out of parallel concerns about untrammeled exploitation in global supply chains, taking shape as corporate codes of conduct, factory auditing programs, collective initiatives such as the Fair Labor Association, and certification of factories to Social Accountability International's SA8000 standard. Reactions have ranged from celebratory to highly critical, but often the heated debates have made it difficult to see what these codes accomplish on the ground.[76]

These are two of the most prominent and influential fields of transnational private regulation, but they have rarely been examined together, perhaps due disciplinary specializations that have made land and labor, despite Polanyi's diagnosis, separate spheres of study. Comparing them allows for a clearer picture of transnational private regulation as a general form of governance. In both cases, reformers have sought to counteract exploitative commodification by infusing markets with moral principles and "orders of worth" beyond price.[77] As the Polanyian perspective would expect, private regulatory initiatives emerged in the shadow of scandals that illustrated the destructive consequences of globalizing markets. In addition, as we will see, the implementation of sustainability and fair labor standards continues to be beset with tensions springing from the fictitious commodity character of land and labor.

CERTIFYING SUSTAINABLE FORESTRY

Perhaps no form of private regulation has been as influential as the certification of sustainable forestry. The story begins with the search for "good wood" and "positive alternatives" to the tropical timber boycotts waged in Europe and the US in the late 1980s. Small, craft-based woodworking firms in the US and Europe were among the first to suggest that "to ensure that timber that is marketed with the label 'sustainable' indeed confirms to certain production standards, and to separate genuine companies from opportunists, a watchdog

---

[75] Cashore, Auld, and Newsom 2004:4.

[76] See Fung, O'Rourke, Sabel, Cohen, and Rogers 2001 for an optimistic appraisal, Seidman 2007 for a critique, and Locke 2013 for an analysis that lies somewhere between.

[77] Guthman 2007; Boltanski and Thévenot 2006. On market- and moral-valuation more generally, see Fourcade and Healy 2007, Zelizer 2013, Beckert and Aspers 2011.

in the form of an independent monitoring organization will be necessary."[78] They joined with a group of foresters, representatives of environmental NGOs, certification bodies, and a handful of retailers to convene meetings for what would soon become the Forest Stewardship Council (FSC). WWF quickly became what one participant called the "incubator and surrogate mother" of the FSC, pushing the organization forward to its official founding in 1993.[79]

The FSC's standards set a high bar for the ecological and social dimensions of forest management, including requiring loggers to safeguard soil, water, and biodiversity; maintain "high conservation value" areas, and respect the customary land rights of indigenous communities. Very quickly, the FSC faced competition from "homegrown" industry- or government-sponsored programs in US, Canada, Germany, Sweden, Malaysia, Brazil, and several other countries, which would later unite under the umbrella of the Programme for the Endorsement of Forest Certification (PEFC).[80] The outcomes of this competition varied across countries, but the FSC's stringent standards for forest management generally survived.[81] Something of a "race to the middle" ensued, as industry-driven initiatives made reforms to increase their credibility and the FSC revised its labeling rules to increase its market share.[82]

Contrary to the idea that consumer demand drives eco-labeling initiatives, the FSC and its supporters had to work very hard to "make the market" for certified wood and paper products. While the Ford Foundation, Rockefeller Brothers Fund, and other foundations helped WWF organize "buyers' groups", the Rainforest Action Network, ForestEthics, and other activist groups aggressively campaigned against large retailers and brands—generating a kind of "good cop–bad cop" dynamic.[83] Companies such as The Home Depot, Staples, Kimberly-Clark, and Ikea agreed to promote FSC certification in their supply chains, although many others adopted sourcing policies that accepted certification by either the FSC or its competitor, PEFC.[84]

Much of the initial growth in certified land occurred in northern countries, especially Sweden, Poland, and the US, where existing management practices

---

[78] Ecological Trading Company 1990.

[79] Phone interview with NGO representative, 8/9/02.

[80] These included the Sustainable Forestry Initiative in the US, the Canadian Standards Association's sustainable forestry standard, PEFC affiliates in Germany and Sweden, the Malaysian Timber Certification Scheme, and the Brazilian Forest Certification Programme (CERFLOR).

[81] Cashore 2002; Cashore, Auld, and Newsom 2004; Cashore, Egan, Auld, and Newsom 2007; Gulbrandsen 2005; Auld, Gulbrandsen, and McDermott 2008; McNichol 2006; Espach 2006; Espach 2009; Nebel, Quevedo, Jacobsen, and Helles 2005.

[82] Overdevest 2010; Conroy 2007.

[83] Sasser, Prakash, Cashore, and Auld 2006; Conroy 2007; Carlton 2000; Auld 2006; Caplan 2005; Bartley 2007a.

[84] See Auld 2014; Conroy 2007.

17

were not too distant from the FSC's standards. This provoked a number of projects to extend the FSC's reach, including a partnership between WWF and the World Bank with an ambitious growth agenda. As large increases occurred in Russia, Brazil, and Canada, watchdogs worried that the FSC's standards were being watered down.[85] On the other hand, the FSC's prohibition on clearing natural forests for timber plantations, its requirements for reduced-impact logging, and its support for forest-dwelling communities continued to make it a challenging set of standards for timber companies in many places.[86] Rigorous multi-stakeholder processes to localize the FSC's global standards were held in a few locations, though certainly not everywhere they were needed.[87]

The FSC's influence has stretched far beyond forestry, especially as WWF became an enthusiastic carrier of the certification model. WWF copied many aspects of the FSC when it co-founded the Marine Stewardship Council for the certification of sustainable fisheries in 1997, and it went on to develop a number of "commodity roundtables" for the certification of sustainable palm oil, biofuels, aquaculture, soy, sugar, beef, and cotton.[88] These initiatives tweaked the FSC's model in various ways, but they have been subject to many of the same dynamics. Advocates have built market support by pushing large corporations to require certification in their supply chains, getting Wal-Mart and McDonalds to support Marine Stewardship Council certification and Nestlé to support the Roundtable on Sustainable Palm Oil.[89] Elaborate structures and norms of "best practice" have emerged as these initiatives have sought to legitimate themselves and fight off challenges from exporting industry associations.[90]

Scholars of sustainable forestry have largely focused on the conditions under which timber industries, especially in Europe and North America, have taken an interest in the high-bar of FSC certification, highlighting

[85] Rainforest Foundation 2002. See Klooster 2010 for a critical but ultimately approving account of the FSC's ability to withstand pressures to water down its original principles.

[86] See McDermott 2012; Tysiachniouk 2012; Malets 2013; Cerutti, Tacconi, Nasi, and Lescuye 2011; Cashore, Gale, Meidinger, and Newsom 2006.

[87] Tollefson, Gale and Haley 2008. As of 2006, there were FSC-certified forests in seventy-three countries but only thirty-four national initiatives and twenty-three approved national or subnational standards (http://www.fsc.org/en/about/accreditation/accred_fss, accessed June 28, 2006). In some countries—including Indonesia and China, as we will see—attempts to start a national initiative proved contentious and unsuccessful. Even in countries with functioning national initiatives, auditors retain a significant amount of discretion and may consider themselves "agents of change," not merely assessors (Malets 2015; Tysiachniouk 2012).

[88] These are the Roundtable on Sustainable Palm Oil, the Roundtable on Sustainable Biomaterials (previously the Roundtable on Sustainable Biofuels), the Aquaculture Stewardship Council, the Roundtable on Responsible Soy, Bonsucro, the Global Roundtable for Sustainable Beef, and the Better Cotton initiative.

[89] Auld 2014; Ponte 2012.

[90] Ponte 2014; Schouten and Glasbergen 2011; Boström 2006; Boström and Hallström 2010; Loconto and Fouilleux 2014.

particular combinations of export dependence, domestic political support, and weak footholds for competing "homegrown" initiatives.[91] Some have used counts of certified forests to generate a rough measure of consequences in different countries.[92] Only a few have looked at how sustainable forestry auditors translate global standards into concrete rules and request improvements from forest managers.[93] More broadly, research on sustainability standards has highlighted biases that keep small and marginalized producers from reaping the rewards of certification, while research on environmental management systems has analyzed its mixed effects on pollution reduction.[94]

AUDITING LABOR STANDARDS

Private regulation of labor standards arose through a similar but largely independent set of processes. As the production of apparel, footwear, and toys for American and European markets shifted more fully to Asia and Central America in the early 1990s, a wave of anti-sweatshop campaigns and media exposés revealed child labor, dire working and living conditions, abuse and sexual harassment, forced pregnancy tests, and repression of workers' attempts to unionize.[95] Levi Strauss, C&A, Reebok, and several other companies adopted codes of conduct early on, becoming leaders in the project to privately protect human rights and improve working conditions. By the late 1990s, most large apparel and footwear brands in North America and Europe had adopted codes of conduct and were sending auditors to check suppliers' compliance. As industry advisors put it, these steps might address the variety of "public black eyes for the garment industry" and perhaps "put a muzzle on these watchdog groups".[96] Reputation protection was elusive, though, as activists and scholars continued to reveal harsh, dangerous, and repressive conditions, sometimes passed over by poorly trained or negligent auditors.[97] Moreover,

---

[91] Cashore 2002; Cashore, Auld, and Newsom 2004; Cashore, Egan, Auld, and Newsom 2007; Gulbrandsen 2005; Espach 2006; Nebel, Quevedo, Jacobsen, and Helles 2005.

[92] Gullison 2003; Auld, Gulbrandsen, and McDermott 2008; Gulbrandsen 2010; Marx and Cuypers 2010.

[93] Malets 2013; Malets 2015; McDermott 2012; Tysiachniouk 2012; Cerutti, Tacconi, Nasi, and Lescuye 2011. Research examining the "corrective action requests" provides one method (Newsom, Bahn, and Cashore 2006; Newsom and Hewitt 2005), but one must be careful not to assume that the reforms recorded by auditors are necessarily substantive and durable. For a rare longitudinal study of certification and land use, see Heilmayr and Lambin 2016.

[94] On sustainable agriculture, see Ponte 2008; Ponte 2014; Silva-Castañeda 2012; Fortin 2013. On environmental management system certification, see Prakash and Potoski 2006b; Potoski and Prakash 2013.

[95] See Armbruster-Sandoval 2005; Brooks 2007; Spar and LaMure 2003; Rodríguez-Garavito 2005; Ross 2004; Bartley and Child 2014.

[96] WWD 1996:1; Rolnick 1997:72.

[97] For exposés showing that codes of conduct were often not even posted in factories or exposing shoddy monitoring by accounting firms, see Campaign for Labor Rights 1997; O'Rourke 1997; Shaw 1999.

factory managers were complaining of "audit fatigue," as each brand conducted its own oversight.

It was in this context that groups of companies and NGOs formed collective initiatives to coordinate and lend credibility to factory auditing. One of these, the Fair Labor Association, grew out of the Apparel Industry Partnership convened by President Clinton in 1996, which brought Nike, Reebok, Liz Claiborne, and a handful of other brands together with NGOs, such as the International Labor Rights Fund and the Lawyers' Committee for Human Rights (now Human Rights First), and initially the Union of Needletrades, Industrial, and Textile Employees (UNITE), though it soon dropped out in protest.[98] The FLA's critics in the labor and anti-sweatshop movement created their own program, the Worker Rights Consortium, to conduct independent and thorough investigations of factories producing for the collegiate-licensed market. Although it occupies a small niche, this organization became a key player in highlighting the repression of union rights and mobilizing pressure on selected companies.[99]

Around the same time, the Council on Economic Priorities, a US-based non-profit advocate of responsible investment and consumption, joined with Toys R Us, Avon, Eileen Fisher, SGS, and a handful of others to develop the SA8000 (Social Accountability 8000) standard and begin certifying factories.[100] The SA8000 standard was more stringent than most in calling for a "living wage" and for "parallel means" of worker representation where independent unions are outlawed. Although there is no on-product label—an option that was rejected by the Fair Labor Association as well—certified factories and participating companies can advertise their use of the SA8000 standard. SA8000 certification grew quickly in India, China, and especially Italy, where regional governments and national agencies were promoting and sometimes subsidizing it.[101] More than other labor-centered initiatives, the SA8000 standard became integrated into the larger world of sustainability standards, positioning itself as a peer of the FSC, Marine Stewardship Council, Fair Trade Labelling Organization, and others.[102]

These are just a few corners of the crowded, fragmented field of voluntary labor standards. Some brands and retailers have joined other multi-stakeholder

---

[98] See the end of Chapter 2 on how the exit of UNITE and the Interfaith Center on Corporate Responsibility shaped the FLA and perhaps the broader field of labor standards.

[99] Rodríguez-Garavito 2005; Ross 2006; Esbenshade 2004.

[100] The Rugmark certification program was founded earlier, in 1994, through the work of Indian and German activists, but it had a narrow scope, focusing only on rugs woven in South Asia. See Chowdhry and Beeman 2001 for the origin story and Seidman 2007 for a critique.

[101] Corporate Register 2012; Carey 2008.

[102] The accreditor for SA8000 certification, Social Accountability Accreditation Services, is a member of the ISEAL Alliance, along with the Forest Stewardship Council, Marine Stewardship Council, and other multi-stakeholder initiatives.

initiatives, such as the UK-based Ethical Trading Initiative, while others have relied on initiatives spawned by industry associations, such as the European-based Business Social Compliance Initiative and the US-based Worldwide Responsible Apparel Production program. Meanwhile, many companies, including mega-retailers such as Wal-Mart, Target, and Macy's, have relied primarily on their own codes and auditing, sometimes aided by audit information clearinghouses, such as the Fair Factories Clearinghouse and Sedex (the Supplier Ethical Data Exchange).

As exposés of exploitation spread to other industries, so did private regulation. The electronics industry was next in line. Even before worker suicides brought Foxconn's factories in China into the spotlight, labor-rights activists were proclaiming that "Apple is the new Nike" and exposing the use of toxic chemicals and excessive overtime in electronics factories.[103] Dell, HP, and IBM joined with their suppliers to develop the Electronics Industry Citizenship Coalition (EICC), which soon gained additional participants and began requiring factory auditing.[104] In addition, HP supported SA8000 certification for several years, and Apple joined the Fair Labor Association in 2012.[105] Labor standards have also come to occupy a central role in codes and certification initiatives for extractive industries—such as the Initiative for Responsible Mining Assurance and its industry-driven counterpart, the Responsible Jewelry Council—and some sustainable agriculture programs.[106]

Labor scholars have mainly focused on the limits of private regulation. Some research has traced the history of codes of conduct in different locations, arguing that they obscure the essence of labor-rights struggles, spur evasion, and only rarely promote a "culture of compliance" among manufacturers.[107] As this field has matured, it has become clear that the evolving approaches of leading apparel, footwear, and electronics brands do generate some improvement, but perhaps only to the extent that fierce competition can be replaced with strong relationships and productivity-enhancing innovations.[108] There is also evidence that unions can "leverage" corporate codes of conduct, at least given particular combinations of brand image, grassroots mobilization, and

---

[103] CAFOD 2004; Frost and Burnett 2007.

[104] Raj-Reichert 2011; Fransen and Conzelmann 2015.

[105] For more on HP, see Locke 2013; Distelhorst, Locke, Pal, and Samel 2015; Nadvi and Raj-Reichert 2015.

[106] While some view Fair Trade as a labor standards initiative, its origins and emphasis lie in supporting owners rather than workers—that is, owners of cooperative farms, who can receive a premium price if certified. More recently, Fairtrade International has added standards for hired labor. See Raynolds 2014. For more on the evolution of the fair trade model, see Auld 2014; Jaffee 2012; Lyon and Moberg 2010.

[107] Seidman 2007; Esbenshade 2004.   [108] Locke 2013.

cross-border solidarity.[109] Researchers are learning more about the changes spurred by factory auditing and the correlates of compliance through analyses of data obtained from brands and auditors.[110] Note, though, that this data does not allow a comparison to factories that are subject to little or no private regulation—or a consideration of how auditors define compliance.[111] Most research, though, focuses not on implementation but on the adoption of labor standards, the dynamics of competing initiatives, and the rise of corporate social responsibility in affluent countries.[112]

TOWARD A COMPARISON

Likewise, to the extent that scholars have looked across industries, issues, or fields, they have mainly focused on the emergence, design, and support of private regulatory initiatives, not their on-the-ground consequences.[113] It is clear from this research that certification of forests, fisheries, and coffee farms evolved differently, and that the local conditions that support one sustainability certification initiative may fail to support another.[114] Practitioners have sometimes wanted to assess the performance of certification across issues and industries, but the necessary evidence has been sparse.[115]

A comparison of sustainable forestry and fair labor standards captures two of the most prominent and influential attempts to privately govern land and labor. For those interested in how far private authority can go, these cases provide a wealth of material, intersecting with issues of indigeneity, environmental justice, climate change, biodiversity, property rights, human rights, union rights, gender discrimination, and workplace health and safety. We should not expect private regulation to work identically in these fields, but we should certainly see some parallels, given the role of retailers and brands in pushing standards, the widespread use of auditing, the challenges of credibility, and the "fictitious commodity" character of land and labor.

---

[109] Rodríguez-Garavito 2005; Armbruster-Sandoval 2005; Ross 2006. See Brooks (2007) on how this strategy can be counterproductive when it does not include organized grassroots actors.

[110] Distelhorst, Locke, Pal, and Samel 2015; Locke, Amengual, and Mangla 2009; Locke, Qin, and Brause 2007; Locke 2013; Toffel, Short, and Ouellet 2015.

[111] For analyses that do include negative cases, see Oka 2010a; Bartley and Egels-Zandén 2015. For a study that does examine auditors' understandings of compliance, see Kim 2013.

[112] See Fransen 2011; Fransen 2012; Fransen and Burgoon 2011; O'Rourke 2003; Brammer, Jackson and Matten 2012; Matten and Moon 2008; Campbell 2007; Vogel 2005; Mundlak and Rosen-Zvi 2011.

[113] Büthe and Mattli 2011; Büthe 2010; Verbruggen 2013; Bartley 2007b; Fransen and Conzelmann 2015. Some strands have been brought together in edited volumes and summary overviews, such as Potoski and Prakash 2009; Graz and Nölke 2007; Vogel 2008. For studies that have some consideration the "on the ground" effects of different types of standards, see Vogel 2005, Dauvergne and Lister 2012, Bartley et al. 2015, and Tampe (forthcoming).

[114] Auld 2014; Gulbrandsen 2010; Espach 2009.

[115] RESOLVE 2012; Ward and Ha 2012.

Democracy and authoritarianism

If transnational rules can truly bypass the state and transcend domestic governance, then they ought to work in similar ways in different countries. To the extent that domestic governance channels and reconfigures private regulation, though, we should see transnational rules becoming intertwined with the state and civil society in distinctive ways in different countries. A comparison of Indonesia and China contributes both substantive significance and analytical leverage.

Both countries are important sites for the implementation of fair labor and sustainable forestry projects. They have large export-oriented apparel/footwear and forest products industries that have been at the center of controversies about labor exploitation and environmental degradation. The clearing and burning of rainforests in Indonesia has at various points spread a haze over large swaths of Southeast Asia, while the exploitation of Indonesian workers fueled some of the earliest campaigns equating Nike's swoosh with sweatshops. In China, from the brutal repression of the Tiananmen Square protests to the suicides of workers making iPhones, the rights and well-being of workers have been difficult for foreign observers to ignore. Meanwhile, as China became the "factory to the world" for furniture, paper, and plywood—not only apparel and electronics—its forest products industry became intertwined with illegal logging and land grabs both within and outside the country. The success or failure of fair labor and sustainable forestry initiatives depends in no small part on their effectiveness in these cases.

Analytically, it is important that Indonesia and China differ in their political regimes, with a burgeoning Indonesian democracy since the fall of Suharto and a resilient form of authoritarianism in China.[116] This provides a chance to examine how transnational private regulation intersects with democratic and authoritarian governance at the point of implementation.

A democratic-authoritarian comparison captures two key aspects of the domestic context. First, a democratic setting allows for forms of popular scrutiny and pressure that have been found to amplify private rules. Where there are autonomous NGOs and independent trade unions, they can participate in "brand boomerang" campaigns to push companies to live up to the standards they have adopted.[117] As labor-rights groups press firms to make good on promises to respect freedom of association, environmental justice and land-rights groups may do the same for promises about respecting indigenous people's rights. NGOs can also organize stakeholders to be consulted by auditors or contest controversial decisions about certification, which may

---

[116] See, for instance, Aspinall 2005; Perry and Heilmann 2011.
[117] Seidman 2007; Anner 2009; Armbruster-Sandoval 2005. See Keck and Sikkink 1998 for the original, more state-centered account of the boomerang effect in transnational advocacy.

shape auditors' assessments of compliance.[118] The existence of autonomous local NGOs may also enhance the possibilities for collaborative projects that produce more meaningful corporate reforms.[119] Some evidence also suggests that compliance with private regulation is higher in countries with greater press freedoms, perhaps because the media enables popular scrutiny.[120] Of course, NGOs and journalists can expose problems and pressure companies in all but the most closed authoritarian countries too, but they will face much tighter oversight and control from the state. Watchdogs are widespread, but they should generally be on sounder footing in democratic than authoritarian regimes.

Second, a strong authoritarian state is likely to be more difficult for transnational private regulators to bypass. Truly bypassing the state may prove impossible in nearly every case, but the more encompassing the state's power is, the more private regulators should be dependent on its consent. Authoritarian regimes often govern through deep ties between political leaders, the military, trade associations, and leading companies. In some cases, these ties have been organized into effective developmental states, as in South Korea and Singapore, while in others, the heavy hand of the state has led to predation and corruption.[121] In democratic regimes, administration tends to be more fragmented, again producing dynamism in some countries and dysfunction in others.[122] The implication for transnational private regulation is that democratic settings should be more permeable, allowing actors from standard-setting bodies, international NGOs, and transnational corporations to become integrated into the strategies of domestic industries. Authoritarian regimes are likely to police this boundary more aggressively.

This does not exhaust the significance of democracy and authoritarianism for transnational private regulation. My case studies of land and labor in Indonesia and China will turn up some unexpected—and seemingly perverse—ways in which the contentiousness of democracy and the repressiveness of authoritarianism shape private certification efforts.

Indonesia and China obviously also differ in ways that go beyond democracy and authoritarianism. China's market size and dominant manufacturing position are unmatched.[123] Export-oriented industrialization in each country rested on "great migrations" of young people—especially women—from rural

---

[118] Malets 2013; Tysiachniouk 2012.

[119] Distelhorst, Locke, Pal, and Samel 2015. In their analysis of HP's social compliance audits, they find that the rate of compliance is significantly lower in China than in other countries with HP suppliers, including middle-income countries with more autonomous civil society, such as Mexico. They also describe a case in which a Mexican NGO worked with a brand to promote a higher bar of compliance.

[120] Toffel, Short, and Ouellet 2015. [121] See Evans 1995; Wade 1992; Amsden 1989.

[122] Chibber 2002; Rodrik 2007. [123] See Hung 2009.

to urban settings.[124] But there are important differences in the status and settlement of internal migrants, as we will see. Forest land is governed somewhat differently, although there is significant "institutional ambiguity" surrounding forest boundaries and uses in each case.[125] Indonesia's large extractive industries (oil and mining) and majority Muslim population have each, in their own ways, shaped the country's politics and governance.[126] One can rarely control for all the differences between substantively important cases. Thus, rather than relying on a static comparison, the case studies in this book will try to show *how* democratization in Indonesia and resilient authoritarianism in China intertwined with the implementation of private rules.

Interestingly, China and Indonesia are interdependent cases with regard to the fields studied here. Orders for apparel and footwear have shifted back and forth between the two countries—along with a handful of others—as wages and labor unrest have risen and fallen. A different sort of interdependence exists in the forest products industry, where voracious demand for imported timber arose in China as political change was fostering illegal logging in Indonesia, making Indonesia a major source of the illegal timber flowing through factories in China. These intertwined paths reveal some of the evolving interdependencies in the global economy and world of transnational governance.

THE POLITICS OF PRODUCTION IN CHINA AND INDONESIA

China's place in the global economy requires little exposition. Market reforms in the 1980s made China the "factory to the world" by the 1990s. Mainland China became the world's leading exporter of clothing in 1994, and by 2006 it was exporting more clothing than the next six countries combined.[127] In addition to the boom in export-oriented production of clothing, footwear, and electronics, China's forest products industry greatly expanded in the 1990s and 2000s. Plywood exports increased by a massive 4,600 percent from 1996 to 2006, making China the world's top producer by 2003.[128] As China's furniture, flooring, and lumber industries similarly expanded, they rapaciously consumed logs from Russia, Burma, Malaysia, and Indonesia, raising concerns that Chinese production was driving unauthorized logging and timber smuggling networks. There are large tracts of forest land within China—the fifth largest amount in the world—but several

---

[124] Meng and Manning 2010. On the gendered character of migration and industrial development, see Wolf 1992 on Indonesia and Lee 1998 on China.

[125] Ho 2001; McCarthy 2004. Xu and Jiang 2009.

[126] See, for instance, Rinaldo 2013; Mujani and Liddle 2004; Rosser 2007.

[127] WTO export value data for SITC 84, clothing.

[128] Chinese Academy of Forestry 2007; Sun, Wang, and Gu 2004.

rounds of devastation have led to new controls, reforestation campaigns, and massive new timber plantation projects.[129]

In the midst of market reforms, the resilient Communist Party of China has kept a tight grasp on the Chinese polity, promoting a "harmonious society" while working to strictly regulate information and association. Political authority in China has often been described as a kind of "fragmented", "soft", or "adaptive" authoritarianism, which allows flexibility for local policy innovation and multi-level governance, while maintaining single party control and strong coercive state powers.[130] Since the 1990s, there has been an active "semi-civil society" in China, including a range of environmental and labor NGOs. But they are overseen by the state and face repression if they cross the fuzzy line into "political" activities.[131] With the growth of wildcat strikes, anti-pollution protests, and other so-called "mass incidents", the Chinese regime has developed a kind of "bargained authoritarianism" that uses a mix of concessions, cooptation, and repression to maintain control.[132] Since 2013, under President Xi Jinping, the repressive components of the central government's strategy appear to have become much stronger, as activists and NGO leaders have increasingly been detained.[133]

Indonesia is the world's fourth most populous country, but this archipelago of over 13,000 islands often seems invisible to social scientists in North America. Those who cite Benedict Anderson's *Imagined Communities* or James Scott's *Seeing Like a State* rarely remember their Indonesian points of reference.[134] Although there have been several prominent analyses of Indonesia's democratization and navigation of the Asian financial crisis, the country is often neglected in American sociology.[135]

Indonesia has long been a major exporter of forest products, with "timber barons" benefitting from tight links to the military and central government— as well as Japanese and American corporations—during the Suharto regime.[136] As Indonesia surpassed Malaysia to become the top Asian exporter of forest

[129] Food and Agriculture Organization (FAO) 2010; Food and Agriculture Organization (FAO) 2006; Robbins and Harrell 2014; Trac, Harrell, Hinckley, and Henck 2007.
[130] Lieberthal and Lampton 1992; Mertha 2009; Perry and Heilmann 2011.
[131] Spires 2011; Stern and O'Brien 2012; Chang, Ngok, and Zhuang 2010.
[132] Lee and Zhang 2013.
[133] See Mitchell 2016. In its various forms, the "authoritarian resilience" of the Chinese government has attracted a great deal of scholarly attention (Nathan 2003; Stockmann and Gallagher 2011; He and Warren 2011).
[134] Anderson 1983; Scott 1998.
[135] For exceptions, see Gellert 2005, Slater 2009, Halliday and Carruthers 2009, and Rinaldo 2013. A search of abstracts of articles in the *American Sociological Review* and *American Journal of Sociology* from 1975 to 2013 reveals just three that mention Indonesia, compared to fifty-seven for China, thirteen for India, and fourteen for Brazil. To be sure, social scientists in some parts of Europe—especially the Netherlands—and in Australia are much more attentive to Indonesia, due to colonial history and proximity.
[136] Dauvergne 1997.

products in 1988, the industry was shifting from raw commodities to manu-
factured products, such as plywood and furniture, including teak and mahog-
any furniture made by clusters of small craft-based producers.[137] Pulp and
paper companies were also setting up massive mills in Indonesia, often fueled
by the destruction of old-growth natural forests.[138] Forests cover nearly half of
the country's land—amounting to the third largest topical forest area and
eighth largest forested area in general—but natural forest land has been at a
high risk for clearing, burning, and conversion to oil palm and timber
plantations.[139]

In addition to its natural resource industries, Indonesia became a major
exporter of footwear and apparel, facilitated by foreign investment from
South Korea, Hong Kong, Taiwan, and Japan in the 1980s.[140] By the mid-
1990s, Indonesia was one of the top five exporters of footwear worldwide and
one of the top six clothing exporters in Asia.[141] Its apparel industry benefitted
from US quotas—in the form of the Multi-Fiber Arrangement—that kept
clothing imports geographically dispersed, at least until these quotas were
eliminated in 2005. This left the Indonesian apparel industry in a precarious
but still competitive position, as wages remained relatively low.[142]

General Suharto rose to the Indonesian presidency amidst a bloody purge
that killed 500,000 to a million suspected leftists between 1965 and 1967. The
thirty years of his so-called New Order regime combined a deeply militarized
and coercive state with the *Pancasila* ideology of national harmony.[143] Then,
in 1998, in the wake of the Asian financial crisis, an El Niño-driven draught,
student protests, violent riots, and the fracturing of his coalition, Suharto
resigned.[144] The new administration, headed by Vice President Habibie,
quickly began a process of *Reformasi*, expanding party competition, press
freedoms, civil and labor rights, and scheduling new elections. Indonesia's
score on the Polity IV scale of democracy—a −10 to +10 scale—swung from −7
to +6 from 1998 to 1999.[145]

---

[137] FAOStat database, total export value of forest products. In 2005, Indonesia was surpassed by
China as the largest exporter of forest products in Asia. On the furniture industry, see Posthuma
2008; Morris and Dunne 2004.

[138] Dauvergne and Lister 2011; Barr 2001.

[139] Food and Agriculture Organization (FAO) 2010; Food and Agriculture Organization (FAO)
2006; Barr 2001; McCarthy and Cramb 2009; Ruslandi, Venter, and Putz 2011.

[140] Dicken and Hassler 2000.

[141] Scott 2006; WTO export value data for SITC 84, clothing. Indonesia has been in the top
fifteen clothing exporting countries (by value) nearly every year since 1991, although its position has fluctuated with the value of the currency and the changing costs of production in other
parts of Asia.

[142] In part due to rising wages elsewhere in Asia, Indonesia remained among the top six apparel
exporters in Asia in 2013, according to WTO export value data for SITC 84, clothing.

[143] Dove and Kammen 2001; Hadiz 1998; Vickers 2005.

[144] Aspinall 2005; Slater 2009; Liddle and Mujani 2013.

[145] In contrast, China has retained a Polity score of −7 since 1976.

The scars of the past were by no means quickly erased, and new power elites emerged, but Indonesia became a burgeoning democracy with an active civil society. Domestic NGOs, which had been tolerated to some degree under Suharto, found new space to press claims about human rights, indigeneity, and environmental justice.[146] Independent trade unions blossomed, although the labor movement quickly became highly fragmented and had to contend with the "legacy union" of the Suharto era.[147] Local strongmen and corrupt officials make Indonesian democracy far from rosy, but the country's human rights record has seen marked improvement, especially since 2006.[148]

Researching private regulation in practice

To examine fair labor and sustainable forestry standards in Indonesia and China, I conducted 145 interviews with practitioners between 2007 and 2014.[149] They included auditors, consultants, representatives of domestic and international NGOs, compliance staff for brands and retailers, managers of apparel, footwear, and timber companies, garment workers, trade union leaders, and local researchers. Starting with contacts gained from prior research and other scholars, and then recommendations from those I interviewed, I expanded my list of practitioners and sought interviews that would help to triangulate information about key events and processes.[150] To get beyond surface-level portrayals, it helped to talk in specifics rather than generalities, so I let the semi-structured interview move into the person's particular area of expertise, and I probed for the details of specific cases.[151] Corporate compliance representatives and auditors were well aware of the critiques of their work, and many talked candidly about problems and potential solutions. Because many of these individuals operated in organizational worlds where English is the *lingua franca*, approximately two-thirds of the interviews could be conducted in English. The others were done with the help of local interpreters.

[146] Ford 2009; Peluso, Afiff, and Rachman 2008.
[147] Caraway 2008; Juliawan 2011; Tjandraningsih and Nugroho 2008.
[148] Cingranelli, David L., David L. Richards, and K. Chad Clay. 2014. "The CIRI Human Rights Dataset." Version 2014.04.14. http://www.humanrightsdata.com. On the rise of local strongmen since democratization, see Hadiz 2010.
[149] Forty-seven interviews focused on labor standards in China, twenty-four on sustainable forestry in China, thirty-two on labor standards in Indonesia, and thirty-eight on sustainable forestry in Indonesia. Four interviews were with practitioners who straddled the two fields without fitting clearly into one or the other.
[150] I also interviewed approximately sixty practitioners in North America and Europe between 2002 and 2004 to gather information about the emergence of fair labor and sustainable forestry initiatives.
[151] These were informant interviews rather than attempts to capture the subjective experiences of actors in a population. I sought to follow Weiss's (1995) approach to conceptualizing informant interviews and building rapport.

A rich trove of secondary sources, including practitioners' reports and specialized research literatures, has helped me contextualize and supplement the interviews. I also coded publicly disclosed audit reports and have analyzed two factory-level datasets that were graciously shared by the local researchers who collected them.

In studying forest certification in Indonesia, I interviewed auditors, sustainable forestry consultants and researchers, representatives of competing certification initiatives (including the homegrown Lembaga Ekolabel Indonesia), international and domestic NGOs, and timber companies. Most were interviewed during several stays in Jakarta and in Bogor, the home of the Center for International Forestry Research (CIFOR) and several other relevant organizations. In Yogyakarta, I interviewed the heads of small craft-based home furnishings companies and the consultants that were helping them reach "green" markets. In East Kalimantan, a once-richly forested region now suffering from severe deforestation, I joined a team of auditors and experts as we took a boat up the river to visit an oil palm plantation that was considering certification.

In Jakarta, an early interview with a labor-rights NGO quickly spawned a long taxi ride through the city's infamous traffic to meet with a group of factory-level union leaders. This began a series of interviews with unions and other participants the "code of conduct network" that had engaged in bottom-up monitoring of brands' standards.[152] Over the course of several visits, I also interviewed brands' compliance staff, auditors, trade association leaders, corporate social responsibility consultants, researchers, and representatives of NGOs, mainly in the greater Jakarta area, Bandung, or Bogor, the traditional manufacturing centers. I interviewed several groups of garment workers as we sat on the floors of their homes or cramped union offices, and I worked with a local research assistant to gather additional information on key cases. In addition to a practitioner's conference and audit observation, I gained access to survey data on factories that are and are not subject to codes of conduct. (See Chapter 6 for a complete description.)

In China, I began with a series of interviews with labor-rights NGOs and apparel/footwear brands in Hong Kong and Shenzhen. Later, during a three-month stay in Guangzhou and several visits to Beijing and Shanghai, I interviewed labor standards auditors, NGO leaders, factory managers, researchers, and the local staff of apparel and footwear brands and private

---

[152] Some were conducted in tandem with Niklas Egels-Zandén, my collaborator on one part of the project. Graduate students working with him conducted a number of additional interviews and follow-ups, which enhanced our work but are not counted in the number of interviews reported above.

regulatory initiatives.[153] I followed along as an observer on two audits, attended practitioners' conferences, and worked with local research assistants who conducted short interviews with garment workers outside several certi-fied factories—sites where my own presence would have been extremely conspicuous. I also gained access to survey data collected by researchers from Peking University that allows for a rigorous assessment of differences between SA8000-certified and uncertified factories.[154] (See Chapter 5 for a complete description.)

Studying sustainable forestry standards in China took me mainly to Beijing, where most key practitioners are based, in part because of this field's links to the State Forestry Administration and its northern forests. Over several visits, I interviewed some of the most active auditors, foresters who were involved in public and private policy discussions, as well as representatives of certification initiatives, international NGOs, sustainability consultancies, and a trade asso-ciation. As we will see, sustainable forestry in China was in flux—and facing profound challenges—as I was studying it, so media coverage, NGOs reports, and follow-up interviews were also important for fleshing out several cases. The public summaries of audit reports for FSC certification proved also valu-able for understanding forest certification in both China and Indonesia.

This multi-method research provides a number of points of evidence about the outcomes of transnational private regulation. As international relations scholars have argued, identifying the "outcomes" of a regime means docu-menting the observable changes made by its targets. Studying "outputs", in contrast, would simply involve collecting written agreements, rules, and standards. Rigorously identifying "impacts" is incredibly difficult, since it requires systematic measures over time and the ability to rule out alternative explanations.[155] The case studies in this book will document changes made by factory and forest managers in response to private rules and auditing; steps taken to evade or resist this scrutiny; and re-interpretations of the rules that occur along the way. Some systematic comparisons are possible—of SA8000-certified and uncertified factories in China, for instance—but many of the central insights will come from narrative reconstructions of key cases and events, as revealed through a combination of interviews, documentary

---

[153] During this period at least, a foreign scholar of labor standards could make contacts with little interference. I was told by one recent university graduate at a dinner, casually and with a smile, that he had been assigned to watch me. But I encountered no obvious interference in meeting with labor NGOs and scholars.

[154] This and much of my other evidence on labor standards in China comes from Guangdong province, the traditional center of export-oriented manufacturing and thus of private regulatory activity, although interesting new dynamics may emerge as companies move inland in search of lower wages.

[155] Biermann and Bauer 2004; Underal 2002.

evidence, and secondary sources. The case studies seek to make the contexts and consequences of private rules intelligible and engaging.

A Shared Diagnosis and Set of Differences

Looking across the cases, we will see that domestic governance is far more than an empty space; it channels and reconfigures transnational private regulation in distinctive ways. The hope of transcending domestic governance and bypassing the state is illusory. For instance, state repression of migrant workers' rights in China led practitioners of private regulation to either ignore rules about workers' freedom of association or to redefine them in domestically friendly ways. In the forestry case, transnational standards asked timber companies to respect the customary land rights of indigenous people, but this was difficult if not impossible to do in Indonesia, since the state grants forest concessions to companies with little regard for customary claims. In China, the Forest Stewardship Council received a powerful reminder that there is no bypassing the state, when new regulations threatened its ability to continue operating in the country just as it was facing new competition from a home-grown, state-sponsored program.

As practiced in Indonesia and China, private regulation of land and labor has at best been a source of marginal change in industries that remain highly exploitative. At worst, this approach has accepted small and cosmetic changes as evidence of market transformation. Reforms that would be needed to live up to the most rigorous transnational rules often cut against deeply entrenched cultures of production and modes of domestic governance. At times, private actors were simply *incapable* of altering systems of land governance and rights regulation that were grasped as tightly as possible by the state. Certainly, in comparison to cases where transnational private regulation has significantly altered the normal operation of business—such as accounting, food safety, and professional qualifications—fair labor and sustainable forestry standards must be considered failures.[156]

The failings stem in part from transnational corporations' mixed incentives for rigorous enforcement of rules. Simply put, brands and retailers wanted assurances of decency, safety, and sustainability to protect and build their reputations, but they often wanted extreme flexibility and ever-lower prices from their suppliers as well. But the case studies suggest another, less-often-recognized source of the failures: Transnational private regulation sets rules for what constitutes a decent workplace or well-managed forest management

---

[156] Büthe and Mattli 2011; Cafaggi and Janczuk 2010; Fuchs and Kalfagianni 2010.

enterprise, but it brackets what lies *beyond* the factory walls and forest boundaries. It papers over the sourcing practices of brands and retailers, who are treated as the enforcers rather than the targets of regulation. It ignores the domestic political economy in which factories and forests are embedded, and it pretends to bypass the state rather than grappling with the messy but essential character of state-based governance.[157]

Despite this shared diagnosis, there is notable variation across locations and fields, as depicted in Figure 1.1. Democratization in Indonesia allowed civil society actors to push for "maximalist" constructions of compliance with private rules. Unions and labor-rights NGOs pushed Nike, Adidas, and other brands to truly respect workers' freedom of association—by allowing insurgent independent unions in their suppliers' factories, for instance. Indigenous rights and environmental justice NGOs in Indonesia likewise argued that timber companies should not be certified unless the contested rights to Indonesian forest land could somehow be resolved. As we will see, activists rarely won these debates, but their persistence put collective labor rights and community rights at the center of private regulators' attention, and occasionally spurred surprising achievements.

		TRANSNATIONAL FIELDS		
		Fair labor	**Sustainable forestry**	
NATIONAL SITES OF IMPLEMEN-TATION	**Indonesia**	"Contentious Codes" • bottom-up monitoring/ leveraging • precarious industry	"Purity and Danger" • push for high standards • unsettled land tenure, messy democratization	*Civil society push for maximalist constructions of compliance; but little certification*
	China	"Beneath Compliance" • low-quality auditing • impossible to guarantee collective rights	"The State Strikes Back" • dependence on the state • certification despite land grabs	*Contained, minimalist constructions of compliance; higher rate of certification*
		Lax but widespread private regulation	*More rigorous private regulation (with blind spots)*	

Figure 1.1. Summary of the cases

[157] Practitioners of private regulation could adapt transnational standards to domestic governance, but the logic (and economic reality) of their work militated against asking whether domestic governance was so deeply in conflict with transnational standards as to render the latter ridiculous.

In China, in contrast, there were few countervailing forces to prevent transnational corporations, suppliers, and auditors from using minimalistic constructions of compliance. Independent unions did not exist, and migrant labor NGOs were in a precarious position, facing repression if they became too political. Rural residents had little power to resist land grabs orchestrated by companies and local governments, even if external actors were watching. Auditors and other practitioners of private regulation—even those who were conscientious and experienced—routinely accepted weak assurances in this context. In a sense, they were not forced to look hard at the vexing issues of land and labor rights in authoritarian China.

This suggests a perverse way in which transnational private regulation is shaped by democratic and authoritarian contexts. The kind of open contention that is facilitated by democratic governance and an autonomous civil society can *impede* certification to rigorous multi-stakeholder standards. When activists push for maximalist definitions of compliance, expose weaknesses in implementation, and link up with international watchdogs, certification becomes more costly and time-consuming. Because authoritarian governance contains, absorbs, or represses contention, it can make it easier for companies to be certified to a high standard, since auditors may not even see the underlying conflicts. Ironically, it has turned out to be easier for firms to get credibly certified as sustainable, fair, and rights-respecting in authoritarian China than in democratic Indonesia.

Land and labor are similar as fictitious commodities, but there are notable differences across these two fields of transnational governance. On the whole, private regulation has been more rigorous for sustainable forestry than for fair labor standards. The Forest Stewardship Council's standards for forest management have remained expansive and challenging, despite several pitfalls and blindspots—including weak enforcement of rules about labor rights in the forest. SA8000, the most rigorous factory certification standard, has suffered from inconsistent auditing and poor quality control in China and a puzzling lack of application in Indonesia, where collective labor rights are legally protected. Apparel and footwear brands and retailers have pushed a number of other rules as well, generating widespread scrutiny. But often auditing has been weak, and enforcement has been geared toward creating plausible deniability if problems arise rather than promoting meaningful improvements.

The difference across fields, I will argue, cannot be explained by simplistic ideas about corporate greening as an efficiency-enhancing "win-win", which are an especially poor fit with the costs and conflicts involved in sustainable forestry. Instead, I will argue that the pattern stems from differences in the power of non-industry groups in the initial design of private regulatory initiatives, the relative mobility and visibility of industries, and the framing of labor and environment relative to the global public good. While leading strands of organizational and field theory are reluctant to make substantive distinctions, I will argue that fairly durable features of industries, products, and issues set fields on different paths.

Beyond forests and apparel/footwear factories

The two fields of transnational private regulation covered in this book do not represent the full landscape of land and labor standards, though they should capture some general tendencies. Observers of sustainable agriculture and responsible mining should, for instance, find significant points of connection in this study of sustainable forestry, particularly when it comes to land grabs, ecosystem impacts, and negotiations to control natural resources that are fixed in place.[158] On the other hand, forest land has more multi-faceted uses—for timber harvesting, hunting and collection of non-timber forest products, the conservation of biodiversity, and the mitigation of climate change—than most land used for agriculture and mining. The Forest Steward-ship Council's participatory decision-making structure also sets it apart from most other multi-stakeholder initiatives.

Similarly, scholars of labor standards in other manufacturing industries or in labor-intensive agriculture will notice some common enforcement chal-lenges, such as widespread subcontracting, a search for lower-wage work-forces, and the vulnerability of workers who are marginalized by migrant status, gender, ethnicity, and/or race.[159] On the other hand, the apparel industry is less capital-intensive and more mobile than many others, making it especially difficult to have significant increases in labor costs without spur-ring exit. Industries with more complex production processes, greater place-based agglomeration effects, or higher barriers to entry should be somewhat less challenging to regulate, whether publicly or privately. On the other hand, the progression of outsourcing and franchising has generated "fissured" pro-duction architectures in surprising places.[160]

What lies ahead

The next chapter builds from a critique of "empty spaces" imagery in theories of transnational governance to the contextual and substantive approach devel-oped in this book. While many treat governance in poor and middle-income countries as so weak, corrupt, or illegitimate as to be analytically irrelevant,

---

[158] See Ponte 2014; Fortin 2013; Silva-Castañeda 2012; Djama, Fouilleux, and Vagneron 2011.
[159] See Nadvi and Raj-Reichert 2015; Coslovsky and Locke 2012; Tampe (forthcoming); Barrientos 2016.
[160] Weil 2014.

I argue that it is better to start from the opposite premise and look closely at the intersections of domestic governance, global production networks, and transnational fields. A series of theoretical propositions, which have been abstracted from my case studies, further specify a substantive and generalizable theory of transnational governance.

The empirical studies begin in Chapter 3 ("Purity and Danger"), with the case of forest certification in Indonesia. Although the field of forest certification was created in large part to counteract deforestation in Southeast Asia, few forests in Indonesia were certified to the standards of the Forest Stewardship Council. Those that did often struggled to reform destructive logging practices and tense relationships with communities. This chapter asks why forest certification was underdeveloped and what kinds of reforms were made. It shows how "certifying in contentious places" turned out to be quite difficult.[161]

As the next chapter ("The State Strikes Back") shows, China saw faster growth in forest certification, even as the operations of private regulators were constrained and threatened by the Chinese state. This was possible because of what I call the "dual logic of certifying in authoritarian places", in which the state crowds the space of private regulators but also edits out the messiness and contention that can otherwise impede certification. Among other things, this chapter will argue that authoritarian governance suppressed conflicts over land rights, making it easier for apparent land grabs to be certified as compliant with the Forest Stewardship Council's high standards.

Chapter 5 ("Beneath Compliance") examines the practical meanings of labor standards and corporate social responsibility in China. SA8000 certification initially made waves in China by proposing stringent rules and strong respect for labor rights. But as this chapter shows, oversight was weak, and SA8000-certified factories proved not especially different from others. More broadly, despite some provocative projects, brands and initiatives (such as the Fair Labor Association) responded to government restrictions on workers' rights largely by constructing "compliance" in stripped-down, managerialist terms, which were compatible with authoritarian governance.

Labor codes of conduct took a different trajectory in Indonesia, as the next chapter ("Contentious Codes") will show. Although democratization, independent unions, and progressive labor law did not turn Indonesia into a locus of responsible apparel and footwear production (or SA8000 certification), unions and NGOs were able to engage in bottom-up monitoring and leveraging of brands' codes of conduct. Yet the modest improvements that resulted were overshadowed by several larger defeats. This chapter shows how the

---

[161] See McCarthy 2012 for the initial use of this terminology.

mobility of the apparel industry and the factory-centered logic of private regulation impeded greater gains.

The final chapter ("Re-centering the State: Toward Place-conscious Transnational Governance?") considers the possibilities for improving transnational governance of land and labor. Rather than rejecting supply chain scrutiny entirely, I argue that it could be made more effective by acknowledging the spatial and temporal dimensions of corporate responsibility/sustainability, and by "re-centering" the state. This is not a starry-eyed call for strong but responsive governments to somehow emerge, but rather a call to extend potentially empowering reforms that are already underway. A new, binding transnational timber legality regime holds great promise, along with some pitfalls, and perhaps lessons for projects—including the ILO-IFC Better Work programs—that seek to improve the enforcement of labor standards.

2

A Substantive Theory of Transnational Governance

How do global norms and rules make a difference on the ground? It is surprising how few good theoretical answers to this question exist, at least when it comes to rules that flow through private channels. Theories of transnational advocacy networks and the globalization of law speak mainly about state policy and inter-governmental organizations, while theories of private regulation have focused largely on standard-setting and the design of voluntary programs.[1]

This chapter moves toward a theory of the outcomes of transnational private rules, especially as they are put into practice in poor and middle-income countries. It begins with a critique of several paradigms that treat poor and middle-income countries as essentially "empty spaces" waiting to be filled by global norms. It then builds the foundations for an alternative approach that starts from the opposite premise—namely, that places of implementation are crowded with actors and agendas. The key task, then, is to examine the intersection of transnational structures (networks and fields) and the crowded spaces of domestic governance. Some insights can be gleaned from existing research, but much of the necessary work remains to be done. This is the purpose of my case studies of fair labor and sustainable forestry standards in Indonesia and China (Chapters 3–6). Their central findings are summarized and extended here into eight propositions that flesh out a "substantive" theory of transnational governance.

---

[1] See Keck and Sikkink 1998 and Tarrow 2005 on transnational advocacy, and Halliday and Carruthers 2009 for a model of the globalization of law. For useful collections of theoretical perspectives on private regulation, see Quack 2010, Büthe 2010, and Potoski and Prakash 2009. Recently, scholars have developed frameworks for studying "interactions" (Eberlein, Abbott, Black, Meidinger, and Wood 2014) and "intermediaries" (Abbott, Levi-Faur, and Snidal 2017) in transnational governance. The "interactions" agenda is distant from points of implementation and the "intersections" that are at the center of this study. The "intermediaries" agenda moves closer to implementation processes, but mainly by highlighting the role of auditors.

The Problem of Empty Spaces

Transnational private regulation rose to prominence amid a discourse of "bypassing the state". In various ways, advocates for this model argued that states were unwilling or unable to regulate directly and that private actors should step in to fill the void. They pointed not only to the failure of inter-governmental agreements, but also to low capacity and high corruption in developing countries. The architects of forest certification, for instance, cited the "failure of international organizations that ought to have had the remit to enforce, to implement and develop good forestry standards" and national governments that were corrupt or captured by the timber industry.[2] Some argued that the private sector represented a "fast track" to change, in contrast to the slow gridlock of governmental processes.[3] Developers of private labor standards initiatives similarly made their case by pointing to a "lack of resources, corruption in government, governments wanting to make sure the product is sold," as one practitioner put it.[4] As another practitioner diagnosed the problem, there is "weak enforcement at a local level, weak enforcement—no enforcement—at an international level, and in...the US and Western Europe...there's not a political will to hold the companies responsible by law."[5]

Theorists of private regulation have in some respects rejected the image of private actors bypassing the state. They have pointed out that governments have been supporters, endorsers, and "orchestrators" of nominally private and transnational initiatives.[6] The US, UK, and European Union governments, for instance, have supported or endorsed a range of private and voluntary initiatives for labor, food safety, biofuels sustainability, and beyond.[7] Many sustainability initiatives would not exist if not for delegation and support from governments and international organizations.[8]

But in other ways, especially as they have looked at poor and middle-income countries, theorists of transnational governance have supported an image of states as essentially irrelevant. An emphasis on transnational standards being exported to fill "regulatory voids" and "governance gaps" has contributed to a vision of essentially empty spaces at the point of implementation. This

---

[2] Interview with certification initiative representative, Oaxaca, 7/25/02. Bernstein and Cashore 2004; Bartley 2007b.

[3] Elliott 2000.

[4] Interview with NGO representative, Washington, 2/19/04. Interview with initiative representative, Washington, 6/27/02.

[5] Interview with NGO representative, New York, 7/18/02.

[6] Djelic and Sahlin-Andersson 2006b; Bartley 2007b; Drezner 2007; Quark 2013; Abbott and Snidal 2009a; Büthe and Mattli 2011; Green 2013; Gulbrandsen 2010; Auld 2014.

[7] Schleifer 2013; Verbruggen and Havinga 2016; Kinderman 2016.

[8] See Green 2013; Abbott and Snidal 2013 on delegation and orchestration in environmental policy arenas.

misleading image can be seen in several of the most prominent paradigms in the field.

"Areas of limited statehood"

Research on "governance in areas of limited statehood" provides the starkest example. This paradigm sees private action as nearly the sole source of social order in widespread regulatory voids in poor and middle-income countries. In developing this approach, Tanja Börzel and Thomas Risse (2010) start with a dilemma: Self-regulation and private governance seem to require the "shadow of the state" in order to motivate participants and keep them from shirking. Yet the places where private governance is most needed are those places where effective states are absent—that is, "areas of limited statehood." The solution, they argue, is to recognize that other factors, including firms' need for public services (e.g., security, education, public health) and their defense of corporate reputations in the face of NGO campaigns, can motivate and discipline private governance. "Limited statehood does not equal the absence of governance," these scholars assert, since foreign projects, private regulation, and corporate social responsibility initiatives often emerge to fill the void.[9]

Strikingly, this paradigm assumes that essentially all societies "outside the world of developed and highly industrialized democratic states" can be characterized as areas of limited statehood.[10] This does not necessarily mean that entire countries are lacking statehood. Areas of limited statehood can refer particular territories, domains, or populations in which governments "lack the ability to implement and enforce rules" or do not have a monopoly on coercion.[11] But Börzel and Risse and colleagues rely on a stylized contrast between areas of limited statehood and the full-fledged "consolidated states" of affluent democracies.[12] They lump together a huge array of places as characterized by limited statehood, including war-torn "failed states", newly democratic countries, and authoritarian regimes. They note similarities between Somalia, Brazil, Indonesia, and even China—where "government lacks the capacity to enforce its own laws, particularly with regard to environmental protection."[13] Case studies in this paradigm have examined domain-specific areas of limited statehood in South Africa, widespread institutional voids in Afghanistan and the Democratic Republic of the Congo, and challenges of service provision in India and Bangladesh.[14]

---

[9] Risse 2013:9.   [10] Börzel and Risse 2010:118.   [11] Ibid: 119.

[12] Börzel and Risse 2010; Risse 2013. Even when studies identify variation in the effectiveness of interventions, there is little theoretical consideration of whether diverse areas of limited statehood might be more different from one another than they are from affluent, consolidated states.

[13] Börzel and Risse 2010:119.

[14] Risse 2013; Thauer 2014; Beisheim, Liese, Janetschek, and Sarre 2014.

Apart from external interventions, the places of interest are portrayed as either as regulatory voids—that is, "environments where the state is unwilling or incapable of setting high standards, providing essential services, or enforcing legal obligations"—or as containing only primitive forms of authority.[15] Tellingly, the only time that Börzel and Risse (2010) suggest something other than empty spaces, they invoke images of traditional authority, briefly discussing how private governance can be disciplined by "traditional communities with their own social standards" or "clan structures sharing certain standards of appropriate behavior that include the provision of governance".[16] As we will see, this is perhaps the most explicit example of an imagery that runs deep in the literature on globalization and transnational governance.

Orchestration, experimentation, and transnational new governance

In less stark terms, a growing body of research on "orchestration" and "experimentation" in transnational arenas often assumes away governance in poor and middle-income countries. This research celebrates the possibilities for interactions between multiple rule-makers and watchdogs to transform gridlock into discovery. Kenneth Abbott and Duncan Snidal (2009a; 2009b) argue that experimentation with multiple approaches can facilitate more responsive forms of regulation and avoid capture by a single set of powerful actors. From a different tradition, theorists of "experimentalist governance" paint a similar picture. Charles Sabel and colleagues (2000), for instance, argue that global labor standards can be "ratcheted up" through benchmarking of multiple rule-makers and monitors.

These approaches portray government action as important for steering, "orchestrating", and benchmarking, so that multiplicity and flexibility breeds learning and improvement rather than confusion and laxity.[17] But while calling for some governments and inter-governmental organizations to orchestrate or benchmark experimentation, these researchers often diagnose governments in developing countries as incapacitated—and thus largely irrelevant. The goal of "new governance", in John Braithwaite's (2006) words, is to find ways of "networking around these capacity deficits."[18] Extending this approach, Abbott and Snidal (2009b) argue that "developing countries are often inadequate regulators due to insufficient capability or willingness."[19] It is because "many states involved in worker rights, environmental, and human rights issues are not democratic, but authoritarian and

---

[15] Thauer 2014:34.   [16] Börzel and Risse 2010:125.
[17] Abbott, Genschel, Snidal, and Zangl 2015; Abbott and Snidal 2009b; Sabel 2007; Zeitlin 2011; Overdevest 2010.
[18] Braithwaite 2006:884.   [19] Abbott and Snidal 2009b:538.

corrupt" that the "comparative participatory advantages of Transnational New Governance" must be taken seriously.[20] For Sabel and colleagues (2000), the challenge is that governments usually lack the "extensive inspectorates and other administrative capacities to monitor firms, sanction violators, and counter their evasion efforts," especially in developing countries.[21] Their approach therefore "sidesteps these customary standard setting bodies."[22]

The problem is that these accounts too easily conflate administrative capacity, democratic legitimacy, and analytical relevance. They turn a diagnosis of states in developing countries as weak and/or undemocratic into a reason to push them to the background of the theory. Even where the capacities for effective and democratically legitimate regulation are limited, there may still be *uneven or illegitimate* enforcement of law and regulation. For instance, the Chinese government may not effectively enforce its environmental laws, but it does enforce laws that prevent environmental activists from organizing collective social movements.[23] A government may not uniformly enforce land rights or even have a clear system for registering property boundaries, but if a putative landholder can call on police or military forces to expel others, this is an exercise of state power. Or, while resource constraints may keep regulators from policing an entire industry, they may regulate particular segments or locations relatively effectively.[24] In addition, as scholars of law and society have pointed out, even if the "law on the books" is poorly enforced, it can shape the expectations of citizens and workers.[25] There is rarely a true "regulatory void", although there can be a great deal of variation in the substance, style, and strength of regulation.

Sidestepping these aspects of domestic governance, research on orchestration and experimentation has focused largely on the transnational architectures of rule-making and revision. To be sure, some research in the experimentalist governance tradition has looked at the development of new regulatory agendas and capacities as poor and middle-income countries get enmeshed in systems of goal-setting, benchmarking, and review.[26] This research may be abandoning some of the earlier stylized assumptions, but its emphasis remains squarely on the architecture of experimentation and learning, not on the conditions for reform within poor and middle-income countries. A shift in attention, it must be said, might also push this paradigm to

---

[20] Ibid.:557.   [21] Sabel, O'Rourke, and Fung 2000:13.
[22] Ibid.:5.   [23] Cai 2008; van Rooij, Stern, and Fürst 2016.
[24] Examining labor and environmental regulation in Argentina, Amengual (2016) argues that "when the state apparatus does respond to violations in basic rules with enforcement, weak institutions can become 'activated,' and rules that were previously ignored can have a substantial impact" (p. 5).
[25] Ewick and Silbey 1998.   [26] Overdevest and Zeitlin 2014a; Overdevest and Zeitlin 2014b.

acknowledge entrenched interests more than the continuous discovery and revision of preferences. In any case, in most of the work on orchestration and experimentation, poor and middle-income countries are treated as "empty spaces" not by definition, as in the previous paradigm, but by omission.

World society theory

A third image of essentially empty spaces comes from the neo-institutionalist "world society" paradigm in sociology. This approach argues that the "western cultural account" of rationality, individualism, science, and progress has become a taken-for-granted and "transcendent level of social reality" in an increasingly integrated world society and polity.[27] As a result, governments have subscribed to norms about environmentalism and human rights even when there is little domestic demand or "functional need" to do so.[28] Research in this paradigm has traditionally focused on public policy adoption, but it is expanding into analyses of corporate social responsibility and private governance, while also beginning to theorize reforms on the ground.[29]

Sites of reception and possible implementation, especially in poor and middle-income countries, appear to be little more than vessels waiting to be filled by cultural principles that are globally legitimate but completely foreign to the locals.[30] Consider what is perhaps the key trope of this paradigm—the image of a government in a poor country adopting a policy to create an environmental ministry, protect human rights, or expand higher education solely because of the country's exposure to a highly legitimated world culture. John Meyer and colleagues (1997) develop this image through a telling allegory of what would happen if an unknown society on an unknown island were discovered in the current era:

> A government would soon form, looking something like a modern state with many of the usual ministries and agencies.... The society would be analyzed as an economy, with standard types of data, organizations, and policies for domestic and international transactions. Its people would be formally reorganized as

[27] Boli and Thomas 1999b:3. Similarly, Meyer, Pope, and Isaacson (2015) state that "world society transcends particular national states and societies" (p. 34), while Loya and Boli (1999) argue that standards are "designed to activate transcendent purposes oriented around global progress," rather than to privilege parochial, local goals. See Mattli and Büthe (2003) for a critique.

[28] Meyer, Boli, Thomas, and Ramirez 1997; Frank, Hironaka, and Schofer 2000; Boli and Thomas 1999a.

[29] On CSR, see Lim and Tsutsui 2012; Meyer, Pope, and Isaacson 2015. For a theory of accretive and gradual change on the ground, see Hironaka 2014; Schofer and Hironaka 2005.

[30] An exception comes in the work of Boyle and colleagues (e.g., Boyle, Songora, and Foss 2001), which adopts some of the world society paradigm but looks much more closely at how they are received and resisted in particular places.

citizens with many familiar rights, while certain categories of citizens—children, the elderly, the poor—would be granted special protection.[31]

Thus, "without knowing anything about the history, culture, practices, or traditions that obtained in this previously unknown society, we could forecast many changes that, upon 'discovery,' would descend on the island under the general rubric of 'development'."[32]

World society research has proceeded in this mold, conducting numerous cross-national quantitative studies of the adoption of global principles with only rudimentary attention to the receiving context. Analyses typically include crude measures of domestic "functional need" but find that ties to world society prove to be better predictors.[33] Some analyses have measured domestic "receptor sites" that are especially open to world cultural influences, such as scientific and ecological associations that speed the adoption of global environmentalism.[34] But these sites are treated as otherwise inert or as themselves a *product* of world society.[35]

Critics have often charged this paradigm with neglecting issues of power and implementation.[36] World society scholars have responded by further theorizing the effects of global norms, but they have done so in a way that says little about the places where these effects are supposed to occur. For instance, Evan Schofer and Ann Hironaka (2005) argue that the effects of global norms depend on the structuredness of the global arena, its persistence over time, and the "penetration" of the global model into the everyday routines of government, firms, and citizens. Only the last factor speaks to domestic contexts, and it treats them merely as nodes in a global network. It seems that the assumption of essentially empty spaces—the undiscovered island—has persisted even as the paradigm has become more sophisticated.

Filling in the spaces

Despite their differences, these paradigms share a portrayal of poor and middle-income countries as little more than empty spaces waiting to be filled

---

[31] Pp. 145–6. Illustrating the foreignness of principles such as mass education, Meyer et al. write that "children who will become agricultural laborers study fractions; villagers in remote regions learn about chemical reactions; members of marginalized groups who will never see a ballot box study their national constitutions" (pp. 149–50).

[32] Meyer et al. 1997:146.

[33] Frank, Hironaka, and Schofer 2000; Schofer and Meyer 2005.

[34] Frank, Hironaka, and Schofer 2000.

[35] Frank et al. (2000) note that "without external stimuli, receptor sites remain inactive" (p. 103). Longhofer and Schofer (2010) find that world society ties have a large effect on the subsequent founding of environmental associations in "non-industrialized" countries. Thus, this literature argues for a top-down seeding process in which "global movements and networks spawn domestic analogues" (Schofer and Longhofer 2011:578).

[36] See, for instance, Buttel 2000.

by transnational standards. To be sure, these are not the only ways of analyzing transnational governance. Other traditions highlight intense conflicts between elites in affluent countries and governments, experts, or social movements from the global south. As several streams of research have shown, actors from poor and middle-income countries rarely win outright, but the negotiations can nevertheless shape the development of global rules.[37] The theory of "recursive" global rule-making developed by Terence Halliday and Bruce Carruthers (2009), for instance, springs from the back-and-forth between international financial institutions and the governments of South Korea, China, and Indonesia in the wake of the Asian financial crisis. Some researchers have amended this approach to account for cases with greater change in global norms, while others have extended it in to the domain of private standards, primarily by analyzing rivalries between competing standard-setters.[38] In a similar vein, Tim Büthe and Walter Mattli's (2011) "institutional complementarity" theory argues that winning standards wars has less to do with sheer power than with the fit between domestic institutions and the global standard-setting body.[39]

These power-and-negotiation approaches provide a corrective to images of empty spaces and transcendent globalism. Their basic point—that global orders are shaped by unequal but consequential conflicts over whose rules will be globalized—should be a starting point for any account of transnational governance. But many additional gaps must be filled in if we are to understand the implementation of private rules in global production networks. What we learn from many existing accounts turns out to be about negotiations over law, to be adopted and implemented by governments. A fully state-centered and "methodologically nationalist" approach is less appropriate when examining private rules that travel through global production networks. In turn, the accounts that focus on private standards speak primarily about the power to *set* standards, not about their implementation. If implementation flows automatically from the standards on paper, then the power to write the standards may be all that matters. But if private standards are adjusted, reinterpreted, watered down, or ratcheted up in the course of implementation and assessment, then we need additional tools.

In the next section, I will develop the foundations for theorizing the implementation of transnational private regulation, drawing in part from strands of research that *have* attended to domestic contexts. This includes an emerging body of research on domestic sources of compliance with global

---

[37] In addition to the works cited below, see Rodríguez-Garavito and Santos 2005; Dezalay and Garth 2010a.

[38] Chorev 2012; Quark 2013; Botzem and Dobusch 2012.

[39] For a more determinist "great powers" account, see Drezner (2007).

labor standards, which highlights the role of public inspectorates and civil society.[40] It also includes research on the uptake and legitimation of transnational sustainability standards, which focuses on domestic coalitions that support high-bar standards.[41] Because my goal is to theorize multiple types of private regulation, I will attempt to integrate these insights into several general points of orientation. In addition, I will depart from most of the existing research in arguing that the significance of domestic governance lies not merely in boosting or depressing rates of uptake or compliance, but in reconfiguring the very meaning of transnational standards.

From Empty Spaces to Intersections: Foundations for an Alternative Approach

Crowded spaces

Instead of seeing transnational standards as filling in otherwise empty spaces, it is more fruitful to start from the opposite premise—namely, that sites of implementation are crowded with actors, agendas, and rules. These actors include an array of firms competing for orders and investment, international and domestic NGOs, and a variety of government agencies. The rules include locally based private agreements, such as those developed by industry associations; informal but strong norms about how business is done, which may add up to a distinctive culture of production; and perhaps most importantly, national law.

All countries that are linked to global production networks have their own sets of laws about land, labor, and the rights of citizens. The laws may be weak, contradictory, or contrary to the goals of transnational reformers, but they can nevertheless structure managers' and workers' expectations, and undergird particular cultures of production. For instance, the Chinese model of industrial production rests on the state's channeling of foreign investment, restrictions on workers' rights, and the land and internal migration policies that created a mass of "floating" migrant workers.[42] Extractive industries in Nigeria, Ghana, Indonesia, and a number of other countries depend on state security complexes that ensure a steady supply of oil, minerals, or timber while repressing the land and resource claims of indigenous communities.[43] Endemic conflict may make these spaces appear un-governable, but this is a result of competing sets of rules and claims, not a generalized lack of social

---

[40] Locke 2013; Distelhorst, Locke, Pal, and Samel 2015; Toffel, Short and Ouellet 2015; Coslovsky and Locke 2012; Amengual 2010.
[41] Cashore, Auld, and Newsom 2004; Cashore, Egan, Auld, and Newsom 2007; Espach 2009; Peña forthcoming; Prakash and Potoski 2014; Malets 2013.
[42] Gallagher 2005.   [43] Hilson and Yakovleva 2007; Watts 2004; Peluso 1992.

order.[44] The image of an "institutional void" is nearly always a myth that obscures existing norms and legal structures.[45]

In some settings, domestic laws may not be as weak or repressive as they first appear. For instance, a review of forestry law around the world finds a dense set of national regulations that have typically "become more restrictive and more demanding, as governments have given progressively greater weight to the environmental values of forests."[46] In the domain of labor standards, nearly all countries have laws on minimum wages—whether specified or bargained by sector—maximum working hours, and minimum ages.[47] Although documented labor-rights abuses increased globally from the 1980s to 2000s, laws on collective labor rights got stronger over time in some regions, especially following democratization in East Asian and Eastern European countries.[48] In Latin America, there has been a "renaissance" of labor inspection, and in a range of locations, labor and environmental regulators have sought to bolster their capacities by working with other parts of government or with civil society.[49]

To be sure, enforcement capacities may be quite limited in some locations, different levels of government may be working at cross-purposes, and officially *illegal* actions may be strongly embedded in cultures of production. Still, in all but the most extreme "failed states" and hinterland locations, one is more likely to find a plethora of half-enforced and contradictory rules than a true regulatory void. Domestic governance is often uneven and inconsistent, but it is rarely irrelevant. By "domestic governance", I mean the set of laws and regulations, informal norms, and power relations that combine to define the relationship between the economy, society, and polity in a given country. The purpose in using this broad concept is to acknowledge that the law on the books may be contradictory, unevenly enforced, or routinely subverted without assuming that the domestic social order is irrelevant.

---

[44] Watts 2004.

[45] See Horner 2015, who argues domestic institutions that are defined away as a void may actually be well-suited to the goals of domestic firms and policymakers.

[46] McDermott, Cashore, and Kanowski 2010:5.

[47] ILO 2014; Mosley 2011. President Obama assumed a regulatory void when mistakenly stating in 2015 that "under this agreement [the Trans-Pacific Partnership], Vietnam would actually, for the first time...have to set a minimum wage" (https://obamawhitehouse.archives.gov/the-press-office/2015/05/08/remarks-president-trade). Vietnam has had a minimum wage since 1995.

[48] Caraway 2009; Mosley 2011. Caraway shows that laws on collective labor rights in East Asia tended to get stronger during this period, primarily due to democratization. Mosley's indicator of overall labor rights shows a modest global decline from 1985 to 2002 but increases in Central and Eastern Europe and some parts of the Asia-Pacific.

[49] See Amengual 2010; Schrank 2009; Piore and Schrank 2008; Amengual 2016; Coslovsky 2011; Samford 2015; Pires 2013, as well as Perez-Aleman 2013; van Rooij and McAllister 2014; McAllister 2008.

Intersections with global production networks and transnational fields

Simply acknowledging domestic governance is an important step. But a fully state- or place-centric approach is a poor fit with transnational arenas, which after all are filled with "multiple and overlapping networks of supply chains, multinational firms, transgovernmental relations, international organizations, civil society organizations, and private regimes and governance systems."[50] To borrow Manuel Castells's (2016) terminology, we must attend to both the "space of places" and the "space of flows" and the "tension and articulation" between the two. The "space of places" refers here to the social, political, and ecological context at the point of implementation, including national and subnational legal orders, the local organization of companies, workers, and citizens, and the de facto power of different actors. The "space of flows" refers here to the movement of rules and assurances—as they accompany orders and products—through global production networks.[51] When brands and retailers request or require that their suppliers comply with a particular set of rules, a series of transnational flows ensue: Rules flow to suppliers, assurances of compliance flow back, and both buyers and suppliers become enmeshed in transnational arenas where the meaning and legitimacy of those rules and assurances are being continuously debated.

Put differently, the consequences of transnational private regulation depend on the intersection between domestic governance and transnational structures of two types—namely, global production networks and transnational fields.

THE FLOW OF RULES AND ASSURANCES THROUGH GLOBAL PRODUCTION NETWORKS

Global production networks have become infrastructures for spreading and enforcing rules, not only about product characteristics but about the decency and sustainability of production processes. In what Michael Vandenbergh has dubbed the "new Wal-Mart effect", large lead firms are using their power not only to push down prices, but to push standards.[52] Sourcing contracts may stipulate that suppliers are required to comply with a code of conduct (although the lead firm generally retains discretion over how strictly to enforce this), or a lead firm may require all of its suppliers to be certified to a

---

[50] Kobrin 2008:266.

[51] My goal is more modest than those, like Castells, who seek to re-write the entirety of social theory in terms of "flows" and "places." And it is more focused on governance than ecological modernization theorists who highlight flows of "material and energy" through ecosystems and economies (Mol and Spaargaren 2006). See Tysiachniouk 2012 for a compatible adaptation of this terminology.

[52] See Vandenbergh 2007 as well as Scott 2012, who puts enforcement through contracts in a broader context.

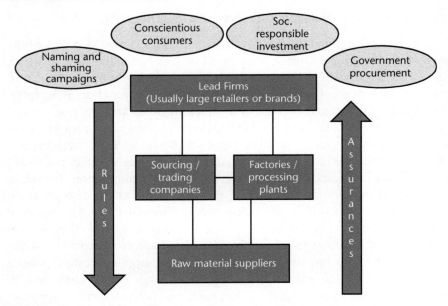

Figure 2.1. The flow of rules and assurances through global production networks

particular standard. This is what auto manufacturers do with the ISO 14001 environmental management system and what some toy brands do with labor standards certification by the International Council of Toy Industries CARE Process.[53] For more challenging, performance-based standards, though, a brand or retailer is more likely to provide incentives for suppliers to get certified—such as increased orders, premium prices, or subsidies for the cost of certification—than to demand it across the board.[54]

Consider the highly simplified global production network at the center of Figure 2.1, which stretches from "lead firms"—quite often retailers and brands that are close to consumer markets—to the companies that extract or harvest natural resources. In between are a variety of processors and manufacturers, that is, factories that make the final products (e.g., garments, furniture, computers) and those that make inputs and "intermediates" of various sorts (e.g., textiles, lumber, semiconductors). In some situations, a sourcing agent or trading company may sit in between, and often there will be subcontractors or sub-subcontractors doing some of the work. If rules are pushed vigorously through this structure, they have the potential to influence large swaths of a production process, from the extraction of raw materials to the final processing and assembly of consumer products. In practice, it seems that brands and

---

[53] McGuire 2014; Yang 2014.

[54] Even for lower-bar management system standards, such as ISO 14001, there is evidence that demand from buyers is an important determinant of certification (McGuire 2014).

retailers often push half-heartedly and unevenly.[55] After all, corporations' interests in promoting sustainability and fairness are generally ancillary to their interests in keeping production costs low, maintaining flexibility, and innovating in design, marketing, or distribution.[56]

Nevertheless, as depicted at the top of the figure, four types of demands can create incentives for firms to push rules through their supply chains. The demands of activists—through "naming and shaming" or "market campaigns"—represent one pressure point. Firms may also be responding to observed or expected demand from "conscientious consumers", although the influence of this factor varies significantly across products and countries.[57] Often, recognizable consumer demand has come only *after* the emergence of certification initiatives and their "market-making" projects.[58] Socially responsible investment funds and institutional investors also play an important role. As responsible investment groups have shifted from negative screens that exclude all companies in objectionable industries to "best in class" models that score corporations' "environmental, social, and governance" (ESG) programs, they have created incentives for corporations to adopt supply chain standards, promote credible certification, and issue detailed sustainability and social responsibility reports.[59] Investors often look to specialized raters of corporate responsibility, who in turn look for existing measures of leadership, including processes and standards that companies have adopted.[60] Finally, in some cases, NGOs have convinced government procurement offices to include preferences for certified products, using the power of governments as large consumers if not as direct regulators.[61]

To appeal to these audiences, companies generally have to provide some assurance that rules are being enforced. Thus, as rules flow from lead firms to suppliers, assurances are constructed and sent back, making their way from auditors at the site of production to compliance managers at corporate offices and ultimately to external audiences. The assurance may consist of a formal certification of compliance to the standards of a third-party initiative—such as the Forest Stewardship Council or Social Accountability International—but it can also take the form of a relatively "clean" audit report, documented evidence that suppliers are using relevant management standards and "best practices", or at least evidence that progress is being made.

---

[55] Locke, Amengual, and Mangla 2009.
[56] On the management and measurement of competing demands by "pro-social" organizations, see Child 2015; Barman 2016.
[57] See Bartley, Koos, Samel, Setrini, and Summers 2015.
[58] Gulbrandsen 2006; Conroy 2007.
[59] Dyck, Lins, Roth, and Wagner 2015; Avetisyan and Gond 2013; Arjaliès 2010.
[60] Delmas, Etzion, and Nairn-Birch 2013; Chatterji, Levine, and Toffel 2009.
[61] Overdevest 2010; Auld, Gulbrandsen, and McDermott 2008.

This flow of rules and assurances constitutes the fundamental mode of enforcement for most forms of transnational private regulation. Indeed, what is "regulatory" about this form of governance is that specific rules are promoted and verifiable assurances are demanded. The stringency of rules and the credibility of assurances may vary, but this basic structure of scrutiny can be found in a number of cases, from fair labor and sustainable forestry projects to those focused on sustainable agriculture, responsible mining, and product safety.

Actual global production networks are far more complex and varied than the stylized version depicted in the figure. Some involve relatively atomized companies buying and selling simple or substitutable inputs (e.g., some types of textiles and timber) or complex but standardized "modular" inputs (e.g., semiconductors, bicycle parts). Others require more durable collaborative relationships between firms; and in some industries "hierarchical" supply chains persist, in which multinationals use subsidiaries and joint ventures for manufacturing or resource extraction.[62] There are reasons to believe that the structure of production will influence the flow of rules and assurances. Research on labor standards has argued that improvement is more likely when buyers and suppliers have long-term, collaborative relationships, which allow for joint problem-solving over time, whereas "hit-and-run" demands for compliance tend to provoke evasion.[63] On the other hand, as these same scholars recognize, long-term relationships are scarce in many global industries, and it is the growth of highly competitive, rapidly changing, and "fissured" supply chains that has generated the demand for new forms of regulation.[64]

Moreover, as research on sustainability standards has emphasized, global production networks encounter different structures of ownership and production as they reach into different countries. Some have argued that concentrated industries should be more receptive to transnational standards, essentially because fewer companies must be convinced.[65] But the existing evidence points in both directions, since concentrated industries have also had the power to fight off transnational standards that are perceived as a foreign intrusion.[66] Further attention to the flow of rules through different structures of production is needed.

Assurances of compliance likewise require further scrutiny. They typically rest on audits that assess whether standards on paper can be verified in practice. As various scholars of the "audit society" and "audit culture" have

[62] Gereffi, Humphrey, and Sturgeon 2005.

[63] Locke, Amengual, and Mangla 2009; Frenkel and Scott 2002; Sabel 2007.

[64] Weil 2014.   [65] Cashore, Auld, and Newsom 2004.

[66] Espach 2006. His analysis of coalitions in support of the Forest Stewardship Council finds greater support in the "heterogeneous and diffuse" Brazilian forestry sector than in Argentina, "where high industry concentration leaves the program vulnerable to the opposition of two major firms" (p. 82).

pointed out, this approach has particular tendencies and biases. At the most general level, audits are a form of checking, not deep investigation, that rely on readily available and quantifiable indicators to produce simplified, decontextualized versions of truth.[67] More specifically, researchers have identified particular blind spots in social and environmental auditing, such as a blindness to deep categorical inequalities of gender and ethnicity, and an acceptance of the authority of written but not verbal forms of proof.[68] Private regulatory initiatives and their accreditors may specify specific indicators for auditors to check and best practices for doing so, but there is nearly always enough ambiguity about the meaning of rules—and enough complexity in a crowded space of implementation—that compliance must be seen as an interpretive accomplishment, not a technical one.

In the larger body of research on regulation, it has become common to argue that compliance is constructed and negotiated by inspectors, managers, lawyers, and "street level bureaucrats".[69] But recent research on private regulation seems to be ignoring the construction of compliance. Instead, scholars have accepted auditors' designations of compliance as their own, using data from audits to explain variation in compliance rates.[70] If auditors' understandings of what is necessary and feasible depend on the domestic setting in which implementation occurs, then the constructed meanings of compliance may vary substantially across countries.[71] Indeed, there is some evidence that auditors cobble together transnational rules and local understandings in deciding how to judge factories and forests.[72] In short, private assurances, like rules, may seem like a transcendent form of scrutiny, but the judgments behind them necessarily occur in particular, non-empty places.

STRUCTURE AND SUBSTANCE IN TRANSNATIONAL FIELDS

If global production networks are the infrastructures for pushing rules, transnational fields are the arenas in which rules and assurances are formulated, debated, and overseen. In general, a field can be defined as a relatively coherent though not strictly bounded arena in which organizations and individuals

---

[67] Power 1997; Strathern 2000; Espeland and Vannebo 2007.

[68] On the limited understandings of gender discrimination in private regulation, see Barrientos, Dolan, and Tallontire 2003; Barrientos and Smith 2007. On auditors' interpretations, see Silva-Castañeda 2012; Fortin 2013.

[69] Edelman, Uggen, and Erlanger 1999; Huising and Silbey 2011; Hawkins 1984.

[70] Toffel, Short, and Ouellet 2015; Locke 2013; Marx and Cuypers 2010; Distelhorst, Locke, Pal, and Samel 2015; Prakash and Potoski 2006a.

[71] Recent work by Prakash and Potoski (2014) suggests one version of this process. They argue that the value and impact of ISO 14001 certification is maximized where domestic regulation is lax and pollution is highly visible. This argument should apply most clearly to systems-based certification with few performance requirements, rather than high-bar performance standards. I will follow a different, more constructivist route in theorizing variation in the meaning of compliance.

[72] Malets 2013; Malets 2015; Kim 2013; Coslovsky and Locke 2012; Amengual 2010.

interact in pursuit of a common project. Fields emerge as "participants take one another into account as they carry out interrelated activities."[73] The rise of transnational governance has gone hand in hand with the structuring of transnational fields, in which actors from different national settings become enmeshed in communities of practice and webs of dialogue and debate.[74] The emergent field of sustainability standards, for instance, includes a number of certification initiatives, umbrella "meta-governance" organizations, practitioners from corporations and NGOs, auditing and certification bodies, and various other consultants, experts, and watchdogs.[75] The shared project that defines a field need not be consensual. Indeed, fields are usually structured by a mix of mutual attention and deep conflict, and private regulatory fields are no exception. Competing initiatives, such as the Forest Stewardship Council and Programme for the Endorsement of Forest Certification, have paid close attention to one another as they have competed, engaging in some mutual adjustment while vying for legitimacy and market share.[76]

Private regulatory fields face a distinctive set of challenges: As private actors—whether NGOs, companies, or a mix of the two—attempt to set standards, they inevitably face questions about their authority to do so. Questions of "who watches the watchdog?" or "who certifies the certifier?" fuel a "spiral of trust".[77] Private regulators can look to a variety of structures and practices to enhance their credibility, including multi-stakeholder governance arrangements, information disclosure, and credentialing and accreditation systems for auditors. But the same questions can be asked of these activities—that is, "who certifies the certifier of the certifier?"[78] Competing initiatives further fuel the spiral of trust, raising questions about the credibility of their rivals as they attempt to shore up their own systems.

As a result, credibility is a constantly moving target. Its arbiters include formal overseers, such as accreditation bodies and umbrella organizations that codify best practices, external watchdogs that publicize controversial decisions, and "critical insiders" that use internal governance processes or

---

[73] McAdam and Scott 2005:10. This conception comes from neo-institutional theories of organizations, but it overlaps to some degree with Bourdieusian conceptions of fields, which emphasize competing forms of knowledge and power (Fligstein and McAdam 2012; Bourdieu and Wacquant 1992).

[74] Djelic and Sahlin-Andersson 2006b.

[75] Dingwerth and Pattberg 2009; Bartley and Smith 2010.

[76] Cashore, Auld, and Newsom 2004; McNichol 2003; Meidinger 2003; Overdevest 2010.

[77] Shapiro 1987; Djelic and Sahlin-Andersson 2006b. Because states can claim a monopoly on authoritative rule-making within a territory, the spiral of trust is deeper and more endemic to private than public regulation.

[78] The ISEAL Alliance plays this role for a number of certification initiatives focused on sustainability and/or fairness. Its members include the Forest Stewardship Council, Marine Stewardship Council, the Roundtable on Sustainable Palm Oil, and Fairtrade International and accreditation service providers such as Accreditation Services International and Social Accountability Accreditation Services.

external publicity to keep their initiatives honest. The power of watchdogs and critical insiders can vary, though, with some initiatives and fields being more open to "voice" than others.[79]

A growing body of research on transnational fields, epistemic communities, and governance "interactions" focuses on the ways in which these dynamics play out in transnational spaces, whether in face-to-face meetings or more dispersed forms of dialogue, debate, comparison, and benchmarking.[80] But it is important to remember that these transnational debates are also intertwined with events at the point of implementation. For instance, competing global standards may reflect on-the-ground struggles over the feasibility of particular reforms, the proper role of the state, and control over the definition of sustainability and decency in a particular setting.[81] In addition, the rigor of transnational standards depends not only on credibility contests and formal structures of oversight in transnational fields, but also on assessments made on the ground, additional forms of scrutiny in the surrounding environment, and the links between local and global watchdogs. Research on the architecture of transnational fields is often quite optimistic about the feedback between local implementation and transnational rule-revision processes, but those who have observed implementation often find perversions and blind spots that go unresolved.[82]

Sociological analyses of fields, both domestic and global, have blossomed in recent years, but they often emphasize the form and structure of fields more than their contents. Most prominently, Neil Fligstein and Doug McAdam's (2012) general theory of "strategic action fields" focuses on generic "incumbents" and "challengers" who vie on unequal footing for control over the field. "Challengers" in their account ends up referring to a highly varied set of actors—from civil rights groups fighting for racial equality to entrepreneurial mortgage brokers taking on large financial institutions. The type of broad parallel they draw between the "field of racial politics" and the mortgage market is not uncommon in organizational sociology.[83] But treating these

---

[79] Auld 2014. Note that the flow of rules and assurances also characterizes fields of transnational private regulation themselves, running through umbrella organizations (e.g., ISEAL Alliance), accreditors (e.g., Accreditation Services International), standard-setting programs (e.g., FSC, MSC), and certification bodies (e.g., SmartWood, SGS). One outcome of transnational private regulation is clear—the hyper-production of assurances.

[80] On transnational epistemic communities, see Djelic and Quack 2010; Adler 2005. For agenda-setting pieces on "transnational business governance interactions," see Eberlein, Abbott, Black, Meidinger, and Wood 2014; Wood, Abbott, Black, Eberlein, and Meidinger 2015.

[81] Cashore, Auld, and Newsom 2004.

[82] For an architectural account of feedbacks, see Zeitlin 2011. For some contrasting findings on the ground, see Ponte 2008; Vandergeest 2007; Mutersbaugh 2005; Malets 2015.

[83] For instance, organizational sociologists have identified similarities in field-building projects for gay identity, total quality management, environmental sustainability, and alternative dispute resolution, as well as similarities in collective action for civil rights, shareholder rights, nouvelle

diverse projects as the "same kind of stuff" may be taking a toll, leaving scholars to assume that *what* organizations and field-builders are working on is irrelevant.

In looking at transnational private regulation of land and labor, this study examines two similar fields, but it finds important differences in the organization of scrutiny, the integrity of standards, and the trajectory of reform. In place of organizational sociology's reluctance to make substantive distinctions, I will argue that the *content* of rules and field-building projects makes a difference. Put differently, a sound theory of transnational governance must attend to the substance of particular rules and the understandings of justice, progress, and the common good that animate fields.

This study of course also finds cross-national differences, as these fields and associated global production networks intersected with newly democratic Indonesia and authoritarian China. "Community rights", "natural forests", "freedom of association", and the operational space for private regulation itself meant different things as the same standards were put into practice in different contexts. At the same time, some constraints—especially those linked to the state—could not be overcome in any of these settings. All of this would be missed if we assumed transcendent norms, empty spaces of implementation, and simple measures of compliance.

A Substantive Theory of Transnational Governance: Propositions

Building from these foundations and the case studies that follow, I have developed a "substantive" theory of transnational governance, which makes claims about the modal consequences of private regulation, the intersection of transnational and domestic governance, and the content of rules. The eight propositions described in this section are an attempt to abstract insights from the case studies and provide claims that can be applied and tested elsewhere. The case studies were developed decidedly not through a deductive testing of theory, but rather through a back-and-forth of ideas from prior research (as summarized above) and the events and patterns I could discover through interviews, documents, and quantitative analyses. Only once the case studies were researched and written was it possible to develop these propositions. They provide a glimpse into some commonalities and differences in my cases, a typology of rules that goes well beyond these cases, and an attempt to make sense of some remaining puzzles.

cuisine, and HDTV standards. See Rao, Morrill and Zald 2000; Davis, McAdam, Scott, and Zald 2005; Armstrong 2002; Lounsbury, Ventresca, and Hirsch 2003.

The theory is "substantive" in three senses. First, rather than seeing transcendent norms and empty spaces of un-governance, the theory fills in the places of implementation. Second, the theory makes claims about the particular kinds of outcomes that are most and least likely to spring from transnational private regulation. Third, the theory argues that the content of rules, the ideas that animate transnational fields, and even features of the relevant products can shape the outcomes of private regulation. I will begin with propositions about the flow of rules and assurances through global production networks, then proceed to intersections with domestic governance, and then consider the content of rules and fields.

The flow of rules and assurances

PROCESS OVER PERFORMANCE

1. *Transnational private regulation most often leads to additional policies and systems, record-keeping, or other forms of documentation, even if the rules appear to require more substantive changes in performance.*

The specific outcomes of private rules vary from case to case, and occasionally rules are so lax as to spur no noticeable change, but the use of auditing, verification, or certification means that some concrete reforms will normally be required to produce an assurance of compliance or progress.[84] The general pattern might be called "process over performance". When rules about performance are subject to formal auditing, they are often operationalized as assurances about management systems and processes. For instance, rules might state that employees must not face discrimination, that communities' rights must be respected, or that certain plant or animal species must be protected. But auditing and certification bodies frequently construct assurances by pointing to management systems, such as formal hiring procedures, community dispute resolution procedures, or systems for considering species protection when drawing up management plans. For managers, it is typically less costly and disruptive to create or improve record-keeping and management systems than to alter core employment and production processes. Just as importantly, creating new systems and processes generates the kind of clear documentation that auditors need to collect to generate assurances of compliance.

A substitution of process for performance will be seen at a number of points in the case studies. To assess relationships between timber companies and

[84] Bromley and Powell (2012) highlight this kind rationalized scrutiny and evaluation to argue that "decoupling" between an organization's policies and practices is increasingly difficult to sustain. The theory developed here views rationalized verification as driving *particular kinds* of changes but still leaving a sizable gap between policy and practice, since auditing organizations have an easier time measuring the former than the latter.

communities, sustainable forestry auditors in Indonesia and China often checked to see if a company had a well-defined *system* to address community complaints or manage "free and informed consent" processes. In the FSC-certified Stora Enso plantation in China, assessing the company's improved dispute resolution system was simpler—and more amenable to the certification model—than delving into the thorny "historical" issues of corporate-state land-grabbing and the evolving context of Chinese land governance. In Indonesian forest concessions, companies such as PT Sumalindo and PT Intracawood could receive certification in the midst of community conflicts because auditors prioritized documented agreements and consultations, not the full resolution of conflicts.

Similarly, in the private regulation of labor standards, human resource management systems and occupational health and safety committees have been treated as ways of complying with rules about labor relations and workplace safety. This is especially clear in China, where narrow channels of worker–management communication have been substituted for collective labor representation, which is restricted by law. (As I will argue in Chapter 5, this is a highly contained and managerialist redefinition of labor rights, which may struggle to keep up with workers' expectations.) As can be seen in factories audited under the auspices of the Fair Labor Association or certified to the SA8000 standard, private regulation has put a premium on formal human resource management systems. By emphasizing systems and processes, private regulators have been able to construct factories as sufficiently compliant even when the relevant performance standards—such as those pertaining to freedom of association, working hours, or domestic legal compliance—are essentially out of reach for the entire industry. Here, the logic of auditing coincides with the business interests of private regulators and lead firms, who would suffer if large swaths of key markets were considered off limits.

Beyond the case studies in this book, there is a growing body of evidence on how the auditing model is remaking the world in its own image.[85] Auditing requires the world to be auditable—that is, it seizes on issues for which documentation is available and downplays issues that are illegible. In research on sustainable agriculture, one can see auditors privileging written forms of proof while struggling to process the testimony of residents about customary land rights.[86] In other research on labor standards, there is evidence that private regulation has mostly brought the "institutionalization of paperwork", as factory managers create more and more records to be shown to auditors.[87]

---

[85] Power 1997; Espeland and Sauder 2006.
[86] Silva-Castañeda 2012; Djama, Fouilleux, and Vagneron 2011; Fortin 2013.
[87] Sum and Pun 2005.

As discussed below, documentation, policies, and management systems are not the only outcomes of transnational private regulation, but they are the most likely, especially when performance is difficult to assess and/or few suppliers can meet the relevant performance standard. One implication is that the distinction between performance-based and systems-based standards, which has been at the center of many debates, is blurrier on the ground than it appears from afar.[88]

NETWORK CONDITIONS FOR IMPROVEMENT

2. *The likelihood of more substantive changes in performance is related to (a) the "network distance" between the demander and ultimate target of rules and (b) the durability of their relationship.*

Although new documentation and management systems are the most likely outcomes of transnational private regulation, substantive behavioral changes certainly occur too. As shown in Chapters 3 and 4, auditors' "corrective action requests" for FSC certification from 2001 to 2010 resulted in behavioral changes in the field roughly 42 percent of the time in Indonesia and 32 percent of the time in China. As shown in Chapter 5, Yue Yuen and other footwear factories in China phased out toxic chemicals and improved their working environments in response to scrutiny from brands and auditors. As shown in Chapter 6, unions in Indonesia were sometimes able to "leverage" codes of conduct to get abusive managers dismissed, increased payments to the social security system, or decreased use of short-term contract workers.

The likelihood of reform is related in part to the domestic context, as described below, but it also seems to be related to two features of the global production network through which rules flow. First, the case studies reveal several instances in which the flow of rules dissipated as it traveled through intermediary nodes. In Indonesia, some vertically integrated plywood producers—who engaged in harvesting, manufacturing, and marketing—responded effectively to market demand for FSC certification. In contrast, market demand had nearly evaporated by the time it passed from furniture manufacturers to their timber suppliers to logging companies. In the case of labor standards, large first-tier suppliers to leading brands got cleaned up—becoming "window factories", as one practitioner in China put it—but far worse conditions persisted in subcontracted factories. Brands and retailers have often asked their first-tier suppliers to police working conditions further

---

[88] As Prakash and Potoski (2006b) put it, systems- or process-based approaches tend to be "predicated on the belief that if appropriate processes and internal systems are in place, the desired outcomes will follow" (p. 26). But because they are generally easier to comply with, systems-based standards are more likely to be promoted by the backers of "business as usual." Indeed, what makes the FSC and several other initiatives stand out in a sea of greenwashing is their stringent performance standards.

up the supply chain, but the resources and time devoted to this do not appear to be proportional to efforts in the first tier.

Similar patterns have been noted in other research. For instance, the codes of conduct of electronics brands are all but invisible in their second- and third-tier suppliers.[89] In addition, companies that require environmental management systems typically apply this requirement only to first-tier suppliers.[90] The general principle can be stated in terms of the "network distance" that rules must travel—that is, the number of intermediate nodes through which they must flow to get to their ultimate targets. Other things being equal, the greater the network distance, the weaker the flow of rules.

Second, the likelihood of meaningful reform seems to depend on the durability of the tie between the demander and target of rules. As a growing body of research has found, if brands and retailers demand compliance from factories that they have only fleeting, market-based relationships with, factory managers are likely to resist or evade the rules. When the relationships are more durable and interdependent, then collaborative problem-solving and meaningful improvements are more likely.[91] It is worth noting, though, that in many industries, supply chain linkages change quite quickly, reducing the likelihood of gradual reforms. One can see both ends of the spectrum in my case studies, including the rapid churning of apparel factories, more long-standing ties in some parts of the forest products industry, and an intermediate situation in the footwear industry, where some factories were cast aside as other became "core" suppliers to major brands. This part of the proposition also springs from evidence from other industries, such as coffee production, that durable, long-term relationships can foster more meaningful application of standards.[92]

Of course, simple and durable supply chain linkages are not guaranteed to produce meaningful improvements. A variety of other factors—including price and speed pressures, lax scrutiny, and domestic governance—routinely get in the way. But to the extent that private regulation is rigorous and resources for improvement are available, network structures can make a noticeable difference.

Intersections with domestic governance

Some research has begun to show how domestic governance depresses or boosts compliance with private regulation. High state capacity and independent civil

---

[89] Nadvi and Raj-Reichert 2015.   [90] Vandenbergh 2007.
[91] Locke, Amengual, and Mangla 2009; Lim and Phillips 2008; Frenkel and Scott 2002; Oka 2010b.
[92] See Raynolds 2009; Child 2015.

society, for instance, have been found to increase the rate of compliance with labor codes of conduct.[93] The case studies in this book suggest that the influence of domestic governance is more profound: It channels and reconfigures the meanings of transnational private regulation, shaping the practical meaning of rules and definition of compliance. The propositions below focus on how domestic civil society shapes the construction of compliance and on what happens when there is a "clash of rules" between transnational standards and domestic governance.

THE POLITICAL CONSTRUCTION OF COMPLIANCE

3. *Compliance tends to be constructed in more demanding terms in locations where domestic civil society is active and autonomous. Where civil society is weak or repressed, auditors are likely to accept more minimalistic definitions of compliance.*

In most private regulatory systems, auditors and certifiers are paid—either directly or indirectly—by brands and retailers that are pushing rules through their supply chains and seeking assurances of compliance. As we will see, there is clearly variation in their integrity, independence, and skill, with evidence of laxity and corruption plaguing some fields. But even conscientious and skilled auditors and certifiers often fall back on professional and personal understandings of what is feasible and sufficient in a particular context. In some circumstances, they have access to standards and indicators that have been tailored to the particular context, but even then, it is nearly impossible for all aspects of a complex judgment to be codified in advance. Moreover, auditors have incentives to operationalize rules in "realistic" and "pragmatic" ways, since overly strict interpretations usually clash with their employers' business interests.

As a result, definitions of compliance tend to be constructed and crystalized based on a combination of the rules as written (which may in some cases be quite detailed), the definition of best practices in the relevant transnational field (including characteristic emphases and blindspots), and importantly, the normal ways in which business is conducted in the place of implementation. For instance, we will see auditors for FSC certification in China falling back on domestic definitions of "natural forests", of the unproblematic character of land tenure, and of the legitimacy of the state-sponsored All-China Federation of Trade Unions (ACFTU). In Indonesia, sustainable forestry auditors only occasionally problematized the common practice of timber companies paying off community elites to guarantee access to forest land. Auditors of labor standards in China knew it was nearly impossible for factories to meet the widely flouted legal limit on working hours, so they pushed at most for

---

[93] Toffel, Short, and Ouellet 2015; Distelhorst, Locke, Pal, and Samel 2015.

compliance with the sixty-hour standard set by many brands—in spite of the fact that most codes of conduct also call for legal compliance.

More importantly, the case studies suggest that domestic civil society has shaped what auditors are forced to see and how seriously they have to grapple with it. In Indonesia, where civil society is active and autonomous, bottom-up pressures have forced private regulators to pay attention to vexing issues of collective land and labor rights. This can be seen in the "code of conduct network" through which unions and labor NGOs pushed brands to support insurgent independent unions (see Chapter 6); and it can be seen in attempts by environmental and indigenous rights NGOs to use "indigeneity as a vehicle to counter dispossession" from forest land (see Chapter 3).[94] In China, where labor NGOs were in a precarious position and land-rights NGOs were virtually non-existent, problems could be more easily swept under the rug, and even careful auditors would simply find few independent stakeholders to consult with. Partially as a result, minimalist constructions of compliance allowed SA8000 and other standards to grow quickly in China (see Chapter 5). More strikingly, some Chinese timber projects created through apparent land grabs could be certified to the stringent standards of the FSC (see Chapter 4)—and quite quickly in comparison with the conflictual and drawn-out processes in Indonesia.

This is not to say that what private regulators do and do not see is determined by domestic civil society. There may be characteristic omissions—such as a blindness to gender discrimination in many labor standards auditing efforts—and points of emphasis that are shaped by distant watchdogs and constituents.[95] The key point is that there are nearly always complex, historically rooted tensions surrounding the fictitious commodities of land and labor; these are pushed into the foreground in some settings but submerged in others. The autonomy and strength of domestic civil society largely determines how reliably these tensions come into the fore.

Ironically, if open contention is suppressed or submerged, auditors are more likely to quickly and easily designate a particular site of production as compliant with transnational rules. A location where civil society is weak or repressed can, perversely, be fertile soil for the implementation of seemingly stringent transnational standards. (This is one side of the "dual logic of certifying in authoritarian places" described in Chapter 5.) Certification is more arduous and rare when domestic activists can push for "maximalist" definitions of compliance. In general, we should expect countries with strong

---

[94] Li 2010:399.
[95] I thank Stephanie Barrientos for pointing out that auditors of labor standards routinely ignore gender discrimination in employment, seemingly because gender hierarchies are so deeply taken for granted in a number of settings.

civil society to be contentious and often difficult places for transnational private regulation to be implemented but also the site of the most significant consequences when implementation occurs.

While other research does not go as far in theorizing the construction of compliance, some studies provide congruent evidence. Analyzing the implementation of FSC standards in Russia, Olga Malets (2013) finds that "the early and effective involvement of NGOs with forest certification has so far helped to keep FSC an instrument with some bite and did not allow companies and certifiers to water down certification requirements."[96] Environmental NGOs in Russia have repeatedly appealed certifiers' decisions, organized stakeholders, and otherwise pushed for stringent interpretations of transnational standards.[97] Growing government restrictions on civil society in Russia, though, raise questions about whether NGOs will be able to continue pressing for maximalist definitions of compliance.[98] There may be opportunities here and elsewhere to test this proposition by tracing sustainability assurances over time as governments crack down on civil society linkages.[99]

THE CLASH OF RULES

4. *When transnational standards clash with domestic governance, the latter will usually retain primacy.*

As transnational standards are put into practice, there will inevitably be some "clash of rules"—that is, a situation in which transnational and domestic norms are directly contradictory. Usually this involves transnational rules that call for companies to take actions that cut strongly against domestic law and cultures of production.[100] For instance, FSC standards ask companies to respect the customary rights of communities, but the Indonesian state grants timber companies the right to harvest land without acknowledging community claims. Similarly, while most labor codes of conduct and factory certification initiatives ask companies to respect workers' freedom of association and collective bargaining rights, these rights are heavily restricted by law in China. If transnational standards can trump domestic governance, then private regulation may be able to create sites of production that truly transcend their local contexts and live up to global best practices. It appears, though, that transnational standards rarely "win out" when a direct clash occurs.

---

[96] Malets 2013:319.   [97] Tysiachniouk 2012.
[98] See Malets 2015 on the declining quality of forest certification in Russia.
[99] See Dupuy, Ron, and Prakash 2016.
[100] As described earlier in this chapter, I define domestic governance as the set of laws and regulations, informal norms, and power relations that combine to define the relationship between the economy, society, and polity in a given country. Law is an important part of this combination, but it is quite possible for the violation of a law on the books to be deeply embedded in the informal culture of production, as with working hours in China.

Other scholars of global norm conflicts have treated the outcome as contingent on whichever party is more powerful in a given arena. For instance, Bruce Carruthers and Terence Halliday (2006) argue that conflicts between governments and international organizations turn on how "distant" a government is from the global norm and how much power it has to resist or revise it.[101] When dealing with reforms promoted by *private* regulators, though, we can make a bolder prediction: Domestic governance will almost always have primacy when a clash of rules occurs. Practically speaking, this means that auditors and other private regulators will ignore, dampen, or redefine transnational standards to allow them to be implementable in that domestic context.

The basic reason is twofold. First, it is difficult for firms to make reforms without a supportive socio-political context. Firms might take locally counter-normative actions to follow a transnational rule, but these can easily be stymied by government agencies or business partners that are not subject to the transnational rule. Second, as discussed above, private regulators typically prefer "realistic" and "pragmatic" definitions of compliance, rather than saying "no" to all firms in a particular location. Their job, when a clash of rules occurs, is to find ways to reinterpret the problematic rule in a locally acceptable fashion.

We will see the primacy of domestic governance in the assessment of forest land rights in both Indonesia and China. Despite differences in constructions of compliance, auditors tended to take the state's designations as authoritative. As one practitioner in Indonesia put it, "when we come to the certification, the assumption is that if the company gets a concession from the central government, it is legal to operate," despite the possibility of customary land claims.[102] In the case of labor rights in China, we will see that domestic governance was strong enough to lead private regulators to either abandon freedom of association rules or redefine them in terms of communication. In a different way, the primacy of domestic governance will be seen in the mismatch between Indonesian unions' "in the streets" power and the factory-centered logic of labor codes of conduct.

Beyond these cases, there is further relevant evidence from research on forest certification in Russia. FSC-certified companies there have occasionally implemented practices that go against state regulation, but the evidence "points mainly towards the restrictive effect of the interactions between domestic regulations and auditing practice."[103] Put differently, certifiers have become more flexible and lenient when they have run up against

---

[101] Carruthers and Halliday 2006.   [102] Interview with auditor, Bogor, 9/8/10.
[103] Malets 2015:355. In the same setting, Tysiachniouk (2012) similarly concludes that transnational standards that conflict with national legislation are often not fully implemented.

domestic governance. To be sure, reforms that cut against domestic governance are not impossible, especially if they can made relatively cheaply and unilaterally by the targeted firm. But they are unlikely—and made even more so by particular issues, as discussed next.

TERRITORY, RIGHTS, AND DE-CENTERED AUTHORITY

5. *Domestic governance is especially likely to retain primacy when a transnational rule focuses on territory or rights.*

Saskia Sassen's (2006) language of "territory, authority, and rights" helps to think further about the conditions under which transnational private regulation is subsumed to domestic governance. My case studies of land and labor in Indonesia and China suggest that a transnational rule will be especially unlikely to trump, bypass or transcend the state when it concerns territory (e.g., control of land), rights (e.g., workers' rights to unionize or be treated equally in hiring), or the combination of the two (e.g., the land rights of individuals or communities).[104]

In a variety of ways, the rapidly growing body of research on transnational governance and private regulation shows that authority has been significantly decoupled from the nation-state. States have not been eclipsed, but there has been a pluralization of authority both within and across states, such that "state regulators are increasingly embedded in and interplay with many other regulatory actors."[105] As seen in this book, transnational corporations now routinely exercise a type of authority by pushing rules through their supply chains. Their power to do so can be legitimated by referencing demands from consumers and investors, reputational risks, and strategic partnerships with NGOs. In this sense, semi-autonomous arenas of private authority have emerged alongside nation-states.

Territory and rights, though, appear to have remained much more strongly tied to the state. It is difficult for a private actor on its own—such as a corporation, auditing organization, or NGO—to systematically and reliably control territory. A private regulator can enforce other kinds of rules—defining what pesticides can be used in agriculture, what solvents can be used in manufacturing, or even what workers ought to be paid—by directing a client or business partner to simply change its practices. If a private regulator wants to enforce rules over territory, though, it must in some fashion work through the state, which remains the sole actor with the legitimate capacity to delineate, register, and protect land. Directing a business partner to alter the

---

[104] Conversely, to the extent that a clash of rules does not centrally concern territory or rights (e.g., reducing energy usage, reforming the organization of production, protecting workers from danger, eliminating toxic chemicals), then there is a greater chance for private regulatory rules to make a difference, albeit subject to the other complications discussed above.

[105] Djelic and Sahlin-Andersson 2006a:377. See also Slaughter 2004; Black 2001.

boundary of a given piece of territory is likely to fail unless others—especially the relevant government agencies—accede to this change. To be sure, non-state actors such as separatist movements can sometimes wrest territorial control away from states, but they invite violent, coercive responses in doing so. It is difficult to imagine the coalitions of firms and NGOs that populate fields of transnational private regulation risking deligitimation or state violence by taking such steps.

Likewise, to the extent that private regulators want to protect rights—such as human rights, labor rights, community rights, or property rights—they ultimately depend on legal and judicial systems provided by states. Private regulators can of course demand that a supplier or business partner respect the rights of employees and community members, but if that company fails to do so, the only recourse is to cease the business relationship. If one wanted to force respect for rights, some kind of binding legal action would be necessary. The point is not that states—or courts—are always good protectors of rights; it is that private regulators can be no better.

It may be that reliable alternative mechanisms for governing territory and rights will emerge as political structures continue to evolve, but it is difficult to find them in the current period. The spectacular rise of private commercial arbitration demonstrates that private parallels to traditional courts are viable, but this system still depends on national legal professions and the enforceability of contracts in courts.[106] In the forests of Indonesia, we will see some participatory boundary-mapping projects led by NGOs, but for these boundaries to become authoritative, they would need to be incorporated in state cadastral systems and official maps.

Collective rights—such as the rights of workers to form unions or the rights of communities to control land—appear to be especially problematic for private regulators. In large part, this is because the expansion of collective rights is usually unpalatable to both local elites and to the transnational corporations that are charged with enforcing private rules. For lead firms, having collectively organized workers and communities in their supply chains increases the threat of disruption and decreases the managerial flexibility of their suppliers. Brands and retailers routinely adopt rules that call for collective rights to be respected, but as we will see in the case studies, they rarely demand rigorous definitions of compliance or prioritize these rules over others. Other research on labor codes of conduct has found them to be at their weakest when it comes to workers' freedom of association and collective bargaining rights.[107] In addition, the collective land rights of indigenous people have been folded into sustainability discourses to a remarkable degree, but research on

---

[106] See, for instance, Dezalay and Garth 1996; Drahozal 2009.
[107] Barrientos and Smith 2007; Egels-Zandén and Merk 2014.

sustainable agriculture similarly finds that these rights are frequently endorsed but rarely rigorously enforced.[108] Respect for collective rights *can* improve when local and global pressures are combined over time, but this is perhaps the least common outcome of transnational private regulation.

The content of rules and fields

BEYOND LAND AND LABOR: A TYPOLOGY OF RULES
6. *Private rules that coordinate markets or regulate product characteristics will be more vigorously enforced than rules that restrict suppliers' production processes and methods (e.g., most labor and environmental standards).*

Considering the content of rules can help to account for the limits of both fair labor and sustainable forestry standards in comparison to some other cases of transnational private regulation. Studies of accounting standards, technical standards, and food safety portray private regulation as significantly reshaping the everyday practices of firms and industries.[109] A simple typology of rules helps to make sense of the differences.

First, rules may be primarily market-coordinating or market-restricting. Market-coordinating rules are usually intended to harmonize inconsistencies across national jurisdictions, sectors, or firms in order to facilitate trade, investment, or other forms of market integration. For example, harmonized accounting standards have been essential for the expansion of global financial markets; technical standards have facilitated global production and consumption of electronics; and quality standards have gone hand in hand with the globalization of markets for cotton and other commodities.[110] Here, conflicts and "standards wars" are endemic, as different firms and national industries vie for the power to set the global standard, but the conflicts center on *which* standards are to be used, not *whether* standards are attractive to transnational corporations.[111]

Market-restricting rules, in contrast, seek to rein in practices that could be profitable but that would expose consumers, workers, or citizens to undue burdens or hazards.[112] These include most labor and environmental standards, as well as standards for product safety and ethical business practice.[113] To

---

[108] Fortin 2013; Silva-Castañeda 2012.
[109] Meidinger 2009; Havinga 2006; Büthe and Mattli 2011; Cafaggi and Janczuk 2010; Rysman and Simcoe 2008; Lytton 2014.
[110] Dowell, Swaminathan, and Wade 2002; Büthe and Mattli 2011; Murphy and Yates 2009; Quark 2013.
[111] Ibid.; Dezalay and Garth 1996; Mügge and Stellinga 2015.
[112] There is admittedly some blurriness, since restrictive rules may prevent market failure and allow markets to function (see Fligstein 2001). In general, market-regulating rules "raise the bar of acceptability" while market-coordinating rules simply "put everyone on the same page."
[113] Verbruggen and Havinga 2016; Fuchs and Kalfagianni 2010; Verbruggen 2013; Boddewyn 1985.

the extent that companies have an interest in enforcing these standards, it typically comes from a risk-management rationale. Restricting otherwise profitable activities can reduce the risk of scandals and accidents that would produce negative publicity, sales losses, or stock market penalties.

A second dimension concerns the focus or target of rules. Some rules pertain to the products themselves, including their quality, safety, or inter-operability. Other rules concern the production process and methods.[114] They may focus on how workers are treated, how natural resources are extracted and utilized, how pollutants are disposed of, or even how assets, income, and profits are calculated. Nearly all labor standards are concerned with production processes, as are most environmental standards, except for those that focus on the health consequences of a product.

This dimension is important for the study of private regulation because it highlights *where* the risks of non-compliance are most directly felt. For product-based rules, hazards travel with the product to the end users, thus having a direct and potentially severe impact on a retailer or consumer brand. A serious lapse in food safety, for instance, will be felt by the consumers of the product and can usually be linked to the brand or retailer whose name is on the product, even if discovering the ultimate source of the safety breach is more difficult.[115] This should strengthen the interest of brands and retailers in cracking down on potential safety problems in their supply chains. This may not be sufficient to guarantee product safety in complex global production networks, but it at least provides a baseline of

---

[114] There is of some blurriness in the product-process distinction as well. Standards for organic food pertain to both the production process (i.e., restricting the use of pesticides in farming) and the product (i.e., reducing pesticide residues on fruits, vegetables, coffee beans, etc.). The distinction is practically and politically important, though. The GATT and WTO have been more accepting of governments imposing product standards than standards pertaining to process and production methods, as seen in the 1991 "tuna-dolphin" decision (Wessells, Cochrane, Deere, Wallis, and Willman 2001). Later decisions (e.g., the "shrimp-turtle" case) allowed process-based import restrictions, but only under very particular conditions, including proving that the restriction is non-discriminatory and "necessary to protect human, animal or plant life or health" (GATT Article XX). Howse and Regan (2000) argue that the real question is whether products can be considered "unlike" on the basis of their production methods. But as Kysar (2004) notes, the threshold of acceptability is still much higher for production process standards than for product standards, such that "the process/product distinction survives in modified form within international trade law" (p. 547). See also DeSombre and Barkin 2002; Bernstein and Hannah 2008.

[115] This appears to be one reason why public food safety systems in Europe and North America have been able to rely heavily on imperfect but reasonably effective private-certification systems. See Verbruggen and Havinga 2016. See Cheit 1990 for a different case of effective private regulation of product safety driven by risk-management and liability concerns. See Lytton 2014 for an account of how kosher certification blurs the product-process distinction, although it is worth noting that a violation here would be felt by the consumer, making it more akin to a product standard.

private scrutiny and remediation efforts, which can be bolstered by government regulation and legal liability provisions.[116]

For process-based rules, on the other hand, many hazards of noncompliance remain at the point of production. Production workers and local communities, not distant consumers or transnational corporations, bear most of the risks of hazardous workplaces, industrial pollution, and over-exploitation of natural resources. This distance seems to temper risk-management rationales for vigorous enforcement. The reputational and sales damage that can be done by distant scandals is enough to lead brands and retailers to push standards through their supply chains, but that push is often weak, inconsistent, or easily trumped by other business priorities.

If we cross these two dimensions, as shown in Table 2.1, we would expect transnational corporations' interest in stringent enforcement to be the weakest for market-restricting, process-based rules (quadrant 4)—that is, the types of rules for land and labor that are the focus of this book. They should have much stronger interest in market-coordinating rules, whether pertaining to products or production processes, since these bring the prospect of market expansion.[117] Market-restricting, product-focused rules (quadrant 3) are an intermediate case, since they may raise costs or decrease flexibility but may also help consumer-facing firms manage direct and potentially severe risks.[118]

Table 2.1. The content of rules

		Focus of rules	
		Product	*Process and production methods*
Purpose of rules	*Market-coordinating*	1 e.g., quality standards, inter-operability standards	2 e.g., accounting standards, ISO management systems
	Market-restricting	3 e.g., product safety standards, environmental standards with consumer health implications	4 e.g., most labor and environmental standards

[116] See Baker 2009; Bamberger and Guzman 2009, who argue that legal liabilities could be structured to strengthen product safety oversight by companies in WTO-compliant ways.

[117] Transnational corporations may have the strongest interest in enforcing market-coordinating rules that pertain to the production process (quadrant 2). Market-coordinating product-based standards (quadrant 1) could, if taken to the extreme, turn products into undifferentiated commodities (or modules), reducing the ability of firms to capture quality or brand-based premiums.

[118] It seems that the cases that scholars point to in portraying this as a "golden era of regulation" (Levi-Faur and Jordana 2005) are market-coordinating standards, while a hollowing out of regulation is more apparent when looking at market-restricting standards. See Streeck 2009 for an account of "Williamsonian" and "Durkheimian" rules that overlaps with the distinctions made here. In addition, product-based regulations should be more easily carried by trade (see Vogel 1995) than process-based regulations. But see Greenhill, Mosley, and Prakash 2009.

One implication of this theory, then, is that the content of rule-making projects shapes the strength of enforcement by firms and thus the outcomes of transnational private regulation.

LAND OVER LABOR

7. Among market-restricting, production process-focused rules, those focused on land and environmental standards tend to be more rigorously enforced than those for labor.

Despite serious problems, sustainable forestry standards have generally had more integrity than have fair labor standards. As the case studies will show, a number of large retailers and brands have promoted the FSC's challenging standards for forest management, even though the less stringent standards of the Programme for the Endorsement of Forest Certification have also expanded. On the ground, auditing of forests has had serious blind spots, but it has not been plagued by the deception and fraud that is common in the labor standards case. In both Indonesia and China, getting and staying certified to the FSC's standards has been a significant challenge for forest managers, often requiring years of preparation and the meeting of numerous corrective action requests. This meant not only creating new policies and monitoring systems but also making behavioral changes in the field, such as altering harvesting practices, increasing ecological buffer zones, eliminating certain pesticides, and negotiating new boundaries and compensation amounts with local communities.

In contrast, high expectations and rigorous monitoring existed mainly on the margins of the fair labor standards field. Small initiatives in particular niches, such as the Worker Rights Consortium and the Fair Wear Foundation, have sought to uphold stringent standards, sometimes working with local NGOs and unions to engage in "bottom-up" monitoring, as we will see in the Indonesian apparel and footwear industry. In addition, several leading brands, such as Nike and Adidas, developed their internal compliance departments and worked with key suppliers to improve factory conditions over time. But more commonly, factory managers were able to meet the requirements of brands, retailers, and private regulatory initiatives with modest improvements. Auditing often turned into a "cat and mouse game", as auditors chased information from evasive factory managers and workers. Some SA8000-certified factories in China were better than others, but as a group, they were not systematically different from similar uncertified factories in some respects. (See the analyses in Chapter 5.) In addition, the available evidence suggests that it typically took managers a matter of months, not years, to prepare for SA8000 certification.

Beyond the case studies in this book, there is ample evidence of the failures of private labor regulation.[119] In 2013, the Rana Plaza complex of garment factories in Bangladesh, some of which had been audited by brands and private initiatives, collapsed—killing more than 1,100 workers. This provided a stark reminder of the failures of corporate social responsibility, and it spawned some new initiatives, which are described in this book's final chapter. The year before, a fire killed nearly 300 workers at the Ali Enterprises factory in Pakistan, many of whom were trapped behind blocked doors and windows. The factory had just been approved for SA8000 certification, as had many others in Pakistan, where the government was aggressively subsidizing SA8000.[120] The certifier in question (the Italian firm RINA) lost its accreditation to work in Pakistan—but remained eligible to grant SA8000 certification elsewhere—and Pakistan remained a leading location for SA8000.[121]

The sustainable forestry field is not without its own controversies, including the violence perpetrated by Perum Perhutani and the attempt by Asia Pulp and Paper to capitalize on the FSC logo, both of which are described in Chapter 3. The Danzer Group's subsidiary in the Democratic Republic of the Congo got FSC-certified despite residents facing violence from the logging company, police, and military forces. But the FSC's decision to dissociate from Danzer following a complaint by Greenpeace—much as it had done with Asia Pulp and Paper in Indonesia—is the sort of move that has not been paralleled in the labor standards field.[122]

Notably, the FSC's standards on the rights of forest workers have been weakly implemented and audited, much like other labor standards. In China, as we will see, sustainable forestry auditors almost never noted the problem of workers lacking the right to join or organize their own unions. In Indonesia, similarly, they almost never focused on freedom of association, despite the fact that unions in logging operations have been subject to intimidation or retaliation and undermined by subcontracting and informal employment.[123] It may be the *issues*, not just the initiatives, industries, or fields that shape the outcomes of private regulation.

---

[119] Seidman 2007; Locke 2013.

[120] Theuws, Huijstee, Overeem, Seters, and Pauli 2013; Walsh and Greenhouse 2012.

[121] Social Accountability International 2012. As of the end of 2015, Pakistan had the fifth highest number of employees in SA8000-certified facilities and the eighth largest number of facilities (SA8000 certification by country as of December 31, 2015).

[122] Forest Stewardship Council 2013b. The decision to re-associate with a supposedly reformed Danzer fifteen months later raised many eyebrows, but nevertheless, the practice of dissociation and the public documentation of re-association have no parallel in the labor standard field (FSC Watch 2014).

[123] Interview with union representative, Jakarta, 6/30/09; Anam 2010; International Labour Organization 2010. In fifty-three audits for FSC certification in Indonesia from 2000 to 2010, only three minor and one major corrective action requests were made related to workers' freedom of association, making this one of the least problematized of all of the FSC criteria. If we weigh

WAS POLANYI WRONG? MAKING SENSE OF DIFFERENCES
BETWEEN LAND AND LABOR

One way to interpret the uneven implementation of rules is to presume that there are *inherent* differences between labor and environmental issues. Perhaps Polanyi was wrong to portray land and labor as similar fictitious commodities. And yet, most attempts to specify the difference fall short. As the case studies will illustrate, the notion that environmental issues are "natural" or "technical" while labor issues are "social" proves to be a very poor fit with the dynamics of forestry.[124] Similarly, one might speculate that environmental improvements are a "win-win" for companies and residents while labor issues are more "distributional", but this fails to appreciate the deep distributional conflicts over forest land and resources.[125] More generally, it is tempting to equate environmental standards with win-win efficiency enhancements—for energy efficiency, for instance.[126] But most standards for sustainable forests, fisheries, and farms bring no clear cost savings or efficiency enhancements, at least in the short- and medium-terms.[127] If consumers were willing to pay higher premiums for environmental than labor standards, this might help explain the performance of private regulatory systems. But the existing evidence here is mixed—with no clear advantage for sustainability labels that do not promise health or energy-saving benefits.[128]

Rather than presuming inherent differences, the proposition and discussion below uses insights from my case studies to explain the divergence between fair labor and sustainable forestry standards—and perhaps land and labor more generally.[129]

"minor" corrective action requests at half the level of "major" requests, workers' freedom of association (FSC criterion 4.3) ranked 45th out of 58 total FSC criteria in Indonesia and 41st in China.

[124] This point is made in a variety of literatures on forestry, from political ecology to common-pool-resource accounts. See Agrawal and Gibson 2001; Larson and Ribot 2007; Ostrom 1990.

[125] See Locke 2013 for a brief reference to this presumption.

[126] Mayer and Gereffi 2010 do so in suggesting that it is easier for firms to comply with environmental standards because doing so will save them money in the long term, citing Wal-Mart's energy efficiency reforms as an example.

[127] Instead, they ask managers to set aside conservation areas, protect endangered species, and ensure the livelihoods of forest-dwelling people. One can argue that forest products companies should have an enlightened interest in maintaining viable supplies over time, but it appears that this goal can largely be met through less costly "sustained yield" approaches that do not dwell on biodiversity or the livelihoods of local residents as sustainable forestry standards do. See Prudham 2007.

[128] Although the studies are not perfectly comparable, estimates of consumer demand for sustainability and fairness labels suggest they are similar in size and sensitivity to price increases. See Anderson and Hansen 2004; Hainmueller, Hiscox, and Sequeira 2011; Hiscox and Smyth 2007; Aguilar and Vlosky 2007. One meta-analysis suggests that consumers may be *more* willing to pay premiums for labor standards (Tully and Winer 2014).

[129] See also Evans and Kay 2008.

8. *Private rules tend to be more rigorously enforced to the extent that (a) non-industry groups occupy powerful positions in multi-stakeholder initiatives; (b) industrial operations are immobile and visible; and (c) the content of rules resonates with the main constituents and watchdogs in the field.*

Power and scrutiny in multi-stakeholder initiatives

The fair labor and sustainable forestry fields have seemingly similar forms of "multi-stakeholder" involvement in private regulation, but there are important differences in the practical power of industry outsiders. NGOs such as Greenpeace, the Rainforest Action Network, and Cultural Survival, as well as community forestry experts, were involved in the early discussions that spawned the FSC, and WWF quickly became its key organizer and promoter. Early fears of a corporate takeover led several smaller NGOs to disengage, but it also led the FSC's leaders to partition representation, voting, and administration so that actors with "economic" interests in forests were balanced with actors with "environmental" and "social" interests in forests.[130] This governance structure—though derided by some observers as producing "psychotic democracy"—has allowed the FSC's stringent forest management standards to persist over time, even as the program expanded and "mainstreamed".[131] In addition, the FSC's requirement that detailed summaries of forest management audits be publicly posted has enabled critical insiders such as Greenpeace and external watchdogs such as the Rainforest Foundation, FSC Watch, and a variety of domestic NGOs to appeal decisions, issue critical reports, and campaign against controversial decisions.[132] As the competition between the FSC and Programme for the Endorsement of Forest Certification (PEFC) heated up, the PEFC also began to require public disclosure of audit reports, making this type of transparency a field-wide norm.[133]

Non-industry groups were much less powerful in the development of multi-stakeholder initiatives for labor standards. When the Fair Labor Association (FLA) was being developed, unions and NGOs with ties to the labor movement (e.g., the International Labor Rights Fund, Interfaith Center for Corporate

---

[130] Synnott 2005. Initially, the FSC apportioned voting power into an "economic" chamber (25%) and a social and environmental chamber (75%), with each chamber further split into those from the global north and south. This was later revised into a three chamber system—economic, environmental, and social—with each holding one-third of the voting power and again split into northern and southern representatives.

[131] Interview with foundation official, New York, 3/5/04. See Klooster 2010 on how the FSC's organizational democracy restrained its mainstreaming. The most significant revisions to the FSC's model involved the opening to percentage-based claims, the new concept of "high conservation-value forests," and the addition of a principle on timber plantations in 1996, which was revised in 1999 and kept most of its key features in its 2012 revision.

[132] See Auld and Gulbrandsen 2010 on the distinctiveness of the FSC's approach to transparency.

[133] Overdevest 2010.

Responsibility) were at the table. But in this case, concerns about a corporate takeover led most of them to walk away in protest, having lost battles over the meaning of "independent monitoring" and freedom of association.[134] The remaining NGOs got one-third of the seats on the FLA's board of directors, but with the other two-thirds going to companies and university licensing representatives, NGOs could easily be outnumbered.

Social Accountability International (SAI) was a spin-off of a non-profit organization, the Council on Economic Priorities, and other stakeholders were invited to join an advisory board, not a membership structure. The initial advisory board that helped to develop the SA8000 standard, included representatives of companies (e.g., Toys R Us, Reebok, Eileen Fisher), certifiers (SGS and KPMG), unions (the International Textile, Garment, and Leather Workers Federation), and NGOs (the National Child Labor Committee and the Association François-Xavier Bagnoud). But the union representative did not have the full backing of his federation, and these NGOs were marginal to the labor rights/anti-sweatshop movement.[135] Once SAI became its own organization, NGOs were relegated to an advisory board that was split into business and non-business representatives.[136] Perhaps an indication of NGOs' weak position, the non-business side has been sparsely populated at times, with representatives of Amnesty International, the Maquila Solidarity Network, and other prominent NGOs coming and going.[137]

In contrast to the FSC's disclosure of audit reports, SAI discloses only a list of SA8000-certified facilities, with no information on the auditing process. There is a channel for complaints and appeals, but watchdogs would have to mobilize their own documentation.[138] The FLA releases basic summaries of audit reports—sufficient for my coding in Chapter 5 but without identifying information about the factory or details of the auditing process. In general, transparency is lower and less specific in the labor standards field, leaving critics to deride the entire endeavor but making it difficult to appeal or publicize particular controversial cases.

---

[134] Esbenshade 2004; Bartley 2007b. The International Labor Rights Fund's decision to stick with the FLA caused internal strife and the severing of some of its ties with the labor movement.

[135] The National Child Labor Committee focuses largely on youth employment in the US, and the Association François-Xavier Bagnoud has focused largely on the rights and well-being of children affected by the HIV/AIDS epidemic.

[136] Social Accountability International IRS 990 form, 2000; http://www.sa-intl.org, accessed February 24, 2001.

[137] In recent years, the seven-member non-business group has included someone from an industry association (the Foreign Trade Association, a body made up of European companies), the president of SAI itself, and several academics (http://www.sa-intl.org/index.cfm?fuseaction=Page.ViewPage&pageId=494, accessed May 11, 2016). For earlier members, see Leipziger 2001.

[138] Social Accountability Accreditation Services 2008.

The power of industry outsiders at the moment of founding seems to have had a profound and lasting impact on the stringency of rules and shape of transparency. Note, though, that the FSC's founding constituency and main watchdogs have been environmental and indigenous rights NGOs, not labor rights NGOs or trade unions.[139] This may help to account for the weak enforcement of labor rights in the forest.[140] It must be said that the *desire* of NGOs to engage with private regulatory systems also seems to vary across the labor and environmental domains. International environmental NGOs have typically been willing to work with market-based approaches, whether because they have accepted the "compromise of (neo-)liberal environmentalism" or because they hope to build markets for alternative production models.[141] But with the exception of "union label" promotion, unions and labor-rights NGOs have been more suspicious of market-oriented paths to reform, whether because of more deeply seeded capital versus labor narratives, the checkered and paternalistic history of consumer-worker alliances, or ambivalence about the emerging global trade regime.[142] For better or worse, labor-rights advocates have tended to criticize the entire project of transnational private regulation, while environmental advocates have been willing watchdogs and arbiters of the credibility of particular initiatives and decisions. We will see evidence that watchdogs matter at several points in the case studies.

Mobility and visibility of production
The difference between labor and environmental standards should not be viewed only through an organizational lens. The terrains of private regulation appear to have varied in their openness to scrutiny and their receptiveness to reform. In particular, fair labor standards, especially in the apparel industry, have been implemented in a rapidly globetrotting industry, the conditions of which are difficult to see from outside the factory walls. Sustainable forestry standards, in contrast, operate in an industry in which at least some

---

[139] A handful of unions and labor organizations had become FSC members by 2000, but these amounted to a small fraction of the roughly 300 organizational members at the time (Forest Stewardship Council 2000). Over the next decade, the Building and Woodworkers International union federation and some of its affiliates became involved with the FSC.

[140] In 2016, an Indonesian union organizer was elected as the chair of the FSC Board of Directors (Building and Wood Worker's International 2016). This may signal a change in the status of labor rights in the FSC, but for most of the organization's history they have been on the margins of the certification process.

[141] Bernstein 2001.

[142] See Frank 2003; Evans and Kay 2008. In a comparison of labor and environmental standards in NAFTA, Evans and Kay argue that the US labor movement was comparatively ineffective in pushing for enforceable standards, shifting clumsily between insistence on standards and opposition to the entire agreement. For examples of tensions over corporate engagement in the labor-rights NGO world, see Athreya 1998a; Compa 2008.

operations are more fixed in place and visible to external scrutiny. Gradual reforms and rigorous monitoring are more likely, though certainly not guaranteed, in the latter situation. Time and visibility seem to enable stringent private regulation.

The "supply-chain revolution" enhanced the mobility of production for a wide array of consumer products, but this is more constrained in some industries—and for some products—than others. Rudimentary apparel factories can be opened with modest investments in locations that have a pool of low-cost and modestly skilled workers (with the industry especially attracted to young women), decent infrastructure for power and transportation, and favorable tariff treatment for exports to major consumer markets. Thus we see the historical migration of apparel production from Japan, Hong Kong, Taiwan, and South Korea to Central America, the Caribbean, Southeast Asia, China, and Vietnam—and from Western Europe to Eastern Europe and North Africa as well. [143] In the past two decades, much production has moved to Bangladesh, India, and other parts of South Asia, while Kenya and Ethiopia now appear to be the next frontiers.[144]

Like many extractive industries, the forest products industry has been tied to a smaller number of places. To be sure, many types of lumber are widely produced, and pulp and paper companies have built new frontiers with massive plantations in various parts of the global south.[145] But some forest products are far more constrained in their movement. High-value tropical timbers, including teak and ramin, can only be harvested in a handful of locations after decades of growth. The top three teak producing countries—India, Indonesia, and Myanmar—were the same in 1990 and 2010, with only minor shuffles in the next tier.[146] Even softwoods grown in temperate forests come mainly from a handful of forested countries, such as Canada, the US, Russia, and Finland.

Without resorting to determinism, we should recognize that production processes differentially bind global production networks to particular places over time. And as we will see in the case studies, time is important for meaningful solutions to complex problems.[147] The long engagement between Perum Perhutani and the FSC, for instance, brought reforms that would have been difficult to forge without a stable stock of teak. Even in the threatened forests of Indonesia's outer islands, some concessions were stable enough to

---

[143] Rosen 2002; Bonacich and Waller 1994; Gereffi 1999. The shifts can also be seen in trade data compiled by the WTO (http://www.wto.org/english/res_e/statis_e/statis_e.htm).

[144] Morris, Plank, and Staritz 2015.

[145] Dauvergne and Lister 2011.

[146] Kollert and Cherubini 2012. Ghana and Nigeria moved into the top five, but the top ten to fifteen producers were quite similar at these two points of time.

[147] This might also help to explain the relative success of Fair Trade coffee, which rests on decades of capacity-building of producer cooperatives in a limited number of high-elevation locations where specialty coffee can be grown.

allow indigenous rights activists, when aided by the international spotlight, to gain ground. In contrast, unions' bottom-up monitoring and leveraging of labor standards in the Indonesian apparel industry was often undermined by factory shutdowns, the loss of orders from brands, and the migration of the industry to different regions or countries.[148] Products that can be made essentially the same way in a variety of places are more prone to globetrotting orders, "hit and run" rule implementation efforts, intense price competition, and hard-fought gains that are quickly nullified.[149]

Relative immobility does not guarantee effective implementation of rules. Indeed, entrenched governance of fixed natural resources is often highly corrupt, repressive, and destructive. But if one wants private regulation to foster learning, collaboration, and productive forms of contention, then one ought to look for ties that bind a global production network to a particular place.

The quality of private regulation can also be shaped by the visibility or direct observability of production processes. When auditors visit a forest or timber plantation, they can observe some of its relevant features directly—such as the species of trees, the conditions of other plant life in the forest, the condition of logging roads, and the size of ecological buffer zones. They may only observe a sample of locations, but they can nevertheless use their direct observations to judge many indicators of compliance. Some aspects of forest management can be observed from outside the forest—for instance, through satellite imagery that may be available to auditors and external watchdogs alike.[150] Although sustainable forestry auditors also rely on company-provided records and interviews with managers, workers, and community members, these sources can be triangulated with other forms of evidence. Community members, moreover, may provide an alternative perspective on the company. In a sense, auditors of land can engage in multi-method research.

In factories, auditors are more reliant on records and testimony. They can of course look for fire escapes, safety guards, and hazardous materials, but much of their evidence must come through company-provided records (e.g., of wages and hours) and through interviews of workers, who are routinely coached to give the "correct" answers and may in any case be reluctant to risk the loss of orders if they blow the whistle. This makes the "cat and mouse game" severe. Some brands and initiatives have responded by setting up hotlines to allow anonymous complaints, but few have been willing to pay

---

[148] Similar events have occurred when unions have sought to leverage codes of conduct in Thailand and the Dominican Republic. At the BJ&B factory in the Dominican Republic and the Gina Form Bra factory in Thailand, independent unions gained ground through "brand boomerang" campaigns only to see the factories shut down within several years. See Clean Clothes Campaign 2007; Worker Rights Consortium 2006a.

[149] See Anner, Bair, and Blasi 2013 and Schrank 2004 on the downward pressure on the prices that suppliers receive in the highly mobile apparel industry.

[150] For an example, see Greenpeace 2014a.

extra for off-site interviews with workers, which would increase the quality of the information. To be sure, laxity in the private regulation of labor standards is not due to poor auditing alone, but even if we assume high standards, supportive supply-chain relationships, and experienced auditors, the potential for evasion and "gaming" the system will be high when production processes are difficult to see directly.

Labor, environment, and the global common good
Finally, even if land and labor are not *inherently* different, they may be different types of public issues. One study found that American and European corporations have been more engaged with environmental issues than with labor and human rights, perhaps because environmental norms have "become more embedded in global markets than the social norms that underpin labour and human rights."[151] Land and labor share important similarities as fictitious commodities—not only are they resistant to complete commodification, they are dynamic in ways that make the certification of compliance problematic, as the case studies will reveal. But environmental and labor issues have been framed in policymaking and advocacy communities in different ways, especially vis-à-vis the global common good. References to "our common future" stretch from the Brundtland Commission's initial statement on sustainable development to current accounts of climate change and biodiversity preservation.[152] Whether considering Garrett Hardin's influential telling of the "tragedy of the commons" or Elinor Ostrom's alternative account, scholars have broadly and authoritatively treated environmental problems as problems of preserving public goods.[153] Policymakers may disagree on the seriousness of a problem or the right steps to solve it, but few question the basic premise that environmental problems "affect us all".

The "carbonization" of forests—that is, an emphasis on forests' role in mitigating climate change—has tied them even more strongly to conceptions of the global common good. The full effects of the "forest-carbon cycle" are complex, varying across forest uses, forest types, and even over time.[154] But the powerful stylized point is that, as a UN Environment Programme report put it, "the entire global population depends on forests for their carbon-sequestering services."[155]

---

[151] Favotto, Kollman and Bernhagen 2016:24.

[152] Brundtland Commission 1987; Daly and Cobb 1994. The scientific conference preceding the UN Conference of the Parties meeting in Paris in 2015 was titled "Our Common Future under Climate Change."

[153] Hardin 1968; Ostrom 1990.

[154] Schimel, Stephens, and Fisher 2015; Bellassen and Luyssaert 2014.

[155] United Nations Environment Programme 2011:3. In addition, the destruction of forests worsens climate change, most dramatically when peat swamp forests are drained and burned,

Framings of decent labor conditions as a global common good are far less accepted, at least in expert and policymaking arenas. "Workers of the world unite" has of course been a powerful frame historically, and perhaps the shadow of communism has something to do with the current reluctance to see labor standards as a global common good. Orthodox accounts of the global economy treat labor standards almost exclusively as private goods, the benefits of which would flow to the most privileged workers in the global economy. Thus, the specter of protectionism is used to discredit many calls for global standards and cross-border solidarity.[156] Even seemingly progressive economists and pundits fiercely attacked anti-sweatshop activists, arguing that they were driven by misguided paternalism or protectionism, and were ignoring the widespread benefits of free trade—even if a country's comparative advantage is rooted in workers' desperation.[157] As Dani Rodrik (2011) points out, this is odd, since within affluent democracies, labor standards are accepted as ways to prevent the desperation of some workers from undermining the conditions for decent work in general.[158] But when experts and policymakers have turned their attention to the global economy, this rationale has often disappeared or faded into a hope for voluntary, non-binding norms.

In academic circles, the "race to the bottom" thesis represents one way of conceptualizing labor conditions as a collective good, which can be undermined by unrestrained competition in a world of profound inequality.[159] The best empirical evidence is mixed: certain types of international trade relations have been associated with declining labor rights while others have been linked to greater stringency in law and/or practice.[160] But scholars appear to have a penchant for attacking this collective good framing of labor standards—often on the spurious basis that companies do not necessarily migrate to the *least* stringent environments or that the race to the bottom thesis is driven by protectionist interests.[161]

The International Labour Organization (ILO) has since the late 1990s, attempted to distance global labor standards from charges of protectionism and frame "fundamental labor rights" (freedom of association and the elimination of forced labor, child labor, and employment discrimination) as a global public good. But as Gary Fields (2003) has noted, this agenda was resisted

---

which releases massive amounts of of carbon dioxide and methane (Jauhiainen, Limin, Silvennoinen, and Vasander 2008; Sedjo and Sohngen 2012).

[156] See Fields 2003 for a review.   [157] Krugman 1997; Kristof and WuDunn 2000.
[158] See also Freeman 2005 for a review of the evidence of market-wide effects of unions in the US.
[159] Chan and Ross 2003.
[160] See Mosley 2011; Greenhill, Mosley, and Prakash 2009; Blanton and Blanton 2016.
[161] See Srinivasan 2013 for a critique of global labor standards as protectionist on the basis of an appraisal of the race to the bottom thesis.

by powerful international organizations—even those that had accepted sustainability agendas. "International financial institutions—in particular, the World Bank and the International Monetary Fund...—have not endorsed or worked actively to support these core labor standards,...apparently [because of] opposition to freedom of association and collective bargaining."[162] Eventually, the World Bank and its private lending arm, the International Finance Corporation (IFC), began to incorporate core labor standards in their screening of projects.[163] The IFC soon joined with the ILO to sponsor the Better Work initiative, which is described in the final chapter of this book. International organizations are perhaps becoming more accepting of "common good" frames for labor, but this comes roughly two decades after these organizations incorporated environmental sustainability frames into their work.[164]

For both labor and environmental standards, it seems that some benefits tend to be more concentrated (e.g., improved local soil and water quality, increased wages) while others tend to be more diffuse (e.g., regional air quality, mitigation of climate change, reduced inequality, or a culture of respect). Yet with odes to "our common future" in one case and condemnations of protectionism and misguided paternalism in the other case, it is perhaps not surprising that private regulation of labor standards has been shaky. We will see some indications of this in the case studies—in half-hearted commitments by leading companies, the movement of production to labor-repressive environments, and the precarious position of domestic labor-rights advocates. In the book's conclusion, the question of issue-differences and reform coalitions will return as I consider possibilities for moving beyond the failures of transnational private regulation.

The image of global standards descending into otherwise empty spaces runs deep in writing about transnational governance. The case studies that follow show what can be learned by instead delving into the crowded places of implementation. In many respects, the case studies can stand alone as accounts of sustainable forestry or fair labor standards in Indonesia or China. The similarities and differences across cases were the inspiration for the propositions developed in this chapter. Rather than testing propositions, the case studies provide rich narratives of the contexts and consequences of private regulation—weaving together evidence from my interviews, documentary sources, and some quantitative analyses—solving several case-specific puzzles along the way.

---

[162] Fields 2003:66.   [163] Murphy 2014.
[164] Bernstein 2001; Goldman 2005.

3

Purity and Danger

The Dilemmas of Sustainable Timber in Indonesia

> *"Consumers have a huge responsibility, perhaps more so in the case of Indonesia than many other sources of tropical timber, because we have seen again and again that Indonesia itself is unable to control this problem. If the market doesn't help then there's no hope for Indonesia's forests."*
>
> Nigel Sizer, The Nature Conservancy[1]

> *"It wasn't so long ago that people were going to laugh the FSC out of the country for certifying Perhutani."*
>
> Interview with forestry researcher[2]

The tropical forests of Indonesia resemble neither the isolated "wilderness ideal" imagined by preservationists nor the stable, "legible" forests constructed by scientific foresters.[3] They are places in which the enrichment of timber barons, the rise of agricultural industries, and the survival strategies of villagers have collided to produce a sense of "illegibility" and a number of dramatic changes. To what extent can credible sustainability assurances be made in a setting such as this, where the governance of land is ambiguous, contested, and unstable?

From 1990 to 2005, Indonesia lost 31 percent of its primary forest cover—that is, relatively undisturbed native forests—and 24 percent of all forested land.[4] While deforestation was slowing in many parts of the world, Indonesian forests were rapidly being cut or burned in order to be converted to plantations for timber or oil palm. This was one reason for the forest fires that spread a haze over much of Southeast Asia in 1997 and 1998. Illegal logging and timber smuggling threatened many of the forests that remained,

---

[1] Quoted in Greenpeace 2003:22. [2] 8/14/08. [3] Cronon 1996; Scott 1998.
[4] Food and Agriculture Organization (FAO) 2006.

and by the early 2000s, researchers and environmental NGOs were highlighting massive losses in biodiversity, new threats to the habitats of orangutans, tigers, and other endangered species, as well as rising greenhouse gas emissions from the burning of peat forests.

The 1990s were also a time of great political change. After ruling the country for thirty years, the Suharto's authoritarian "New Order" regime gave way to an era of democratization and *Reformasi*. This period created space for civil society and competitive elections, but it also produced great uncertainty, new power struggles, and ultimately destructive consequences for Indonesian forests.[5] Meanwhile, the remnants of Dutch colonial-era and Suharto-era ways of managing forest land persisted in many respects. For two centuries, central authorities have appropriated Indonesian forest land—usually ignoring or displacing local people—and allocated harvesting rights to well-connected companies. The links between timber companies, the military, and paramilitary groups from the Suharto era did not fall away easily in the transition, and much of the timber trade remained an opaque world of complex financial entanglements and front companies.

Many environmentalists, foresters, community-rights advocates, and entrepreneurs within and outside Indonesia have embraced the hope that the country can shed its reputation for forest destruction and become "known as a source of sustainable products," as one practitioner put it.[6] In Europe and North America, activists and their retail targets made a market for Forest Stewardship Council-certified products that grew to $20 billion in sales by 2007.[7] Within Indonesia, forestry consultancies and NGOs sought to help timber companies get certified and tap into this market. Their hope is that certification can reward companies and community-based operations that are logging responsibly, make other logging practices less destructive, and provide a disincentive for forests to be cleared and converted to agricultural land.

Yet as the international market for certified forest products grew, the vast majority of Indonesian forestry operations remained unaffected. Indonesia was the site of one of the first experiments with forest certification—the 1990 certification of Perum Perhutani's teak plantations by SmartWood. But by 2009, less than 2 percent of the area designated as "production forest" in Indonesia was FSC-certified, a great disappointment for certification's champions and a stark contrast to the 15–20 percent rate of FSC certification in Brazil, Russia, and several other major timber exporters. Indonesia's

---

[5] See McCarthy 2004; Casson and Obidzinski 2002; Tsing 2005; Hadiz 2010.

[6] Interview with sustainability consultant, Yogyakarta, 6/23/09. Both neoliberal reformers at the World Bank and environmental NGOs have sought to restructure Indonesian timber markets, often in strikingly similar ways. See Barr 2001.

[7] Forest Stewardship Council 2010.

"homegrown" initiative, Lembaga Ekolabel Indonesia, had mainly certified the same forests as the FSC, so less than 3 percent of production forest land was certified under either system. The forests that did get certified faced recurrent problems, suspensions, and critiques from watchdogs. In spite of these challenges, the FSC and its certifiers pressed on, in hopes of introducing a host of best practices to the tumultuous terrain of Indonesian forests.

Understanding forest certification in Indonesia means addressing two types of puzzles. First, with a growing market for certified products, why did Indonesian forests remain largely untouched by the certification model? As we will see, the answer is partially about how demand was limited or disarticulated in the export markets that were most important to Indonesian producers. But a full answer cannot be based on foreign markets alone; it requires delving further into the domestic political economy of Indonesian timber—and even the way in which forest property is constituted. There is a deep contradiction between the domestic governance of forests and the transnational standards for certification, and despite the hopes of sustainability advocates, this barrier has not been washed away by the growth of green markets.

The second puzzle has to do with the forests that were certified. To receive and retain certification, managers had to make a number of changes—to harvesting practices, conservation areas, and relations with communities, for instance. How far could such changes go in rectifying the problems that face Indonesian forests? As discussed in the introductory chapter, many accounts suggest that "pushing" standards through global supply chains can, in a sense, "pull" particular operations out of destructive and conflict-ridden settings and make them operate by a different logic. The case of Indonesian forestry casts doubt on this notion. With the promise of market premiums, the glare of global scrutiny, and assistance from experts, companies did make some meaningful changes in order to get certified. But they also reproduced existing modes of appropriation and exploitation of forest land—in a form that was perhaps gentler but still quite distant from demands for land rights and environmental justice.

I will begin with the story of Perum Perhutani's dramatic certification, de-certification, and re-certification. Next, I will expand the scope to describe the development and implementation of certification in Indonesia, taking up the two puzzles in turn. The first requires a look at the limits of foreign market demand, the domestic political economy of timber, and the ways in which forest property evolved into especially ambiguous and contested terrain. The second involves looking at the changes made to get certified, how auditors assessed them, and the constructions of compliance that ensued. As we will see, FSC certification was difficult to achieve, but it nevertheless promoted shallow resolutions to deep conflicts.

Certifying Violent Spaces: The Case of Perum Perhutani

From colonial conquest to certified sustainability

In the pre-colonial period, control of Javanese teak forests was fluid, and peasants negotiated with local nobles for rights to clear land for agriculture.[8] The Dutch East Indies Company in the seventeenth to eighteenth century and especially the Dutch colonial administration in the nineteenth century greatly centralized control of Javanese teak forests and introduced scientific forestry methods to manage them in the orderly style of German and French foresters.[9] While forests on the outer islands would not be consolidated as "state forests" until the twentieth century, the colonial authorities quickly established control of Javanese land and pushed local people to migrate to less populated islands.[10] Once Indonesia became an independent nation-state (1945–9), the state retained control of the forests, mixing populist rhetoric with forestry laws that were often borrowed from the colonists.

After General Suharto's bloody rise to power (1965–7), the state forestry company, Perum Perhutani, was founded to foster an "Indonesianization" of earlier systems. But, Nancy Peluso (1992) argues, "its 'personality' in the field, from the perspective of forest villagers, remain[ed] that of a foreign institution seeking to control the extraction of local resources."[11] The company's guard-ianship of the forests had a militaristic tone, with teak plantations being protected by armed forest guards and paramilitary "mobile brigade" (*Brimob*) police.[12] Their role was to stop what Peluso calls the "counter-appropriation" of teak by local people, who were denied legal access to the land and struggled to subsist on the small-scale agriculture allowed by the *tumpang sari* system of inter-cropping, which had been adopted from the Dutch and revised through "social forestry" experiments in the 1970s.[13] Black-market entrepreneurs fun-neled teak into the furniture districts of Central Java or smuggled it out of the country, while villagers assisted or looked the other way, since they had "no incentive to help the state monopolize access to the most valuable forest resource on Java."[14]

Given this history, it might be surprising that Perhutani was among the first operations certified by the Rainforest Alliance's SmartWood program. But many foresters saw the Perhutani's scientific agroforestry model as one to be emulated, and the company had participated in social forestry projects sponsored by the Ford Foundation and others.[15] The Rainforest Alliance, a non-profit organization founded in 1987, built its SmartWood program with

---

[8] Peluso 1992.   [9] Scott 1998.   [10] Peluso and Vandergeest 2001.
[11] Peluso 1992:129.   [12] Ibid.   [13] Ibid.   [14] Ibid.:231.
[15] Peluso and Poffenberger 1989; Sunderlin, Artono, Palupi, Rochyana, and Susanti 1990; Donovan 2001.

support from Smith & Hawken, an eco-conscious furniture company that was using Indonesian teak.[16] With 75 percent of Perhutani's exports going to Western Europe or the US, the company depended on "eco-sensitive" markets and hoped to differentiate itself from controversial teak from Burma/Myanmar.[17] In 1990, SmartWood certified all of Perhutani's 2.5 million hectares of forest land, pointing to the company's "innovative, socially oriented plantation management program".[18]

SmartWood soon became a founding member and accredited certifier of the FSC, and Perhutani began the process of getting several districts FSC certified.[19] Five districts, a select group of the company's full fifty-seven districts, were certified between 1998 and 2000. Peluso, the sociologist, who had chided environmentalists for seeing Perhutani's plantations as "exemplars of good management, without understanding their... history or the political implications of this form of management", was enlisted as a peer reviewer of the certification process, and the auditors did fret somewhat about company–community relations.[20] Nevertheless, the certifications were granted, and by 2000, FSC-certified timber from Perhutani forests was flowing through more than thirty Indonesian furniture firms that had received "chain of custody" certification.[21]

But the political context was in the midst of dramatic change. Suharto's regime had fallen in 1998, and although many companies retained military linkages, the "withdrawal of the New Order army as the guarantor of corporate greed," as Anna Tsing (2005) puts it, meant that "illegal resource extraction suddenly overwhelm[ed] the legal."[22] In addition, to implement decentralization reforms pushed by the World Bank, Indonesia devolved some control of forests from the central to district governments, which as we will see later, had disastrous consequences for forests throughout the country. In the Javanese teak plantations, local "counter-appropriation" and black-market entrepreneurship flourished. Sometimes this had political undertones, with lootings referred to as "*demo kayu*" (timber demonstrations) as well as more conventional protests against Perhutani.[23] The economic incentives for illegal logging were substantial, since one stolen mid-sized teak log might be worth three months of wages for an agricultural worker and could be sold to manufacturers at half to two-thirds of Perhutani's price.[24] The cluster of

---

[16] Taylor and Scharlin 2004.   [17] Elliott 2000:100.   [18] Donovan 2001.
[19] This had to wait until the FSC decided to allow the certification of plantations in 1996, which are lower in biodiversity than natural forests but which sometimes help to take pressure off of natural forests.
[20] Peluso 1992:5.   [21] Muhtaman and Prasetyo 2006.
[22] Tsing 2005:42. See Human Rights Watch 2010 on persisting military connections.
[23] Schiller and Fauzan 2009:32; Fauzi 2003.   [24] Schiller and Fauzan 2009:31, 34–5.

craft-based furniture makers in Jepara became known as the "vacuum cleaner" for illegal teak.[25]

Perhutani's armed forest guards clashed with what the company viewed as "timber mafias", as well as local government officials who could profit from illegal logging.[26] After the company's guards killed one alleged illegal logger, villagers burned down a Perhutani regional office. In another village, a person detained for illegal logging died in the hospital after allegedly being tortured by company officials.[27] Perhutani would eventually be accused of killing thirty-one people from 1998–2008 and injuring many more.[28] The long-tense relationship between villagers and Perhutani had been a "time bomb waiting to explode", as one district representative called it, and democratization and decentralization had ignited it.[29]

Suspension—and redemption?

In 2001, SmartWood announced that it was suspending Perhutani's FSC certificates, citing violence, rampant illegal logging, and the company's unwillingness to rethink its production sharing model, which had proven inadequate next to the profit potential from illegal teak sales.[30] The suspension was not entirely a surprise, since SmartWood auditors had previously noted social unrest, hostage situations, deaths, and volumes of timber theft that went far beyond the annual allowable cuts in some districts.[31]

It is clear that being FSC certified was far from sufficient to guarantee decent and sustainable conditions in the forest. Perhutani's social forestry projects were no match for the challenges that were unleashed by *Reformasi* and decentralization, and the company responded in militaristic ways. The suspension left the makers of FSC-certified furniture without a reliable source of teak and raised larger questions about whether certification was appropriate in the Indonesian context.

Starting in 2003, Perhutani began a long process to redeem itself by getting several districts re-certified. With help from WWF and The Forest Trust (a consultancy sponsored largely by European furniture retailers), Perhutani embarked on two main initiatives. The first was a new production-sharing system (PHBM, *Pengelolaan Hutan Bersama Masyarakat*, or Community Based Forest Management), which allowed villagers to receive a portion of the profits

---

[25] Jarvie, Kanaan, Malley, Roule, and Thomson 2007; Posthuma 2004. It seems furniture makers prioritized short term profits even if it undermined their long-term prospects, believing that new forms of fast-growing teak and other species would save them in the future (Schiller and Fauzan 2009:35).

[26] Interview with company official, Jakarta, 9/17/10.

[27] Colchester, Sirait, and Wijardjo 2003.   [28] World Rainforest Movement no date.

[29] Quoted in Schiller and Fauzan 2009:32.   [30] Donovan 2001.

[31] SmartWood 2001a.

from teak—up to 25 percent depending on species and time of involvement.[32] Prior to the suspension, auditors had noted that "joint management and production sharing of the teak resource has been off limits" in practice in some districts.[33] In the re-certification, auditors from the company's new FSC-accredited certifier, the UK-based Soil Association, demanded several improvements in implementation before judging that the system provided real opportunities for "engagement and benefit sharing" and even "participative planning in some areas."[34] The breadth and depth of implementation is not entirely clear, but as one observer pointed out, previously "the idea of giving money or sharing product with communities would have been unthinkable."[35] On the other hand, villagers remained dependent on rules of access controlled by Perhutani.[36]

The second major change was a "drop the guns" policy. Even where killings had not occurred, villagers complained about company officials intimidating them by "always hav[ing] guns and hold[ing] weapons when they talk with us."[37] The company made progress in disarming forest guards in the districts to be certified, but then a killing occurred in a different district, and some forest managers argued that they needed to remain armed.[38] The Soil Association auditors pressed the company to change its approach. Ultimately, they were satisfied with a 2008 policy that pushed out the *Brimob* forces, restricted the use of guns to "critical conditions" that cannot be "handled by hand", and specified detailed procedures to be followed if a gun was used.[39]

The remaining barriers to re-certification were about the risk of certifying a few districts if others remained troubled. Under the FSC's approach to "partial certification", the company would need to "demonstrate a long-term commitment to adhere to the FSC Principles and Criteria", including on lands not being certified. As we will see later, the FSC's dealings with pulp and paper companies in Indonesia had made it especially sensitive about companies using small areas to greenwash their larger images. The Soil Association—which traces its origins to the organic movement in the UK—was described as "scared shitless to issue to certification" to Perhutani.[40] Another certifier, SGS, was in charge of supplementary audits in a sample of other districts.

[32] Interview with company official, Jakarta, September 17, 2010.
[33] SmartWood 2001b:25.
[34] Soil Association 2011: section 2. The FSC-accredited certifier for a different set of districts, SGS, similarly approved of the new system, though they appear to have scrutinized it less. In language that reflected little change in approach, the SGS report noted that "Indigenous peoples do not have any control of forest management since it is state land. . . . Communities are employed to carry out activities such as planting and tending and in return they are permitted to cultivate their crops on the forestry land in a system known as 'Tumpang sari'" (SGS QUALIFOR Programme 2012:38).
[35] Interview with NGO representative, Jakarta, 9/21/10.   [36] Maryudi 2012.
[37] Quoted in Colchester, Sirait and Wijardjo 2003:188.
[38] Interview with company official, Jakarta, 9/17/10; interview with auditor, Jakarta, 9/20/10.
[39] Soil Association 2011.   [40] Interview with forestry consultant, Jakarta, 9/22/10.

Ultimately, these audits, along with consultations with the FSC International secretariat, allowed two districts to be FSC certified in 2011, with three more finalized in 2012.[41]

The story of Perhutani's suspension and re-certification raises a number of questions about forest certification in Indonesia. Can transnational standards be meaningfully implemented when land rights are shifting and contested? How deep are the reforms promoted through certification? There is no doubt that Perhutani made reforms in the re-certification process, but the underlying tensions surrounding Javanese teak plantations did not disappear. In their re-assessments, auditors discovered that illegal logging had decreased since the "period of political instability, 1997 to 2003" but was still more severe than in the years prior to that period.[42] Recent reforms do not easily wipe away a troubled and brutal past or make Perhutani teak "clean" of exploitation, unless one wants to deny history entirely. As we will see in this chapter and the next, dilemmas of current practice and past injustice hang over many attempts to certify land.

Sustainable Forestry in the Tropics: The Development and Under-development of Certification in Indonesia

Indonesian timber was a central target of environmental boycott campaigns in Europe and North America in the late 1980s. This was the context not only for the pioneering certification by SmartWood and the eventual emergence of the Forest Stewardship Council, but also for an interesting "homegrown" certification initiative in Indonesia. When a 1992 Austrian law threatened mandatory labeling of tropical timber products and a 70 percent increase in import tariffs, Indonesian government and industry leaders quickly organized what plywood magnate and Suharto crony Bob Hasan announced as "a committee for the formulation of sustainable forestry guidelines for Indonesia."[43] The association of forest concession companies (APHI, Asosiasi Pengusaha Hutan Indonesia) began working on a certification component, with help from the multinational testing firm SGS and the Ministry of Forestry.

But in 1993, the Minister of Forestry changed course and asked the respected former Minister of Environment, Emil Salim, to set up an independent organization, Lembaga Ekolabel Indonesia (LEI).[44] Salim convened academics and NGOs to develop the program. This was "quite amazing in an undemocratic situation," one observer noted, "since the group was consulting

[41] Interview with NGO representative, Jakarta, 9/21/10.   [42] Soil Association 2011: part 2.
[43] Elliott 2000:99. On the Austrian laws, see Elliott (2000) and Varangis et al. (1995).
[44] Elliott 2000:101.

broadly with stakeholders.... It was quite taboo to do this."[45] In contrast to most other homegrown systems, such as the Malaysia Timber Certification Council and the state-led system that we will see in China, LEI had challenging standards and relationships not only with industry and government but also with advocates of community-based forest management, allowing for a "consideration of local knowledge" in the certification process.[46]

Lembaga Ekolabel Indonesia and the Forest Stewardship Council co-evolved and sometimes cooperated. A "joint certification protocol" from 2000 to 2005 allowed companies to be simultaneously audited for both systems, usually leading to an initial LEI certification and a set of additional steps needed for FSC certification. LEI standards are similar in many respects to the FSC's, but two key differences have proven practically important.[47] First, while the FSC prohibits certification if conversion of natural forests has occurred since 1994, LEI does not have a blanket prohibition of this sort. As a result, the controversial pulp and paper giants—Asia Pulp and Paper (APP) and Asia Pacific Resources International (APRIL)—have been able to get some timber plantations certified by LEI. Second, unlike the FSC, LEI allows high performance on some criteria to compensate for lower performance on others.[48] Though FSC and LEI agreed to further cooperation in 2010, differences in constituencies and certifiers have impeded a closer relationship. Notably, though, LEI did not affiliate with the FSC's global competitor, the Programme for the Endorsement of Forest Certification (PEFC), as most other "homegrown" initiatives have. Perhaps as a result, its influence was subtle and limited.[49]

Whether considering FSC or LEI standards, no more than a tiny fraction of Indonesian forests have been certified. Perhutani's districts were FSC-certified in 1998, and two other companies (Xylo Indah Pratama and PT Diamond Raya) followed within three years, but only nine enterprises covering 1.09 million hectares were FSC-certified as of 2009. This is not a trivial amount of land, but it accounts for less than 2 percent of Indonesia's roughly 59 million hectares of land designated as "production forest".[50] A bit more land was certified by LEI, but more than half of this was also certified by FSC, so the

---

[45] Interview with forester, Bogor, 7/1/08.

[46] Maryudi 2009; interview with forestry researcher, 8/14/08; interview with certification representative, Bogor, 7/1/08.

[47] Muhtaman and Prasetyo 2006; Hinrichs and Prasetyo 2007.

[48] Interview with certification representative, Bogor, 7/1/08.

[49] In 2014, PEFC endorsed a different homegrown initiative, Indonesian Forestry Certification Cooperation, which had been formed several years before by a new coalition of actors from the timber industry, academic institutes, government, and domestic civil society.

[50] 1.09 million hectares is roughly 2.7 million acres, equivalent to approximately half the size of the US state of New Jersey or ⅓ the size of Belgium. The 2% figure is calculated with data from the Ministry of Forestry reported in Prasetyo, Hewitt, and Keong 2012. The rate of FSC certification is closer to 1% if one counts the additional 23 million hectares of forest land eligible for harvesting or conversion to other uses.

total area certified as of 2009–10 was roughly 1.7 million hectares, or less than 3 percent of all production forest.[51] Most of the certified areas were natural forest concessions—that is, areas of native forest where the state has granted companies the right to harvest—so the rate of certification for concessions was slightly higher: Approximately 3.8 percent of Indonesia's 29 million hectares of natural forest concessions was certified to the standards of FSC, LEI, or both.[52]

A few comparisons put these figures in perspective. Worldwide, roughly 7.5 percent of eligible land (that is, forest land designated for production or multiple use) was FSC-certified as of 2010.[53] In Brazil, 17.6 percent of natural forest area available for harvesting (the equivalent to Indonesia's concessions) was FSC-certified at that point, and nearly 100 percent of planted forests were certified by either FSC or its domestic competitor, CERFLOR.[54] In Russia, 20 percent of forest land leased for logging was FSC-certified by 2010, and this climbed to 25 percent by the end of 2011.[55] Cameroon went from having no forests certified in 2005 to having 15 percent of managed forest land FSC certified in 2009.[56] Although Malaysia has a low level of FSC certification, the homegrown Malaysian Timber Certification Council had certified nearly 39 percent of production forest area by 2009.[57]

Indonesia's laggard status prompted an aggressive growth campaign. Several consultancies, including The Forest Trust (supported largely by European companies), the Tropical Forest Foundation (supported by American companies and linked to the Smithsonian Institution), and WWF's Global Forest and Trade Network, had been helping Indonesian companies move toward certification since the late 1990s. In 2010, international supporters of the FSC extended these efforts by creating The Borneo Initiative, which more generously subsidized the costs of certification, paying roughly $2 per hectare to companies preparing to get certified. One observer speculated that "if this doesn't work, maybe there will be no more forest certification in Indonesia."[58] The Borneo Initiative and related efforts did help to increase the amount of FSC-certified forest land in Indonesia to 1.6 million hectares by early 2013. But this still amounted to less than 3 percent of total production forest area and included just 4.8 percent of forest concession land.

Alongside this stunted growth in certified land, the FSC's multi-stakeholder process for developing regional or national versions of its global standards

---

[51] See ibid. for the amount certified by LEI.
[52] Aside from the jointly certified forests, LEI had certified one additional concession, two plantations, and twelve small community forests by 2010 (Prasetyo et al. 2012).
[53] Food and Agriculture Organization (FAO) 2010.
[54] Blaser, Sarre, Poore, and Johnson 2011.
[55] Malets 2013; Food and Agriculture Organization (FAO) 2012.
[56] Cerutti, Tacconi, Nasi, and Lescuye 2011.   [57] Malaysian Timber Council 2011.
[58] Interview with forestry consultant, Jakarta, 9/21/10.

never occurred in Indonesia. In part, this was due to disagreements about whether LEI should play a role or perhaps even become an FSC-affiliated national initiative.[59] In addition, as one practitioner put it, the FSC-International secretariat had a diverse membership that "was pulling it in different directions", so it was not able to prioritize key countries like Indonesia.[60]

In any case, the lack of an FSC-endorsed national standard was a "huge glaring problem".[61] It arguably limited the growth of certification, and it meant that difficult issues, such as the rights of indigenous communities, were open to ad hoc interpretations by auditors and certification bodies.[62] In comparison, negotiations over a regional FSC standard in British Columbia, Canada, proved difficult but crucial for clarifying indigenous rights, although stakeholders there also had reference to an evolving body of court decisions.[63] Forest certification might have taken a different path in Indonesia if an FSC-approved national standard had been developed. As we will see, though, a number of factors made this difficult terrain.

Pushing Standards: The Market for Sustainable Forestry

Consistent with the image of retailers and brands "pushing" standards through their supply chains, one can trace most FSC-certified forests in Indonesia to a request or promise from a large buyer in North America or Europe. In the early 2000s, The Home Depot "sent clear signals about its preference to companies here [in Indonesia], and certainly offered price premiums, although that wasn't public at the time," as one practitioner noted.[64] The company had once promised environmentalists that it would stop selling tropical meranti plywood due to concerns about Indonesian deforestation, but it later decided to "remain at the table" with producers that would get FSC-certified.[65] This included PT Intracawood, an Indonesian plywood manufacturer with a marketing arm in the US—Taraca Pacific, which came to sell exclusively to The Home Depot. After failing its first attempt, Intracawood got its concession in East Kalimantan FSC-certified in 2005. Sumalindo, a producer of meranti plywood and veneers soon followed with the certification of a concession in East Kalimantan (Sumalindo Lestari Jaya II). The company

[59] Interviews with NGO representative, Jakarta, 7/8/08, forestry consultant, Jakarta, 9/22/10, forestry researcher, 8/14/08.

[60] Interview with forestry consultant, 6/23/08.

[61] Interview with forestry researcher, 8/14/08.

[62] One practitioner complained that "when you have the certifier both developing and auditing their own standards, there are going to be conflicts of interest, and when pressed, the certifier will just end up being defensive" (interview with auditor and consultant, Bogor, 7/2/08).

[63] Tollefson, Gale, and Haley 2008.   [64] Interview with forestry consultant, 6/23/08.

[65] Lawrence, Toyoda, and Lystiani 2003:26.

was "seeking to upgrade its forest management standards to meet the demand from the US market, notably The Home Depot" and also saw certification as a chance to improve its market share and corporate image.[66]

The Danish timber trading company DLH (Dalhoff Larsen & Horneman) faced criticism for its involvement in conflict zones in Africa, but it also became "the biggest exporter of FSC-certified mouldings out of Indonesia" after the 2007 FSC certification of Sari Bumi Kusuma's logging concession in Central Kalimantan.[67] DLH sells certified bangkirai decking, known for its durability, to retailers at a 20–30 percent premium, and Sari Bumi Kusuma is known to get a "significant" premium for these solid wood products.[68] Yet because DLH was also selling seemingly identical uncertified bangkirai decking for a lower price, some worried that it was undercutting the certified version.[69]

PT Diamond Raya, which harvests ramin, the "most valuable timber species found in Indonesia" for use in fine furniture, picture frames, and mouldings for the US and European markets, began exploring FSC certification to please buyers in the UK.[70] The twist in this case is that because ramin grows in fragile peat forests and habitats for endangered tigers, the Indonesian government had gotten it listed as protected under the Convention on International Trade in Endangered Species (CITES). But it provided an exception to this export ban for Diamond Raya's certified ramin, making this company the only legal exporter from Indonesia. The wood fetches a high price, but the company reported that the 5 percent premium it was receiving had "been a disappointment" compared to the 35 percent premium it initially hoped for.[71]

The limits of market demand

As these cases suggest, the flow of rules through global production networks was accompanied by material incentives for certification. A reliable and straightforward linkage between demand and supply was more the exception than the rule, though.

Premiums were available for some products and companies, as the examples above illustrate. But by one estimate, retailers and manufacturers were rarely

---

[66] Colchester and Ferrari 2007:16; Jurgens 2006; interview with company representative, Jakarta, 6/26/08.

[67] DLH 2011:22; Forests Monitor 2001; Global Witness 2010.

[68] WWF-UK 2011; interview with forestry consultant, Jakarta, 9/22/10.

[69] WWF-UK 2011. Suka Jaya Makmur, which makes solid and plywood products and is owned by the same parent company as Sari Bumi Kusuma, was FSC-certified in 2010.

[70] Van Assen 2005; Tacconi, Obidzinski, and Agung 2004; interview with forester, Bogor, 7/1/08

[71] Quoted in van Assen 2005:309. In a different niche of the market, the German pencil-maker Faber-Castell's early embrace of FSC certification led its Indonesian supplier, Xylo Indah Pratama, to have its plantation certified.

willing to offer a premium of more than 5 percent, which would barely cover the costs of certification for many operations.[72] An initial forest management certification could cost between $35,000 and $100,000 including various consultations and pre-assessments, and the costs of implementing the required practices can be significantly higher.[73] When one Indonesian forestry firm (PT Irma Sulindo in Papua) entered discussions about certification, it claimed that it would need to receive more than double the market price for its merbau furniture to make certification worthwhile.[74]

More generally, demand for FSC certification was limited because of the markets to which Indonesian forest products are exported. Approximately 25 percent of plywood exports (by value) from 1997–2005 went to countries where environmental campaigns targeting retailers were prominent (the US, Canada, EU countries, Australia, or New Zealand); but 38 percent went to Japan, where the market for certified wood has been built much more slowly.[75] Japanese timber conglomerates have long played a powerful role in Indonesian forests, but they have resisted many calls for "greening" of timber operations, in part because corporatist arrangements have insulated them from public pressure and in part because they "have a great deal to lose from the widespread adoption of FSC certification," which conflicts with their own logging and production models.[76]

One Indonesian plywood company, PT Erna Djuliawati, which exports almost exclusively to Japan and elsewhere in East Asia, did get its logging concession in Central Kalimantan FSC-certified, but it was apparently idiosyncratic in its motivation—since it was "never focused on a premium" and doing it as a matter of "personal pride" of the top executives, as explained by a forestry consultant.[77]

Beyond plywood, China is a major export destination for Indonesian forest products. It received 35 percent of sawnwood, 45 percent of wood pulp, and 29 percent of paper exports (by value) from Indonesia between 1997 and 2005 (see Figure 3.1). China's imports are not completely divorced from green markets in Europe and North America, since perhaps up to half of forest products imports to China are then processed and re-exported to markets with greater demand for sustainability assurances.[78] The character or

[72] Tacconi, Obidzinski, and Agung 2004.
[73] Interview with forestry consultants, Jakarta, 9/17/2010, 9/22/10. For debate on whether practices like Reduced Impact Logging are truly more costly than conventional practices, see Durst and Enters 2001.
[74] Jurgens 2006.
[75] Owari and Sawanobori 2007; interview with auditor, Jakarta, 9/20/10. This and other calculations in this section are based on data from the FAO's Forestat database.
[76] Gale 2006:16; Dauvergne 1997.
[77] Interview with forestry consultant, Jakarta, 9/22/10.
[78] Tacconi, Obidzinski, and Agung 2004 estimate that China's total re-exports of forest products in 2003 were 35 million cubic meters RWE, which would be nearly half of the roughly 70 million

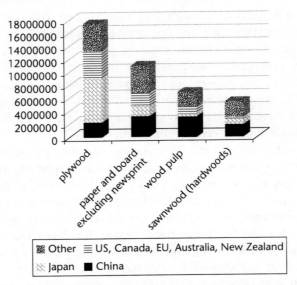

Figure 3.1. Value of Indonesian forest products exports (in thousands of USD) to different markets, 1997–2005
Source: FAOSTAT Forestry Trade Flows data

complexity of these supply chains, though, appears to have buffered demand for certification. Tellingly, none of the companies in the first wave of FSC certification in Indonesia was exporting primarily to China.

Of course, even in countries where some retailers and manufacturers have promoted FSC certification, most have not. Among the five largest American importers of plywood from Indonesia in 2001–2, three companies accepted less stringent forms of certification or were linked to the FSC's American industry-driven competitor, the Sustainable Forestry Initiative (a PEFC affiliate); and one company appears to have no sustainable sourcing policy at all.[79] The European Timber Trade Federation, which represents many tropical timber importers, claims to support certification (by either FSC or PEFC), but it reported almost no certified wood being imported from Asia to the EU in 2011.[80]

Demand for "green" furniture might have spurred a growth in forest certification, since a majority of Indonesia's roughly $1 billion in wood furniture

cubic meters RWE of forest products imports to China in that year. This kind of re-exporting is especially common in the production of furniture and paper/cardboard packaging (Wagner 2007; Sun, Cheng, and Canby 2005).

[79] Based on Lawrence, Toyoda, and Lystiani 2003, these were Georgia Pacific, North Pacific Lumber, Far East American, IHLO Sales and Imports, and Taraca Pacific. I gathered information on sourcing policies from the companies' websites.

[80] European Timber Trade Federation 2011.

exports goes to Europe or the US.[81] But the demand that existed was disarticulated from the supply of sustainable forestry standards within Indonesia in several ways. For instance, a few large furniture retailers made high-profile commitments to FSC certification, but it is difficult to find any practical influence on Indonesian forests. Ikea committed to using FSC-certified timber in its supply chain in the early 2000s, and several other furniture retailers, such as Maisons du Monde, Crate & Barrel, Williams Sonoma, and Wal-Mart, soon followed suit with similar though less ambitious commitments.[82] (As we will see in the next chapter, Ikea's commitment proved quite influential in China, where much of its manufacturing and some of its timber supply were located.)

One can find both small craft-based furniture manufacturers in Central Java and larger factories in East Java that have sold furniture to retailers with preferences for certification. But the links to Indonesian forests have been much more tenuous. Some small manufacturers reported selling products at premium prices to European buyers—but using FSC-certified wood imported from other countries, where the supply was greater.[83] Some craft-based furniture makers had been using certified teak from Perhutani, but when that certificate was suspended, they turned to alternative materials, such as reclaimed teak from traditional Javanese houses.[84] Other similar manufacturers turned to "verified legal" timber—a weaker substitute but one that allowed them to continue to highlight their green credentials in negotiating with retailers—or to small teak plantations certified by LEI.[85]

For small manufacturers, the allure of green markets was often tempered by the tendency of large buyers to squeeze tightly on prices. Several companies and consultants portrayed Ikea as especially demanding in this regard.[86] Even larger manufacturers that could handle retailers' price pressures did not necessarily control forest management operations. As one practitioner describes it,

---

[81] For export values and destinations, see ASEAN Affairs 2009:39–41; Prasetyo, Hewitt, and Keong 2012.

[82] Gunther 2008. By 2008 only 5–6% of Ikea's wood supply was FSC-certified, but the company pledged to increase that to 30% in the following years (Gunther 2008). By 2012, this had increased to 23%, still shy of its target but ahead of most competitors (Kelly 2012). The other companies listed here expressed preferences for FSC-certified products at various points and were members of The Forest Trust or WWF's Global Forest and Trade Network.

[83] Interview with furniture manufacturer, Solo, 6/19/09; interview with forestry researcher, 8/14/08. One Javanese furniture company sells an FSC-certified product using certified timber imported from the US.

[84] Interview with furniture manufacturer, Yogyakarta, 6/22/09. Some such houses were demolished by the 2006 earthquake that killed nearly 6,000 people in Central Java (interview with sustainability consultant, Yogyakarta, 6/22/09).

[85] Interview with sustainability consultant, Yogyakarta, 6/23/09; interview with furniture manufacturer, Yogyakarta, 6/23/09.

[86] Interview with furniture manufacturer, Yogyakarta, 6/24/09; interview with sustainability consultants, Yogyakarta, 6/23/09, 6/24/09. Some put Pier 1 in the same category, but one argued that IKEA was more aggressive on price than Pier 1, Cost Plus, Pottery Barn, and several others.

timber from forest concessions is usually sold in bulk, and furniture manufac-turers rarely have the cash-flow necessary to purchase enough to steer timber traders and forest managers toward certification.[87]

Looking at forest management operations, out of a total of 351 natural forest concessions that existed in 2001, it seems that fewer than 25 percent participated in any kind of certification or pre-certification activity, such as trainings or orientation settings, and far less than this maintained any involvement. This rough estimate is based on information disclosed by the leading pre-certification programs (The Forest Trust, Tropical Forest Founda-tion, Global Forests and Trade Network, and The Borneo Initiative). [88] It concurs with comments by one practitioner that there was a "big flurry of scopings and pre-assessments" around 2000, but "most companies just dropped it."[89] Another observer put the number of concessionaires "interested in certification and long-term forest management" at less than 5 percent.[90] As described by practitioners, companies that expressed initial interest often stalled or dropped out because of an insurmountable gap between current practice and certifica-tion standards, because the parent company failed to invest in serious improve-ments, or because instability in companies required the process to "have to restart over and over".[91]

With at least some pockets of demand and only weak competition from the homegrown LEI, why was there not more interest in certifying Indonesian forests to the FSC's standards? After all, while some exports went to markets with little demand for certification, others were going to some of the most "eco-sensitive" markets in Europe—namely, the UK, Germany, and the Neth-erlands.[92] The puzzle remains only partially solved unless one digs deeper into the domestic political economy of timber and forest land, which as we will see, did not bend easily to the hopes of foreign buyers and NGOs. The kinds of forest enterprises imagined by sustainable forestry projects and the kinds of

[87] Interview with auditor, Jakarta, 9/20/10.
[88] The detailed records of pre-certification consultancies are confidential, but their public reports often list companies involved, allowing for rough estimates of the rate of participation. I counted forty-one different concession management enterprises that were known to be working with The Forest Trust, Tropical Forest Foundation, the Global Forests and Trade Network, or The Borneo Initiative, or that received FSC certification between 2000 and 2012. Tacconi et al. (2004) counted twenty-nine concessionaires involved in an earlier working group, but many appear to also be in the group counted above. Since some companies may have dropped out quickly, leaving little trace of their participation, we may assume that the total is somewhat higher than the fifty to sixty-five companies that have been recorded—but most likely not more than eighty-five in total, or 24% of all concessionaires. See also Prasetyo, Hewitt, and Keong 2012.
[89] Interview with forestry consultant, Jakarta, 9/22/10.
[90] Interview with forester, Bogor, 7/1/08.
[91] Tacconi, Obidzinski, and Agung 2004. Interview with forestry consultant, Samarinda, 7/6/09; interview with forestry consultants, Jakarta, 9/17/10.
[92] Elliott 2000:84.

enterprises operating in Indonesia were difficult to match, especially in the tumultuous late 1990s and early 2000s.

Irreconcilable Forces? Transnational Standards and the Political Economy of Indonesian Forests

The organization of firms and production processes

Achieving FSC certification requires firms to invest in a range of new practices—including "reduced impact logging", monitoring of soil and water quality, and setting aside "high conservation value" areas. But many companies that manage Indonesian forest concessions use the forest as a "fundraising process" for other activities, like financial investments, agriculture, or mining.[93] One observer estimated that only around 10 percent of concessionaires are planning to stay in that business for the long term, while most are just looking for "quick profits from the forest".[94]

Timber conglomerates, such as Barito Pacific, The Bob Hasan Group, and Djajanti, led by "forest kings" with familial or political ties to Suharto, had been extremely powerful during the New Order era. The Ministry of Forestry awarded forest concessions as a matter of patronage, and firms reaped extraordinary rates of profit from the state's largesse.[95] When the Asian financial crisis of 1997 left timber and paper firms deeply indebted, many were deemed "too big to fail" and bailed out.[96] Under pressure from the World Bank and IMF, Indonesian officials did open up the allocation of concessions and break Bob Hasan's plywood monopoly, but large timber companies retained a privileged position. A Barito Pacific executive explained that "the government won't let the industry collapse from lack of raw materials because plywood is too important for the economy."[97]

As international demand for certification grew, many timber companies were more interested in feeding their over-built plywood mills—as well as newer pulp and paper mills—than in investing in sustainable management of concessions. Some vertically integrated firms—such as Intracawood and Sumalindo, as mentioned above—were in a good position to respond to retailers' requests for certified wood, since they controlled the process from the stump to the mill. In contrast, the smaller concession companies that had emerged since *Reformasi* were less likely to be vertically integrated and more likely to be "just selling their wood to a trader, who doesn't care about any of these certification schemes," as one practitioner put it.[98] With traders and manufacturers "aggressively guard[ing] their upstream supply chain

---

[93] Ibid. [94] Interview with NGO representative, 7/3/08. [95] Broad 1995; Brown 1999.
[96] Barr 2001. [97] Quoted in ibid.:40. [98] Interview with NGO representative, 7/3/08.

information," market incentives did not travel smoothly from buyers to forest managers.[99] Here we can see evidence of the flow of rules dissipating as it travels through complex production networks.

Furthermore, small and large concessionaires alike had fewer "slack resources" to devote to certification. In the early 1990s, concession companies were estimated to be producing logs for $67 per cubic meter and selling them for $145 per cubic meter on average.[100] By the 2000s, the costs in Kalimantan had risen to around $80 per cubic meter and the average price had fallen to $122 per cubic meter.[101] Large concessionaires could still make sizable returns, but "companies with smaller, less productive, and/or remote concessions have been operating much closer to the margins of profitability."[102] As one consultant noted, certification is "at the mercy of the cash flow of the company," and companies are not "rolling in money anymore. Businessmen are putting down everything they have on a concession, and they have to get their timber out as quickly as possible."[103]

The rise of illegal logging also undercut the market for sustainable forestry. Indonesian manufacturers faced a choice between searching for high-cost certified wood, buying conventional uncertified wood from authorized concessions, or buying cheaper wood from unknown sources. Estimates suggest that illegally harvested wood could be delivered to a mill for $32 per cubic meter, or far lower if purchased directly from a roadside trader, while a similar type of legal wood cost $46 to $85 per cubic meter.[104] Even firms with their own forest concessions, such as Barito Pacific and Kayu Lapis, routinely purchased additional logs; according to one expert, "even the best companies don't really know where all their timber is coming from."[105] "We buy logs from a broker. Sometimes they have documentation, but often they do not," one plywood executive admitted. "We generally do not know where the logs come from."[106] The danger of this strategy became apparent when Sumalindo, which had one FSC-certified concession, was accused of having "absorbed 3,000 logs from illegal logging activity."[107] The company was selling certified logs to others at a premium while purchasing cheaper logs to feed some of its own mills.[108] The Sumalindo executives were later found not guilty, but its

---

[99] Jurgens 2006:26.
[100] Elliott 2000:108. The rate of profit was even higher before a ban on log exports was imposed in 1985 to support domestic plywood manufacturing and Bob Hasan's plywood monopoly. This ban was lifted under IMF pressure and to generating foreign currency in 1998, then reimposed in 2001. It remains in effect, although it has often been criticized by economists and companies. See Goodland and Daly 1996 for a parial defense of log export bans.
[101] Ruslandi, Venter, and Putz 2011. [102] Barr 2001:52.
[103] Interview with forestry consultants, Jakarta, 9/17/10.
[104] Tacconi, Obidzinski, and Agung 2004; Kishor and Lescuyer 2012.
[105] Interview with forestry researcher, Bogor, 7/1/08; Greenpeace 2003; Barr 2001.
[106] Quoted in Barr 2001:47. [107] Indonesia Today 2010.
[108] Interview with forestry consultant, Jakarta, 9/22/10.

production model had put it in a risky situation, and it ultimately let its FSC certification expire.[109]

The pulp and paper giants

Some firms were nearly impossible to certify to FSC standards, because practices that were unambiguously prohibited by the FSC were at the core of their production models. The FSC prohibits certification of areas that have been converted from natural forests to plantations in the recent past (since 1994) in order to ensure that monoculture tree plantations are not built at the expense of biodiverse natural forests. Large pulp and paper companies—most notably, Asia Pulp & Paper (APP) and Asia Pacific Resources International (APRIL)— routinely cleared natural forest land for acacia plantations. Looking at this part of the market reveals both the challenge of entrenched production practices and the risks of "greenwashing".

To promote pulp and paper manufacturing, the Indonesian government distributed more than $400 million in subsidies and authorized 4.3 million hectares for plantation development during the 1990s, mostly for the conversion of "degraded" natural forests.[110] The "mixed tropical hardwoods" that could be harvested while clearing these forests quickly became a crucial source of supply for pulp and paper companies' overbuilt manufacturing plants. In some cases, a "plantation hoax" occurred, in which forests were cleared and the resulting wood was used, but the plantation was never developed.[111] Perversely, the "load of money" to be made from conversion gave companies an incentive to ruin their own concessions so that they could be declared degraded and eligible to be clear-cut.[112] Once valuable timber was removed, loose affiliates of companies sometimes used fire as a cheap way to clear the land.[113]

In the eyes of ecologists, environmental NGOs, and certification bodies, many officially "degraded" areas were in fact rich, biodiverse forests.[114] Many could meet the FSC definition of protected natural forests as "areas where many of the principal characteristics and key elements of native ecosystems such as complexity, structure and diversity are present."[115] Furthermore, many areas designated for conversion were peat forests, which release large amounts of carbon dioxide when cleared, contributing to Indonesia's move

---

[109] Indonesia Today 2011.   [110] Barr 2001: 64,80.
[111] Human Rights Watch 2006; Ekawati 2009.
[112] interview with NGO representative, Jakarta, 7/8/08; Jenkins and Smith 1999:258.
[113] Dauvergne 1998.
[114] See Edwards, Larsen, Docherty, Ansell, Hsu, Derhé, Hamer, and Wilcove 2011 on biodiversity in "degraded" forests in Malaysian Borneo.
[115] Forest Stewardship Council 2002:12.

from 20th to 12th place in the world in total carbon emissions from 1999 to 2009.[116]

Facing aggressive activist campaigns and denunciations from environmentalists and neoliberal reformers alike, the pulp and paper giants began to develop sustainability plans that would reduce their reliance on state-subsidized mixed tropical hardwoods and illegal logging.[117] But since these plans relied heavily on the conversion of peat swamps, they were poor candidates for FSC certification.[118] Interestingly, though, as pressure mounted and the market for certified paper products grew, the pulp and paper giants started to engage in various ways with the FSC and its constituents.

In 2003, Asia Pulp & Paper (APP) began working with WWF on the assessment of "high conservation value forests" (HCVF), but WWF soon pulled out and urged APP's clients to exert greater pressure. As the Office Depot, Metro Group (a German retailer), and others dropped APP as a supplier, the company turned to SmartWood, which conducted HCVF assessments until ending the relationship three years later.[119] In addition, APP received FSC "chain of custody" certification for several pulp mills and passed a "controlled wood" assessment for one forest, which allowed the company to combine pulp from that forest with certified pulp purchased from elsewhere and label the resulting paper as "FSC Mixed".[120]

When this was publicized in a *Wall Street Journal* article, the FSC quickly stepped in to salvage its reputation and force APP to cease using the FSC label.[121] The affair drew attention to the perils of the FSC's growth and the risks of greenwashing, and it ultimately led the FSC to develop a new "policy for association of organizations with the FSC", which allowed the organization to distance itself from companies engaged in illegal or highly destructive logging. For APP, the affair brought a new round of canceled orders—this time, from Staples and Woolworths (Australia), as well as Mattel and Levi Strauss, who had used APP products in their packaging. Some observers argue that APP has become recalcitrant and "doesn't give a shit", though its 2013 promise to stop clearing natural forests generated a new wave of assessments, this time led by The Forest Trust.[122]

Another pulp and paper giant, Asia Pacific Resources International (APRIL), got one plantation certified by LEI in 2006 and was reportedly "trying to do everything they can to get FSC certified".[123] As a substitute, it too worked with

---

[116] Based on World Bank data.   [117] Raitzer 2008.   [118] Barr 2007.

[119] Raitzer 2008; Jurgens 2006.

[120] "Controlled wood" must be legal, not genetically modified, and the harvesting process must not violate traditional rights, threaten high conservation value forests, or convert natural forests.

[121] Wright and Carlton 2007.

[122] Interview with NGO representative, 7/3/08.

[123] Interview with forestry consultant, 6/23/08.

WWF on an assessment of "high conservation value forests", leading some to worry that this concept had become a "greenwashing tool".[124] APRIL also got one LEI-certified plantation approved by SmartWood under the FSC's "controlled wood" standard, allowing it to be mixed with certified pulp and given the "FSC Mixed" label. Less than eighteen months later, though, SmartWood suspended the certificate, finding that the company was not living up to its commitments and fearing that the project was being used as cover for conversion of natural forests.[125]

In sum, the big pulp and paper companies were not prepared to abandon their harvesting practices, but they did navigate the margins of FSC certification in search of sustainability assurances. The FSC and its constituents, in turn, further policed these margins to retain their credibility, especially when prompted by external scrutiny. As theorized in the previous chapter, the rigor of transnational private regulation depends in part on scrutiny from external and internal watchdogs. As we turn to the contentious issue of land rights, we will see more of the extent and limits of this type of scrutiny, as well as another set of factors that inhibited the growth of forest certification in Indonesia.

Problematic property: the shifting, ambiguous, and contested character of forest land

FSC standards call for stable, clear, and legitimate land-use rights, but in several ways the rights to use forest land in Indonesia are unstable, overlapping, and contentious. First, because there were sizable incentives to convert forested land into oil palm plantations, forests were in a real sense fleeting—and whatever premiums might be gained by getting certified were far too low to reverse this trend. The Indonesian government began supporting fast-growing oil palm plantations in the 1980s by helping foreign investors secure land in "frontier" areas, often suppressing or displacing local smallholders.[126] Land designated for oil palm increased by more than 600 percent from 1990 to 2010, and Indonesia became the world's largest producer of palm oil in 2007.[127] Palm oil was an increasingly popular ingredient in processed foods and cosmetics, as well as a cooking oil in China and India. As prices and export volumes rose in the 2000s, governments and investors could earn far more from converting forests into oil palm plantations than from managing them for logging.[128] One conservative estimate put the value per hectare of a

---

[124] Interview with forestry consultant, 9/14/10.
[125] SmartWood 2010b; Eyes on the Forest 2011; Donovan 2010.
[126] McCarthy and Cramb 2009.
[127] Carlson, Curran, Ratnasari, Pittman, Soares-Filho, Asner, Trigg, Gaveau, Lawrence, and Rodrigues 2012; McCarthy and Cramb 2009.
[128] Koh and Wilcove 2007.

logging operation in Kalimantan at roughly \$2,300 and of a well-run oil palm plantation at roughly \$6,800.[129] When the FSC was first created, its supporters hoped that certification could "add value" to managed forests and thus decrease the incentive to convert them to agricultural uses.[130] But even if companies were to receive 10–20 percent premiums from forest certification, it would be difficult to match the profits available in agricultural development.

Oil palm development quickly became a major source of fires and deforestation—the "worst stuff" according to one forester—and forest certification was powerless to affect this.[131] More than half of Indonesian oil palm expansion from 1990–2005 came from the conversion of forests.[132] Like timber plantations, oil palm plantations are supposed to be developed on "degraded" land, but as the price of oil palm increased, local and district governments sometimes succeeded in getting forests re-categorized as eligible for conversion.[133] Once again, some areas were cleared of timber but not actually turned into plantations.[134] To promote improvement in this industry, WWF teamed up with several global brands (e.g., Unilever, Sainsbury's) and palm oil producers (e.g., the Malaysian Palm Oil Association) to form a new certification initiative, the Roundtable on Sustainable Palm Oil, in 2004. Modeled to some degree on the FSC, this initiative has faced similar challenges related to land-tenure and community rights, though with a cozier relationship with large plantation companies and a greater risk of fires in certified areas.[135] The key point for the current analysis is that as the Roundtable on Sustainable Palm Oil was gaining support, the incentives to convert forest land to oil palm plantations remained overwhelming.

A second complication was that forest property was ambiguous, such that the thing to be certified—a bounded forest management unit with clear legal standing—could not be assumed. "Seeing like a state", in this period at least, produced a fuzzy and muddled view. The same piece of forest land might be claimed by one company that received a logging concession from the central government, another company that received a permit from the district government to clear the forest, and indigenous communities invoking customary law. Some overlapping permits were "horizontal" in origin, with one government agency issuing a permit for forest management and another issuing a

---

[129] Ruslandi, Venter, and Putz 2011.

[130] Johnson and Cabarle 1993; but see Gullison 2003.

[131] Interview with forestry researcher, Bogor, 6/30/08.   [132] Koh and Wilcove 2008.

[133] Interview with forestry researcher, Bogor, 6/30/08; interview with NGO representative, Jakarta, 9/21/10.

[134] Gellert 2005:1352; Elson 2011.

[135] There is a rapidly growing body of research on this initiative and industry. For examples that resonate with this chapter's analysis of forest certification, see Silva-Castaneda 2012, McCarthy et al. 2012, and Dauvergne 2017. On fires in RSPO-certified oil palm plantations, see Cattau, Marlier, and DeFries 2016. See Bartley et al. 2015 for a review of RSPO and other commodity roundtables.

permit for mining or agriculture.[136] This was partly the outcome of the 1999 Forestry Law, which created overlapping authority between the Ministry of Forestry and the Ministry of Energy and Natural Resources, which could authorize mining in forested areas.[137] So if a forest concession has coal deposits or is suitable for oil palm "and you're not 100% clear on the situation with the other departments", it could be quite difficult to pursue certification, explained one practitioner.[138]

Overlapping permits could also be "vertical" in origin, with central, provincial, and district governments issuing different permits for the same land.[139] This became especially common following the 1999 decentralization reforms. To move governance "closer to the people", the Indonesian government adopted a package of reforms pushed by the World Bank, which included provisions to devolve the right to issue small forest concessions from the central Ministry of Forestry to district governments. Interestingly, the choice to devolve rights to districts rather than provinces was in part a strategy to prevent secession and maintain Indonesian nationhood.[140] Corruption was not new, but it increasingly shifted from centralized political-military power to more localized strongmen.[141]

For forests, decentralization led to what observers called the "proliferation of small logging permits within large forest concessions," as "local entrepreneurs, timber brokers, and community elites voiced the opinion that large-scale concession holders had never had legitimate claims to the areas they had logged" and local officials traded licenses for political support.[142] Entrepreneurs raced to exploit this ambiguity and cut as much timber as possible in this "volatile socio-legal configuration."[143] One set of researchers described the devastation in forest concessions in Sumatra and Kalimantan in 2000:

> In the concessions we visited, illegal logging gangs were operating freely along logging roads. Large areas of forest had been newly cleared and burned to create new agricultural plots. Numerous piles of sawn timber indicated extensive portable saw mill operations within the forest. . . . Concessionaires claimed that logging gangs would gang up to burn camps and logging trucks if a company attempted to interfere with their illegal activities.[144]

As decentralization's disastrous consequences became apparent, control over forests was partially re-centralized from 2002 to 2004.[145] Districts lost the

---

[136] Blaser, Sarre, Poore, and Johnson 2011; interview with forestry consultant, Jakarta, 9/21/10.
[137] Boulan-Smit 2002.   [138] Interview with forestry consultants, Jakarta, 9/17/10.
[139] Interview with forester, Bogor, 7/1/08.
[140] Fitrani, Hofman, and Kaiser 2005; Liddle and Mujani 2013.
[141] Hadiz 2010.   [142] Tacconi, Obidzinski, and Agung 2004:12.
[143] McCarthy 2004.   [144] Jepson, Jarvie, MacKinnon, and Monk 2001:860.
[145] Barr, Dermawan, McCarthy, Moeliono, and Resosudarmo 2006.

right to issue permits, though some refused to accept this change.[146] Decentralization had provided "opportunities for various players to take advantage of the confusion, and they got licenses that have since been declared as illegal", as one practitioner put it.[147] Put differently, decentralization fostered unruly logging, and re-centralization declared more of it illegal.

Overlapping land uses directly impeded some certification efforts. One company in Kalimantan had a pre-certification scoping, but because local government officials had issued permits for oil palm in some parts of the concession and "oil palm companies were somehow supporting farmers to encroach on [those] areas," the process was halted.[148] Sumalindo, the plywood company discussed earlier, was on its way to getting a second concession (SLJ IV) certified, but part of the concession was taken away against the company's wishes after the provincial government announced it wanted to convert that area to agriculture.[149] Since "almost all concessions have a chunk of 'conversion forest' within them", one practitioner explained, disruptions of this sort are not atypical.[150]

Conflicts between companies and forest-dwelling communities also made forest property highly problematic. At least 12 percent of Indonesians live in forested areas, but for reasons discussed below, the state largely denies them rights to claim forest land, and the Ministry of Forestry routinely grants concessions to companies without regard to the communities around or within the forest.[151] It thus falls to timber companies and community elites to negotiate boundaries, compensation, and uses by villagers—or else face a range of unauthorized uses. In some instances, companies have called on paramilitary forces to intimidate or punish villagers, and villagers have used blockades, property destruction, or violence to press their claims, leading some observers to argue that Indonesian wood is often "conflict timber".[152] In 2002 alone, the association of timber concessionaires in East Kalimantan recorded eighty-one conflicts in twenty-three different forests in that province, involving "camp burning, beatings, equipment seizure, blockades and demonstrations."[153]

To better understand land conflicts and their implications for transnational private regulation, we must consider the *adat* system of customary land rights, which has been reinvigorated by movements for indigenous rights and

---

[146] Human Rights Watch 2009; Larson and Ribot 2009.
[147] Interview with forestry consultant, 6/23/08.
[148] Interview with NGO representative, Jakarta, 9/21/10.
[149] Interview with forestry consultant, Samarinda, 7/6/09.
[150] Interview with forestry consultant, Jakarta, 9/22/10.
[151] See Colchester 2004a for the 12% estimate.
[152] Jarvie, Kanaan, Malley, Roule, and Thomson 2007.
[153] Jarvie, Kanaan, Malley, Roule, and Thomson 2007:62. An estimate from 2013 suggested that as many as 20,000 villages nationwide were involved in conflicts over forest land (Butler 2013).

environmental justice in post-Suharto Indonesia. These customary forest rights are endorsed by the FSC and many other transnational sustainability standards, but they have been suppressed or denied in the Indonesian state's official governance of forest land.

INDIGENEITY AND AUTHORITY

Adat evolved from the Islamic sultanates of the thirteenth century, through Dutch colonialism in the seventeenth century, to the development of the Indonesian nation-state in the twentieth century. While early forms were "complex, flexible, and negotiable" across situations, a particular form of *adat* was institutionalized during colonialism.[154] As Tania Li (2010) has argued, Dutch authorities invoked stereotypes of an "Asiatic form of collective landholding" to dissemble individual property rights and control their subjects.[155] The notion of *hak ulayat* allocated collective rights to land based not on ownership but on things like what was being cultivated, the amount of work individuals put into the land, and community consensus.[156]

The use of Dutch law for colonists and the adaptation or imposition of *adat* for their subjects would eventually spawn scholarly debates about "legal pluralism"—and as Indonesian independence came onto the horizon, political debates about whether *adat* was a relic or a viable basis for governing land. The Indonesian constitution of 1945 ended up retaining some space for *adat* law, while the Basic Agrarian Law of 1960 sought to unify the legal system around western-inspired rights of ownership grounded in *adat* and the "social function" of land.[157] A central achievement of the nationalist government led by Sukarno, the Basic Agrarian Law was passed with great fanfare and "acquired almost sacrosanct status from its inception".[158] But in subsuming *adat* rights to the "national interest", this law created a path for them to be suppressed.

Suppression became dramatic when Suharto's New Order regime came to power after 1965. It refashioned the national interest as the "state interest", and began a project of "reverse land reform".[159] In 1967, the Indonesian government passed a Basic Forestry Law that declared essentially all forests to be "state forests", removed them from the jurisdiction of the Basic Agrarian Law, and effectively nullified customary rights. To that point, timber operations had focused largely on Javanese teak forests, but the Suharto administration "carved forest concessions out of the county's periphery" and distributed harvesting licenses to military elites and their foreign business

---

[154] von Benda-Beckmann 1989:138.   [155] Li 2010.
[156] von Benda-Beckmann and von Benda-Beckmann 2009:181–2; Fitzpatrick 1997.
[157] Fitzpatrick 1997.   [158] Lucas and Warren 2003:95.   [159] Ibid.:95.

partners.[160] By the 1970s, the Ministry of Forestry had taken jurisdiction of 70 percent of all of Indonesian land. Forest-dwelling people were labeled backwards and "isolated people", expelled, or treated as squatters, and "trans-migrants" from Java were sent to work in the outer islands.[161] As Peluso (2005) puts it, "hundreds of villages that fell within the broad jurisdictions of forests mapped from an office in Jakarta or Bogor, were simply left off the map."[162] The Village Law of 1979 further gutted the *adat* system by standardizing village administration and disrupting grassroots organizational capacities.[163]

With democratization and decentralization in the late 1990s came a resurgence of *adat* claims. These increasingly linked up with transnational movements to use "indigeneity as a vehicle to counter dispossession" and frame causes in terms of environmental justice and human rights.[164] *Adat* claims arose in villages where land had been seized by colonial authorities, taken over by the Suharto regime, or given up "voluntarily" under authoritarian power structures.[165] Networks indigenous rights NGOs—most notably, the Alliance of Indigenous People of the Archipelago (AMAN, Aliansi Masyarakat Adat Nusantara)—emerged in the late 1990s, forging important but sometimes uneasy alliances with peasant and environmental NGOs, such as the Consortium for Agrarian Reform (KPA, Konsorsium Pembaruan Agraria) or the Indonesian Forum for Environment (WALHI, Wahana Lingkungan Hidup Indonesia).[166] Indigenous communities that claimed to be protectors of the forest could ally with domestic and international environmental NGOs, but the use of cultivation to claim customary rights also made for some tense relationships between villagers and environmentalists.[167]

The 1999 Forestry Law, which replaced the 1967 law, recognized the category of *hutan adat* (customary forests) but defined this as "*state forests* located in the areas of custom-based communities" (emphasis added), thus continuing to assert the state's control of all forest land. Some new channels for claiming *adat* rights were opened, but as John McCarthy and Carol Warren (2009) put it, "potent interests and incentives pushed in the other direction [and] the reforms failed to improve villagers' local position significantly with respect to customary rights over resources."[168]

[160] Broad 1995:323.
[161] Resosudarmo, Atmadja, Ekaputri, Intarini, Indriatmoko, and Astri 2014; Center for International Environmental Law 2002.
[162] Peluso 2005:10. Moreover, Peluso notes that "In the cases where some nod might be given to local people's presence, compensation to local people with resources and land within political forests was never a recognition of territorial rights, but of rights to trees" (p. 10).
[163] Kato 1989:113.   [164] Li 2010:399; Peluso, Afiff, and Rachman 2008.
[165] Bakker and Moniaga 2010.   [166] Li 2001; Peluso et al. 2008.
[167] Resosudarmo, Atmadja, Ekaputri, Intarini, Indriatmoko, and Astri 2014.
[168] McCarthy and Warren 2009:7–8.

CONTESTED PROPERTY AS A BARRIER TO CERTIFICATION

The contentiousness of land rights exposed a central contradiction in the certification of sustainable forestry in Indonesia. The FSC says that companies must respect customary rights, but the state ignores them when granting concessions. FSC Principle 2 stipulates that "local communities with legal *or customary* tenure or use rights shall maintain control, to the extent necessary to protect their rights or resources, over forest operations unless they delegate control with free and informed consent to other agencies," and principle 3 protects the resources and customary rights of *indigenous* people specifically.[169] So transnational standards endorse customary law but do so by asking companies to implement rights that are systematically denied—both historically and currently—by the state. "Jakarta's rights sit on top of traditional community rights," as one practitioner put it, and the Ministry of Forestry routinely grants forest concessions without regard to customary claims.[170]

It is not just *adat* claims that are ambiguous and contested. Domestic and international NGOs have questioned the legitimacy of the vast majority of Indonesian forest concessions. The 1999 Forestry Law required the Ministry of Forestry's "designation" of a forest area to be followed by a process of "boundary demarcation and mapping", to be done by the holder of the permit (i.e., a company) in consultation with government agencies and local residents. Only then can forest boundaries be officially "enacted". But the second step has been neglected or stalled in most forests, partly due to cost and partly because of ongoing conflicts. The government "offloaded responsibility to the forest sector," as one practitioner put it, but this only led to 10–14 percent of state forest land being fully delineated.[171] In this sense, most Indonesian forests lack the "clearly defined, documented, and legally established" land-tenure and use rights that the FSC requires. As we will see, certifiers typically accept the Ministry of Forestry's designation as sufficient, which effectively redefines and waters down the FSC's requirements.

Some NGOs have argued that the ambiguous and contested character of forest property make credible FSC certification in Indonesia impossible.[172] In response, the FSC commissioned a 2003 study by the Forest People's Program, an international NGO, and temporarily paused certification. The study concluded that "the current Indonesian forest policy environment is difficult for, even hostile to, certification to FSC standards," but the FSC

---

[169] LEI also includes community rights in its standards and it arguably has closer ties to community forest operations than the FSC does, though some subtle differences kept LEI's standards from unambiguously supporting customary *adat* rights (Colchester et al. 2003).

[170] Phone interview with forestry consultant, 6/23/08.

[171] Interview with forestry consultant, Jakarta, 9/22/10; Colchester, Sirait, and Wijardjo 2003; interview with forestry researcher, Bogor, 9/7/10.

[172] See Down to Earth 2001 for WALHI's call for halting FSC certification in Indonesia.

pressed on, allowing certifiers to continue work in Indonesia.[173] Some practitioners admit that "doing FSC 100% would require changing the national regulation," while others put a great deal of faith in the consultation and "informed consent" processes that the FSC requires if companies are to use land with customary claims.[174] As one advisor put it, "anything can be resolved. Some [forest conflicts] may be so deep that it's difficult, but if there's enough will, something can be done. It's a mentality thing, and companies aren't paying enough attention to it."[175] As we will see in the next section, auditors and companies were often forced to pay attention to community conflicts, but many questions surround the resolutions that they reached.

Can Certification Repair Indonesian Forests? Accomplishments and Dilemmas

Forest management enterprises that seriously pursued certification usually achieved it, but only after making changes in their harvesting methods, environmental management systems, and relations with surrounding communities. As seen in the case of Perum Perhutani, auditors made "corrective action requests" and scrutinized firms' response to them, both in the initial certification audit and in follow-ups. Most firms had also had consultants perform confidential pre-certification scoping and training activities, so it often took several years' worth of changes from an initial engagement to a successful FSC certification. FSC certification was not easy to achieve, but there were also incentives for auditors to take a "pragmatic" approach, accepting incremental changes as sufficient for certification.

What kinds of changes have companies made in the certification process, and to what extent do these resolve the underlying problems and create an alternative logic of production? To what extent are certification's supporters right to look at the conditions of Indonesian forests and claim that "anything can be resolved . . . if there's enough will" on the part of companies?[176]

Changing practices to achieve FSC certification

All FSC-certified forest management enterprises had to make some changes. For example, PT Erna Djuliawati set aside an additional 1,800 hectares of

---

[173] Colchester, Sirait, and Wijardjo 2003:18. The FSC later responded with a mild note that "the positive impact of FSC certification requires time" and that stakeholders' complaints can be dealt with by the certified company or used to improve the practices of certifiers (Karmann and Smith 2009).

[174] Interview with forestry researcher, Bogor, 6/30/08.

[175] Interview with forestry consultant, 9/14/10.

[176] Interview with forestry consultant, 9/14/10.

conservation area and improved its Reduced Impact Logging practices.[177] Suka Jaya Makmur reduced erosion from road construction and log removal in order to get certified, and Xylo Indah Pratama stopped using several pesticides that were banned by the FSC and Indonesian law in order to keep its plantation certified.[178] "Major" corrective action requests—which must be resolved in order to get or stay certified—were most commonly related to the monitoring of environmental impacts and forest conditions (FSC criteria 8.1 and 8.2), to erosion and pesticides (6.5 and 6.6), to forest management plans (7.1), and to respect for domestic law (1.1). "Minor" corrective action requests were most commonly related to the "chain of custody" of wood as it leaves the forest and to employee health and safety (criterion 4.2), and these were usually resolved without needing to be "upgraded". Minor problems related to environmental impacts of forest management (criterion 6.1) were a bit more difficult to resolve, with ⅓ of these being upgraded to major concerns.[179]

Escalating corrective action requests sometimes led to temporary suspensions. For instance, SmartWood suspended Intracawood's certification in 2008 after the company failed to make required improvements in erosion control, community relations, and several aspects of logging operations.[180] They later reinstated the certificate but admitted that the same issues remained problematic and issued new corrective action requests with similar concerns.[181] Auditors sometimes avoided suspending certificates by continuing to issue a series of similar corrective action requests without letting them escalate too far.[182]

Overall, companies with FSC certified forests took actions sufficient to "close" a total of 293 corrective action requests between 2000 and 2010. Table 3.1 shows that 42 percent of these involved implementing some concrete behavioral change in the field.[183] In other words, FSC certification was

---

[177] SmartWood 2005a.

[178] Control Union Certifications 2011; SmartWood 2007b; SmartWood 2009c.

[179] Similarly, 23% of minor problems with the forest management plan (7.1) and 21% of minor problems with the monitoring of forest conditions (8.2) were upgraded to major concerns.

[180] SmartWood 2008b.

[181] SmartWood 2008d; SmartWood 2008a. They found, for instance that "though the details [of a corrective action related to Reduced Impact Logging] have been addressed there were issues beyond the scope of the specific focus of this verification audit that need to be noted," and went on to describe further weaknesses in the RIL system (ibid.:3–4).

[182] SGS raised two major concerns about Diamond Raya Timber's management plan prior to certification, but these and many others were "downgraded" to minor concerns upon certification, only to be followed by several new minor corrective action requests related to the management plan in the six years after certification (SGS QUALIFOR Programme 2000; SGS QUALIFOR Programme 2009).

[183] To generate this summary, a research assistant read the descriptions of evidence used to close-out corrective action requests as shown in the public summaries of audit reports and coded the actions taken by the forest management enterprise as being of one or more of the following types: (1) producing, revising, or disclosing a written policy (including a management system), (2) implementing or improving monitoring or documentation of existing activities, and (3)

Table 3.1. Types of actions taken to resolve auditors' "corrective action requests" for FSC-certified forests in Indonesia

Producing, revising, or disclosing a written policy	Improving monitoring or documentation	Implementing behavioral change in the field (beyond monitoring)	Total CARs resolved
32%	44%	42%	293

N=53 audits of 9 forest management enterprises with CARs closed from 2000 to 2010. Actions are not mutually exclusive.

not an easily granted seal of approval for practices that companies were already using; it routinely required reforms in the field. Still, just as often— around 44 percent of the time—corrective action requests were met by improving the monitoring or documentation of existing practices and impacts. In addition, 32 percent of the requests were met by producing, revising, or disclosing a written policy.[184] These findings are consistent with the idea that transnational private regulation leads to the elaboration of formal policies and management systems, although they also reveal a significant degree of behavioral change—slightly more than we will see for FSC certification in China (see Chapter 4) and more than is typical in the certification of labor standards (see Chapters 5 and 6, although comparable data on changes is not available for the labor standards cases).

Land and community rights

Looking at the particularly thorny issue of land and community rights provides some additional insight into the kinds of behavioral changes made in the certification process. Given the political context—the ambiguous and shifting governance of land use, as well as the rising claims of indigenous rights and environmental NGOs—it should not be surprising that auditors were often forced to address issues of land-tenure and community rights. Six of the seven large FSC-certified forests in Indonesia (as of 2010) faced conflicts with communities or serious questions about land tenure during the certification process.[185] This provides an opportunity to examine how auditors navigated

implementing some concrete action or change in behavior (beyond monitoring) in the field. Some audit reports were clearer and more detailed than others in describing the changes made, but the data reported in the table provides at least an approximation of the frequency of different types of changes.

[184] See Nussbaum and Simula 2004 for similar evidence that the adoption of policies and management systems as sufficient for compliance with FSC standards.

[185] The six were Intracawood, Sumalindo Lestari Jaya II, Diamond Raya, Erna Djuliawati, Sari Bumi Kusuma, and Suka Jaya Makmur. Community conflicts did not come up in the certification of Xylo Indah Pratama's plantations. The other three certified operations were small community forestry operations.

FSC requirements for clear land tenure, respect for community/indigenous rights, and the resolution of disputes.

AUDITING RIGHTS

As the previous discussion shows, Indonesia is a challenging environment in which to certify forest management companies as having clear tenure and respecting the customary rights of forest-dwelling people. Permits issued by the Ministry of Forestry are contestable due to the incomplete delineation of boundaries, and some degree of community conflict is the norm. FSC standards speak of communities giving "free and informed consent" to companies for the use of customary lands, but how should "free consent" be judged in the midst of massive power differentials and historical acts of dispossession? Moreover, how are certifiers to judge the legitimacy of different parties' claims and make sense of "community" in the midst of the diverse priorities of individual actors?[186] As we will see, auditors often recognized the difficulty of "certifying in contested spaces", but they adopted approaches that understated the severity of contestation and minimized its interference with certification.[187]

One problem that auditors face is how to judge the legitimacy of a company's permit from the Ministry of Forestry. One auditor admitted that "formally none of the HPH [concession permits] are valid: none of them were granted with consent."[188] But auditors usually accept the Ministry of Forestry's designations as legitimate nonetheless. As one described it:

> The constitution grants rights [to indigenous people] with some conditions... But the constitution is also clear that all forest land belongs to the state. When we come to the certification, the assumption is that if the company gets a concession from the central government, it is legal to operate.[189]

Another explained that "our basic agenda is to go as far as possible in the current framework."[190]

This pragmatic approach represents one side of a debate about who is responsible for past injustices. Critics charge that "companies have gotten themselves in the breach just by following legal procedure [and] it's pretty much stolen land already and you have to rectify it."[191] But certifiers and

---

[186] See Li 2010.   [187] The phrase comes from McCarthy 2012.
[188] Quoted in Colchester, Sirait and Wijardjo 2003:239.
[189] Interview with auditor, Bogor, 9/8/10.
[190] Quoted in Colchester, Sirait and Wijardjo 2003:240. LEI similarly must deal with the conflict between customary law and "positive law." One LEI participant admitted that "in the positive legal approach, the people on the land don't really have rights there," but explained that their approach is to "work on a positive legal basis, and look to see if there are conflicts, opportunities for new mapping, and try to resolve the problem" (interview with LEI representative, Bogor, 9/8/10).
[191] Phone interview with NGO representative, 6/18/09.

consultants tend to argue that companies are not responsible for prior illegitimate acts by the state. "Whose fault is it that the community was ignored in land use rights originally?" asked one rhetorically.[192] Another suggested that the "problem is where you [a company] as a rights holder come up against an ineffective government. I've done what I can. Is that good enough? Or are you going to hold me ransom?"[193]

Instead of holding a company "ransom" and effectively halting certification, auditors usually encourage companies to negotiate with the leaders of communities. By FSC standards, a company must receive "free and informed consent" from communities with customary claims in order to use a given area of land. Practically, this means having a written agreement on compensation that is to be paid to villagers and potentially on how the boundaries of the forest (and the uses of different areas) are defined. In the best cases, auditors do not rely on written documents alone, since they can be faked, and they devote substantial energies to navigating this terrain:[194]

> If the local community has clear claim over a portion of the area, we have to assess how the companies deal with such a claim—if there's fair compensation, if it was freely negotiated. We do this through interviews, public consultation, focus group discussions...[and] documentary evidence...But I recognize that in past years it was not easy for the community to say no. And there may not be documentation.[195]

Auditors also recognize that it can be difficult to spend enough time on the ground to understand company–community relations. "You're lucky if there's an NGO there," or it can be difficult to learn the situation, explained one participant in auditing teams. [196] In addition, practitioners often counter the "puffy stuff" of romanticized images of communities with reminders that it is "survival of the fittest" on the ground.[197] Most communities are "very pragmatic" and eager for compensation, while only a few "still have strong leadership and institutions and are not as interested in the monetary compensation."[198]

It is easy to point out that the agreements forged through certification rarely reflect a deep sociological analysis of "free and informed consent" and all of its power-laden complications. As the FSC has shifted to the more demanding notion of "free and *prior* informed consent" (FPIC)—as a 2012 revision mandates—the concept must be further stretched. As one practitioner

---

[192] Interview with NGO representative, Jakarta, 7/8/08.
[193] Interview with forestry consultant, Jakarta, 7/3/09.
[194] Colchester, Sirait and Wijardjo 2003.   [195] Interview with auditor, Bogor, 9/8/10.
[196] Interview with forestry researcher, Bogor, 6/30/08. On how companies can exploit intra-community conflict and distrust in ways that are difficult for outsiders to see, see Colchester and Ferrari (2007) and Jarvie et al. (2007).
[197] Interview with NGO representative, Jakarta, 7/3/08.
[198] Interview with auditor, Bogor, 9/8/10.

pointed out, "I don't believe FPIC can be implemented in Indonesia without modification."[199] "The 'prior' part is the difficulty," another explained. "The company already has the concession. To really do FPIC, you'd need the company to consult with the community at the beginning."[200] But what *is* accomplished when certifiers encourage new or expanded agreements between companies and community leaders? The cases described below provide some insights.

CERTIFYING IN CONTESTED SPACES—A CLOSER LOOK

PT Intracawood, which supplied certified plywood to The Home Depot, had a tense relationship with indigenous communities in its concession in East Kalimantan. Intracawood had received the concession through a 1988 partnership with the state-owned company PT Inhutani, and while the company compensated communities to some degree in the early 1990s, it was accused of doing so "sporadically and unevenly ... [such that] resentments, confusion, and unmet demands were high."[201] One villager claimed that "when PT Intracawood first came here, we were not brave enough to say anything, because it was during the New Order regime. Since *Reformasi* we have spoken out."[202] In one village in 2002, community members seized machinery and destroyed buildings in a dispute over compensation, leading several to be imprisoned. In another, villagers called for Intracawood to leave the area, blockaded roads, and destroyed a company camp. Intracawood called in the *Brimob* and other forces, who "came fully armed to the village and demanded that the blockade be lifted."[203]

The legal standing of Intracawood's concession was also problematic. The company had only finished delineating certain parts of the forest boundaries, and some boundaries had been mired in confusion for years.[204] During decentralization, district governments used their new authority to issue a number of small logging permits within the concession, and village leaders signed deals with entrepreneurs giving roughly $2 per cubic meter of timber in compensation for supporting these permits.[205] Intracawood successfully got these permits voided in the midst of recentralization in 2002.[206]

Auditors from SmartWood had noted this problem when they first assessed the concession in 2001. They made it a pre-condition for certification that the company conduct a "community survey to document and map community

---

[199] Ibid.   [200] Interview with NGO representative/researcher, Bogor, 9/8/10.
[201] Lawrence, Toyoda, and Lystiani 2003:26.
[202] Quoted in Colchester, Sirait, and Wijardjo 2003:211.   [203] Ibid.:212.
[204] Ibid.:205–7.   [205] Ibid.:215–16.
[206] Villagers' resentment of Intracawood may have been related to its attempts to cut off the small operators that were compensating communities to receive permits to log within the concession.

land claims, resource use, and sites of special community interest within the concession", and establish a "consultative community forum" to set guidelines and resolve land disputes.[207] In follow-ups, the auditors found that the offending permits had been voided and that sufficient progress had been made on the survey and forum, although they required the company to improve and expand these activities after certification. But just days after issuing the certificate in 2003, SmartWood suspended it, after the Indonesian Minister of Forestry issued a letter halting operations on Intracawood's concession, saying that it was mistakenly granted in the first place.

Personal lobbying by Intracawood's owner—the prominent businesswoman, Siti Hartati Tjakra Murdaya, whose holding company also owns the Nike suppliers PT Hasi/PT Nasa discussed in Chapter 6—got the permit reinstated.[208] SmartWood revived the certification process and finally certified Intracawood in 2005. Concerns about community relations continued to trail the company, though, as auditors asked Intracawood to implement the results of the community survey, "establish a standard procedure for negotiating a written agreement with communities prior to commencement of operations," and to make "significant progress to resolve all community disputes dating from prior to certification."[209]

In follow-ups, the auditors found that several participatory mapping exercises had been done (though not fully used) and that "most local people interviewed feel that the communication between Intracawood and local communities has improved."[210] The community forum had helped in negotiating compensation agreements with several communities, amounting to payments of 2,500 rupiah (roughly $0.27) per cubic meter of log volume in the village areas, plus various contributions to village infrastructure and education.[211] The fee per cubic meter amounts to roughly 0.3 percent of the cost of production or 0.2 percent of the average log price received by timber concessionaires in Kalimantan.[212] It is likely higher than what communities were receiving in the early 1990s, when military force loomed over company–community relations (though the amount of compensation at that time is not known). But it is of course far lower than the $2 per cubic meter that loggers were willing to pay to communities to secure rights to the land in 2002.

---

[207] SmartWood 2006c.   [208] Tempo 2012.   [209] SmartWood 2006c.
[210] SmartWood 2008b; SmartWood 2006a.
[211] SmartWood 2006a. This is based on a rough exchange rate of 9200 rupiah to the dollar in 2006.
[212] 2500 rupiah in 2006 was roughly $0.27. If we use Ruslandi et al.'s estimate that companies in Kalimantan produced logs for around $80 per cubic meter and sold them for around $122 per cubic meter, this means the payment to the community was around 0.3% of the cost of production, or 0.2% of the price received.

Intracawood continued to struggle with community relations—as well as its logging practices—and had its certificate briefly suspended in 2008 and again in 2010. In each case, the company showed enough evidence of improvement to get reinstated but not enough to entirely clear up lingering concerns. By 2011, auditors were assessing claims that the company was not fulfilling its agreements and failing to respect the district government's partial recognition of indigenous rights.[213]

Similar dynamics occurred in the certification of Sari Bumi Kusuma in Central Kalimantan and Sumalindo Lestari Jaya II in East Kalimantan. Activists accused Sari Bumi Kusuma of initially securing land by enlisting military help to intimidate indigenous people, and SmartWood's auditors noted that "the concession was granted originally by the government without adequate consultation with local people, a common practice under the previous political regime."[214] The auditors pushed the company to improve boundary mapping, compensation, and "avoid future instances of overlapping land use" without precluding certification. While the company began to allow indigenous people to use some traditional sites within the concession, the language of "free and informed consent" fell out of the auditors' discourse.[215]

In the case of Sumalindo, while many celebrated this certification, indigenous rights activists were critical.[216] In earlier clashes with Sumalindo, indigenous villagers had been arrested and pressed to accept a low level of compensation.[217] During a two-year certification process, SmartWood auditors met with a variety of local actors and pushed the company to further delineate the forest boundaries and better communicate with communities.[218] After certification, the company supplied maps of customary land claims—to be used "for calculation of compensation sharing for the community"—that were signed by government and village leaders and found to be accepted in the villages.[219] But an NGO's report charged that the auditors had relied on just two interviews in one village, overlooked intra-community divisions, and ignored evidence of possible intimidation.[220] Furthermore, as one auditor noted, since consultations were done after operational plans were made, this did not really constitute "free and prior informed consent."[221]

While villagers, local NGOs, and foreign watchdogs often pushed auditors to attend to community rights, close attention was not guaranteed. When SGS certified Diamond Raya's concession in Riau, auditors reported that there were

---

[213] SmartWood 2012.   [214] SmartWood 2007c.
[215] Ibid.; SmartWood 2008c; SmartWood 2009a.
[216] Clifford, Tashiro, and Natarajan 2003.
[217] Jarvie, Kanaan, Malley, Roule, and Thomson 2007.   [218] SmartWood 2006b.
[219] SmartWood 2007a.   [220] Colchester, Sirait, and Wijardjo 2003.
[221] Interview with auditor, Bogor, 9/8/10.

no customary claims and that community conflicts were negligible, consistent with the forest's image as more isolated than most.[222] But the company had previously called in *Brimob* troops to address illegal logging, and international NGOs later showed that SGS had been aware of a "major dispute over the boundaries of the concession" but had downplayed it.[223] In follow-ups, SGS disputed the idea that customary claims were present, but it did find that the company was not disbursing the agreed-upon amount to communities, asking the company to rectify this, improve dispute resolution processes, and establish an internal "community development division."[224]

RESOLVING RIGHTS THROUGH CERTIFICATION: THE MEANING AND LIMITS OF RESOLUTIONS

These cases suggest that villagers and their advocates have influenced the certification process, but this has resulted more in the *management* of conflicts than in a resolution of competing claims. Certifiers sometimes spurred marginal improvements in boundary-mapping, occasionally extending projects for "participatory mapping"—or "counter-mapping" of forest boundaries— that arose from indigenous rights movements in Kalimantan in the 1990s.[225] Typically, though, auditors could help companies facing a conflict "resolve it through terms of compensation."[226] It is likely that scrutiny from auditors helped villagers get higher levels of compensation that they would have otherwise, and overt repression by military forces was unlikely to be repeated under the watch of certifiers.

But of course that watch is selective and temporary. It is not clear whether agreements on boundaries and compensation did or would survive if the company ceased to be in the spotlight. Villagers might find other points of leverage, yet even with the help of certification and transnational advocacy networks, they are typically in a weak bargaining position. Many indigenous communities have what one auditor described as "very fragile institutions" traceable in part to the disorganizing reforms of the 1979 Village Government Law.[227] In addition, as John McCarthy (2009) has pointed out, they have not had the "shadow of the law" on their side, given the ambiguous legal status of *adat* claims.[228] Given the maze of regulations, one legal analysis concluded that the best answer to the question, "can we get *hak ulayat*?" (recognition of

[222] SGS QUALIFOR Programme 2000; van Assen 2005.
[223] Colchester, Sirait, and Wijardjo 2003:199–200; Ginting and Counsell 2001; Klein, Thies, Maráz, and Brune 2004:3.
[224] SGS QUALIFOR Programme 2005; SGS QUALIFOR Programme 2003. See also van der Vist and Heringa 2010 on the certification of Suka Jaya Makmur.
[225] Deddy 2006; Peluso 2005.
[226] Interview with NGO representative/researcher, Bogor, 9/8/10.
[227] Interview with auditor, Bogor, 9/8/10.   [228] McCarthy 2009:188.

customary rights), is that "according to formal law, probably nobody can. But do not let that deter you."[229]

In mediating company-community conflicts, it appears that certifiers have yet to make a strong break from the practice of companies buying off village leaders. During the New Order regime, large timber companies could rely on military and political power to ensure access to the forest, but in the *Reformasi* period, they came to rely more on monetary contributions. Industry actors often resent having to "pay a fee to the community", especially to people who would "rather sit back and take the money" than work for the company.[230] "We received a legitimate permit from the district head and our concession area falls within the state forest," one complained. "You have to understand, the claim of the community is economically motivated."[231] Nevertheless, timber companies routinely make payments to avoid or resolve conflict, raising concerns that "the resolution is between the company and the elite of the community."[232] Certifiers often try to assess whether non-elite villagers accept and benefit from this type of agreement, but this nevertheless operationalizes "free and informed consent" in terms of ad hoc compensation agreements.

As such, even the most rigorous certification processes have tended to sidestep the question of durable rights, bracket past injustices, and reproduce a logic of forest use in which the Ministry of Forestry and concession companies are privileged while villagers remain dependent.

Conclusion: Progress or Regress?

How one judges the accomplishments of sustainable forestry standards in Indonesia depends to a great extent on the comparisons made. Comparing Indonesia to other timber-exporting countries, it is clear that only small amounts of Indonesian forest land have even been candidates for the FSC's high-bar standards, despite the lack of a strong homegrown competitor. As this chapter has shown, Indonesia's laggard status is related not only to its export markets but also to the domestic political economy of timber, the rapidly changing political context, and the contested character of forest property.

---

[229] Bakker 2008:5.
[230] Interview with company representative, Jakarta, 6/26/08.
[231] Quoted in Yasmi, Guernier and Colfer 2009:103.
[232] Interview with NGO representative, Jakarta, 9/24/10. This was said with reference to PT Finantara Intiga's plantation development in West Kalimantan, which others have portrayed as a best case example of fair compensation (interview with certification representative, 9/8/10; Schneck 2009) and which was certified by LEI.

If one compares the FSC's standards on paper to their practical implications on the ground, it is clear that many compromises have been made in the implementation process. To be sure, companies have made behavioral changes to get or remain certified, as well as adopting many new policies, management systems, and monitoring plans. As we have seen, auditors have been forced to attend to thorny issues surrounding the rights of communities, but their "pragmatic" approaches have privileged state designations and ad hoc agreements, and some companies have been able to receive or retain a certified status while struggling to manage community conflicts.

Compared to areas that are being burned and cleared for agriculture, FSC-certified forest management companies are almost certainly superior in terms of biodiversity, the protection of animal habitats, soil and water resources, and many other virtues of managed natural forests. The tighter comparison of certified and uncertified natural forest concessions is much more difficult to make. Practitioners have noted variation in each group. For instance, on the use of reduced impact logging techniques, one consultant noted that "some non-certified [companies] are actually doing quite good things...and some certified [companies] are not doing well at all."[233] One recent study that compared villages near FSC-certified and uncertified concessions in Kalimantan found that certification was linked to greater forest cover, a reduced likelihood of air pollution, and some measures of villager well-being, though there were no discernible differences in the incidence of forest fires or the development of community health and safety infrastructures.[234]

If these were the only comparisons made, one could reasonably conclude that forest certification has improved the governance of Indonesian forests, even if only on a small scale and not completely reliably. If one compares forest certification to other ways of handling the relationship between timber, forest land, and people, though, some deficiencies of private solutions come into clearer focus.

The profit sharing system that Perum Perhutani developed to get re-certified represents a step forward from the company's earlier versions of the *tumpang sari* system of intercropping.[235] But Perhutani avoided—and indeed, sought to nullify—another path forward that gave villagers greater control. In the village of Wonosobo in Central Java, the local parliament passed a regulation in 2001 that allowed community groups to actively manage state forest land.[236] Villagers' effectiveness in protecting these lands amid the upsurge in illegal logging had made the district government receptive to their calls for greater rights. The "Wonosobo regulation" allowed villagers to decide what species of trees to plant and required negotiation on the rate of profit-sharing, whereas

---

[233] Interview with forestry consultant, 9/22/10.   [234] Miteva, Loucks, and Pattanayak 2015.
[235] Mayers and Vermeulen 2002.   [236] Bakker and Moniaga 2010; Nomura 2008.

Perhutani's system kept those decisions in the hands of the company.[237] The company first ignored the Wonosobo regulation, then lobbied aggressively to have it rescinded, pressuring villagers and officials and labeling its adversaries "communists", "which is still 'fatal' for civil society groups in Indonesia," as one representative noted.[238] Under pressure from the Ministry of Forestry and the Minister of Home Affairs, the Wonosobo villagers had to accept Perhutani's terms—or else take the risky step of "holding out for complete control."[239] Strikingly, the alternative model suggested by the Wonosobo regulation appears to have been completely ignored by certifiers, who portrayed Perhutani's system as the only way forward.

On Indonesia's outer islands, where land rights are even more unsettled, there are scattered examples of communities receiving recognition of land claims from governments, rather than just through agreements with companies. The Guguk community in Jambi province, with help from the NGO Warsi, reclaimed land that had been harvested by a timber company (PT Injapsin) and received endorsement of their *hutan adat* from the district governor.[240] In a fascinating case with a different twist, the indigenous community in Sungai Utik in West Kalimantan sought certification from LEI in hopes that it would help secure formal recognition for customary forest lands. The villagers had protected the land as illegal logging overtook surrounding areas, though it is not clear whether this protection—or the certification by LEI— would be sufficient for formal recognition from regional or central government agencies.[241] Of course, the project to link sustainability, indigenous rights, and community forestry carries its own dilemmas. As Tania Li (2001) points out, "land and resource rights *made contingent upon stewardship* are a pale version of the rights other citizens enjoy."[242] Tensions between collective and individual rights, as well as the rights of women, are often ignored in sustainability and indigeneity advocacy.

In various ways over the past century, development projects in Indonesia have left forest-dwelling people scrounging for the least valuable forest products and unable to secure robust rights to land. As Michael Dove (2011) argues, "What the smallholders need above all else are the means to hold on to their lands, their natural resources; and this entails political empowerment at the local level and wider development of the institutions of civil society."[243] To the extent that transnational private regulation has addressed the land rights of rural people in Indonesia, it has left them ambiguous or subject to fragile agreements between companies and community leaders.

---

[237] Nomura 2008.   [238] Quoted in ibid.:181.   [239] Macqueen 2010:21.
[240] Abubakar 2009.
[241] Down to Earth 2006; interview with certification representative, Bogor, 7/1/08; interview with certification representative, Bogor, 9/8/10; phone interview with forestry researcher 8/14/08.
[242] P. 671, emphasis added.   [243] P. 258.

There are signs, though, that other processes are increasing the space for recognition of community rights. In 2013, the Indonesian Constitutional Court ruled that the 1999 Forestry Law was wrong to define customary forests as a subset of state forests. This called into question whether the Ministry of Forestry—which has since been renamed the Ministry of Environment and Forestry—can continue to exercise control over land with *adat* claims.[244] Meanwhile, between 2011 and 2015, the Indonesian government introduced several moratoriums on the granting of new logging concessions in primary forests, partly to participate in climate change mitigation initiatives and to respond to a new wave of dangerous haze from forest fires. The moratoriums have been rife with exceptions, failed promises, and the continued clearing of biodiverse "secondary" forests.[245]

Nevertheless, indigenous rights and community forestry advocates may be able to gain leverage from the government's expanding set of pledges, especially combined with the Constitutional Court decision and a new transnational timber legality regime that is described in this book's final chapter. Unlike forest certification, this form of transnational governance "re-centers" the state—rather than trying to transcend it—and may better empower domestic reformers.

---

[244] Natahadibrata 2013; Down to Earth 2013.
[245] Saturi, Sigit, Nugraha, and Jacobson 2015; The Economist 2016.

4

The State Strikes Back

Forest Certification in Authoritarian China

"They're the government and they can change and there's not much we can do about it."

Interview with certification initiative representative, speaking
of changing administrative requirements for certifiers[1]

"The primary problem and greatest threat to tenure security of farmers is government intervention—plus either intended or unintended companies standing behind. In [the] Stora Enso [case], the company set up a state owned company with the sole purpose of acquiring land."

Interview with NGO representative[2]

The terms "China" and "environment" conjure images of thick smog, belching smokestacks, and polluted rivers. But China also has the world's fifth largest amount of forest land, befitting its large land mass, and the third highest number of plant species, behind only Brazil and Indonesia on this measure of biodiversity.[3] Much of China's forest cover was lost prior to the twentieth century, but a wide variety of forest types remain, from the temperate forests of the north to tropical and subtropical forests of the south.[4]

The upheavals of the twentieth century brought "three great cuttings" to the forests of China.[5] First, the collective forests that Mao established after the revolution were cut rapidly during the Great Leap Forward (1958–61)—often, to fuel the hundreds of thousands of backyard iron and steel mills that were supposed to rapidly industrialize China. After the Great Famine that resulted from this disastrous industrialization project, the Chinese government put a renewed emphasis on agricultural development. A second great cutting followed, with many natural forests being clearcut and converted to farms during

---

[1] 12/26/10.   [2] 3/13/14.   [3] Ho 2006.
[4] Kram, Bedford, Durnin, Luo, Rokpelnis, Roth, Smith, Wang, Yu, Yu, and Zhao 2012.
[5] Trac, Harrell, Hinckley, and Henck 2007; Shapiro 2001.

the Cultural Revolution (1966–76).[6] The market reforms of the 1980s brought a third wave of deforestation. As individual households were granted greater rights to use collectively owned forests, many responded by cutting as much as possible, fearing that they would soon lose these tenuous and partial rights, while local governments turned to logging to generate revenues.[7] When the timber trade was liberalized in 1985, ending the state-run monopoly, demand for logs skyrocketed.[8] "Highly skilled and productive lumberjacks became local heroes," according to one account, "felling trees as swiftly as possible to meet the growing domestic and international demand for China's timber products."[9]

The consequences became painfully clear in the summer of 1998. Floods of the Yangtze and other rivers killed nearly 4,000 people, displaced millions, and caused $20–30 billion in damages.[10] Heavy rainfalls precipitated the floods, but it was deforestation and soil erosion that made the rain especially devastating.[11] The central government demonstrated a "sudden concentration of political will" in response, developing a major campaign to promote conservation and afforestation.[12] A new National Forest Protection Plan banned logging altogether in some Yangtze River areas and tightened logging quotas in other areas, while a "Grain for Green" program subsidized farmers to re-convert agricultural lands to forests, especially on sloping land prone to erosion.[13] Adding an element of popular mobilization, the government issued "a flood of nationally televised environmental awareness campaigns that stressed the dangers of erosion and desertification" and organized teams of school children, corporate employees, and local residents to participate in tree-planting campaigns.[14]

Yet during the same period, China was becoming a top exporter of forest products. Exports of wood furniture, paper products, and plywood increased by 527 percent, 856 percent, and a whopping 4,600 percent respectively, from 1996 to 2006.[15] Most were headed to the US, Japan, or EU countries, with the

---

[6] Dai, Wang, Su, Zhou, Yu, Lewis, and Qi 2011.

[7] Zhang and Kant 2005; Dean and Damm-Luhr 2010; Trac, Harrell, Hinckley, and Henck 2007; Ho 2006; Robbins and Harrell 2014. Sichuan province, which had been heavily forested, lost roughly half of its forest cover from the 1970s to 1980s (Economy 2010:65).

[8] Zhang and Kant 2005.   [9] Economy 2010:64.

[10] Zhang and Kant 2005; Ho 2006.

[11] Zong and Chen 2000. The day before the floods, state TV had shown an undercover report on illegal logging in Yunnan province, making the link to deforestation especially salient in public discourse (Economy 2010: 157–9).

[12] Strauss 2009:1172.

[13] Miao and West 2004; Trac, Harrell, Hinckley, and Henck 2007. Official data portrays these reforestation programs as a massive success, but the research by Trac et al. (2007) casts doubt. Looking closely at one area of Sichuan province, they found barren land where reforestation efforts were supposedly occurring, a poor choice of species, weak implementation, and incentives for local cadres to over-report success.

[14] Strauss 2009:1172.   [15] Chinese Academy of Forestry 2007.

US alone eventually accounting for 35 percent of China's forest products exports.[16] Timber demand within China was also growing, with domestic construction consuming six times more than furniture production.[17] With booming demand, both large state forestry bureaus and small farmers had strong incentives to exceed their official logging quotas.[18] Other companies raced to acquire large tracts of land for fast-growing timber plantations, even if it meant strong-arming local residents to give up whatever land-use rights they had. Given limits on the domestic wood supply, manufacturers also relied heavily on timber imported from Russia, Malaysia, Indonesia, and elsewhere, much of it of suspicious or illegal origin.[19] In short, the boom in forest products manufacturing in China rested on an array of interrelated and often destructive modes of forest management, both within and beyond Chinese borders.

No one claimed that the certification of sustainable forestry within China could resolve all of these challenges, but many advocates argued that it could at least recognize sound forest management practices and prevent plantation projects from eradicating biodiversity. Large, experienced state forest bureaus would make "a good [place] for the FSC [Forest Stewardship Council] to be implemented in China, a showcase of what forest management could be like," explained one NGO representative.[20] Moreover, if retailers and brands would demand certified products, then timber from certified forests, whether near or far, would displace the flow of illegal timber through Chinese factories.[21] Because the central government was interested in promoting sustainable forest management, the State Forestry Administration supported the Forest Stewardship Council's entry into China in the early 2000s, while WWF, Ikea, and other international supporters began helping forest enterprises in China get certified.

Despite a comparatively late start, FSC certification in China grew rapidly. The first forest management certificate was awarded in 2001, and the second came only in 2004. But by 2010, there were twenty-nine FSC-certified forests in China, covering approximately 1.75 million hectares, or 2.0–2.7 percent of the eligible land.[22] This almost doubled by 2014 to 3.4 million hectares, or 4.0–5.3 percent of the eligible land. Even more striking, the number of FSC

---

[16] Sun, Cheng and Canby 2005; White, Sun, Canby, Xu, Barr, Katsigris, Bull, Cossalter, and Nilsson 2006.

[17] Sun, Wang, and Gu 2004; Kaplinsky, Terheggen, and Tijaja 2011.

[18] Strauss 2009.

[19] White, Sun, Canby, Xu, Barr, Katsigris, Bull, Cossalter, and Nilsson 2006; Robbins and Harrell 2014.

[20] Interview with NGO representative, Beijing, 12/8/10.

[21] Monument 2008; Greenpeace 2007.

[22] If we take the FAO 2010 estimate of 84.8 million hectares of production forest in China, the rate of FSC certification would be 2% in 2010 and 4% in 2014. Using the FDA's estimate of 64.2 million hectares of timber production forest, the rate of FSC certification was 2.7% in 2010 and 5.3% in 2014 (USDA Foreign Agricultural Service 2009).

"chain of custody" certificates—which allow factories to label products as made with FSC-certified timber—skyrocketed to more than 1,000 in 2010 and surpassed 3,000 in 2013.

The FSC's stringent standards, backed by foreign NGOs and retailers, seem to have gained an important foothold within China. And yet, even as the amount of certified land grew, some industry and state officials—including some from the same agencies that had originally welcomed the FSC—were charging the FSC with being "illegal" in China and promoting a homegrown alternative, dubbed the China Forest Certification Council (CFCC). As it became increasingly difficult for the FSC and its constituents to operate in China, the amount of FSC-certified land began to fall—to 2.2 million hectares by January of 2015 and then to 1.5 million hectares by June of that year.[23]

This chapter seeks to explain the rapid rise and partial fall of FSC certification in China. How did the FSC's standards become prominent in this setting? How were they translated into practice? And how were they constrained? As we will see, global retailers spurred the initial growth of FSC certification in China, consistent with the view of transnational corporations pushing standards through their supply chains. But both the practical interpretation of standards and the operation of the FSC system proved to be deeply dependent on the state, belying any idea of bypassing it.

I will argue that the authoritarian character of governance in China has had a dual consequence for forest certification. On one hand, the strong authoritarian state threatened the operational autonomy of the FSC system, especially as state agencies put their weight behind a homegrown initiative. The FSC's auditors faced new burdens of state authorization; NGO allies had to temper their support; and supply-chain linkages could be quickly cut by government decisions. In these ways, the state was a constraint on private authority. Here, this case study resonates with other research on the "authoritarian logic of regulatory pluralism" in Chinese environmental governance. As researchers are increasingly recognizing, a wide range of actors within China—including NGOs, journalists, and informal citizen groups—have taken on the task of enforcing environmental law. But their activities are constrained by "continued party-state dominance and a schizophrenic recognition [by government officials] that new actors are both necessary and, at times, threatening".[24]

---

[23] This is based on the data reported in "FSC Facts and Figures" except for the January 2015 figure, which comes from the 2015 "Market Info Pack" (Forest Stewardship Council 2015b). FSC published the Facts and Figures document monthly from February 2012 to November 2014, except for July and August of 2014; and then again from June 2015 to December 2015.

[24] van Rooij, Stern and Fürst 2016:9. See also Yee, Lo, and Tang 2013; Johnson 2016; Marquis, Zhang, and Zhou 2011.

On the other hand, though, authoritarian governance also *enabled* the ground-level certification of sustainable forestry in some respects. This was especially the case in the plantation projects of south China. Land tenure in these collectively owned areas could be complicated, and land grabs by timber companies and the local state were more than possible. This might have impeded certification to the FSC's standards, which require clear land tenure and respect for communities' rights. But land conflicts were repressed, suppressed, or highly contained by the authoritarian setting, allowing auditors to construct plantation projects as compliant with the FSC's high standards. Thus, the case of sustainable forestry in China displays what I call the "dual logic of certifying in authoritarian places"—that is, *constrained* operational autonomy combined with *contained* constructions of compliance that facilitate rapid certification.

I will begin with the initial growth, implementation challenges, and implications of forest certification in China. I will then show how the rise of a state-sponsored competitor threatened the FSC's ability to operate in China. This section strongly contradicts the notion that private regulators can become legitimate authorities solely on the basis of market demand and conformity to global norms. Next, I will make the case that authoritarian governance also enabled FSC certification in some respects. Here, we will see China's shifting land-tenure arrangements, the potential for land grabs, and the certification of troubled plantation projects managed by Sino-Forest and Stora Enso.

Certifying Sustainability in Chinese Forests

As the project to certify sustainable forestry came to China, its first wave of candidates came mainly from the north, where forest land is mostly owned by the state and managed by large state forestry bureaus. The remainder of forest land in China, roughly 60 percent of the total, is held by village collectives, with land-use rights sometimes devolved to individual households or small groups of villagers. The State Forestry Administration regulates the rate of logging in state-owned forests, and these quotas are often extended to collectively owned forests as well. But as one sustainable forestry practitioner explained, "Chinese traditional forest management practice pays little attention [to] environmental impacts and social impacts...As a result, Chinese FMUs [forest management units] need to learn to adapt the requirements of environmental and social aspects of FSC standards."[25]

[25] Email communication with forestry researcher, 4/2/14.

The rise of FSC-certified forest management

A handful of international NGOs and retailers, working in cooperation with the State Forestry Administration (SFA) and the Chinese Academy of Forestry, led the project to introduce the FSC's principles into China. Central to these efforts was Ikea, which was using timber from Chinese forests to feed its factories there. Roughly 20 percent of Ikea's products were being made in China, using a mix of domestic and imported (especially Russian) timber.[26] As Ikea witnessed environmental campaigns against retailers in the 1990s, it "realized it would soon be a major target."[27] The company developed its "Iway" code of conduct in 2000 and soon began working with WWF to promote FSC certification in its global supply chain.[28]

To develop a supply of FSC certified wood in China, Ikea looked to several large state forestry bureaus in the northeast. Two such forests—the Baihe Forest Bureau in Jilin province and the Youhao Forest Bureau in Heilongjiang province—received FSC certification in 2005, amounting to roughly 425,000 hectares of certified land. For these two cases and several others, Ikea subsidized the cost of certification, giving funds to WWF for this purpose.[29] Over time, Ikea is said to have sponsored roughly 90 percent of the forestry operations in China that were FSC-certified by 2010 and eventually to have "directly or indirectly supported about 2 million hectares in China for FSC certification."[30]

Ikea's pricing strategies, on the other hand, did not leave much slack for its suppliers to invest in sustainability. As one observer put it, "Ikea wants it [FSC certification] but doesn't pay well."[31] "They shift suppliers often; they are changing too much," another complained.[32] "Ikea's business model is always to be 20% lower than others," one practitioner explained, noting also that "Ikea decreases the price every year . . . It's a dilemma for Ikea—on one hand

---

[26] Ivarsson and Alvstam 2010; interview with certification representative, Beijing, 7/18/11. Ikea's suppliers are generally responsible for accessing their own raw materials, but Ikea provides short-term loans and sometimes assistance in identifying sources (ibid.). In a survey of 195 Ikea suppliers in China, 95% said that Ikea provided "technical consultations on product characteristics," but only 41% said that Ikea provided advice or assistance in obtaining raw materials (ibid.).

[27] Interview with certification representative, Beijing, 7/18/11.

[28] In 2005, Ikea pledged to have 30% of its wood products made of FSC-certified timber within four years, but two years later, it had only reached the 4% mark (Goodman and Finn 2007).

[29] Interview with certification representative, Beijing, 7/18/11; interview with certification representative, Beijing, 12/8/10; phone interview with certification representative, 12/26/10; interview with forester, Beijing, 7/21/11.

[30] Interview with certification representative, Beijing, 12/8/10; interview with sustainable forestry consultant, Hong Kong, 3/10/14. By one estimate, Ikea provided a 5 million yuan (roughly $750,000) to hold workshops and trainings to prepare companies for FSC certification (interview with forester/auditor, Beijing, 3/14/14).

[31] Interview with NGO representative, Beijing, 12/10/10.

[32] Interview with industry association representative, Beijing, 3/17/14.

pushing down the price but on the other hand telling them to get certified."[33] In addition, even while Ikea was promoting forest certification, it was struggling to trace where all the wood in its supply chain was coming from, making it difficult to reduce the risk of using illegal timber.[34]

Beyond those supported by Ikea, FSC certification was granted to the Changhua Forest Farm in Zhejiang province, which was introduced to the idea by an American client, and to Sino-Forest, which pursued certification to build its reputation in the financial sector, as described later in this chapter.[35] The Badaling Forest Farm, near a heavily visited part of the Great Wall, was the site of several ecological demonstration projects prior to its certification, and WWF identified it as "a good place to promote FSC because it's a famous place."[36] Several bamboo producers pursued certification in order to better reach green markets for flooring and furniture. This was complicated by bamboo's ambiguous status as a "tree-like grass" that is considered a grass by some and a tree by others and by the risks of erosion, pesticide over-use, and declining biodiversity on large monoculture bamboo plantations.[37] As one sustainable forestry auditor put it, "the FSC initially thought bamboo didn't produce forest eco-services, but they're convinced now that some types can."[38]

The market for certified paper and packaging also contributed to the first wave of FSC certification in China, with the Fujian Yong'An Forest Group's certification supported by Tetra Pak, the multinational food packaging company.[39] Unlike the state forest bureaus of the north, the land in this case was under a mixture of state and collective ownership.[40] Foreshadowing the complicated cases that would follow, a representative of WWF-China noted that "the complex situation in the forested areas in Southern China makes it difficult to carry out large-scale FSC forest certification" but praised Yong'An as "a good example for forest certification and sustainable forest management in the south."[41]

Practical implications of certification

Although the amount of FSC-certified land increased, the material benefits for forest management companies were less than most had hoped. By one estimate, only around one-fourth of the timber from certified forests was being sold as certified—that is, to buyers who would use it to make certified

---

[33] Interview with certification representative, Beijing, 7/18/11.   [34] Ibid.
[35] Interview with auditor, Beijing, 7/14/11.
[36] Interview with forester, Beijing, 7/21/11; Beijing Forestry Society 2012.
[37] Buckingham and Jepson 2015.   [38] Interview with auditor, Beijing, 7/14/11.
[39] Liu 2009; Environmental Panorama International 2009.
[40] Chen and Innes 2013; SGS QUALIFOR Programme 2008.
[41] Quoted in WWF-Global 2008.

products.[42] It could sometimes fetch price premiums, but these varied substantially. At the high end, one forest bureau reported selling certified wood at 10 percent more than the normal market price, and several others reported a 5–15 percent premium.[43] But one practitioner estimated that as the supply of certified wood increased, premiums were amounting to only around 20 yuan ($3.20) per cubic meter—or roughly 0.5 percent to 1.5 percent of the raw log price.[44] According to one practitioner's study, the direct costs of auditing were usually 200,000–300,000 RMB (roughly $32,000 to $48,000), with an additional 200,000–300,000 RMB in indirect costs (that is, the costs of making the required changes), and totals of 1 million RMB (roughly $160,000) or more for large forests.[45]

To what extent did forest managers have to change their practices to get (or stay) FSC-certified? To answer this, we can once again look at auditors' corrective action requests (as in Chapter 3). One finds a range of issues, from erosion control and the elimination of banned pesticides to employee health and safety protections. Table 4.1 summarizes the types of changes made, looking across all corrective actions that were completed from 2001–10. For 43 percent of the completed requests, forest managers could comply by adopting a new policy or other document. For instance, the Kaihua Forest Farm had to create a new policy on the use of safety equipment for different types of harvesting activities.[46] 44 percent of the time, managers could comply by

Table 4.1. Types of actions taken to resolve auditors' "corrective action requests" for FSC-certified forests in China

Producing, revising, or disclosing a written policy	Improving monitoring or documentation	Implementing behavioral change in the field (beyond monitoring)	Total CARs
43%	44%	32%	303

Based on 38 audits of 18 forest management enterprises with CARs closed from 2001 to 2010. Actions are not mutually exclusive.

[42] Interview with forester/auditor, Beijing, 3/14/14.

[43] Zhao, Xie, Wang, and Deng 2011; email communication with forestry researcher, 4/2/14. Another practitioner who studied certified forest management companies in China found only one that got a large benefit, while most others were hopeful that they could reap benefits in the future in the market or with government (interview with forester, Beijing, 7/15/11).

[44] Interview with forester/auditor, Beijing, 3/14/14. The percentage is a rough estimate assuming that domestic logs would sell for as low as 1300 yuan and as high as 4000 yuan per cubic meter, depending on the species and size (Global Wood 2014). Throughout this chapter and book, I will generate dollar estimates using an approximate exchange rate of 6.2 rmb to the dollar during the 2013–15 period, 6.7 rmb to the dollar during the 2009–12 period, and 8 rmb to the dollar from 2000–8.

[45] Email communication with forestry researcher, 4/2/14. The manager of one large forest farm estimated that the total costs in his case were much higher, around 4 million RMB (Yao 2014).

[46] Institute for Marketecology 2009.

improving the monitoring or documentation of existing practices. For instance, Sino-Forest had to expand its monitoring of water quality and availability in its plantation areas to retain its certification.[47] Somewhat less commonly, 32 percent of the time, forest managers had to make behavioral changes in the field. For instance, in order to control erosion, the Muling Forestry Bureau had to begin re-converting several agricultural areas near riverbanks into forested areas.[48]

Overall, this initial wave of FSC certification in China did require forest managers to make behavioral changes in the field, though at a somewhat lower rate than in Indonesia. The greater frequency of policy and monitoring changes should serve as a reminder, though, that auditors' requests could often be satisfied with improved documentation and formal management systems.

Challenges and blindspots

A closer look reveals several significant gaps in the implementation and auditing of the FSC's principles. For instance, there were mundane but important challenges of monitoring compliance in large and complex forests.[49] The large forestry bureaus of the north had established systems of documentation and "lots of people doing monitoring and patrolling," as one practitioner put it, but they also had experience in exceeding their logging quotas.[50] "State forest bureaus show you GIS and have sophisticated information, but they manipulate it... [They can] show you the good parts," one practitioner claimed.[51] "The forest management [enterprise] may say a chosen site [a site chosen by the auditor] is too far, too hard to get to," another explained.[52] By some accounts, the challenges of auditing were magnified by the fact that most lead auditors were foreigners who did not speak Chinese.[53] "If you're Chinese, you know better how to translate and make [standards] relevant to this region. If it's a foreign auditor with a translator, it takes double-time."[54]

---

[47] SmartWood 2005b.   [48] SmartWood 2009a.

[49] An instance of deception by the Baihe Forest Bureau was discovered two years after certification when auditors found that the company was "producing documents that weren't specifying the full supply chain" (email interview with certification representative, 12/26/10). This led to a withdrawal of the certificate, which was later reinstated (interview with sustainable forestry consultant, 7/18/11).

[50] Interview with NGO representative/auditor, Beijing, 3/11/14.

[51] Interview with forestry researcher, Beijing, 7/15/11.

[52] Interview with certification representative, Beijing, 12/8/10.

[53] Especially during the first decade of FSC certification in China, lead auditors typically flew in from abroad and did not speak Chinese, although their auditing teams always included Chinese foresters as well.

[54] Interview with auditor, Beijing, 7/14/11.

Looking at three particular challenges helps to clarify the blindspots and limits of FSC certification in China. One pertains to the prohibition on clearing "natural" forests; another to labor rights in the forest; and a third to "chain of custody" certification.

WHAT COUNTS AS A "NATURAL" FOREST?

"This was a pioneering certificate, then suddenly it was all over," said one observer about the suspension of the Yong'An Forest Group's certificate just over a year after it was first granted.[55] The problem arose when a follow-up audit concluded that the company's clearcutting for plantation development had violated the FSC's prohibition on the clearing of natural forests (after 1994). Since it contained planted conifer trees, the original auditors had not considered this area a natural forest. Instead, it fit the definition of a planted forest that is common among Chinese foresters and government agencies.[56] "Forest authorities define it just based on origin: if it's planted, it's called a plantation."[57] But the follow-up audit team concluded that the converted area had been "semi-natural" forest, the clearing of which was prohibited by FSC standards.[58] As one observer explained, the planted trees were "all local species and [the forest managers] had been using semi-natural management style for 20 years."[59]

The company, with assistance from WWF-China, appealed unsuccessfully to Accreditation Services International (ASI), the body that oversees all FSC-accredited auditors. "The definition of natural forest is different here," one practitioner complained.[60] "Forest authorities encourage planting of native species and transforming of low-yield forests. They may want to harvest everything in a low-yield forest and plant fast-growing species," another explained.[61] Indeed, the government's "conversion of low quality forest" policy can pose problems for companies seeking FSC certification, since that low-yield, mixed-species forest could be defined as a natural or semi-natural forest.[62]

This kind of definitional conflict is supposed to be addressed by developing FSC-endorsed national standards that tailor global principles to the domestic context. As we will see, though, that process quickly got caught up in struggles over the power of the state and private regulators.

---

[55] Interview with sustainable forestry consultant, Hong Kong, 3/10/14.
[56] Interview with auditor, Beijing, 7/14/11; interview with NGO representative/auditor, Beijing, 3/11/14; interview with auditor, Beijing, 12/10/10; interview with NGO representative, Beijing, 12/10/10.
[57] Interview with forester/auditor, Beijing, 3/12/14.   [58] Ibid.
[59] Interview with NGO representative, Beijing, 12/8/10.
[60] Interview with NGO representative, Beijing, 12/10/10.
[61] Interview with forester/auditor, Beijing, 3/12/14.
[62] Interview with NGO representative/auditor, Beijing, 3/11/14.

IGNORING LABOR RIGHTS

The FSC's principles cover both labor protections—including health and safety protection—and labor rights—such as the right to form unions. In practice, auditors often asked for improvements in labor protections but almost never problematized labor rights. In fact, the most common corrective action request made in audits from 2001 to 2010 focused on the criterion (4.2) that requires that "forest management should meet or exceed all applicable laws and/or regulations covering health and safety of employees and their families." (See Table 4.2.) Auditors often pushed for better personal protective equipment (PPE) for forest workers, although some auditors admitted that "when we audit, we can tell that the equipment is brand new and just used for the audit."[63] "In such cases, as an auditor, you need to be concerned about which are the most important issues for certain enterprises," another auditor explained. "If you're very strict, nearly every enterprise couldn't get FSC certified in China."[64]

While auditors were at least attentive to issues of worker safety, they were almost completely blind to the problem of labor rights in China. FSC criterion 4.3 states that "the rights of workers to organize and voluntarily negotiate with their employers shall be guaranteed as outlined in Conventions 87 and 98 of the International Labour Organization (ILO)." ILO Convention 87 says that workers must be able to "establish and . . . join organizations of their own choosing," and that "the public authorities shall refrain from any interference which would restrict this right or impede the lawful exercise thereof." As

Table 4.2. Most common criteria for corrective action requests, FSC-certified forests in China, 2001–10

Top criteria, ranked by frequency of corrective action requests

1. Employee health and safety (criterion 4.2)
2. Other/no specific criterion (e.g., forest group management issues)
3. Documentation for chain of custody (c8.3)
4. Assessment of environmental impacts and integration into management system (c6.1)
5. Training in forest management plan (c7.1)
6. Banned pesticides (c6.6)
7. Requirements for the forest management plan (c7.1)
8. Erosion, road construction, water protection guidelines (criterion 6.5)
9. Requirements for monitoring forest management (criterion 8.2)
10. Social impact evaluations (criterion 4.4)
. . .
. . .
41. Workers' freedom of association (criterion 4.3)

Ranking of 58 criteria in total, based on a weighted sum of major (1) and minor (0.5) corrective action requests.

[63] Interview with forester/auditor, Beijing, 3/12/14.
[64] Interview with auditor, Beijing, 12/10/10.

described further in the next chapter, the monopoly of the state-backed All-China Federation of Trade Unions (ACFTU) makes it nearly impossible to comply with global norms on freedom of association.[65]

By a strict definition, virtually no enterprise in China can meet the FSC standards for workers' rights. Using a less strict definition, one might expect to see auditors looking for ways around this contradiction. This is what auditors in the apparel and footwear industry have done, as we will see in Chapter 5. But the FSC's accredited auditors usually ignored the problem altogether. In eighty-four audits for forest management certification from 2001 to 2010, auditors issued only four corrective action requests (all categorized as minor) related to criterion 4.3. Two called for the establishment of grievance procedures; one simply required that the "FME [forest management enterprise] shall have the copy of ILO Conventions 87 and 98;" and another stated that "an employee must be appointed for communication with unions and other workers' organizations."[66] In the more recent certification of a Stora Enso plantation in Guangxi province, the auditors blithely reported that "there was no evidence that the rights of the workers to organize and voluntarily negotiation with their employers were not guaranteed as outlined in Conventions 87 and 98 of the International Labour Organisation (ILO)."[67]

In interviews, several auditors confirmed that they see management- and state-controlled ACFTU unions as satisfying the FSC standard. "In the northeast state forest bureaus, it's no problem, because the forest bureau is also the government, so the workers' union is no problem," explained one auditor, going on to describe it as a good thing if union representatives are in management positions.[68] Another auditor mentioned ILO conventions, but ignored conventions on freedom of association, instead pointing to conventions on child labor and forced labor to note that "most of those things are not happening in China," at least in forests.[69]

Although the FSC's constituents and watchdogs have rarely focused on labor rights in China, one stakeholder complaint was made to Accreditation

---

[65] China has not ratified ILO Conventions 87 or 98 and is widely seen as diverging from international norms about freedom of association. China has ratified conventions on four of the ILO's eight "fundamental labor rights," but not those covering union rights and forced labor.

[66] SmartWood 2009a:11; Institute for Marketecology 2010:18.

[67] Bureau Veritas Certification 2012:64. In this case, the auditors did recognize a hotline that the company had set up, suggesting that perhaps the sustainable forestry field was beginning to incorporate the CSR practices that had emerged earlier in the labor standards field.

[68] Interview with forester/auditor, Beijing, 3/14/14.

[69] Interview with auditor, Beijing, 7/14/11. The auditor said that forced labor cannot happen, since dissatisfied workers will simply leave. It is unclear whether forced labor is used in forests in China, but given the import of workers from other regions to work in remote timber plantations, it is certainly a possibility. Like the two auditors above, a third auditor did not mention questions about the legitimacy of ACFTU unions when asked about enforcing the FSC's labor standards (interview with auditor, Beijing, 12/10/10).

Services International in 2014 regarding the Wuhua Eucalyptus Forest in Guangdong province.[70] It questioned whether the certifier had actually assessed criterion 4.3 on workers' rights. After investigating, the oversight body concluded that auditors had not properly guaranteed confidentiality when interviewing workers, but it did not discipline the certifier, and it declined the chance to take a stand on the legitimacy of the ACFTU union. "During the witnessed audit these aspects could not be fully evaluated due to the sensitivity of this information in the Chinese context," the report stated.[71] As discussed in Chapter 2, although the FSC's constituents may be beginning to pay more attention to labor rights in the forest, this has often been a blind spot in the implementation of sustainable forestry standards.

MISSING LINKS IN THE CHAIN OF CUSTODY?

Beyond the forest, the market for FSC-certified products rests on "chain of custody" certification. This is simply "a system certification of the company's ability to handle certified product," explained one practitioner.[72] It allows a manufacturer of paper, plywood, flooring, furniture or other forest products to put the FSC label on product lines made from the required amount of FSC-certified wood or pulp.

The number of FSC chain of custody certificates in China went from roughly 250 in 2006 to more than 1,000 in 2010, then tripled to more than 3,000 by 2013.[73] This might be an indication of rising global demand for FSC-certified products, and indeed part of the increase can be attributed to growing demand for FSC-certified paper products and the expanding paper and publishing industries in China.[74] But there are also signs that factories have gotten chain of custody certificates while using few if any certified inputs.

One practitioner estimated a third of the companies in China with FSC chain of custody certification were not producing FSC-certified products, while another suggested that the number could be much higher.[75] "A retailer might just ask a supplier to get certified but not demand the [certified] products themselves," another practitioner explained.[76] Unlike certification of

---

[70] Accreditation Services International 2014; Yap 2010.

[71] Accreditation Services International 2014:6.

[72] Interview with sustainable forestry consultant, Hong Kong, 3/10/14.

[73] Monument 2008; Forest Stewardship Council 2013c. It stood at approximately 3,8000 in 2015 (Forest Stewardship Council 2015b).

[74] Interview with sustainable forestry consultant, Beijing, 7/18/11. The growth of FSC-certified paper products is linked to the development of the "FSC Mix" label and changes in the way certified volumes can be calculated. See Bartley et al. 2015 for a description of this evolution.

[75] Interview with forester, Beijing, 7/15/11; interview with sustainable forestry consultant, Beijing, 7/22/11.

[76] Phone interview with certification representative, 12/26/10.

forest management, chain of custody certification is "easy to get—there's a template and it's easy to adapt. So it's a marketing tool, like a reward that can be bought."[77]

Some such companies may be hoping to use FSC-certified inputs in the future, but some may be seeking "cover" or engaging in greenwashing.[78] After a fairly simple system certification process, manufacturers can tout their green credentials to clients. They are not supposed to publicly advertise their chain of custody certification if they are using no certified wood, and auditors will check companies' website to guarantee this.[79] But there are gaps in the chain of custody system that have allowed some companies to use the certificate for marketing purposes without actually using certified wood. "The certification body is relying on company-produced documentation . . . If they really want to cheat you, it's very easy," one practitioner explained.[80] A manufacturer could buy an invoice from a certified forest management company but not actually buy the wood. "We have heard this—some FMEs [forest management enterprises] have told us," explained this person.[81] Or they could buy a small amount of certified timber and then falsify the documented volumes. As one auditor explained, "it's impossible to go to the forest to check how much timber is sold to the company and match it to the records."[82] Even careful auditors face information problems, as one practitioner explained:

> Manufacturers usually have complex supply chains, and there are several different certification bodies [auditing different parts of this supply chain]. Different certification bodies don't share information. Documents on the amount coming in may not be trustworthy . . . [and] certified and non-certified . . . may not be marked in the raw wood.[83]

---

[77] Interview with sustainable forestry consultant, Beijing, 7/22/11. The most active chain of custody certifier—SGS-Hong Kong—was suspended by ASI for two months in 2013 for irregularities (Forest Stewardship Council 2013a).

[78] Interview with forester, Beijing, 7/15/11; interview with NGO representative, Beijing, 12/8/10. In one intriguing case, the Shanghai Anxin Wood Flooring company garnered a $27.5 million investment and praise for "its forestry protection efforts for sustainable development" from the Carlyle Group soon after getting FSC chain of custody certification for its factory (quoted in Global Witness 2009:52). The following year, marketing representatives from Anxin boasted to investigators from the *Washington Post* that they "had a large and steady supply of Burmese teak" (Goodman and Finn 2007:A01). Nearly all Burmese teak was entering China illegally, and none was FSC-certified, raising suspicions that the company's image was out of line with its practice (Interview with NGO representative, Beijing, 12/8/10).

[79] Interview with sustainable forestry consultant, Hong Kong, 3/10/14.

[80] Interview with forester, Beijing, 7/15/11.   [81] Ibid.

[82] Interview with forester/auditor, Beijing, 3/14/14; similar idea expressed in interview with sustainable forestry consultant, Beijing, 3/14/14.

[83] Interview with auditor, Beijing, 12/10/10.

"If the companies really want to fake the system," another explained, "they can find a way."[84] Some have called on the FSC to develop a shared database that would allow auditors to track certified inputs and outputs, but this has been held up in debates about confidentiality.[85]

The most serious concern is that chain of custody certification has provided cover for illegal timber. Scott Poynton of The Forest Trust, a sustainable forestry consultancy, has argued that factories are pleasing their buyers by getting this credential, but once "the audit is done, the system passes and the factory gets back to normal, untraceable production with no systems at all operating the next day and for the next 12 months."[86] It is not clear whether chain of custody certification has made illegal logging worse, as Poynton charges. But there is certainly room for suspicion in the dramatic growth of chain of custody certification and no doubt that illegal timber remained a problem in China as the field of forest certification grew.

Illegal timber and the problem of traceability

China's log imports increased by roughly 500 percent from 1998 to 2005, with logs coming mostly from Russia, as well as Malaysia, Papua New Guinea, Burma, and Gabon.[87] Much of the timber imported from Malaysia was actually smuggled in from Indonesia, in defiance of Indonesia's 2001 ban on the export of raw logs. Discrepancies in the import-export records suggest that "at the peak in 2003 ... around 1.6 million cubic metres of illegal logs were being smuggled from Indonesia to China each year."[88] On the Burma–China border, land-based illegal logging networks emerged, in which Chinese loggers would cross the border to gain access to teak and other valuable logs from Burma's rapidly deteriorating forests. "You bribe one army and you get the right to cut everything," one Chinese logger said to investigative journalists from the

---

[84] Phone interview with forestry researcher, 12/28/10. In addition, some manufacturers have attached the FSC label to products in a completely fraudulent way, without ever receiving permission. At some point, Wal-Mart, Target, and B&Q all purchased FSC-certified items from China that turned out to be fraudulent (phone interview with certification representative, 12/27/10). This, it should be noted, is not a failing of the chain of custody system so much as an illustration that the FSC has joined the ranks of brands that must be vigilant in policing fraudulent uses of their labels.

[85] NEPcon. 2014. "Tackling FSC fraud: will the Online Claims Platform fail or fly?" http://www.nepcon.net/newsroom/tackling-fsc-fraud-will-online-claims-platform-fail-or-fly-0, accessed May 16, 2016.

[86] Poynton 2013.

[87] White, Sun, Canby, Xu, Barr, Katsigris, Bull, Cossalter, and Nilsson 2006. The 500% estimate is an approximation (by import volume) based on Figure 2 in White et al.'s report. As of 2005, 68% of the imported logs were from Russia, with 6% from Malaysia, 6% from Papua New Guinea, 4% from Burma, and 3% from Gabon.

[88] Lawson and MacFaul 2010:111. This estimate is based on the discrepancy between the official timber exports reported by Malaysia and the total timber imports from Malaysia reported by China.

Washington Post. "Then another army comes and threatens to arrest you, and you have to bribe them, too."[89] The Chinese government soon cracked down on this trade, but investigations showed that traders with *guanxi*—that is, good relationships—could still get illegal timber across the border.[90]

In the far east of Russia, numerous unauthorized logging operations fed into a massive flow of logs toward the Chinese border. As described in one exposé, "freight cars bore loads of Korean pine and linden trees—both protected species—with the cargo bound for furniture factories in China."[91] Chinese authorities considered most timber coming in by train from Russia to be legitimate, but this overlooked a series of questionable transactions and permits within Russia. One NGO estimated that for a cubic meter of Russian timber worth $140 on the Chinese border, $32 would have been spent bribing various officials, from environmental inspectors to customs officials and militias.[92] Some timber traders and sawmills on the Chinese side of the border reported making cash purchases and mafia payouts to access the "dark" trade in Russia.[93] The best available estimate suggests that a total of 145 million cubic meters of illegal wood products, worth $15.8 billion, was exported from Russia to China between 2000 and 2014.[94]

The hope that certified timber would displace illegal timber proved too optimistic, as the same companies that were promoting certification also struggled to trace the sources of timber in their complex supply chains. Wal-Mart was promoting forest certification as part of the WWF Global Forest & Trade Network. But an NGOs' undercover investigation in 2007 discovered suppliers in China—mostly making baby cribs and other furniture—that were using questionable wood from Russia and had never been asked by Wal-Mart about the sources of their timber.[95]

Ikea's suppliers in China often purchased wood from timber traders and lumber mills within China, who purchased wood from timber traders on the China–Russia border, who mixed together wood from numerous logging operations within Russia. As one industry actor described the border area, there are "lots of traders buying from multiple logging companies right off the train. They get an SMS [text message] from the train company when loads

---

[89] Quoted in Goodman and Finn 2007.   [90] Global Witness 2009.

[91] Goodman and Finn 2007.

[92] White, Sun, Canby, Xu, Barr, Katsigris, Bull, Cossalter, and Nilsson 2006.

[93] Khatchadouria 2008.

[94] These estimates are based on the data provided by Chatham House (http://indicators. chathamhouse.org/explore-the-data/china) and reported by Lawson and MacFaul 2010 and Wellesley 2014. Chatham House's method combines data on imports from different countries and estimates of the prevalence of illegal logging in those countries (Chatham House 2013).

[95] Environmental Investigation Agency 2007. Consultancies such as The Forest Trust have focused most of their work in China on the traceability of timber supplies, not on the promotion of FSC certification. As described further in the conclusion, "legality verification" services have become increasingly prominent in a field that was previously focused on sustainability certification.

are arriving."[96] As of 2007, Ikea was inspecting only around 30 percent of the imported wood used by its suppliers in China, and at least one supplier near the border reported receiving little scrutiny: "Ikea will provide some guidance, such as a list of endangered species we can't use, but they never send people to supervise the purchasing. Basically, they just let us pick what wood we want."[97] In the ensuing years, Ikea invested time and personnel in improving traceability, shortening supply chains, and building longer-term relationships with suppliers.[98]

While Ikea became a recognized leader in timber traceability, many parts of the timber trade remained complex and opaque, with manufacturers having little information on their sources. "A company buys wood at market, sometimes from a trader who combines sources and doesn't like to provide information on the sources," explained one forester.[99]

As described in this book's final chapter, new laws passed in the US and EU are forcing retailers and brands to pay closer attention to illegality in their timber supply chains. The certification of sustainable forestry, though, had little bearing on the flow of illegal timber through manufacturing operations. The rise of forest certification meant that small amounts of certified wood were flowing through furniture, flooring, lumber, and packaging plants in China, next to large amounts of wood from unknown sources.

State Power and the Right to Certify

So far, it would seem as if the project to certify forests in China was driven by global retailers and NGOs, connected only tangentially to the Chinese government—through the certification of state forestry bureaus, for instance. In fact, state agencies were key players from the beginning, initially as supporters and then as strong challengers and regulators of the FSC project. In each of these roles, the Chinese state has had a profound influence on attempts to privately certify sustainable forestry in China.

This section shows how the state's influence became exceedingly—and sometimes painfully—clear to the FSC and its constituents in China. The story can be told in four roughly sequential steps. First, actors within the State Forestry Administration shifted from supporting the FSC to helping to create a competing initiative that sought to reclaim the terrain of sustainable forestry. Second, the state agency that regulates certification as a general

---

[96] Interview with certification representative, Beijing, 7/18/11.
[97] Quoted in Goodman and Finn 2007.
[98] Interview with certification representative, Beijing, 7/18/11; interview with sustainable forestry consultant, Hong Kong, 3/10/14.
[99] Interview with forester, Beijing, 7/15/11.

matter (the Certification and Accreditation Administration of China or CNCA) cracked down on the ability of FSC-accredited certification bodies to operate in China. Third, in light of the previous two developments, relationships between the FSC's constituents and state officials became tense, with some state and industry officials arguing that the FSC was "illegal" in China. Fourth, and separately from the other events, a new wave of conservation-inspired state logging bans essentially ended production in some FSC-certified forests. Each of these is described in more detail below.

One can read the state's reassertion of control as an expression of national sovereignty in the face of global private authority, as reflecting concerns about market access for Chinese forest products, as a pragmatic response to rapidly growing markets for certified products, or as stemming from squabbles among a relatively small group of practitioners. A combination of these factors seems to be at play, at least for the first three steps. The logging bans, in turn, reflect a return to the conservation policies first imposed after the 1998 floods and a promotion of plantation development as the next wave of timber supply. Taken together, these events demonstrate the extent to which the operation of a private regulatory initiative was deeply dependent on, and ultimately constrained by, the strong authoritarian state. The ability to "govern through markets", to use to use Benjamin Cashore and colleagues' (2004) language, turned out to depend on the consent of the state.

From state support to state-sponsored competition

The State Forestry Administration (SFA), which oversees forest policy and production, was initially the patron of the FSC in China. Researchers from the Chinese Academy of Forestry had begun looking into sustainable forestry standards in the mid-1990s, as China was preparing to become a full member of the WTO.[100] WWF, which had helped the Chinese government protect endangered pandas and join the Convention on International Trade in Endangered Species in the 1980s, played a key role in introducing Chinese foresters and government officials to the FSC.[101] When individuals from the SFA, Chinese Academy of Forestry, and WWF developed a working group on forest certification in 2001, they gravitated toward the FSC and began to lay the groundwork for it in China. [102] By 2006, the working group was seeking to

---

[100] Buckingham and Jepson 2013.   [101] Economy 2010; Conroy 2007:86.

[102] Interview with forester, Beijing, 7/15/11; interview with NGO representative, Beijing, 12/10/10. At the global level, the FSC faced competition from the PEFC. But it seems that the conflict between these two global coalitions had died down a bit during the period that forest certification was getting off the ground in China, making it easier for the working group to see the FSC as the scheme to support (Buckingham and Jepson 2013). One practitioner noted that the working group did not even know about the PEFC at the time that it began working with the FSC (interview with certification representative, Beijing, 7/18/11).

launch an official FSC National Initiative in China, but it soon became clear that this group would not be recognized as such by FSC-International.[103] The FSC has specific procedures for the endorsement of National Initiatives (later renamed National Offices), which had not been followed by the working group in China. Some participants blame the problem on poor communication and a lack of attention from FSC-International staff.[104]

As it became clear that a formal affiliation with FSC-International was not forthcoming, several of the FSC's previous supporters at the Chinese Academy of Forestry and SFA began to develop a new certification program—the China Forest Certification Council (CFCC). The program was officially launched in 2010 and housed within the SFA, which provided much of the initial funding.[105]

The CFCC was a homegrown alternative to the FSC, but its developers borrowed heavily from the FSC's Principles and Criteria. One practitioner noted that "80% of the wording is similar," while another called the two initiatives "brothers—but separated to different families when born, and [they] look different when grown up."[106] There are several consequential differences, though. Unlike the FSC, the Chinese system does not entirely prohibit recent clearing of natural forests for plantation development or require extensive processes for protecting High Conservation Value Forest areas.[107] In addition, CFCC requires proof of land-use rights, but it does not require "free and informed consent" from communities with customary claims to land, as the FSC does.[108] There were also differences in who would do the auditing. Initially, the only accredited auditor for the CFCC was Zhonglin Tianhe, an organization that grew out of trade association that was part of the SFA.[109] "If you dig inside Zhonglin Tianhe, you find that it is all controlled by SFA," noted one practitioner.[110]

CFCC soon developed a relationship with the FSC's global competitor, the Program for the Endorsement of Forest Certification (PEFC). A PEFC-China initiative was established in 2007, and after several years of discussions, PEFC officially endorsed the CFCC system in late 2013.[111] This gave the CFCC

---

[103] WWF-Global 2006.

[104] Interview with NGO representative, Beijing, 12/10/10; interview with sustainable forestry consultant, Beijing, 7/18/11.

[105] Interview with forester/auditor, Beijing, 3/14/14.

[106] Interview with NGO representative, Beijing, 12/10/10; interview with forester, Beijing, 7/21/11.

[107] Interview with NGO representative, Beijing, 12/10/10; interview with NGO representative, Beijing, 12/8/10.

[108] China Forest Certification Council 2012. In addition, there is a prohibition on pesticides deemed especially hazardous by the World Health Organization, but the CFCC standard provides an exception "where no other viable alternative is available" (ibid.:17).

[109] Interview with certification representative, Beijing, 7/18/11.

[110] Interview with sustainable forestry consultant, Beijing, 7/22/11.

[111] PEFC 2014; PEFC-China 2008.

standards a place in the global market, since wood from CFCC-certified forests could now be sold to buyers with a preference for PEFC certification and used in products bearing the PEFC label.

It is not unusual for governments and trade associations to sponsor home-grown alternatives to the FSC. It has happened in nearly every country in which the FSC operates, and it accounts for most of the PEFC's members.[112] But as we will see, the Chinese state went further than others in regulating the FSC and its supporters—by some accounts, seeking to "kick FSC out".[113] "The officials hate FSC," explained one practitioner, noting also that "in China, if you want to promote something or change something, the government role is very important."[114]

State regulation of private certifiers

US-based SmartWood, Swiss-based Institute for Marketecology, German-based GFA Consulting Group, and the Swiss multinational firm SGS had conducted most of the audits for the first wave of FSC certification in China, while also working in a variety of other locations in Asia, Africa, South America, and Europe. As forest certification grew in China, and especially after CFCC was created, it became clear that these certifiers could not take the right to operate in China for granted.

All certification service providers, regardless of the substance of their work, are subject to oversight from the Certification and Accreditation Administration of China (CNCA), a body created in 2001 to conform to the mandates of the World Trade Organization.[115] In 2003, the Chinese government introduced regulations that required certifiers to have their scope of activity approved by CNCA and to meet certain organizational requirements, such as having official registration in China, capital of at least 3 million yuan (approximately $375,000), and more than ten full-time personnel.[116] For the FSC's smaller certifiers, these requirements would be essentially impossible to meet. Yet it was unclear whether even the large certifiers, such as SGS, could

---

[112] This is the story behind the Malaysian Timber Certification Council and CERFLOR, the Brazilian Forest Certification Program, among others. As discussed in the previous chapter, the homegrown initiative in Indonesia, Lembaga Ekolabel Indonesia (LEI), had closer ties to civil society and did not pursue PEFC membership. More recently, a new initiative in Indonesia, called Indonesian Forestry Certification Cooperation, was formed and achieved PEFC recognition in 2014.

[113] Interview with sustainable forestry consultant, Beijing, 3/14/14.

[114] Interview with forester/auditor, Beijing, 3/14/14.

[115] As one observer noted, until China joined the WTO and had to open its market to foreign service providers, it would have been "unimaginable" to have foreign organizations auditing Chinese businesses (interview with auditor, Beijing, 7/14/11).

[116] *Regulations of the People's Republic of China on Certification and Accreditation*, adopted August 20, 2003. The rough dollar equivalent is based on an approximate exchange rate of 8 rmb to the dollar in the early 2000s.

comply with the regulation, since CNCA lacked a clear procedure for approving forestry as part of a certifier's scope of activity.[117]

FSC-International and CNCA forged an agreement in 2007 that allowed the smaller foreign certifiers to operate in China by partnering with local organizations.[118] This allowed for significant growth in the number of FSC-certified forests in China from 2007 to 2009. But in 2010, CNCA announced that it would strengthen supervision of the FSC's certifiers, in essence tightening enforcement of the 2003 regulation and nullifying the 2007 agreement.[119] By some accounts, this was a response to the massive growth of chain of custody certification and fears that it indicated corruption in the auditing system.[120] CNCA may also have been following the lead of the SFA, which had turned its certification plans inward as described above.[121] In any case, the decision meant that "the rules and regulations certification bodies must adhere to are constantly evolving," creating a great deal of uncertainty.[122]

The crackdown put FSC certification in China in a precarious situation. Some certifiers (e.g., SmartWood and the Soil Association) stopped doing new forest management audits. Another, Scientific Certification Systems, continued until ASI suspended it in 2013 for not having the proper permissions from CNCA.[123] Large, generalist certification bodies (such as SGS and Bureau Veritas) continued to perform audits, since they at least met the administrative requirements and were approved for other activities. But there was still the question of whether they needed to be explicitly approved for forestry by CNCA.[124] As of 2010, only Zhonglin Tianhe, the certifier for CFCC, had been explicitly approved by CNCA for forestry. While the FSC's supporters might have once imagined bypassing the state, they were now forced to acknowledge their ultimate dependence on it. "They're the government and they can change and there's not much we can do about it," one practitioner noted.[125]

Mounting tensions

Questions about the right to certify have fed into a larger set of tensions between backers of the CFCC and FSC. Some individuals within SFA have

---

[117] Interview with auditor, Beijing, 12/10/10; interview with forester, Beijing, 7/15/11; interview with certification representative, Beijing, 12/8/10.

[118] Interview with auditor, Beijing, 12/10/10; phone interview with certification representative, 12/26/10.

[119] Ibid.   [120] See Buckingham and Jepson 2013 p. 291.

[121] Interview with forester, Beijing, 7/15/11.   [122] Buckingham and Jepson 2013:290.

[123] Forest Stewardship Council 2013a.

[124] Interview with certification representative, Beijing, 7/18/11; interview with forester, Beijing, 7/15/11.

[125] Phone interview with certification representative, 12/26/10.

argued that the FSC is "illegal" in China.[126] In addition to the issue of accreditation, they noted that the FSC was not officially registered as an organization in China, having only a regional office in Hong Kong. While the SFA initially supported, then tolerated the FSC, "now SFA would like to drive FSC out [so that] now we only have the national scheme," claimed one practitioner.[127] At one point, a representative of CFCC reportedly claimed that CNCA and the Ministry of Commerce would stop the FSC's work in China, which ironically led to "companies hurrying to get certified by FSC in case it was going to go away or become harder to get," according to one practitioner.[128]

Support for the FSC from international NGOs—most notably, WWF—has been hobbled by their dependence on state sponsors. Globally, WWF is the FSC's most ardent supporter, and the WWF-China office actively assisted in the initial round of FSC certifications in China, as described above. But WWF-China's official and necessary sponsor is the SFA, putting the NGO in an awkward position as tensions mounted. WWF staff were at one point asked by SFA to curtail their assistance to companies seeking FSC certification.[129] WWF has ended up taking an "open" position: "The WWF network supports FSC. But here in China [it] also cooperate[s] with CFCC," explained one practitioner.[130] This makes it the only branch of WWF to actively support a PEFC-affiliated system.[131]

As of 2010–11 some practitioners were hopeful that the FSC's relationships with government would improve, and the FSC's small staff in Beijing was spending much of its time managing relationships with government.[132] By 2014, several reported that the tension had gotten worse, perhaps because of the CFCC program's endorsement by the global PEFC network.[133] Some SFA officials think "if the FSC doesn't want to recognize CFCC, then you should leave the country," one practitioner explained.[134] Several Chinese researchers

---

[126] Interview with certification representative, Beijing, 3/13/14; interview with forester/auditor, Beijing, 3/14/14.

[127] Interview with forester, Beijing, 7/15/11.

[128] Interview with forester/auditor, Beijing, 3/12/14.

[129] Interview with NGO representative, Beijing, 12/10/10.

[130] Interview with NGO representative/auditor, Beijing, 3/11/14.

[131] Buckingham and Jepson (2013) summarize practitioners' view, saying "to criticize the PEFC system would be tantamount to criticizing the Chinese standards themselves, which would risk the ability of INGOs to operate within their borders" (p. 292). Meanwhile, a few NGOs, such as Greenpeace, have been able to operate in China without a state sponsor because they are incorporated as businesses, not an NGO.

[132] Interview with auditor, Beijing, 12/10/10; interview with NGO representative, Beijing, 12/8/10.

[133] Interview with forester/auditor, Beijing, March 14, 2014; skype interview with auditor, 3/27/14. CFCC was now in the international spotlight, and Greenpeace was criticizing the initiative's opaque procedures and weak standards (Greenpeace 2014b.

[134] Interview with forester/auditor, Beijing, 3/14/14.

had to step back from FSC-related projects, and one was told by a boss to stop working as a freelance auditor for FSC-accredited certification bodies.[135]

In 2014, the FSC-China office issued a statement assuring its compliance with Chinese law and promising "increased engagement and sustained ongoing dialogue with high-level officials in the State Forestry Administration (SFA) and the Certification and Accreditation Administration of the People's Republic of China (CNCA)."[136] Nevertheless, in 2015, CNCA and SFA issued a new set of "Forest Certification Rules" that raised the requirements for certifiers of sustainable forestry.[137] The new rules treated CFCC as the authoritative set of national standards for sustainable forestry and did not mention FSC.[138] Practically speaking, this meant that FSC-accredited auditors would have to also become accredited to work in the CFCC system, among other requirements. The FSC has framed this as a path to continued viability in China, reporting that the organization "has received assurance from CNCA and SFA that FSC standards can continue to be used in China," despite not being officially recognized in the new rules.[139]

Since two of the larger FSC-accredited certification bodies—Bureau Veritas and SGS—had already established links to the CFCC system, it is plausible that FSC certification will continue in China.[140] There is little doubt, though, that the Chinese state's strong oversight of certification bodies has been a sharp thorn in the FSC's side, requiring sustained attention from the organization's staff and altering the supply of auditors. Scholars of forest certification have shown how private actors must maneuver to garner acceptance within industries and conformity with global norms.[141] But they have overlooked the more localized, and perhaps more fundamental, challenges of gaining the right to operate within national borders.

Logging bans and the shifting terrain

State policies also had a direct effect on the forest land that was eligible for certification. Following its 2009 National Forest Resource Inventory Report, the SFA announced that timber production would shift away from the

---

[135] Ibid.   [136] Forest Stewardship Council-China 2014.

[137] Certification bodies would need to be explicitly approved for this activity by CNCA and accredited by CNCA's offshoot, the China National Accreditation Service for Conformity Assessment.

[138] China Forest Certification Council 2015; PEFC and SFI 2015.

[139] Forest Stewardship Council 2015a.

[140] As of late 2015, SGS was in the process of becoming one of four accredited auditors for CFCC, joining Zhonglin Tianhe, Jilin Songbai Forest Certification Co. Ltd, Jiangxi Shanhe Forest Certification Co.

[141] Bernstein and Cashore 2007; Cashore 2002; Bernstein and Hannah 2008; Loconto and Fouilleux 2014.

northern forest farms to southern forests.[142] As one practitioner put it, this was a "sweeping" announcement that "northern forests will take a rest; southern forests will be used for production."[143] The share of "mature" forests in the northern province of Heilongjiang had fallen from more than 60 percent in the early 1980s to approximately 10 percent in 1996 to just over 3 percent in 2008, such that, as one researcher put it, "there is almost no forest left to be harvested there."[144] A logging ban was instituted for parts of Heilongjiang province in 2011 and extended to the entire province, along with subsidies for displaced workers, in 2014.[145] The SFA soon implemented logging bans in two other northern provinces—Jilin and Inner Mongolia—and eventually announced that commercial logging in natural forests would be phased out nationwide by 2017.[146]

The initial announcement caught many foresters and companies off guard. "Even the people working in forest industries didn't really know what was happening," explained one observer.[147] The new restrictions were in one sense an extension of the bans and tightened quotas of the 1998 National Forest Protection Plan, as well as an indication that the earlier policies had been insufficient.[148] "Chinese forests have been under great pressure of logging. We have strict rules and regulations in China, but the logging industry has not been following the rules. Possibly this is why they enforced the ban."[149] The shift to the south was also in line with the government's plan to promote large, fast-growing timber plantations, along with some high-value native tree species, as an engine of rural development.[150]

Whatever the environmental and economic consequences, the shift to southern forests clearly changes the terrain for forest certification. "It will have a big impact on FSC," one practitioner noted. "Some forests have to stop [their certification] now, since they can no longer do any cutting."[151] Another practitioner described audits of two northern forest bureaus in 2013: "They knew then that the cutting quota would be reduced by one-third, and they told me that in the next two years it would go to nothing."[152] The new policy also created a problem for Ikea, which had been promoting FSC certification in northern forests[153]. "They will now have to source from south China," explained one practitioner, "but there are more problems [in getting certified] there because the low-yield natural forest policy," which, as

---

[142] USDA Foreign Agricultural Service 2009.
[143] Interview with sustainable forestry consultant, Hong Kong, 3/10/14.
[144] Xu 2013:13.　　[145] Xinhua 2011; Qin 2014.　　[146] China Daily 2015; Xinhua 2015.
[147] Interview with certification representative, Beijing, 3/13/14.
[148] Interview with forester/auditor, Beijing, 3/12/14.
[149] Interview with certification representative, Beijing, 3/13/14.
[150] Interview with forester/auditor, 3/14/14.　　[151] Skype interview with auditor, 3/27/14.
[152] Interview with forester/auditor, Beijing, 3/14/14.
[153] Interview with certification representative, Beijing, 3/13/14.

described earlier, can conflict with the FSC's prohibition on the clearing of "natural" forests.[154]

It is possible that logging bans may end up increasing the amount of land that becomes certified to the homegrown CFCC standards. According to one practitioner, forest bureaus that have to stop logging "will receive subsidies from the government to protect the forest, and government will also provide subsidies to get CFCC—to transfer from FSC to CFCC".[155] Indeed, the Muling Forestry Bureau of Heilongjiang province, which had been FSC-certified since 2008, terminated its FSC certificate in 2013 and was certified to the CFCC standard by Zhonglin Tianhe the same year.[156] A CFCC certificate would mean that the company could export products as PEFC-certified—for now, perhaps only some wood chips and non-timber forest products, but with more substantial volumes possible if logging quotas are relaxed in the future.[157]

The decline of FSC certification?

Some combination of withering market demand, state-imposed logging bans, and questions about the FSC's future in China led to a wave of "terminations" of FSC certificates. This included the Changhua Forest Farm, which had been the first to receive FSC certification in China and had maintained it for eleven years. A total of twenty-nine FSC forest management certificates were terminated between 2010 and 2014, meaning that forest managers had withdrawn from the auditing needed to maintain or renew the certificate. As described by practitioners, forest managers might decide to discontinue certification for a variety of reasons—because price premiums are not sufficient to justify the costs, because few of their buyers are demanding certified wood, or because they simply lack the resources to continue.[158] A rash of twenty-three additional terminations in 2015 included five large forestry bureaus in Heilongjiang province and three in Jilin province, both of which had experienced logging bans.

After reaching a peak of 3.4 million hectares in September of 2014, the amount of FSC-certified forest land in China fell by 35 percent by January of 2015 (to 2.2 million hectares) and by another 32 percent by June of 2015 (to less than 1.5 million hectares by June of 2015).[159] All of the northern forests that had been part of the first wave of certification—including the Baihe and

---

[154] Interview with sustainable forestry consultant, Beijing, 3/14/14.
[155] Skype interview with auditor, 3/27/14.   [156] China Forest Certification Council 2013.
[157] Interview with forester/auditor, Beijing, 3/12/14.
[158] Interview with certification representative, Beijing, 3/13/14; email communication with certification representative, 5/22/14; interview with forester/auditor, Beijing, 3/12/14.
[159] See Forest Stewardship Council 2015b plus FSC "Facts and Figures" for September 2014 and June 2015.

Youhao forestry bureaus that had been supported by Ikea—were no longer certified by the end of 2015.

Authoritarian Governance and the Un-politics of Land Conflicts

Even as state agencies challenged the FSC's operations and logging bans arose in the north, the amount of FSC-certified land in south China grew rapidly between 2010 and 2014. In part, this was because the FSC's certifiers were increasingly being asked to assess the environmental and social impacts of plantation projects in the south. The government's Industrial Base Development Program had promoted fast-growing timber plantations since 2001, eventually giving China the second largest area of eucalyptus plantations in the world. Ecologists have raised many questions about the high water demands of eucalyptus and this non-native species' impact on biodiversity.[160] In addition, as we will see, plantations were often developed on land held by village collectives, and land grabs for plantation development were a real risk.

The FSC's Principle 2 calls for land-tenure and land-use rights to be "clearly defined, documented, and legally established," with additional criteria requiring respect for communities with customary claims to the land, unless they have delegated "free and informed consent" to others (as discussed in Chapter 3). This could be challenging to implement in the collective forests of China, which had been partially and repeatedly reformed to a point of "deliberate institutional ambiguity."[161] In addition, some collective forests were in the midst of a new wave of quasi-privatization reforms, in which long-term rights to use rural land, or lease it to others, could be granted to individual households. Whether land was held by village councils, smaller groups of villagers, or individual households, there was the potential for coalitions of the local state (i.e., municipalities) and land development companies to take advantage of villagers' limited options and restricted political power.[162]

Yet despite land tenure that was complicated, ambiguous, and occasionally contested, FSC certification grew rapidly in the collective forests of China.

---

[160] Williams 2015.   [161] Ho 2001; Ho 2006.

[162] There is an ongoing debate about whether quasi-privatization reforms give villagers more or less power to resist exploitation by the local state, plantation development, and agribusiness interests. On one side, advocates of individual property rights argue that clearer property rights will empower villagers and restrict the ability of developers to gain access to land by simply cutting deals with a few village leaders (Yin, Xu, and Li 2003; Fewsmith 2008). On the other side, critics of privatization point to "distress sales" by desperate rural residents and subsequent landlessness in other countries, the insecurity of quasi-private rights, and cases in which collective ownership seems to have bred solidarity (see Zhan and Andreas 2015; Zhang and Donaldson 2013). For the analysis of forest certification, it is sufficient to note that land grabs are quite possible under either system of land rights, and that auditors may have a difficult time recognizing and assessing them, given villagers' limited space for political representation.

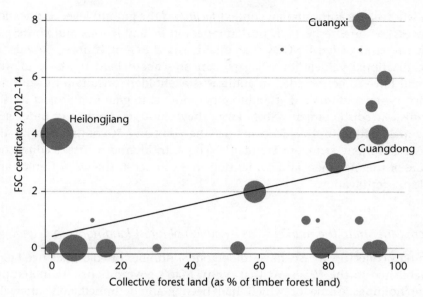

Figure 4.1. Collectively held forest land and the second wave of FSC-certification in Chinese provinces

Several earlier certifications had involved collective forest land, including the certification of Sino-Forest in Guangdong province and several areas in Zhejiang province, where land-tenure reforms were underway.[163] Collective forest land, especially in the south, became the major center of gravity for the second wave of FSC certification in China. As shown in Figure 4.1, provinces in which more of the forest land was collectively owned tended to also have more forests certified as of 2012–14.[164] With the exception of Heilongjiang province in the north, where nearly all forest land is state owned and several areas have been FSC-certified, one can see a pattern of more recent FSC certification in provinces where a greater share of forestland is collectively held.[165]

Looking more closely at collective forest land provides additional insight into the FSC's growth in China and the practical meaning of its standards. As

[163] Robbins 2011.

[164] The figure shows the number of FSC certificates (2012–14) and the percentage of timber-oriented forest land under collective ownership (that is, not directly held by the state) in twenty-five forested provinces, with the size of the circle representing the total amount of timber-oriented forest land in each province. Data on collectively held timber forest land and total timber forest area comes from Annex 1 in Miao and West 2004.

[165] In a supplemental regression analysis that controls for the total amount of timber land, there is still a positive relationship (statistically discernible at the 0.05 level) between the percentage of land that is collectively owned and the number of forests certified in this recent period.

we will see, the authoritarian context *facilitated* the ground-level certification process in some respects. Land tenure could be ambiguous and contested, but the kind of local NGOs that might in a different context provide an organizational vehicle for villagers' concerns about land rights—and who would have to be included in auditors' stakeholder consultations—did not exist. When auditors did attend to a potential land grab in a project for the Finnish-Swedish company Stora Enso, they found few sources of independent information and could construct the company as compliant with the FSC's seemingly stringent standards. The authoritarian context edited out some of the messiness and contention that can get in the way of quick and "clean" certification.

From Maoism to the market? The evolution of forest land rights in China

China's collective forests have undergone a number of changes since being established in the 1950s. At that point, Mao's government eliminated private holdings (some of which had been granted immediately after the revolution) and set up collective forest farms—a total of roughly 8,000 by 1960.[166] Deng Xiaoping's 1979 introduction of the Household Responsibility System marked the first step in a partial de-collectivization of rural land in China. This agricultural reform unleashed farmers from the strict quotas assigned to their collective farms and allowed them to make more production decisions. It is widely credited with boosting agricultural efficiency, though also for laying the foundation for the circular movement of "floating" migrants from the countryside to urban factories and back.[167] In 1981, the government extended the de-collectivization strategy to forests through the so-called "Three Fixes Policy", which sought to clarify several historical ambiguities in forest property and allow collectives to delegate some land-use rights to households.[168] A "dual system of collective land ownership and individual use rights" evolved in the 1980s, granting households some rights to manage forest land themselves or share in the proceeds of management decisions made by the collective.[169] The degree and style of implementation varied across provinces, but by 1986, the management of 69 percent of all collectively owned forest land had been devolved in some fashion to individual households or small groups of villagers.[170] At the same time, though,

---

[166] Zhang and Kant 2005.

[167] Yang 1997; Mullan, Grosjean, and Kontoleon 2011. See the latter for more on the links between forest land tenure, agriculture, migration, and manufacturing employment.

[168] Kram, Bedford, Durnin, Luo, Rokpelnis, Roth, Smith, Wang, Yu, Yu, and Zhao 2012.

[169] Zhang and Donaldson 2013; Robbins 2011; Zhang and Kant 2005.

[170] Wang, Scalise, and Giovarelli 2012.

farmers in many areas faced heavy taxation and seemingly arbitrary quota restrictions.[171]

Ambiguity about the security of forest rights combined with the "overnight liberalization of the [timber] market" in 1985 made this a period of rapid harvesting, illegal logging, and decline in southern forests.[172] By the late 1990s, a series of partial reforms and reversals, within a complex structure of overlapping authority, had created what Peter Ho (2001; 2006) calls "deliberate institutional ambiguity". He argues that this ambiguity "makes the system tick"—in the sense that it makes it impossible to answer the question of "who owns the land?"—and warned that this ambiguity could allow local governments to steamroll over villagers when land values are high.[173]

The Rural Land Contracting Law of 2002—and its extension into forestry in 2003—went a step further in creating quasi-private property rights, while also constraining the actions of village leaders to act on behalf of collectives. This was a milestone for advocates of privatization because it allowed households to transfer land-use rights and make long-term leases of thirty to seventy years.[174] Importantly, it also required collectives' decisions to lease their land rights to be approved by at least two-thirds of the membership.[175] On the other hand, while re-allocation of rights by village leaders was prohibited, it was not entirely eliminated; and as we will see, the two-thirds provision could sometimes be manipulated or ignored.[176]

The quasi-privatization of Chinese forest lands continued with a 2008 statement from the government that further encouraged the leasing of forest land, in part by allowing households to make leasing decisions without seeking permission from their collectives.[177] According to research by Alicia Robbins and Stevan Harrell (2014), pilot projects led to increased incomes for farmers located near forest products industries, but forest-dwelling people in rural China remained among the poorest and most vulnerable in the country. They rely on a mix of cash income and subsistence farming and have often been culturally marginalized as "uncivilized".

---

[171] White, Sun, Canby, Xu, Barr, Katsigris, Bull, Cossalter, and Nilsson 2006.

[172] Zhang and Kant 2005:299; Robbins 2011.

[173] Ho 2001:420. He writes: "The local government would welcome a legitimization of its common practice: robbing the natural village from its land ownership. At this point, there is a high risk that the deliberate institutional ambiguity becomes an instrument in the violation of villagers' interests" (p. 421).

[174] Interview with forestry researcher, Beijing, 7/15/11.

[175] Law of the People's Republic of China on Land Contract in Rural Areas, http://www.npc.gov.cn/englishnpc/Law/2007-12/06/content_1382125.htm.

[176] Mullan, Grosjean, and Kontoleon 2011.

[177] Dean and Damm-Luhr 2010. This is the Communist Party of China's Important Decision on Certain Issues Concerning the Advancement of Rural Reform and Development, also known as the "2008 Decision."

Under the 2008 reforms...such communities have been encouraged to put their collective forest lands out to bid. In our own experience in Liangshan Yi Autonomous Prefecture, Sichuan, this results in a one-time "sale" (as local people term it) to an unknown outside speculator; households receive a lump-sum payment and are unclear about what authority the speculators assume over the forest; in the meantime, households continue to gather firewood and cut timber for construction.[178]

Despite several rounds of reform to increase households' land-use rights and improve rural livelihoods, researchers often note that "rural people continue to lack awareness and confidence in their rights."[179] One group of legal scholars has pointed to interlinked problems of representation, administration, and valuation that undercut villagers' actual rights to benefit from forest land:

> A small group of people at the village and municipal levels usually collude to decide on land sales and acquisition of village assets.... The lack of legal channels for transferring land out of the collective sector—other than through state expropriation—and the lack of a mechanism to transparently assess the market value of the rural properties involved—creates rent-seeking behavior and opportunities for corruption.[180]

Land disputes, rightful resistance, and repression

The ambiguity of land rights and marginalization of rural villagers does not mean that land development has been uncontested. The "growth machine" interests of local governments have been met by thousands of "mass incidents", in which residents protest corrupt land deals made by local officials, unfair distribution of the profits, or the expulsion of local residents. Most mass incidents involving land have occurred in villages near rapidly growing cities, where local officials have welcomed urban land developers in the midst of rising property values.[181]

Most famously, in 2011 residents in the village of Wukan in Guangdong province "chased out Communist Party officials, repelled an assault by police officers and barricaded all roads leading into Wukan with tree trunks" in protest over the deals that village leaders had made with urban land developers.[182] Villagers had been protesting corruption for months and petitioning to the central government for several years before that. The takeover of the town occurred after a protestor suspiciously died while in police custody. As villagers pushed party leaders and police out, police

---

[178] Robbins and Harrell 2014.   [179] Robbins 2011:35.   [180] Zhou and Banik 2014:258.
[181] For a Kafkaesque case in which villagers' apparent land-use rights were trampled for state-led property development, see Pils 2005.
[182] Wong 2011. See also Jacobs 2011.

blockaded the town to stop the entry of food supplies. After ten days, and with heavily armed riot police waiting outside town, a provincial government leader negotiated an agreement that ended the occupation. Notably, the villagers insisted all along that they were challenging only the local government, not the central government. They made signs saying, "We are not a revolt" and "We support the Communist Party. We love our country."[183]

Observing this type of discourse in many settings—though rarely with this sustained degree of revolt—scholars have argued that a repertoire of "rightful resistance" has become central to activism in China, especially in rural areas.[184] By appealing to the ideals espoused by the central government while portraying local governments as corrupt, rightful resistance has found a prominent place in an otherwise repressive political environment. Rightful resistance appears to be more than just a strategic discourse, in that researchers have found that villagers who are dispossessed of land lose faith in local governments but do not have lower trust in the central government.[185]

On the other hand, even rightful forms of resistance are often suppressed or repressed, especially by local governments. Looking at sixty-six cases of collective resistance and suppression across China—including a number focused on "compensation for peasants who lost farmland"—Yongshun Cai (2008) finds that local governments typically responded with police action. Out of nearly 600 individuals who were detained or arrested in these cases, 44 percent were sentenced to jail, some for up to fifteen years. In one land dispute in Guangxi province, police detained twenty-seven activists initially and then 110 additional villagers who called for their release. Seventeen were sent to jail and two to labor camps.[186] In the fishing village of Dongzhou in Guangdong province, villagers who had protested a land grab for a power plant were "reduced to submission" by the deadly shooting of several protesters, the detention and interrogation of many others, and a heavy police presence.[187]

Scholars have also identified more subtle ways in which local governments suppress or absorb rightful resistance. Yanhua Deng and Kevin O'Brien (2013) highlight "relational repression", in which local officials form work teams of allies who systematically use their familial and social ties to cool out protesters. Julia Chuang (2014) highlights "bureaucratic absorption" strategies, through which rightful resistance related to land rights has been muted by government strategies that emphasize monetary gain, frame the relinquishment of land as a modernizing process, and exploit the lure of changing *hukou* statuses, even while stripping away the benefits of that change.[188]

---

[183] Wong 2011. [184] O'Brien and Li 2006. [185] Cui, Tao, Warner, and Yang 2015.
[186] Cai 2008. [187] Cody 2005.
[188] Chuang argues that when rural residents do get converted to urban *hukou*, it is usually in "fiscally challenged townships where [public goods regimes] are becoming increasingly administered through market mechanisms rather than through state channels" (p. 667).

Because of absorption, suppression, and repression, backed by powerful alliances between land developers and local officials, it is difficult to know just how common and severe are land grabs in Chinese forests. As John Gaventa (1982) has argued in a different context, accumulated injustices may never breed observed disputes, since the power of local elites may be enough to keep injustices out of the public eye or even shape the understandings of the powerless. Following Gaventa's lead, the material below will consider both a situation in which conflicts over forest land tenure did come to light and a situation in which conflict is likely to have been hidden and/or suppressed.

As we will see, as investors sought to develop large, fast-growing timber plantations, they worked with local governments to gain the rights to use forest land held by villages or households. Local governments' efforts on behalf of timber companies could be aggressive and swift. When Chenming Paper, a Chinese pulp and paper company, was developing a plantation in Hubei province, the city government promised 67,000 hectares and very quickly delivered most of it, despite the fact that control of the land was supposed to have been devolved to individual households.[189] Similar dynamics occurred in the two cases considered below—except that these two plantations were being certified by the FSC.

The curious case of Sino-Forest

One of the earliest FSC certificates in China was issued in 2004 to Sino-Forest for the company's eucalyptus and acacia plantations in Guangdong province. Sino-Forest was a Hong Kong-based company with numerous subsidiaries, including one (the Jia Yao Forestry Development Company) that was created as a joint venture with the local forestry bureau to manage this plantation.[190] Sino-Forest's decision to seek certification seems to have had more to do with enhancing its status in the financial world than with the associated particleboard factory nearby, which was mostly producing for domestic consumption. Sino-Forest had been listed on the Toronto stock exchange since 1995, and it was reportedly seeking a loan from HSBC, which was promoting FSC certification as part of its sustainability policy.[191] Notably, in the first five years of having its plantation certified, the Sino-Forest subsidiary did not actually sell any logs to its manufacturing subsidiaries as FSC-certified.[192]

---

[189] J. Li 2010.   [190] SmartWood 2005b.

[191] Interview with forester/auditor, Beijing, 3/14/14. In the spring of 2004, HSBC adopted a forestry policy that required clients to have at least 70% of their business certified by the FSC by 2009. Interestingly, HSBC's Deputy Head of Corporate Sustainability (since 2004) is Francis Sullivan, who played a crucial role in creating the FSC in the early 1990s when he was with WWF-UK.

[192] Smartwood 2008e.

Part of the plantation area had been developed through a World Bank project, starting in the early 1990s, to replace low-yield pine species with fast-growing eucalyptus.[193] Other areas were planted by Sino-Forest from 1997 to 2002. At this point, most of the relevant land was collectively held by villages, and Sino-Forest and its partners had forged agreements to give collectives of farmers 30 percent of the timber upon harvesting in return for the use of the land.[194] These agreements may have produced greater benefits for villagers than had the previous pine forests, but it is difficult to see them as entirely voluntary. Sino-Forest was co-founded by a Hong Kong entrepreneur (Allen Chan) and a former Guangdong Forestry Bureau official (Kai Kit Poon, aka Jiajie Pan) who served as a liaison to government officials.[195] Given the various links between the plantation development project and the state, the potential for intimidation and unequal bargaining over land-use rights was significant.

The auditors from SmartWood, however, paid fairly little attention to land rights or the relationship between villagers, collectives, companies, and the state. The auditors visited three villages and interviewed "numerous household and village leaders", but they reported only one concern or complaint emerging from these stakeholder consultations—from an officer of a municipal hydrological bureau concerned about the high water demands of the eucalyptus plantation. In evaluating compliance with FSC Principle 2, which requires clear and legitimate land tenure, the auditors noted that "long-term rights to use the land are as clear and secure as they can be under the existing system," though they did ask the company to create "sufficient mechanisms that can confirm and monitor that villagers receive their contractually agreed share of the harvest."[196] Following up the next year, the auditors reported that the company "claims that they have not had any problem with complaints from the local villagers with regards to payment" and that "SmartWood's stakeholder interviews...have not uncovered any problems with the local villagers getting their share of the harvest."[197]

By the time the Sino-Forest certificate was up for renewal in 2008–9, some of the land was being leased from farmer collectives rather than being used in return for a 30 percent share. In addition, the 2008 national land-tenure reforms had been issued, although they were not yet implemented in this part of Guangdong province. The audit report noted these changes and mentioned "potential tenure conflicts resulting from the reform" in the future.[198] Nevertheless, after interviewing farmers in several locations and reporting no

---

[193] Interview with company representatives, Hong Kong, 12/29/10.
[194] SmartWood 2005b.
[195] Yong 2013; Hoffman and MacKinnon 2011; The Globe and Mail 2012.
[196] SmartWood 2005b:21, 30.   [197] Ibid.:40.   [198] Smartwood 2008e:16.

complaints, SmartWood issued the certificate, this time for an expanded area. The report from the follow-up audit in 2010 made no mention at all of land-tenure issues, and reported no concerns from the six local inhabitants consulted.[199]

In 2011, Sino-Forest's land holdings came under great scrutiny, but not because of FSC certification. A Canadian investor issued a report charging that Sino-Forest had vastly and fraudulently overstated the value of its timber holdings in China in order to drive up its stock price. Sino-Forest had become a "stock market darling" and the largest forest products company traded in Toronto, valued as high as $6 billion at one point.[200] The investor, Muddy Waters LLC, which specialized in short-selling, sent investigators to examine Sino-Forest's web of operations in southwestern China and came back with "smoking gun evidence" that the company had overstated its timber purchases in Yunnan province by $800 million.[201] In both Yunnan and Guangxi provinces, the company allegedly transferred timber holdings back and forth between shell companies to drive up the value of the land.

As Sino-Forest attempted to refute the allegations, it stock price quickly fell from $18 to $5 to less than $1.50. Sino-Forest had begun organizing visits to its FSC-certified plantation in Guangdong to rebut criticism, but investors noted that this amounted to only 6 percent of the company's purported plantation holdings.[202] The company filed for bankruptcy and was delisted from the Toronto exchange in the first quarter of 2012. Although its parent company had imploded, the Jia Yao Forestry Development Company persisted and was incorporated into a new company. Its FSC certificate was renewed in 2013 before being terminated in early 2015.

Some sustainable forestry practitioners within China noted that the investigation had confirmed their prior suspicions about Sino-Forest. "The company is doing more concept than running a business," said one.[203] Another said, "it is a good report. They must have had a very good field researcher working for them in Yunnan—someone who really knew the area." This practitioner added that "many companies in China are using this strategy for finance," explaining that land acquisition is being used merely to drive up financial valuations.[204]

The FSC-certified plantations in Guangdong province were not directly implicated in the Muddy Waters investigation, but as journalists looked further into Sino-Forest's holdings in south China, they uncovered some concerning land acquisition tactics. In several villages in Yunnan, illiterate villagers had

---

[199] SmartWood 2010a.   [200] MacKinnon 2011; Lu 2014.   [201] Muddy Waters 2011.

[202] McDermott 2011.

[203] Interview with sustainable forestry consultant, Beijing, 7/18/11.

[204] Interview with sustainable forestry consultant, Beijing, 3/14/14.

sold long-term leases to middlemen but did not receive documentation or even know exactly who they were selling to. In one distant area, brokers had descended on a village just as households were receiving greater land-use rights. They pushed residents to lease their rights for a low price and offered large bonuses to village leaders who got villagers to cooperate.[205] "They persuaded us by saying, 'The trees are so far from the village, there's no road up', and that this [privatization of forest land] is a new national policy that we should co-operate with," one village leader said. "We sold it too cheap."[206]

In Guangdong province, the same Sino-Forest subsidiary that managed the FSC-certified area (the Jia Yao Forestry Development Company) took advantage of its ties to government to negotiate a sweetheart deal in at least one village. As the agreement with the company shifted from a revenue-sharing model to a leasing model in 2009—just as it had in the certified areas—those who wanted to hold out for a better price were pushed to give in. Even village leaders noted that the company had been "well taken care of" by its high-level *guanxi* with government, such that no other bidders had access. "If we had the chance to rent our land to another company, maybe we could have gotten several hundred [yuan per mu of timber land]. But we had no other choice," one village leader told a reporter.[207]

It is not clear whether villagers in Sino-Forest's FSC-certified plantations had faced severe intimidation—in part because there were few channels through which grievances could reach auditors or other outside observers. The audit reports issued by SmartWood had boilerplate references to stakeholders. But in all of the audits of Sino-Forest's plantations, there is no evidence of any NGOs being consulted.

This is of course because NGOs focused on land rights rarely exist in mainland China. China's "semi-civil society" expanded in the 2000s, including thousands of environmental NGOs focused on conservation and pollution.[208] But land rights, like labor rights, are a "sensitive" issue, meaning that NGOs risk shutdowns or the detention of leaders if they cross into "political" territory.[209] The Chinese government has repeatedly repressed peasant organizing, even as it responded to rising unrest with policies to improve rural livelihoods.[210] When Chinese environmental NGOs *have* used social justice and popular participation frames, such as in campaigning against displacement due to dam-building, they have faced especially strong responses from authorities.[211]

---

[205] MacKinnon 2011.   [206] Quoted in ibid.   [207] Quoted in ibid.
[208] Sun and Zhao 2008.
[209] For more on labor rights as a sensitive issue, see Chapter 5. On the highly sensitive issue of HIV in China, see Long 2013.
[210] Walker 2008.   [211] Sun and Zhao 2008.

One forestry consultant with experience in south China explained that there was "very little" organizing around land rights, partly since, "from the government side, if you have a group for your rights, it will be sensitive."[212] An auditor noted that while the FSC requires stakeholder consultation, "each time I send notice to NGOs, I get nothing back. I send notice to Greenpeace, WWF, but there are almost no local NGOs in these regions."[213] Another practitioner pointed to NGOs focused on women's land rights in Southeast Asia, saying, "there, one way [to respond to injustice] is to organize and fight for rights together. But in China, you don't see it."[214] The threat of repression is not just imagined.

Without vocal watchdogs and a space for independent organizing, it appears to be all too easy for even conscientious auditors to overlook or downplay problems with land-tenure and community rights. One auditor, who had worked on a Sino-Forest audit among others, minimized concerns about land rights, saying "tenure is usually okay," and pointing to other common problems on the social side of the standards—namely labor contracts, workers' equipment, and worker welfare.[215] To be sure, some auditors recognized the potential complications of land tenure. As one explained:

> many enterprises want to rent land in the south of China that's communal or collectively owned. If a large member of the village, a leader, agreed to rent the land to the enterprise, it could be successful. But with recent reform to distribute communal forests to each farmer, each farmer can make a decision of whether to rent or not. So it's possible that...now a conflict emerges with privatization.[216]

On the other hand, this auditor also explained that "if a [forest management enterprise] has a strategy for how to deal with it—at least documented procedures on how to resolve, even if the conflict hasn't been resolved—in such cases the certification can still be successful."[217] In other words, as theorized in Chapter 2, management processes can be substituted for performance requirements when difficult situations arise. Another auditor explained that "with patience and skill, you can get useful information [from farmers]" but also acknowledged that the time for stakeholder consultations is short.[218] Another practitioner acknowledged that stakeholder consultations may be a weak part of auditing in China, since local awareness is low and auditors may not be spending much time on this issue.[219]

---

[212] Interview with sustainable forestry consultant, Beijing, 3/14/14.
[213] Interview with auditor, Beijing, 7/14/11.
[214] Interview with NGO representative, Beijing, 3/13/14.
[215] Interview with forester/auditor, Beijing, 3/14/14.
[216] Interview with auditor, Beijing, 12/20/10.   [217] Ibid.
[218] Interview with auditor, Beijing, 7/14/11.
[219] Interview with certification representative, Beijing, 12/8/10.

The case of Sino-Forest reveals that the large plantation projects of south China can rest on shaky and exploitative foundations. Auditors are not prohibited from investigating these foundations, but neither are they forced to. Because conflicts over land rights can easily remain submerged, auditors are at risk of glossing over the power of plantation developers to set the terms of a "fair" agreement with communities. As we will see, even when strong-arm tactics come to light, this does not preclude the area from being certified to the FSC's seemingly stringent standards.

Stora Enso in Guangxi province: a certified land grab?

Despite the sensitivity of land conflicts, some do get revealed to a larger audience—whether because the conflict is so sustained and intense as to provoke media attention, as in the Wukan case, or because international watchdogs expose it, as in the case of a plantation developed by the Finnish-Swedish pulp and paper company Stora Enso. The company had positioned itself as a leader in sustainability and corporate social responsibility. It promoted both FSC and PEFC certification, and the percentage of certified wood in its supply chain increased from 49 percent in 2005 to 67 percent in 2009, although it had also faced intense criticism for the displacement of local residents by its Veracel joint venture plantation in Brazil.[220]

To feed its growing stock of pulp and paper factories in south China, Stora Enso worked from 2002 to 2009 to acquire land in Guangxi province for fast-growing eucalyptus plantations. Some forested areas in Guangxi were known for having ambiguous ownership boundaries, where "local forestry authorities were simply unable or unwilling to contain 'unauthorized' appropriation of forest land."[221] Roughly 60 percent of the 120,000 hectares of land that Stora Enso intended to develop was owned by the state, while 40 percent was collectively owned by villages, with a few spots having been devolved to individual households. Initially, the company worked with a state-owned company created by provincial authorities (the Guangxi Gaofeng Group) to acquire land-use rights.[222] By early 2006, the company had leased 34,000 hectares at an average price of 25 yuan per mu (a bit more than $3.00 for an area equivalent to 1/15 of a hectare) per year for twenty to thirty years.[223] That same year, the municipal government in Beihai, which had promised to secure approximately 40,000 hectares for the plantation, set up a state-owned company (The Beihai Forestry Investment Company) solely to secure the rights to land from villagers and transfer them to Stora Enso. By 2010,

---

[220] Stora Enso 2009; Kröger 2012.   [221] Strauss 2009:1171.
[222] United Nations Development Program 2012.   [223] Li and Zhu 2007.

Stora Enso had acquired roughly 90,000 hectares of land, including 23,000 hectares in Beihai.[224]

A 2010 report from two US-based NGOs—the Rights and Resources Initiative and Rural Development Institute (aka Landesa)—made it clear that Stora Enso's middlemen in Beihai had used the power of the state and strong-arm tactics to secure a number of leases. Based on interviews with farmers conducted by the NGOs' staff in China, the report revealed a number of questionable practices. In a few instances, local government officials and police arrived to begin clearing land, spurring conflicts with residents who had not had a chance to consent. More commonly, township and village leaders were given quotas for land acquisition and punished if they did not fulfill them.[225] Leases with village collectives were required by the 2002 Rural Land Contracting Law (and by Stora Enso's own policies) to have the consent of two-thirds of the members, but many farmers interviewed by the NGO investigators said they had not been consulted at all. Sometimes, consent was forged or manipulated by village leaders. In one case:

> the party secretary of the administrative village came to his villager group asking villagers to provide finger prints on a piece of blank paper for 'monetary subsidies for hardship' in an amount of 30–50 yuan per person. A couple of days after farmers in this villager group gave their prints, the secretary announced that 500 mu of the villager group's forestland had been transferred to Stora Enso with all farmers' consent.[226]

In villages where middlemen were active, villagers "were told these transfer terms were decided by the government without room for bargaining. The farmers did not have the power to say no."[227]

Stories of intimidation, violence, and misleading tactics had also come out in the Finnish press and were captured in the Finnish documentary film *Red Forest Hotel*, released in 2011.[228] The documentary showed the filmmaker's attempts—often stymied by security personnel—to talk with farmers in Stora Enso's plantation area and with a lawyer, Yang Zaixin, who had begun to document abuses. Villagers shown in the film expressed worries about erosion and the high water absorption of eucalyptus plantations, as well as coercion and trickery involved in land acquisition. According to one villager, "the government cut down our trees by force. We asked them not to. They wanted to make a contract for our lands. We said no. . . . Then the town mayor led a group of people here and cut down our trees. . . . Then they arrested me."[229] The lawyer, Yang Zaixin, was briefly detained during the filming and was then held for more than a year in 2011–12. Ethnographic research conducted by

---

[224] Stora Enso response, included in Li and Nielsen 2010.   [225] Ibid.:22–3.
[226] Ibid.:18.   [227] Ibid.:20.   [228] Tuohinen 2009.   [229] Quoted in Koskinen 2012.

Wen Zhou (2012) also sheds light on the areas where Stora Enso was acquiring land. She found a combination of complaints about the powerlessness of the villagers and stories about how eucalyptus poisons the land and water—which appeared to be a mix of myth and valid concern—as land shifted from agricultural uses to being leased for timber plantations.

The full scope of intimidation, trickery, and resistance is not clear, but there is little doubt that the power of the local state was mobilized to secure land rights for Stora Enso. The power of the local governments and state-owned company virtually guaranteed that the land would be transferred to Stora Enso, and the state's power over villagers ensured that conflicts would be repressed and scattered. As one practitioner noted about this case, "some farmers were punished by local governments" for pushing for higher payments.[230] Another argued that "the primary problem and greatest threat to tenure security of farmers is government intervention—plus either intended or unintended companies standing behind."[231]

In its initial response to the public criticism, Stora Enso admitted that land disputes existed in Guangxi "due to historic reasons and unclear documentation" and vowed to review contracts and promote conflict resolution processes.[232] In addition, the company claimed that some instances of violence were not linked to the company or its contractors and reported that it had walked away from several contested parcels.

In the glare of international scrutiny, Stora Enso began the process of getting its plantation land in Guangxi certified in 2012.[233] Auditors from Bureau Veritas conducted a pre-assessment for FSC certification in May of 2012 and a full audit in September, covering approximately 90,000 hectares in four regions, including Beihai.[234] In this case, the auditors could not ignore the issue of land tenure. They approached it, though, mainly as a matter of procedure. In the pre-assessment, auditors noted that Stora Enso had a database of complaints related to land tenure, but the company "lacked a systematic approach in resolving such disputes and district managers in charge of resolving most disputes had not been adequately trained".[235] This focus on procedure and training would become the main criterion for judging the legitimacy of Stora Enso's land rights.

Over the course of five-day audit, the team from Bureau Veritas met with a range of local stakeholders, from municipal officials to village leaders to ordinary villagers. The procedure, one auditor explained, was to use Stora Enso's

---

[230] Interview with sustainable forestry consultant, Beijing, 3/14/14.
[231] Interview with NGO representative, Beijing, 3/13/14.   [232] Stora Enso 2009:17.
[233] The company had received advice on FSC certification in Guangxi as early as 2008 and had been working with the developers of CFCC as well (Stora Enso response, included in Li and Nielsen 2010; Stora Enso 2009).
[234] Bureau Veritas Certification 2012.   [235] Ibid.:25.

database of conflicts and then go interview companies and farmers in that area. At the same time, the auditor noted, "it's hard to tell if it's the fault of Stora Enso, since there was a third party involved," referring to government middlemen.[236] The auditors fielded complaints about low lease rates and insufficient payments from local authorities to collectives, but the audit team found that Stora Enso was "dutifully paying the appropriate fees to the appropriate local authorities," and framed these concerns as requiring improved communication and dispute resolution processes.[237] An auditor echoed this framing in saying that "in Stora Enso, the problem isn't land tenure but social issues," noting complaints both by and against local villagers.[238]

After a follow-up audit that focused solely on the dispute resolution process, Bureau Veritas granted the certificate in November of 2012, just six months after the pre-assessment. The auditors reported that the company had "revised its procedures, updated its database and trained most relevant people that may have a role to play in the implementation of the company's dispute resolution procedures."[239] The only stakeholder interviewed at this point was a police representative in one village. Ultimately, the decision to certify Stora Enso's plantations in Guangxi rested on the finding that the company had improved its process for managing disputes, and the deciding evidence came from policy statements, record-keeping, and documentation of trainings.

In the first follow-up surveillance audit, the auditors did gather additional information from villagers. As one auditor explained, "we brought a copy of the land lease agreement with villagers' signatures. We would have a meeting with villagers about how they leased the land to middlemen and try to find out if there were any unresolved disputes."[240] But there were some striking limitations to this procedure. Government officials usually were not present for these interviews, but company representatives were. "We have to bring the Stora Enso employees—they help us make connections," the auditor explained. Asked if the villagers can talk honestly in this situation, the auditor said:

> I could feel that some of the village leaders didn't want to tell us everything. But the villagers are frank. They would tell us about depletion of water resources, about not getting paid. Usually we found that Stora Enso isn't directly responsible—it's the middlemen. They are historical issues, not directly attributable to Stora Enso.... As an auditor, what we want to find out is if Stora Enso is directly responsible for these complaints.[241]

---

[236] Interview with NGO representative/auditor, Beijing, 3/11/14.
[237] Bureau Veritas Certification 2012:61.
[238] Interview with forester/auditor, Beijing, 3/12/14.
[239] Bureau Veritas Certification 2012:95.   [240] Skype interview with auditor, 3/27/14.
[241] Ibid.

The auditors also made contact with the only local NGO they could find—the Beihai Civil Volunteer Association. This is a conservation and social service organization with close ties to the local government and a history of prior cooperation with Stora Enso.[242] Meeting with this type of NGO may be preferable to not meeting with any local NGOs, but one would not expect this NGO to serve as a vigorous representative of villagers who were strong-armed by local authorities.

Researchers from the Rural Development Institute were more sensitive in their interviewing strategies when then returned to Guangxi in 2013 to follow up on their 2010 report. They conducted interviews with farmers in twelve villages, usually in groups and always without government officials or Stora Enso employees present.[243] These interviews confirmed earlier reports of coercion, intimidation, and fraud in land acquisition from 2004 to 2009, but they also confirmed Stora Enso's report that it had put a moratorium on land acquisition in 2009. The vast majority of the farmers interviewed were not familiar with the dispute resolution procedure and hotline that Stora Enso had put in place, but two villages had engaged in negotiations with company staff over low prices in the initial leases. Stora Enso had also pushed the middlemen aside and begun to review the contracts themselves. Although the interviewed farmers were "extremely upset about compulsory takings, the lack of transparency, and fraudulent transactions," they also tended to see Stora Enso as "more flexible and negotiable than other private businesses or government agencies regarding rent."[244] Overall, the follow-up report praised Stora Enso for making changes but noted that the land rights of villagers, especially women, were still quite limited.[245] In addition, with policies giving more forest rights to individual households, the report raised questions about how Stora Enso would navigate the evolving terrain of land tenure in Guangxi province.

Was this a triumph of corporate responsibility or of corporatist disposses-sion, with foreign companies and the local state teaming up to take advantage of villagers? Ultimately, as in the case of Perum Perhutani in the previous chapter, we must view it as a bit of both. Certifiers clearly prioritized recent responsibility-taking in issuing the FSC certificate. The certification depended on the company being "sincere about making things right", as one practitioner

---

[242] Stora Enso 2012; US Consulate General 2009.   [243] Li and Wang 2014.
[244] Ibid.:18.
[245] As reported by Wang et al. 2012 women are often excluded from full membership in their "married-in" village—that is, the village of their husbands—while also being excluded from their birth villages. When land-use certificates are granted to households, usually only the male head of household's name is listed, allowing men to make decisions without their spouses' consent and leaving divorced women without any claim to these resources. As one practitioner noted of forest tenure reform, "if women aren't included and men get more rights, the more vulnerable women will be" (interview with NGO representative, Beijing, 3/13/14).

put it, and on not holding the company responsible for "historical issues" in its land acquisition.[246] If one denies history, then it is not difficult to see how Stora Enso's operation can be held up as a model of a socially responsible plantation. The forest managers were by most accounts knowledgeable and working diligently to respond to issues raised by auditors and watchdogs.

But it is striking how quickly and easily "historical issues" were swept away in this case. The time from pre-assessment to FSC certification was only six months, and villagers who had been intimidated or exploited had few if any channels through which to challenge the process. As described in Chapter 3, when forest management companies in Indonesia sought FSC certification in contested areas, the process could drag on for several years as auditors sought to mediate between companies and local indigenous rights NGOs. Authoritarian governance in China prevented this, making it easy to deny the not-so-distant history of land-grabbing on behalf of Stora Enso.

Conclusion

Rural areas of China have undergone major changes in the past two decades, through ambitious reforestation campaigns, land-tenure reforms, and the abolition of agricultural taxes in 2006, which helped to increase residents' trust in governments.[247] But land grabs have also come to the Chinese countryside, whether as a result of local governments' need for new revenues or China's further incorporation into a global political economy rife with land speculation and peasant dispossession.[248] It would seem that scrutiny from arbiters of corporate sustainability and social responsibility would reduce or mitigate land grabs for large-scale plantation projects. Yet even high-bar standards and multi-stakeholder initiatives are in many respects captive to the contexts in which they are implemented. As we have seen, without independent NGOs or other organized stakeholders to push them, auditors for FSC certification glossed over nefarious land acquisition tactics and framed responsibility in narrow terms, leading to the certification of questionable land as sustainable.

This is one side of the dual logic of certifying in authoritarian places. A strong authoritarian state, with its heavily restricted civil society, leads to constructions of compliance that are quite contained—and potentially blind to severe injustices. At the same time, though, a strong authoritarian state constrains the operational autonomy of transnational private regulators, potentially even threatening their local viability. FSC certification grew

[246] Interview with certification representative, Beijing, 3/13/14.
[247] Michelson 2012.   [248] See Siciliano 2014; Michelson 2012.

160

quickly in China, but it faced strong competition from a homegrown and state-sponsored initiative, new hurdles of state authorization, and sweeping logging bans that ultimately made certification irrelevant.

This stands in contrast to Indonesia, where democratization gave the FSC and its constituents space to operate autonomously, but also made it very difficult for forest management enterprises to get certified. Ambiguous land rights were openly challenged by organized activists and residents in Indonesia, forcing private regulators to look for compromises and sometimes precluding certification. Land rights in China were often ambiguous and occasionally contested, but the suppression of organized challenges allowed forest enterprises to be deemed compliant with the FSC's seemingly stringent standards. In neither case was the domestic context an empty space or regulatory void, but democracy and authoritarianism provided different spaces for the implementation of transnational private regulation.

"The state" in China is of course a complex set of organizations and arrangements. Scholars of contentious politics in China have argued that it must be disaggregated if we are to understand the mix of opportunities, constraints, and restraints that activists face.[249] The same could be said for forest certification and transnational private regulation. It was the central government that initially created the opportunity for the FSC to gain traction in China and then made it increasingly difficult for the FSC to operate once a homegrown competitor had been launched. The local state was most important in clearing the way for timber plantations and keeping villagers' concerns submerged, thus indirectly enabling the certification of some of these areas. The "dual logic", then, may also reflect the interests of different levels of the Chinese state—with the central government being attentive to national sovereignty and administrative control while the local state acts as the repressive growth machine.

The complex, resilient authoritarianism of the party-state in China is unique in some respects. To be sure, few countries have China's combination of market size, global economic integration, and authoritarian state capacity. Nevertheless, as initiatives to certify the sustainability of agriculture, mining, and forestry gravitate toward authoritarian and autocratic regimes in the Congo Basin, Eastern Europe, or elsewhere, they may encounter some of the same challenges, constraints, and perverse growth opportunities found in China. Even in formally democratic regimes where there have been crackdowns on civil society, such as Russia, the ability of local and international NGOs to discipline the certification process is likely to decline.[250] If practitioners are to uphold the integrity of transnational standards, they must not assume that these local settings can be transcended.

---

[249] For example, O'Brien and Li 2006.   [250] See Malets 2013 on their importance to date.

For scholars, the case of sustainable forestry standards in China should bring several general features of transnational governance into sharp relief. Some of these are captured by the propositions in Chapter 2, especially with regard to the primacy of domestic governance, the political construction of compliance, "process over performance" dynamics, and the weakness of labor-rights standards. Two other general implications deserve mention. First, the legitimation of private authority involves navigating the consent of the state, not just the endorsement of industry and global civil society. The legitimacy contests that pervade transnational fields of governance are intertwined with much more localized struggles over the political control of best practices, although these may be less visible from afar.[251] Second, notwithstanding the profound influence of states and domestic civil society, transnational corporations play a central role in pushing standards into particular territories. Ikea deserves much of the credit for bringing FSC certification to China, although there are serious questions about whether its low-cost model is compatible with high-bar sustainability standards. Rather than focusing on dispersed demand for sustainability, fairness, or "environmental, social, and governance" measures, scholars should look more closely at what particular companies are and are not willing to do to push standards through their global operations.

---

[251] See Quack (2010) for a balanced account of legitimation in transnational governance that avoids reifying global civil society.

5

Beneath Compliance

Corporate Social Responsibility and Labor Standards in China

> *"Workers were given model answers about the Labor Law, and they had to memorize them so that when customers' inspectors come and ask, they will deliver the line, 'five-day workweek, eight-hour day, Sunday off, two hours maximum overtime each day and not more than five nights per week. We are all very satisfied with our work schedule.' It's the first time we learned the details of the Labor Law, and what we were not getting."*
>
> Worker in a handbag factory in south China
> (quoted in Lee 2007a:171)

When the Chinese government set up the first "special economic zone" in 1980, Shenzhen was a small city surrounded by agricultural land. By 2000, an influx of migrant workers had helped to make Shenzhen a bustling city of 7 million and growing. Throughout Guangdong province, young women arrived from distant villages to become *dagongmei*—young women "working for the boss"—differentiated from the traditional working class in state-owned enterprises by gender, age, and a strong rural-urban categorical divide.[1] By 1994, mainland China had become the world's top exporter of apparel, with wages that were well below their competitors in Southeast Asia.[2] By the time it joined the World Trade Organization in 2001, China—and especially south China—had truly become the "world's factory".

Underpinning this massive migration and industrialization was a "dormitory labor regime" that provided housing within the factory complex in return for an ability to work long and often unstable hours. The dormitory system provided basic subsistence, but migrant workers were paid far less than official

---

[1] Pun 2005b; Lee 1998.
[2] World Trade Organization data on exports of clothing (SITC 84) by value, stat.wto.org; Yang, Chen, and Monarch 2010.

urban residents, often below the legal minimum wages that were established in 1994, and they endured harsh treatment and safety hazards. Outside the factory, migrant workers were politically marginalized by the *hukou* system of internal registration, which denied them full residency and access to services in the cities where they worked. Wildcat strikes occurred, but representation through unions was essentially impossible. The All-China Federation of Trade Unions (ACFTU) had a legal monopoly on worker representation, and its charge was to control workers more than to represent them. NGOs were springing up to help migrant workers, often with ties to labor-rights groups in Hong Kong, and "semi-civil society" was growing in China. But NGOs dealing with "sensitive" issues like labor were in a precarious situation and faced repression if they crossed the blurry line into "political" issues.[3]

It was in this context that "corporate social responsibility" (CSR) came to China. Early adopters of codes of conduct, such as Reebok and Nike, had begun to press their suppliers to soften harsh treatment and improve factory conditions. When congressional debates about trade with China heated up in the US in the early 1990s—with Tiananmen Square still a vivid memory— companies and their allies argued that codes of conduct could be relied upon to ensure respect for labor rights.[4] By the end of the 1990s, most large American and European apparel and footwear brands and retailers were scrutinizing their suppliers' labor conditions to some degree, whether by hiring external auditors or developing their own compliance departments.

The SA8000 standard—developed by Social Accountability International and backed by Toys R Us, Timberland, The Gap, and others—played an especially important role in bringing CSR to China. This initiative allowed factories to be certified as above the bar, but the standard demanded reduced working hours and payment of a "living wage". Most provocatively, it echoed international norms about workers' freedom of association, calling for "parallel means" of worker representation where independent unions are illegal, as they are in China. SA8000 was just one part of a growing field of CSR and private labor standards. By some accounts, the compliance activities of major brands (e.g., Adidas, H&M, or Wal-Mart) have been at least as influential. Moreover, auditing done under the auspices of the Fair Labor Association, Ethical Trading Initiative, or Business Social Compliance Initiative has added an additional layer of rules and assurances.

How can these types of transnational rules for fair and decent work be translated into practice in a domestic context that systematically restricts migrant workers' rights? It is tempting to answer this question by simply saying that rules have *not* been translated into practice—that is, that they

---

[3] See Spires 2011; Cheng, Ngok, and Zhuang 2010.
[4] Jacobs 1992; Barrett 1994. See Bartley 2005 for more on this period.

have been evaded, resisted, or have been so divorced from the profit-seeking activities of firms as to be meaningless. This is indeed part of the story, and this chapter will offer a diagnosis of this dysfunction. But it would be wrong to say that private rules have been meaningless. Supply chain scrutiny has spawned some reforms, and a few brands and CSR initiatives have undertaken ambitious efforts to bypass the state's restrictions on workers' rights. To delve into the contours and consequences, this chapter will consider two sets of questions.

The first pertains to the influence of codes of conduct, auditing, and factory certification on material conditions within factories. Why have so many problems been impervious to supply-chain scrutiny, while others have proven open to reform? To what extent has the leading form of factory certification— SA8000 certification—surpassed other auditing efforts to mark truly distinctive factories? Interviews with practitioners, along with quantitative analyses of data from workers and managers, reveal just how much the auditing and certification model has faltered in China, where the dormitory labor regime has exacerbated the industry's tendencies toward long working hours, falsified records, and lax or compromised scrutiny.

Second, how have rules about workers' *rights* been operationalized in this context? What can guarantees of "freedom of association" possibly mean in China, where the state tightly regulates both citizen association and labor rights? While some brands and CSR initiatives have simply ignored this contradiction, some have attempted to reconcile claims about labor rights with production in China. This is in line with what the first chapter called the "hope of transcendence"—that is, the idea that global rule-making can create spaces that are autonomous from the domestic context. Looking at these attempts, I will argue that domestic governance has proven resilient, forcing the meaning of private regulatory rules to change accordingly. While purporting to ensure the *rights* of workers, private regulation has become a vehicle for diffusing managerialist scripts about worker-management *communication*.

I will begin with the case of Yue Yuen, the largest athletic footwear manufacturer in the world, a supplier to Nike, Adidas, New Balance, and something of a microcosm of CSR in China. On one hand, this is perhaps the clearest case of meaningful and gradual reform, fostered by brands with leading CSR programs. On the other, recent events revealed the limits of CSR and deep tensions surrounding the status and rights of Chinese workers.

Scrutiny and Reform in the Footwear Industry: The Case of Yue Yuen

The Taiwanese company Pou Chen began manufacturing athletic shoes for American and European department stores and footwear brands in the late

1970s. In 1988, it created Yue Yuen (YY) as a Hong Kong-based company to help expand into mainland China. As labor costs rose in Taiwan in the 1990s, Pou Chen shifted most of its production to YY factories in China, as well as Indonesia and Vietnam.[5] YY's operations grew into a series of enormous factory complexes, running hundreds of distinct production lines for Nike, Adidas, New Balance, Puma, Timberland, and others. Most are located in Dongguan, the bustling industrial city in Guangdong province that has been called "a perverse expression of China at its most extreme."[6] By the mid-2000s, YY employed roughly 280,000 people, mostly in China, and accounted for 17 percent of the world footwear market.[7] By 2013, YY counted 413,000 employees and was producing 300 million to 400 million pairs of shoes per year.[8]

More than most other footwear manufacturers in China at the time, YY had been able to promise large volumes, low prices, staunch protection of brand secrets, as well as "flexibility in adapting with lightning speed to the rapid fashion changes in the shoe industry."[9] Its ability to deliver rested in no small part on the harsh discipline it imposed on migrant workers. Using piecerates, heavy production quotas, and a harsh, militaristic management style, YY engaged in what the author of an otherwise sympathetic account of Nike's ascendance called "management by terror and browbeating."[10] In one early exposé of YY's factories in China, a worker described how the company's demanding precision extended to mealtimes:

> The gate opens at 5:30 sharp. The workers file up the stairs on one side, while those who have finished their dinner descend on the other. When they get to the canteen, they sit eight to a table and wait. Only when the bell rings can they begin to eat. We have 10 to 15 minutes to finish the meal, then we file downstairs again.[11]

YY and Pou Chen's strict discipline also garnered attention when, in 1997, an NGO in Vietnam exposed several incidents at factories producing for Nike: In one, factory managers punished a group of workers by forcing them to run outside the factory, leading some to faint. In another punishment, workers were forced to stand outside in the sun for an hour—and one who refused was fired.[12] In China, a report issued by China Labor Watch in 2002 raised concerns about suicides, disciplinary fines, and production speed-ups at a YY factory producing for Adidas.[13]

---

[5] Cohen 2006.   [6] Chang 2009:27.   [7] Appelbaum 2008; Merk 2008.
[8] Yue Yuen Industrial (Holdings) Limited 2014.
[9] Van Agtmael 2007:116. Over time, Pou Chen also invested in upstream production of leather and other raw materials, as well as in retail distribution, contributing to its remarkable growth and profitability (Cohen 2006).
[10] Katz 1994:157; Merk 2008.   [11] Quoted in Chan 1996:C4.
[12] Vietnam Labor Watch 1997.   [13] China Labor Watch 2010.

As events like these fueled anti-sweatshop campaigns, Nike, Adidas, New Balance, and others pushed YY to soften its management style and comply with their codes of conduct. These large brands had leverage over YY, but they also depended on its production capacity. By one estimate, Nike relied on YY for 15 percent of its shoe purchases, and YY relied on Nike for 28 percent of its sales.[14] As Richard Appelbaum has explained, unlike the rapidly churning world of discount apparel production, where brands frequently switch suppliers, "the higher-end, branded athletic footwear industry requires close cooperation between buyer and supplier, achieved through stable, ongoing relationships."[15] As we will see, these relationships allowed scrutiny to gradually translate into reform in YY's factories.

Recalcitrance and reform

Rules about health and safety generated some reforms. Workers in footwear factories were commonly exposed to toxic chemical in solvents and glues, not only the punctures, cuts, and possible amputations that can occur in apparel factories. In fact, when footwear factories migrated from Taiwan to China in the late 1980s and early 1990s, the heavy use of hazardous chemicals had been the norm. Factories in China relied heavily on adhesives containing the toxin toluene, sometimes mixed with those containing high levels of benzene.[16] Minimal ventilation and protective equipment meant that workers were routinely exposed to serious health hazards.[17] As many poisoned workers suffered in anonymity, a few cases, such as a worker poisoned while producing for Payless Shoes, reached international audiences.[18]

Nike and Reebok took the lead in banning the use of toluene and promoting safer alternatives, with Adidas, New Balance, and other brands soon following.[19] In this way, footwear brands had an important influence on conditions at YY and elsewhere. Compliance was not always complete, though. A 2002 investigation by China Labor Watch revealed that toluene had been partially but not entirely phased out at one YY factory.[20] One brand representative remarked that toluene is "phased out, except when it's not," acknowledging that it often works better than substitutes.[21] Another brand's compliance staff said that toluene is "completely banned, but we do still find it in some factories," explaining that "it's usually new suppliers with problems with banned chemicals."[22]

---

[14] Merk 2008:88. [15] Appelbaum 2008:74. [16] Chen and Chan 1999.
[17] Brown 2003. [18] Pan 2002. [19] Sellnow and Brand 2001.
[20] China Labor Watch 2010.
[21] Interview with brand representative, Shenzhen, 10/15/10.
[22] Interview with compliance staff members, Guangzhou, 11/10/10.

Brand pressure also led YY to shift from the harsh discipline of piecerates to a more rationalized system of hourly pay with production quotas.[23] But the company was also recalcitrant to many of the brands' demands. In 1999, Reebok took the dramatic step of shifting $40 million of orders away from one YY factory because of persistent non-compliance with the brand's code of conduct.[24] One brand's compliance staff acknowledged that YY managers commonly kept two sets of records, one true, the other with wage and hour figures that fit the brand's standards.[25] YY was far from alone in this practice, as we will see.

Over time, though, scrutiny and reforms mounted. YY took part in a 2001 health and safety training project sponsored by Nike, Adidas, and Reebok, as well as Hong Kong-based labor-rights NGOs and US-based safety advocates. Rather than simply promoting health and safety management systems, this project emphasized worker participation in the identification and rectification of safety hazards, and it established some of the first broad-based health and safety committees in Chinese factories. Committees included ordinary production workers, whose pictures were posted in their departments.[26] The coordinating committee praised the initial steps at participating factories, finding that "plant-wide health and safety committees with significant worker participation were...qualitatively changing the character of previous management safety committees."[27]

Yet a follow-up workshop in 2005 was canceled after "several of the [Chinese] NGOs who were to participate...were visited by government security who inquired about their interaction with foreigners and their interest in labor rights...[and other groups] said they could not come to any workshop involving foreign participants on these issues at the present time."[28] This is a stark reminder of the political sensitivity of the project.

Still, the spotlight continued to produce some reform within YY factories. In a 2008 investigation of a factory producing for Adidas, China Labor Watch found off-the-clock work, poor ventilation, and managers withholding women workers' wages in order to keep them from resigning. But the group agreed not to release the report if Adidas would work on improvements. Two years later, China Labor Watch found that unpaid pre-shift meetings had been shortened, ventilation and safety equipment had been improved, and women could resign more easily and without penalty. Working hours remained high—roughly eleven hours per day, six days per week during the peak season.

---

[23] Merk 2008.   [24] Collier 2000.
[25] Conversation with compliance staff members, Dongguan, November 4, 2010.
[26] China Capacity Building Project: Occupational Health and Safety 2002; Szudy, O'Rourke, and Brown 2003.
[27] China Capacity Building Project: Occupational Health and Safety 2002:16.
[28] Brown 2005:4.

But this was closer to compliance with Adidas's standard of sixty hours per week (with exceptions for peak seasons) than most factories had gotten.[29] The NGO concluded that "the improvements are satisfactory" and highlighted YY as a model to be emulated.[30]

Welfare and workers' rights

After years of scrutiny from brands and investigations by watchdogs, YY was becoming a testament to brand-supplier collaboration and a recognized leader in CSR in China.[31] "Management by terror and browbeating" had been replaced by formal policies and handbooks, management training seminars, and internal grievance mechanisms—along with auditable records of these activities. Asked about YY's previous reputation for harsh treatment by supervisors, one brand representative pointed to a wide array of formal structures now in place—a behavior guidebook and "emotion management" assistance for supervisors, an array of channels for workers to lodge complaints, and records showing that abusive supervisors had been punished.[32] In one "counselling room", I watched as the auditor paged through records of workers' visits.[33] The factory was still a stressful place for workers, but the source had shifted from overbearing supervisors to the impersonal stress of "lean production" methods, which require all workers in a production team to maintain the same (fast) pace and thus "makes workers more tense," the brand representative explained.[34]

With the formalization of YY's compliance activities, brands have come to trust YY managers to provide accurate records, operate their own compliance programs, and educate or police subcontractors.[35] Brands now mainly audit YY's own compliance processes rather than policing for violations.[36] YY's parent company, Pou Chen, became a member of the Fair Labor Association (FLA) in 2011—something that would have been unthinkable in the 1990s, when abuses at Pou Chen and YY factories helped to fuel the FLA's formation.[37]

Some YY factories have also established elected "worker welfare committees" at brands' request. At one such factory, committee leaders described their biggest accomplishments as improving the food in the company canteen, getting more TVs and towels in the dormitories, and achieving a small increase

---

[29] China Labor Watch 2010.   [30] Ibid.:10.
[31] Interview with auditor, Shenzhen, 11/12/10; interview with CSR consultants, Beijing, 12/7/10, Guangzhou, 12/18/10.
[32] Interview with compliance manager, Guangzhou, 11/10/10.
[33] Audit notes, Dongguan, 11/4/10.
[34] Interview with compliance manager, Guangzhou, 11/10/10.   [35] Ibid.
[36] Interview with compliance staff members, Guangzhou, 11/10/10.
[37] Fair Labor Association 2012.

in the seniority bonus.[38] On the other hand, committee leaders described wages as beyond their sphere of influence, and when asked about workers with grievances about compensation or termination, they explained that "the committee is not really focused on rights;" this was the union's role, they noted.[39] In addition, although the committee members had been elected by their fellow workers, it is doubtful that especially activist-minded workers would be allowed to win. As one brand representative noted, "if it was a strike leader, almost surely not."[40] Still, worker welfare committees fit well with YY's attempts to soften the hardest edges of the Chinese dormitory labor system. At the factory I visited, the company had built a recreation center with a movie theater, karaoke club, and dance studio, and the company allowed workers to live and eat outside the factory complex if they wanted.

Brand scrutiny, tightening labor markets in coastal areas, and rising worker expectations all combined to foster a number of changes in YY factories. In some respects, one can see a Chinese version of something like the "welfare capitalism" that spread through American industry in the 1910s and 1920s—when employers adopted formal personnel offices, paternalistic management strategies, and company unions to squelch labor-management conflict.[41]

Labor unrest and the limits of CSR

The limits of reform became clear in the spring of 2014, when a massive strike occurred at YY factories in Dongguan. Despite becoming a CSR leader, YY had acted like many other companies in vastly underestimating its legally required contributions to the social insurance fund, which covers unemployment, pensions, and medical care, and to a related housing fund.[42] Most migrant workers do not actually participate in the social insurance program, since it requires employee contributions and its benefits are often difficult to transfer to a new location.[43] But supervisors, who had been with company for many years, were becoming more attentive to their retirement options, and a wide array of workers had reasons to worry about job losses if YY moved its factories to lower-wage inland locations.[44]

A small protest by a few supervisors quickly sparked walkouts in several YY factories in Dongguan. Thousands joined a march behind banners saying "shame on Yue Yuen's illegal activities", and the growing strike ultimately halted work by all 43,000 YY employees in Dongguan for ten days.[45] This was

---

[38] Notes from worker welfare committee presentation, Dongguan, 11/4/10.
[39] Interview with committee members, Dongguan, 11/4/10.
[40] Conversation with compliance staff members, Dongguan, 11/4/10.
[41] Edwards 1979; Jacoby 1997.   [42] China Labor Watch 2014; Sevastopulo 2014b.
[43] China Labor Watch 2014; China Labour Bulletin 2012.   [44] Harney and Ruwitch 2014.
[45] Committee for a Workers' International 2014; Borromeo 2014.

a crucial moment not just for YY, its clients, and its workers, but for migrant workers in south China in general. The YY strike was bigger than a momentous strike of 1,800 workers at a Honda factory in Foshan in 2010, which had garnered a great deal of attention from scholars and journalists.[46] It was bigger than multi-city strike by Pepsi bottling plant workers in 2011, and bigger than the 1,000-person strike that had just occurred at an IBM factory in Shenzhen.[47]

In addition to social insurance and housing funds, the strike tapped into discontent about the wages of production workers. One striker, who had worked at YY for fifteen years, claimed that "the employer reduced our bonus every time the Dongguan minimum wage was increased but the workers just swallowed their indignation.... Other plants in Gaobu township [in Dongguan] can pay more than 3,000 yuan per month [roughly $485] but at Yue Yuen it is just 2,700 yuan or so [roughly $435]."[48]

Moreover, YY strikers began to demand representation—not through a "worker welfare committee", a hotline to brands, or even through the courts—but through free elections of trade union representatives. This was a rare demand, which cut strongly against ACFTU practice. But it is a demand that has emerged in several recent strikes in China—starting with the insurgent rank-and-file unionists at the Ole Wolff electronics factory in northern China in 2006 and continuing with the 2010 Honda strike.[49] In the YY strike, the demand for representation spread in part via activists from domestic labor NGOs, which occupy a precarious position in "semi-civil society" and have often turned to commercial legal service provision, underground networking, or both in order to survive.[50] In this case, individuals from the Chun Feng Labor Dispute Arbitration Counseling and Service Center became involved in the YY strike. Two were detained for questioning by police, and one was later charged with using the internet to create a public disturbance.[51]

After nearly two weeks of unrest, attempts by the ACFTU to reign in the strike, and heavy police presence, the strike came to an end. With prodding from ACFTU and government officials, YY agreed to increase its social insurance contributions (basing them on workers' total pay, not their base pay before overtime) and increase workers' monthly housing allowance.[52] With

---

[46] Chan and Hui 2012; Friedman 2013.   [47] Cheung 2011; Mitchell and Clover 2014.

[48] Quoted in China Labour Bulletin 2014. As in the previous chapter, I have used a rough exchange rate of 6.2 rmb to the dollar during the 2013–15 period and 6.7 rmb to the dollar during the 2009–12 period.

[49] Chan and Hui 2012; China Labor News Translations 2008.

[50] Lee and Shen 2011; Chang, Ngok, and Zhuang 2010.

[51] Sevastopulo 2014a. One of these activists had also been involved in a strike at a Nokia factory in 2013. Interestingly, Lee and Shen (2011) include Chun Feng in their characterization of labor NGOs as an "anti-solidarity machine," promoting only the narrowest conceptions of workers' rights.

[52] Sevastopulo 2014c.

encouragement from supervisors but without a pay increase, workers returned to the factory floors. YY, which had seen its stock price plummet during the work stoppage, estimated that the additional payments would cost $31 million.[53] ACFTU officials vowed to move forward with union elections, though many observers remained skeptical.[54] The strike also led to renewed consideration of a collective consultation regulations (Regulations on Enterprise Collective Consultations and Collective Contracts), which would give workers a channel other than strikes for collective bargaining with employers.[55]

The YY strike will likely go down in history as part of a shift from the "cellular activism" of wildcat strikes to more mature system of industrial relations—and possibly the harbinger of a more coordinated Chinese labor movement.[56] But the strike also laid bare many of the limits of CSR and brand scrutiny in Chinese factories. The reforms that Nike, Adidas, and others were promoting had resulted in more elaborate human resource management systems, but they did not get YY to full legal compliance or keep up with workers' rising expectations. Nor did the growth of management-sponsored communication systems (like worker committees) provide a meaningful vehicle for worker representation. Overall, the YY case suggests that when faced with sustained scrutiny, factories in China can smooth some of the roughest edges of the dormitory labor system. But the deeper tensions of the Chinese production model are not easily relieved.

Implementing and Undermining Rules in Chinese Factories

While the reforms at Yue Yuen are far from the norm, changes of some sorts have been common in apparel and footwear factories in China. For instance, practitioners tend to agree that buyer pressure has improved physical conditions, making factories "shinier".[57] "Before, you could see the dust, smell the glue right away," another noted. "There have been tangible improvements in working conditions—it's very obvious."[58] There have also been improvements in occupational health and safety. Most often, this has meant providing personal protective equipment for workers, creating new management systems, phasing out dangerous chemicals, and creating health and safety committees.[59] On the other hand, as mentioned above, banned chemicals

---

[53] Wall Street Journal 2014.   [54] China Labour Bulletin 2014.   [55] Lau 2014.
[56] Lee 2007a.   [57] Interview with CSR consultant, Guangzhou, 10/26/10.
[58] Interview with CSR consultant, Beijing, 12/7/10. It is also clear from the FLA's tracking charts that factory managers have often had to improve things like lighting, ventilation, or the storage of hazardous chemicals.
[59] Interview with compliance consultant, Guangzhou, 12/20/10; interview with compliance manager, Hong Kong, 12/29/10; interview with CSR consultant, Beijing, 12/7/10; interview with

and dangerous environments can still be found, and rarely do health and safety committees include production workers.[60]

Scrutiny from brands and retailers has also helped to de-legitimate despotic management practices that were once the norm. The practice of essentially bonding workers, by seizing their identity cards or requiring deposits at the time of hiring, was common in south China in the 1990s.[61] It began to fade away in factories governed by codes of conduct.[62] Brand scrutiny has also made managers more careful about checking the age of prospective employees, reducing the incidence of child labor.[63] This is not to say that forced labor and child labor have been eliminated from supply chains governed by codes of conduct. Child labor can persist under the guise of "work study" programs, and prison-made holiday decorations and small electronics have ended up in the supply chains of Kmart and Electrolux.[64] Scrutiny from brands and retailers has helped to push these practices from the mainstream to the margins, but as we will see, this scrutiny has been highly imperfect.

Limits of reform: working hours and the falsification of records

The problem of excessive working hours illustrates both the resilience of some practices and the limits of supply-chain scrutiny. Brands and certification initiatives typically set a limit of sixty hours of work per week, and by calling for compliance with domestic labor law, they indirectly demand an even stricter limit. Chinese labor law, as adopted in 1994–5, defines the normal working time as forty hours per week and limits overtime to a total of thirty-six hours per *month*.[65]

In practice, Chinese workers in labor-intensive industries may work this much overtime in a single week, with hours extending past midnight in some cases.[66] At one lingerie factory certified by the Worldwide Responsible Accredited Production (WRAP) initiative, workers reported working more than twelve hours per day, six days per week, plus a shorter day on Sundays—for a total working week of nearly eighty hours.[67] Some brands

---

supplier companies' staff, Guangzhou, 11/25/10; interview with compliance staff members, Guangzhou, 11/10/10.

[60] Brown 2008.   [61] Chan 2001.   [62] Pun 2005a.

[63] Yu 2008a; interview with compliance manager, Shanghai, 7/13/11; interview with researcher, Guangzhou, 11/8/10.

[64] National Labor Committee 2010; Jiang 2013; Grigg and Murray 2013.

[65] People's Republic of China 1994; People's Republic of China State Council 1995. Factories can apply to local labor bureaus for permission to count overtime hours quarterly or yearly rather than monthly in order to accommodate seasonal variation, but even these limits are quite difficult to meet. The labor law initially set the normal work week to forty-four hours, but this was revised to forty in 1995.

[66] Verite 2012.

[67] Worker interviews, Jiada factory, Panyu, 12/12/10.

and CSR initiatives have sought to reduce working hours by increasing productivity, but the distance from compliance has often remained huge.[68] One such project reported that the *improved* conditions at one factory were 10.5–12.5 hour days, six to seven days per week.[69] Some larger factories have been able to get close to a sixty-hour week, but they can rarely if ever reach compliance with domestic labor law. A factory owner who had worked diligently with the Fair Labor Association and its member companies said, "I can confess that we don't do well according to Chinese law ... We can only get to the 60 hour standard of American and European standards," later admitting that even this standard was sometimes exceeded.[70]

Excessive overtime is common throughout the global apparel industry, largely because unstable production demands lead managers to "sweat" their existing workers rather than add new employees. But the problem is especially pronounced in China, where the dormitory labor regime has limited workers' engagements outside the factory and made it easier for managers to rapidly increase working hours.[71] Moreover, many smaller Chinese factories continue to calculate wages solely on the basis of piecerates and may not even be keeping track of working hours.[72] Complicating matters, provincial minimum wage regulations specify *monthly* minimums but also require premiums for overtime hours—150 percent of the normal wage on weekdays and 200 percent on weekends.[73] Minimum wage compliance can be difficult for both auditors and workers to determine, since workers understand their wages largely as monthly sums, which may include a variety of shifting and opaque piecerates or production bonuses.[74]

The dominant response to these problems has been for factory managers to produce false wage and hour records and to coach workers on the "correct" answers to give to auditors. Workers, hungry for overtime, confused by wage calculations, and/or wary of becoming whistleblowers, have often played along. Auditors and other CSR practitioners in China widely acknowledge that falsified records and coached workers are the norm.[75] As one put it, "it's impossible to meet the overtime law and everybody knows it. The factory

---

[68] Interview with CSR consultant, Beijing, 7/21/10.   [69] Impactt Ltd 2005:22.

[70] Interview with supplier company CEO, Shanghai, 12/13/10.

[71] Data disclosed by The Gap reveals that its suppliers in China were among the least likely to provide a day of rest each week. See also Fair Labor Association 2004; Fair Labor Association 2012.

[72] Interview with CSR consultant, Guangzhou, 12/18/10.

[73] The 2004 *Rules for Minimum Wages* clarified that workers should receive the minimum wage without having to work overtime.

[74] Du and Pan 2009.

[75] Frank 2008; Interview with auditor, Shenzhen, 11/12/10; interview with compliance manager, Shanghai, 7/13/11; interview with NGO representative, Shenzhen, 5/24/07; interview with compliance manager, Hong Kong, 5/22/07. Five out of six factories included in a project to reduce overtime had used falsified records at some point, and the remaining one had not had its hours scrutinized by buyers (Impactt Ltd 2005).

can't do anything except falsify."[76] Another called falsified records "part of the reality of a labor-intensive industry, [since] you need to satisfy both customers and workers."[77]

Like excessive overtime, falsified records are not unique to China. But here too the Chinese context seems to have made the problem especially severe. As some practitioners pointed out, factory managers were already keeping doctored books for tax purposes, so it was a logical extension to do so for compliance purposes as well.[78] In addition, a "socialist audit culture" had existed in China since at least the 1970s, with township and school administrators putting on elaborate shows for their overseers in the party.[79] Perhaps it is not surprising, then, that as scrutiny from brands increased in the late 1990s and 2000s, Chinese factory managers turned to consultants and software developers who were offering to help them fool their buyers.[80]

When auditors have tried to get past falsification, they have wound up playing "cat and mouse" games with factory managers: Auditors, suspecting that they are receiving false or incomplete wage and hour data, chase the real data, which is guarded heavily by factory managers. Auditors look for hints in worker interviews, but they are aware that the workers have been coached. To be sure, there are things that auditors can do to spot falsified records—like looking for those that are "too perfect", as if workers all swiped time cards simultaneously.[81] And there are other indicators of whether factories are operating when they claim to be giving workers time off—like the records of broken sewing needles. "They never remember to fake those," noted one compliance practitioner.[82] Perhaps most importantly, auditors could conduct confidential, off-site interviews with workers, but they are rarely asked to do so. Off-site interviews are not required for SA8000 or WRAP certification, or for the members of BSCI, FLA, or ETI. Brands and initiatives have occasionally requested offsite interviews when evaluating especially important suppliers or recalcitrant managers, but the costs of doing so are high—sometimes double— since auditors must return at night or on a Sunday.[83] Onsite interviews have remained the standard method.[84]

In one audit that I witnessed, experienced auditors working for a leading brand spent much of their time chasing information on working hours,

---

[76] Interview with certification initiative representative, Shenzhen, 11/12/10.

[77] Interview with compliance manager, Hong Kong, 12/29/10.

[78] Interview with CSR consultant, Hong Kong, 12/30/10; interview with factory owner, Guangzhou, 11/25/10.

[79] Kipnis 2008.

[80] Business Week 2006; phone interview with certification initiative representative, 1/5/11.

[81] Interview with compliance staff members, Guangzhou, 11/10/10.

[82] Interview with brand compliance manager, Shenzhen, 10/15/10.

[83] Interview with compliance consultant, Guangzhou, 12/20/10; interview with compliance manager, Shanghai, 7/13/11.

[84] Interview with compliance manager, Hong Kong, 12/29/10.

especially whether work was occurring on Sundays. One auditor selected workers from the shop floor for a mix of individual and group interviews. Some workers asked their supervisors for permission before leaving their stations, and all could easily be seen walking to the interview room, eliminating any possibility of confidentiality. Others on the auditing team examined the records provided by factory management, but by the end of the day-long audit, they had not received the full set of records. Factory managers explained that the records had been lost in a computer crash. Later, when the auditors asked for older paper records (which I had suggested might serve as a substitute), they were told that the person with access to those records had already left for the day. The auditors told me they would report their suspicions to the brand, but they had not found sufficient proof of noncompliance.[85]

Behind the troubles with auditing

Falsification and weak auditing are the surface manifestation of several deeper problems with the ways in which brands and CSR initiatives have implemented their standards. Three types of problems deserve attention—one related to the auditors, a second pertaining to brands' reasons for auditing, and a third showing how brands' business demands limit improvement in factories.

First, to keep tabs on a large number of suppliers, brands and initiatives have often relied on low-cost, high-volume auditing firms. Auditing organizations with experienced employees and a reputation for rigor do operate in China (e.g., the US-based nonprofit Verité and the UK ethical trade consultancy Impactt Ltd), but these high-end auditors have been priced out of most work. Large generalist auditing/certification companies, such as Bureau Veritas (BV), Intertek, and SGS, can cover numerous factories in a variety of locations and offer "bundled" services (e.g., customs compliance plus factory auditing), which helped them to quickly corner the market.[86] Rather than a professional service, factory auditing quickly became commoditized—that is, purchased as an undifferentiated commodity for a relatively standard (low) price. As of 2010, the going rate for external auditors in China was roughly $500–600 per person-day, and a basic one-day, two-person audit was common.[87] Although a multi-day audit by high-end providers may cost only a few thousand dollars more, when multiplied by hundreds of supplier factories, companies' incentives to economize on auditing costs can be significant.[88]

---

[85] Audit notes, Shenzhen, 12/17/10.   [86] Interview with auditor, Shenzhen, 11/12/10.
[87] Interview with compliance staff members, Guangzhou, 11/10/10.
[88] Clifford and Greenhouse 2013.

Allegations of corruption have dogged low-cost factory auditing in China. An undercover investigation by China Labor Watch found BV auditors accepting bribes and extorting money from factory managers.[89] In one instance, factory managers recorded an auditor asking for a bribe, but rather than reporting him, they used the recording to negotiate a lower bribe. They explained:

> Currently it is very common to offer bribes or other services to auditors, and the factory merely hoped to avoid excessive auditor demands....It is reasonable to pay 1,000–3,000 RMB or offer some other services in order to successfully pass a one-time audit....If the factory gave the recording to BV or a customer, the audit would be a failure and a new one would be arranged, which is not in the interest of the factory.[90]

Other auditors report being offered bribes up to 10,000 RMB (roughly $1500). Since simply having auditors return a second time would cost around $1,000–1,200 (6,700–8,000 RMB), bribes up to and above that amount could make economic sense for factory managers.[91] Since auditors are often hired as recent college graduates with few skills—apart from English language skills sufficient to write audit reports—and face long hours and extensive travel, it is not surprising that some have been tempted by bribes.[92]

There have been several attempts to counteract corruption and build professional norms of integrity, but the results are ambiguous. The China Compliance Practitioners Association (formerly China Compliance Professionals Association) outlined plans to professionalize factory auditing in 2008, but six years later, the group was still struggling to gain participants.[93] Intertek began weeding out its corrupt auditors and even collaborated with an undercover investigator arranged by China Labor Watch. But this project ended on a sour note, when Intertek published a statement that both downplayed evidence of corruption and named the undercover individual, exposing him to personal threats and police questioning.[94]

---

[89] China Labor Watch 2009.

[90] Quoted in China Labor Watch 2009:7–8. In another incident involving BV, one apparel retailer discovered a BV employee informing factories about when purportedly "unannounced" audits would take place, giving them time to clean up their operations and perform for the auditors (interview with compliance manager, Hong Kong, 5/22/07). BV ultimately conducted a "sting" operation to collect evidence against this individual.

[91] Audit notes, Shenzhen, 12/17/10; phone interview with certification initiative representative, 1/5/11.

[92] Interview with auditor, Shenzhen, 11/12/10; interview with supplier companies' staff, Guangzhou, 11/25/10.

[93] Interview with CSR consultant, Hong Kong, 12/30/10; interview with compliance manager, Hong Kong, 3/9/14.

[94] China Labor Watch v. Intertek Group PLC 2011.

A second problem is that brands appear to be using audits not so much to discover problems but to create plausible deniability—that is, to collect just enough information to produce assurances of due diligence.[95] For instance, brands and retailers often set a high bar for proof of noncompliance—putting the burden on auditors to find "objective evidence" that something is amiss. Most brands do not accept evidence from worker interviews as sufficient proof of noncompliance, which is why auditors end up in the "cat and mouse" game to find official records.[96] "Auditors can just make conclusions based on objective evidence," explained one former auditor. "If we suspect falsification, we can mention it to the client, but that doesn't affect the audit result."[97]

There does appear to be variation in the pursuit of plausible deniability. Some brands try to "talk to the suppliers honestly...and encourage them to show the real records," while others "are saying [to auditors], 'I only want clean reports, I don't want you to do offsite interviews,'" allowing problems to remain hidden.[98] This inconsistency can itself undermine the integrity of auditing. As one consultant put it:

> one brand might tell a factory to be more open and we'll work with you. Other brands say it's three strikes and you're out—and everything in between, and it's not always clearly understood. So factories are on tippy toes wondering what the impact of the audit will be. It's easier to provide a red envelope with money and take care of it. And brands get audit reports that show that the factory has a clean bill of health.[99]

Third, as other research has emphasized, brands have demanded that suppliers improve while also subjecting them to intense price and speed pressure, as well as significant uncertainty.[100] From a factory manager's perspective, "when you go down to pricing and orders, it's like CSR never happened. They [brands] want this, they want that. But where's the money?"[101] To the standard triumvirate of "quality, delivery, and price" that brands use to place orders, "compliance" has, in theory, been added. But as one brand representative put it, "we both know that's bullshit."[102] Short production deadlines and last-minute design changes lie behind many code of conduct violations, especially

---

[95] Interview with compliance initiative representative, Hong Kong, 12/30/10.

[96] Informal interview with auditor, Shenzhen, 12/17/10.

[97] Interview with compliance manager, Hong Kong, 12/29/10. Factory managers sometimes do not even receive the audit report, or descriptions of problems may be in English rather than Chinese (interview with CSR consultant, Guangzhou, 12/18/10).

[98] Interview with compliance manager, Hong Kong, 12/29/10; interview with compliance manager, Shanghai, 7/13/11.

[99] Interview with CSR consultant, Hong Kong, 12/30/10.

[100] Locke 2013; Lund-Thomsen and Lindgreen 2014.

[101] Interview with supplier company staff member, Guangzhou, 11/25/10. See Anner, Bair, and Blasi 2013 on the *decline* of unit costs during the era of transnational private regulation.

[102] Interview with brand compliance manager, Shenzhen, 10/15/10.

excessive, forced, or under-compensated overtime.[103] Although brands have begun to talk about integrating their compliance and sourcing priorities to address this, progress has been slow. One consultant noted, "I haven't seen one company that's produced information to show this is how we're aligning these functions. Some have moved in that direction...but no one has said they've cracked this."[104]

Relatedly, while some evidence indicates that improvements are most likely when brands have stable, committed relationships with suppliers, these kinds of relationships have been rare.[105] Consider the stunning amount of change in the supply chains of Levi Strauss and Timberland—CSR leaders who are among the few to disclose their full supplier lists. In 2005, Levi Strauss had 187 suppliers in China, but only nineteen of these were still supplying the brand in 2014. Of Timberland's sixty-three suppliers in China as of 2008, only seven were still listed as suppliers in 2013.[106] Or consider the sourcing practices of H&M, a member of the FLA that is often admired for its detailed code of conduct. A former employee described how H&M would "dump the order in front of [several] suppliers and ask them for the price...then choose the lowest price among them. In the middle of the year, they might renegotiate prices again."[107]

Uncertainty about future orders can make factory managers reluctant to invest in changes demanded by a particular buyer. Reflecting on the lack of "buy-in" from factory managers in a training and capacity-building project, one practitioner expressed frustration: "Brands say, 'You must do this, but we can't guarantee business.'"[108] Uncertainty can also drive violations, one practitioner explained, since "factories will take as many orders as they can"—even if meeting them will require excessive overtime—"because no one is really giving them that [long-term] commitment on paper."[109]

To manage uncertainty, price pressures, and perhaps hide harsh conditions, factory managers often rely on subcontractors. It is clear that brands have paid far more attention to their first tier of suppliers than to subcontractors, although it is risky to ignore them entirely, since violations there can lead to

---

[103] Locke, Amengual, and Mangla 2009; Impactt Ltd 2005.

[104] Interview with CSR consultant, Hong Kong, 12/30/10. A compliance officer for one brand suggested that his company does take account of compliance ratings when developing relationships with important business partners, but admitted that for smaller suppliers "it's hit and run" (interview with compliance manager, Shanghai, 7/13/11).

[105] Frenkel and Scott 2002; Locke, Amengual, and Mangla 2009.

[106] I took the oldest and newest lists available for each brand and looked for the initial suppliers on the most recent list. It is possible that some factories changed names but remained suppliers and were thus overlooked by my method. But even if 10–20% of factories changed names, we would still be left with stunningly high rates of turnover.

[107] Interview with compliance consultant, Guangzhou, 12/20/10.

[108] Interview with auditor and consultant, Guangzhou, 12/31/10.

[109] Interview with compliance manager, Shanghai, 7/13/11.

public scandals if exposed. As one brand representative put it, there are "'window factories' that can pass compliance and quality and look beautiful," but satellites and unauthorized subcontractors can be difficult to track: "How do you manage these shops? That's what worries me."[110] Most often, brands ask their first-tier suppliers to disclose and monitor the second tier, and some brands will supplement this with their own occasional audits. [111]

In sum, although brands and CSR initiatives have pushed labor standards onto factories in China, they have also weakened this push in a number of ways, and some brands appear happy to receive bland assurances rather than rigorous investigations.

Are certified factories different? Examining SA8000 in China

Despite these problems, it is possible that factories that have been independently certified are superior to factories that have received less—or worse—scrutiny. SA8000 certification is the most challenging and credible global factory certification standard. It asks factories to pay a "living wage", has strict limits on working hours, and calls for "parallel means" of representation where unions are restricted, among other requirements. To ensure quality auditing, certification bodies are accredited by a separate body, Social Accountability Accreditation Services, which also investigates complaints and conducts periodic surveillance audits of the auditors. If factory certification is a meaningful vehicle for enforcing private rules, then we would expect SA8000-certified factories to be distinctive.

THE GROWTH OF FACTORY CERTIFICATION: RAISING THE BAR?
The challenging nature of SA8000's standards was not lost on Chinese industry and government, and at times it appeared that they would try to derail or coopt this standard. A 2004 article in the *People's Daily* worried that SA8000 would be "a new export barrier...that consumes the profits of Chinese exporters and denies them their biggest advantage in foreign trade, inexpensive labor."[112] That year, the Certification and Accreditation Administration (CNCA)—the state agency that oversees certification—announced that

---

[110] Ibid. Another brand admitted that it discovers unauthorized factories each year (interview with compliance staff members, Guangzhou, 11/10/10).

[111] Informal interview with compliance staff members, Dongguan, 11/4/10. The SA8000 standard requires certified factories to "maintain reasonable evidence that the requirements of this standard are being met by suppliers and subcontractors" (SA8000 2004, 9.8). Raising questions about how often this occurs, though, one SA8000-certified factory in China was found subcontracting to nearby factories with far inferior working conditions (Clean Clothes Campaign 2005:25).

[112] Jin 2004:1.

SA8000 certification would require government approval. But over time, it became clear that the government would not interfere, giving Social Accountability International (which issues SA8000) what one practitioner called a "yellow light", if not exactly a "green light" to operate in China.[113]

In 2005, the Chinese National Apparel and Textile Council (CNTAC), a trade association with close ties to the state, introduced its own standard, CSC9000T (China Social Compliance 9000 for Textile and Apparel Industry). Although CSC9000T coopted the discourse of global standards, it ultimately found its niche as more of a "step toward" SA8000 than a direct challenge to it.[114] Tempering its earlier discourse about protectionism, the Chinese government came to embrace the growing field of CSR—including SA8000 certification—and to incorporate it into the party's promotion of the "harmonious society".[115]

With support from a handful of brands—especially Toys R Us, Eileen Fisher, Timberland, and The Gap—SA8000 certification rose to prominence in China. The twenty-eight factories that were certified as of early 2001 grew to 134 by 2006—representing only a tiny percentage of the thousands of export-oriented factories in China but a significant share (12 percent) of SA8000-certified facilities worldwide.[116] By the end of 2011, the number increased to 440 facilities, or 15 percent of the global total.[117] As we will see in the next chapter, SA8000's growth in China contrasts with its stagnation in Indonesia.

Many observers have suggested that some (if not most) of this growth is attributable to lax auditing by certification bodies, who turned a blind eye to problems in order to expand their markets.[118] They are "not interested in saying 'no' [to factories], since they will lose the business", claimed one CSR consultant.[119] Notably, the certification bodies accredited to assess SA8000 compliance are mainly divisions of generalist auditing firms, including those that have been dogged by charges of corruption in China (BV and Intertek). Because the SA8000 standard has strict requirements for working hours (no more than fifty-two hours per week in China with at least one day off per week),[120]

---

[113] Interview with certification initiative representative, Beijing, 12/8/10. Note the difference in CNCA's approach to labor standards and sustainable forestry standards, as described in Chapter 3. It is not entirely clear why SA8000 got a "yellow light" while the FSC got something closer to a "red light." It may be, though, that the implementation of SA8000 had proven to be lax enough that it was not deemed as threatening to domestic business and political interests.

[114] Ibid.   [115] Lin 2010.

[116] SA8000 Certified Facilities, as of Jan. 2001; SA8000 Certified Facilities as of September 30, 2006.

[117] SA8000 Certified Facilities as of December 2010, December 2011.

[118] Interview with researcher, Guangzhou, 12/1/10; interview with NGO representative, Guangzhou, 12/20/10.

[119] Interview with CSR consultant, Beijing, 7/21/10.

[120] SA8000 requirements on working hours are somewhat complicated in China. The SA8000 standard limits weekly working time to forty-eight normal hours plus twelve hours of overtime (sixty hours total). But it also requires companies to respect stricter national laws. Since the normal

wages, and non-discrimination, "it's hard for companies in China to get SA8000 the normal way."[121]

Although it is unclear how often certifiers have ignored problems or blithely accepted false records, it is clear that SA8000-certified factories can vary dramatically. At the upper end, the Lever Shirt factory in Shenzhen, which produces for Banana Republic (a subsidiary of The Gap), prepared for roughly a year before receiving SA8000 certification in 2006.[122] Two years later, China Labor Watch investigated the factory and issued a report criticizing inequality in the industry, since Lever Shirt workers only received $2.11 for producing a shirt that retails for $49.95. But the NGO found little to criticize in the factory's working conditions, noting reasonable temperatures and working hours and calling Lever Shirt a "class A factory".[123] The US-educated CEO of Lever Shirt's parent company in Hong Kong has been widely profiled in the business press for his hope of combining efficiency, social responsibility, and environmental sustainability.[124] Although the company shifted some production to Vietnam as labor costs rose in south China, the factory in Shenzhen remained open and SA8000-certified, with renewals in 2009 and 2012.[125]

At the lower end, consider two certified factories supplying the German café/retailer Tchibo, an SAI-signatory member. When several suppliers did not seek renewal of their SA8000 certificates, Tchibo asked SAI to investigate, revealing factories that should never have been certified. In one factory in Shandong province, workers were making candles by hand over primitive gasoline bottle stoves, without protective equipment or adequate precautions against fire. As one investigator described it, "the office building was nice and modern, but the factory behind it was like 1980s China."[126] Factory managers said they hoped getting certified would reduce audits from brands.[127] At a factory in Fujian province making women's knitted clothing, the investigators found harsh treatment of migrant workers and a group of under-age workers. "They told of coming to the factory just after primary school. They said it's easy to get a fake ID, and the factory recommended how to do it."[128]

There is also evidence that some SA8000-certified factories are far from compliant with working hour rules. Panyu F&C Garment is a Guangzhou-area producer of sports shoes and pants for Billabong, an SAI supporting member. When several workers were interviewed outside the factory, they

---

working week is defined as forty hours in Chinese law, auditors are asked to treat fifty-two hours per week as the standard in China (SA8000:2004 and SA8000:2008 Guidance documents).

[121] Interview with compliance initiative representative, Beijing, 7/15/11.
[122] Snyder 2009.   [123] China Labor Watch 2008:1.
[124] Snyder 2009.   [125] Chu 2013.
[126] Interview with certification initiative representative, Shenzhen, 11/12/10.   [127] Ibid.
[128] Interview with certification initiative representative, Shenzhen, 11/12/10.

reported working roughly seventy hours per week, typically with ten- to eleven-hour days Monday through Saturday and just one Sunday off per month.[129] The factory likely passed its audit by falsifying records and coaching workers, and/or by scheduling the audit for an especially low point in the production season—which may be a common strategy.[130]

These observations raise doubts about the depth of reform required for SA8000 certification. One former certifier noted that managers rarely had to make extensive changes between the pre-assessment and the official audit except to complete additional paperwork: "It's not hard for them to prepare the paperwork and forms—they can just download them from the web."[131] Another knowledgeable practitioner expressed great uncertainty about how frequently major improvements had been made and wished that the SAI office in New York had been paying closer attention to the complications of SA8000 certification in China.[132]

ARE CERTIFIED FACTORIES SUPERIOR IN PAYMENT AND TREATMENT?
Still, even if SA8000-certification did not always motivate major improvements, it is possible that certified factories would be superior to those that had not gone through the certification process. While recognizing shortcomings, practitioners have often suspected that "if a factory had certification, protection of workers would be better" and that working conditions and wages would be superior.[133]

Survey data from factories in Guangdong province allow for a partial assessment of this view. The analyses below will examine whether SA8000-certified factories are distinctive their payment and treatment of workers—specifically, wage levels, on-time payment, and the likelihood of verbal abuse. This is based on a survey of workers in factories in five major manufacturing centers of Guangdong (Shenzhen, Dongguan, Zhongshan, Huizhou, and Foshan) conducted in 2010 by researchers from Peking University's Guanghua School of Management and their local partners from Shenzhen University and the Communist Youth League. Using this data, I will focus on eighty-six surveyed factories making apparel/accessories, footwear/sporting goods, or electronics/appliances, since these are the industries in which SA8000 and codes of

---

[129] Worker interviews, Panyu, 12/12/10.
[130] Interview with certification initiative representative, Shenzhen, 11/12/10.
[131] Interview with compliance manager, Hong Kong, 12/29/10.
[132] Interview with certification initiative representative, Beijing, 12/8/10.
[133] Interview with NGO representative, Guangzhou, 12/20/10; interview with researcher, Guangzhou, 11/8/10. On the other hand, some brands with leading CSR programs dismiss SA8000 certification. As one explained about screening factories, "We would ask if a factory has an audit report that is less than six months old. If not, it's not useful. Factories are changing all the time, so trying to certify them isn't really useful" (interview with compliance manager, Hong Kong, 3/9/14).

conduct have been most prevalent.[134] The researchers selected factories from business directories and personal contacts, seeking variation across cities and industries. They deliberately oversampled factories with SA8000 certification, such that 28 percent of factories in the sample analyzed here were certified.[135] Although this is not a probability sample, it provides a rare opportunity to compare conditions in certified and uncertified factories, controlling for a number of other potentially relevant factors. After excluding cases with missing data on wages, we can examine 1,357 workers from these eighty-six factories.

A baseline comparison of wages casts doubt on the idea that SA8000-certified factories are noticeably superior. The average monthly wage in SA8000-certified factories (1920 rmb or roughly $287) was actually slightly lower than in uncertified factories (1973 rmb or roughly $294), though the difference is not statistically discernible.[136] If we trim the top and bottom 1 percent of the wage distribution to eliminate outliers, the average wage in certified factories remains slightly lower than in uncertified factories (1881 rmb versus 1947 rmb).[137]

This simple comparison could of course obscure relevant differences in the types of workers surveyed, as well as other characteristics of these factories. It is important, therefore, to shift to regression analyses that control for both individual and factory-level characteristics. Since the respondents are nested in particular factories, I will use multi-level models that include both individual and factory-level variables.[138] At the individual level, the analyses control for a number of factors that may shape payment and treatment, including sex, position, education, work experience, and *hukou* status (i.e., urban or rural official residency). At the factory level, they control for size, the type of

[134] The original research surveyed workers and managers in more than 170 establishments—mostly manufacturers of various sorts (e.g., metal, plastic, or paper products) as well as some in the service sector.

[135] This was confirmed based on SAI's list of certified facilities as of June 2010. Supplemental analyses show that larger factories and those that primarily export are more likely to be certified, as are those who sell primarily to buyers who ask for compliance with labor standards.

[136] Both a simple t-test for the difference in means and a more appropriate multi-level model with SA8000 certification as the only predictor find no discernible difference (p-value < 0.32 and 0.73 respectively).

[137] Here, a simple t-test suggests that certified factories may pay significantly less (p-value < 0.08) but a more appropriate multi-level model with SA8000 as the only predictor indicates that the difference is not discernible (p-value < 0.54). I will proceed with the trimmed data (excluding the top and bottom 1%, that is, below 500 rmb or above 4850 rmb per month) to guard against the possibility of extreme values obscuring a link between certification and wages. The results remain substantively identical if the untrimmed measure of wages is used.

[138] While having more individual responses per factory would allow more sophisticated multi-level models with random slopes and cross-level interactions, having a reasonable number of groups (in this case, eighty-one factories) is most important for allowing one to estimate basic multi-level models with random intercepts (Robson and Pevalin 2015). The main benefit of multi-level models is that they account for the non-independence of responses within factories while also estimating the amount of variation that lies across factories versus across individuals (Singer 1998).

product, foreign ownership, and export-orientation, in addition to SA8000 certification. The results below are based on responses from 911 to 1,179 individual workers across eighty-one factories (for an average of 11.2 to 14.6 workers per factory, depending on the outcome of interest) that are available after incorporating control variables and cleaning the survey data.[139] Despite its imperfections, this data is extraordinarily valuable for understanding the on-the-ground meanings of factory certification in China. The key results are presented below, and the full models are included in the Appendix.

Note that since workers are often coached to please auditors, one might expect those in certified factories to over-report good conditions and under-report bad ones. Thus, one might find false positives—that is, a correlation between SA8000 certification and wages or working conditions based on differences in reporting rather than differences in performance. This possibility must be kept in mind. But as we will see, the analyses reveal few positive associations with SA8000 certification, minimizing the substantive importance of this methodological challenge. Note also that if a link between certification and wages or conditions were found, this would not necessarily imply a causal relationship. There are numerous challenges involved in inferring causal relationships with the data at hand. Nevertheless, if certification is a meaningful indicator of superior conditions, whether causal or not, then we ought to see signs of this in the data.

The SA8000 standard takes a stronger position on wages than any other voluntary standard—calling for a "living wage" that provides discretionary income and banning all disciplinary fines. Although not a requirement, auditors are also encouraged to examine whether wages exceed the prevailing industry wage (as well as the minimum wage) (SA8000:2004 Guidance document). Are SA8000-certified factories actually distinctive in their wage levels? The results from the multi-level regression models shown in Figure 5.1 suggest that they are not, consistent with the simple comparison of means above. Controlling for relevant individual-level factors (e.g, position, work experience, education, sex, *hukou* status) and factory-level factors (e.g., size, ownership, and

---

[139] Because these were self-administered surveys, it is possible that workers were confused or careless at various points in the survey. With help from a research assistant, I identified four types of problems that could be detected in various parts of the lengthy survey: (1) A logical contradiction (such as choosing "none of the above" *in addition* to other answers, or answering a question that should be skipped as not applicable based on a previous response), (2) a low level of variation (as might be generated by simply marking all answers down a column), (3) a high level of variation where you would not expect it (namely, in several similar questions about the employer, which might reflect arbitrary marking or confusion), and (4) carelessness (namely, in marking similar scores for two questions asking essentially the same thing but in opposite ways—i.e., "managers are honest" and "managers do not do what they say they will"). To maximize the quality of the data without excluding respondents for isolated mistakes, I have dropped any individual who exhibited more than one of these problems. This resulted in dropping ninety-three individuals from the sample.

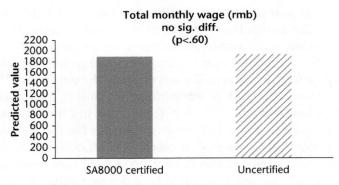

Figure 5.1. Monthly wages: Predicted values in certified and uncertified factories in Guangdong province

exporting), workers' monthly wages are not discernibly different in certified and uncertified factories. (The control variables are held at their means to produce the predicted values in Figure 5.1.) Whether the lowest paid workers in certified factories are receiving a "living wage" is more difficult to say, but there is no evidence of a wage premium for working in a certified factory.

A series of supplemental models (shown in the Appendix) reveal no evidence of a wage premium linked to buyer-imposed labor standards, including but not limited to SA8000. This includes adding a more general measure for whether most of a factory's clients impose labor standards (of any sort), which reveals no evidence of a wage premium and does not alter the results for SA8000 certification.[140] Since it is possible that some of the control variables could be mediating—and potentially obscuring—a relationship between SA8000 and wages, an additional set of models (in Appendix Table 5.2) remove the most likely suspects for this role.[141] Here again, no statistically discernible difference in wages at certified and uncertified factories can be found. In fact, across a number of different supplemental analyses, there is no evidence of a wage premium in SA8000-certified factories.[142]

---

[140] This measure is based on a question asking managers what percentage of their clients set labor standards for the factory. Unfortunately, the question was not asked in a way that allows for a detailed look at buyers' rules or degree of scrutiny, but it does allow for a comparison of factories where the majority of buyers ask for labor standards to those facing less buyer scrutiny. Analyses later in the chapter will show how this matters.

[141] This group of most likely suspects is based on evidence of that a control variable was linked to both SA8000 certification and wages (in either bivariate or multivariate models) and a clear rationale for a confounding role. In particular, certified factories might do a better job than others at retaining workers and providing non-working days and may be more likely among factories that produce primarily for export or have foreign ownership.

[142] The coefficient for SA8000 certification is always negative and usually quite far from statistical significance.

Even if they do not pay more, certified factories may be more likely to pay workers on time, while workers in uncertified factories have to cope with delayed wages. The SA8000 standard requires factories to have formal management systems for social accountability and labor conditions, so one might expect more rationalized and predictable payment practices. An initial look at the survey data, however, shows that approximately 25 percent of workers in SA8000-certified factories and 26 percent of workers in uncertified factories reported having their wages delayed at some point. As shown in Figure 5.2, when controlling for a range of other individual and factory-level factors, the predicted probability of wages being delayed is not significantly different in certified and uncertified factories. The analyses in the Appendix do suggest that wages are less likely to be delayed in factories where most buyers impose some set of standards (with a predicted probability of 0.16 compared to 0.32 for factories without this level of buyer-imposed standards). This is consistent with other evidence in this chapter that private regulation puts a premium on formalization. But there is no evidence that SA8000 is distinctive in this regard.[143]

Finally, certification might mark more humane workplaces. Indeed, the SA8000 standard explicitly prohibits verbal abuse by supervisors, stating that "the company shall not engage in or support the use of corporal punishment, mental or physical coercion, and verbal abuse." If one simply compares the baseline chances of verbal abuse being reported (as witnessed or experienced), it does appear that certified factories are superior to others. Verbal abuse was reported by 21.8 percent of workers in certified factories and 29.9 percent of workers in uncertified factories. But as shown in Figure 5.2, once one controls for other factors that shape the likelihood of witnessing/experiencing abuse— most notably, factory size—there is not a statistically discernible difference between certified and uncertified factories.[144] As with the previous analyses, this finding remains with other adjustments to the models in the Appendix, including the inclusion of the more general measure of standards and the exclusion of potentially confounding mediating variables.[145]

---

[143] The supplemental models in this case remove factory size and industry, since working in smaller factories and in the labor-intensive apparel industry raises the chances of having wages delayed. The findings about both SA8000 and other standards remain the same in these and other supplemental models.

[144] The predicted probabilities in Figures 5.2, 5.3, and 5.6 reflect both the fixed effects and random intercepts from the multi-level models, following the approach described here: http://stats.idre.ucla.edu/stata/faq/how-can-i-estimate-probabilities-that-include-the-random-effects-in-xtmelogit/. The simpler approach of using the "margins" command in Stata produces substantively identical results.

[145] In this case, the most likely confounding mediators are factory size (which is associated with higher rates of observed abuse, perhaps simply due to greater observational opportunities) and industry (with higher rates of abuse observed in footwear/sporting goods factories.)

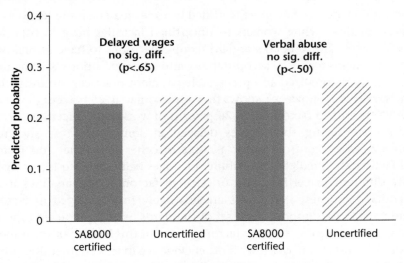

Figure 5.2. Delayed wages and verbal abuse: Predicted probabilities in certified and uncertified factories in Guangdong province

These indicators are not exhaustive, and unfortunately the survey did not ask appropriate questions about working hours and workplace safety. Gaining additional indicators and better causal leverage would be important for a full assessment of SA8000 in China. Nevertheless, these analyses suggest that SA8000 has failed to provide a reliable and systematic symbol of superior wages and working conditions. This does not mean that factory certification is meaningless. Instead, as the next sections will show, the practical meaning of SA8000 and other private labor standards has been defined and redefined through the process of implementation. In particular, as we will see, implementation has diffused particular managerial discourses and practices while sidestepping crucial issues of labor rights. We will see some additional evidence of this in a return to this survey data later in the chapter.

The Problem of Rights

The central contradiction of voluntary labor standards in China is that standards gain global legitimacy by invoking the right of "freedom of association", but this is impossible to guarantee in the Chinese context. The problem is not merely that the Chinese government has laws against unauthorized assembly; it is that the All-China Federation of Trade Unions (ACFTU) is the only authorized union. The ACFTU is not merely a "company union" or coopted by government, it is a bureaucratic arm of the Chinese Communist Party, with a primary purpose to "act as a transmission belt conveying worker concerns and suggestions to higher levels while ensuring that central policies and edicts reach the workplace."[146]

The ACFTU had few outposts in foreign enterprises in the 1980s and 1990s, so the rise of export-oriented factories and dormitory labor regime "emerged in a political context in which ACFTU-subordinate unions were almost entirely absent."[147] As labor unrest increased in the late 1990s and early 2000s, the ACFTU began to establish a presence in foreign enterprises: Typically, local union officials would negotiate with factory owners to establish "paper unions" and appoint a chairperson, often a personnel or human resource manager.[148]

As a result, at the factory level, if a trade union exists, it is typically feeble and akin to a "welfare department" of the company, responsible for sponsoring entertainment or sporting events.[149] At the provincial and district-levels, ACFTU officials are often part of the "total development machine", prioritizing economic growth over other concerns.[150] And at the central level, the ACFTU is deeply connected—"in structure and personnel" to the party-state.[151] Indeed, officials are frequently brought in from other parts of government, preventing the ACFTU from drifting toward greater autonomy.[152]

Central ACFTU officials have promoted important legal reforms, like the 2007 Labor Contract Law, to reign in the precariousness of work.[153] The law strengthened workers' individual rights by requiring written contracts and allowing employees to press legal claims for illegal dismissals and inadequate severance payments. Once the law went into effect, formal complaints against employers skyrocketed, as workers exercised bottom-up enforcement and sought to "use the law as a weapon."[154] But ACFTU officials have been far less supportive of collective demands from workers. When labor unrest occurs, ACFTU officials—especially at local and provincial levels—often play the role of controlling or repressing workers rather than representing them. When Honda workers in Foshan went on strike in 2010, for instance, the local

---

[146] Gallagher 2004:26. Unions in socialist countries in Eastern Europe took a similar form at an earlier point, but while they had to adapt to political liberalization in the late 1980s and early 1990s, the ACFTU did not. In addition, while unions in Singapore and South Korea were coopted by authoritarian states, they were "institutionally distinct from their governments and had to engage in grassroots mobilization to maintain and strengthen their power" (Liu 2010:32). The ACFTU, by contrast, expanded from state-owned enterprises to export-oriented, foreign enterprises in a decidedly top-down fashion.

[147] Friedman 2013:304.

[148] Liu 2011; Friedman 2013; Gallagher and Dong 2011. Occasional attempts by workers to contest this model have been repressed or coopted by union officials, factory management, or both. See Liu 2011 for several examples.

[149] Liu 2011:163.   [150] Gallagher 2004:29.   [151] Gallagher and Dong 2011:14.

[152] Friedman 2013.   [153] Gallagher and Dong 2011.   [154] Lee 2007a; Gallagher 2005.

union federation mobilized thugs to break up the strike and urge workers to pull back.[155]

Although the ACFTU claims a monopoly on the representation of workers, a variety of NGOs intended to assist migrant workers also exist. Activists estimate that there may be as many as 100–150 such labor NGOs in mainland China, and scholars have identified roughly thirty in the largest coastal cities alone.[156] They help migrant workers seek redress from employers, file legal claims, and learn their legal rights—sometimes by operating workers' centers. While some are government-organized NGOs (GONGOs) or heavily coopted by local governments, others have managed their relationship with local governments in ways that allow for a small bit of autonomy.[157] Grassroots NGOs and local governments frequently exist in what Anthony Spires (2011) calls a state of "contingent symbiosis": Local officials will tolerate NGOs so long as they help them to manage local problems, minimize unrest, and avoid scrutiny from higher levels of government, "but if an NGO's work draws too much attention to the failings of local officials or if it oversteps a fuzzy and frequently shifting political line, the organization can be disciplined or even closed down."[158] Control and repression of NGOs appears to have increased as rising labor unrest has touched a nerve in the party. In 2012, twelve NGO-sponsored workers' centers were shut down, mostly by being evicted by their landlord or having their water and electricity cut. As one described it, on May Day in 2012,

> we had some activities in a square, and police took us in and kept us until midnight. After that, our center was asked by the landlord to move out.... Since then, most of us are [staying]—not underground—but low key. We moved upstairs, and since then, not many workers come. The authorities are not ready to remove us but not ready to see us be there.[159]

---

[155] Chan and Hui 2012; Friedman 2013. With continued strikes, rising expectations among workers, and reformist tendencies within the Chinese government, the ACFTU's organizing strategies have become more varied (Liu 2010). But it remains mainly a vehicle of social control. Friedman (2013) dubs it a system of "appropriated representation," in which occasional insurgency at the point of production leads central ACFTU officials to push for stronger regulation but maintains "the atomization of the working class at the point of production, thereby rendering these legislative changes ineffectual" (p. 305).

[156] Meeting with NGO representatives, Hong Kong, 3/10/14; Lee and Shen 2011.

[157] Cheng, Ngok, and Zhuang 2010; Lee and Shen 2011. Some NGOs have found a bit more autonomy by becoming commercial legal service providers. As a representative of Chun Feng Labor Dispute Arbitration Counseling and Service Center—the same NGO involved in the Yue Yuen strike—explained, "If we did this for free, the officials would become very nervous. If you become commercial, they leave you alone. Now, they see that we charge a fee for our service, they thought our organization has changed" (quoted in Lee and Shen 2011:181).

[158] Spires 2011:12.

[159] Meeting with NGO representatives, Hong Kong, 3/10/14. On the other hand, one leader interviewed by Spires expressed a more optimistic view (albeit prior to the crackdown of 2012). "The way our legal system is set up, as long as the government law doesn't prohibit it, we can do it.... We don't work with the ACFTU on anything. They don't interfere with us, either.... you can

Overall, although domestic governance in China has become more responsive to migrant workers than it was in the early 1990s, the Chinese Communist Party has clung tightly to its power to decide how far those rights and protections can go. As Ching Kwan Lee and Yonghong Zhang (2013) argue, in its relationship to citizens and activism, the Chinese regime has evolved into a form of "bargained authoritarianism" in which local government officials "purchase" social stability by buying off protest leaders, coopting them, or resorting to more overt repression if necessary. Late in 2015, authorities embraced the more repressive mode, detaining a number of staff members from labor NGOs in Guangdong province, and ultimately holding and sentencing several from the Panyu Workers' Center.[160] Individual rights have expanded, and strikes have pushed the limits of the dormitory labor regime, but collective labor rights remain heavily controlled, with a grip that has gotten tighter over time.

Navigating the contradiction

Can brands, auditors, and certifiers guarantee workers' rights in this setting? Despite legally restricted association, constraints on NGOs, and the character of ACFTU unions, nearly all private rules endorse freedom of association. On closer inspection, many are written in ways that sidestep the issue in China. For instance, VF's code of conduct simply asks suppliers to "comply with . . . local and national laws and regulations regarding Freedom of Association and Collective Bargaining," which in China would mean a *lack* of freedom of association.[161] The WRAP factory certification program asks only that facilities "respect the right of employees to exercise their *lawful* rights of free association and collective bargaining," similarly subsuming apparently empowering rules to repressive laws.[162]

Yet some initiatives have recognized the contradiction and looked for ways to resolve it—that is, without asking brands to forego production in China. The SA8000 standard calls for freedom of association, invoking ILO Convention 87, but also stated (in the original version) that a company seeking certification "shall, in those situations in which the right to freedom of association and collective bargaining are restricted under law, facilitate

---

bring workers together in other ways to accomplish similar functions to a union. You just can't call it a union, because that would be illegal" (quoted in Spires 2011:23).

[160] Wong 2015; Lai 2016.

[161] VF Global Compliance Principles, https://business-humanrights.org/sites/default/files/webform/VF%20Global%20Compliance%20Principles_0.pdf

[162] WRAP Principles, http://www.wrapcompliance.org/12-principles, emphasis added.

parallel means of independent and free association and bargaining."[163] Practically speaking, "parallel means" came to mean elected worker committees, and by the 2008 version of the SA8000 standard, companies seeking certification in China were simply asked to "allow workers to freely elect their own representatives."[164] Reebok took an ambitious approach in implementing its Human Rights Production Standards in two factories in China, sponsoring elections for factory-level trade union leaders. If successful, these initiatives would suggest that private rules *can* transcend domestic constraints and empower Chinese workers, even if only on the margins. As we will see, though, these efforts have been constrained, reconfigured, and ultimately blunted.

REEBOK'S FORAY INTO UNION DEMOCRACY

Spurred by an ambitious compliance team, Reebok began a project in 2001 to allow trade union leaders at two factories in south China—KTS in Shenzhen and Shunda in Fuzhou—to be elected. Both were relatively large factories (roughly 5,000 and 13,000 employees, respectively) that had long-term partnerships with Reebok and depended on its orders, so the brand had both the relationships and the leverage needed to push its suppliers to accept this groundbreaking experiment.[165]

KTS managers had already made a number of reforms to comply with Reebok's standards, including prominently posting Chinese labor law in the factory.[166] Staff from the factory's Counseling Center helped Reebok's compliance staff to explain the election to workers, solicit nominations, and hold brief speeches by sixty-two candidates. When the election occurred, just over half of the twenty-six individuals who were elected were production workers, and a popular supervisor who had fared well in the election became the de facto chair of the union's executive committee.[167]

Early on, the new committee was able to push management to end monetary penalties and increase workers' benefits. But conflict within the committee

---

[163] The Ethical Trading Initiative's Base Code adopted a similar approach: "Where the right to freedom of association and collective bargaining is restricted under law, the employer facilitates, and does not hinder, the development of parallel means for independent and free association and bargaining."

[164] "When operating in countries where trade union activity is unlawful or where free and democratic trade union activity is not allowed, business partners shall respect this principle by allowing workers to freely elect their own representatives with whom the company can enter into dialogue about workplace issues." BSCI, which is closely linked to SAI, uses similar language. Eventually, the FLA adopted a scaled-down version of this language, asking employers to "not obstruct legal alternative means of workers association" (FLA Workplace Code of Conduct and Compliance Benchmarks, Revised October 5, 2011).

[165] Chan 2009. This section draws on research by Chan and others, as well as information from my interviews, which allows for a fairly detailed reconstruction of the cases.

[166] Ibid.   [167] Ibid.:8.

coincided with a change of ownership in the factory in late 2002—and the new owner took a much harder line, cutting a number of benefits.[168] The committee soon faced recalcitrance from management, a lack of confidence from workers, and little support from Reebok, which had stepped back once the election had taken place. The committee "gradually began to be reabsorbed into the official trade union"—and ACFTU officials rebuffed Reebok's call for a second election in 2003.[169]

Conditions at the Shunda factory had initially been worse than at KTS, with harsh treatment by supervisors and high turnover among production workers. Reebok's team had to push hard to get factory managers to allow the election. Many of the 180 candidates gave short and generic speeches, but a few were more challenging. Workers are "helpless, wronged, and angry that we did not have any means to defend ourselves," said one candidate, with another calling the existing union "just an empty shell."[170] Several of the more challenging candidates ended up being among the thirty-one representatives elected.

Local ACFTU officials had initially acceded to the election, but after the incumbent union chairperson suffered a humiliating defeat, union officials began to co-opt the new leadership and to criticize Reebok, "saying that unionizing is a Chinese government matter of a political nature, and that Reebok should not be taking part."[171] Union officials intervened "to dampen the enthusiasm of the more active elected committee members," while Reebok representatives reminded the elected leaders "not to be so radical.... We suggested they focus on activities to do with employee welfare and entertainment in the first half-year."[172] As relations with factory managers became conflictual, the more demanding elected leaders found they had no organizational backing and remained vulnerable to discipline and harassment from their direct supervisors. As one observer put it, some of the leaders "had real potential... [But] they stayed on the production line and were subject to harassment from management."[173] One leader was forced out of the factory, and the committee chair moved closer to management, rebuffing workers and fellow committee members.[174] When researchers returned to Shunda five years after the election, they found that working conditions had gotten worse—with more intense production targets and long hours, averaging 300 hours per month. Subsequent union leaders had not been chosen through elections, and the union's leadership committee was largely inactive.[175]

As Anita Chan (2009) puts it, in both factories, "democratically elected union committees had become passive and submissive to management and

---

[168] Ibid.:13–14.   [169] Ibid.:17, 14.   [170] Quoted in Chan 2009:11.
[171] Lee 2007b:6; Yu 2008b.
[172] Chan 2009:15; Reebok representative, quoted in Yu 2008b: 290.
[173] Interview with researcher, Beijing, 12/9/10.   [174] Chan 2009:16; Yu 2008b:292–3.
[175] Lee 2007b.

to the upper-level trade unions" within two years.[176] Reebok had stepped back once the elections occurred, while factory management had turned hostile, and trade union officials outside the factory had proven uninterested in—if not hostile to—promoting shop-floor leadership.[177] Ultimately, the Reebok experiment must be judged a failure. There are hints of spillover effects, such as the one elected representative left the factory and began working with labor NGOs.[178] More broadly, the idea of electing factory-level union representatives began to spread, though this appears more directly related to the Honda strike of 2010 and other labor unrest than to CSR experiments.[179] There is also evidence that the pendulum swung back again, as union officials "began to see unauthorized people being trade union representatives—and made sure it didn't happen again."[180] When a reformist leader of Guangzhou Federation of Trade Unions had to assure a group of international scholars that the union will now stand on the side of workers, rather than mediating between workers and managers, it was both a sign of change and a stark reminder of how much would be needed before meaningful worker representation could emerge within the existing structure.[181]

SOCIAL ACCOUNTABILITY INTERNATIONAL AND "PARALLEL MEANS" OF REPRESENTATION

The SA8000 standard asks managers to facilitate (in the original version) or allow (in later version) elected worker committees, but evidence of well-functioning committees in certified factories is scant. In many cases, it appears that auditors have paid little attention to this part of the standard. One practitioner explained that auditors typically assess the status of committees simply by asking managers if a committee exists or perhaps asking for some documentation. "CB [certification body] auditors don't really understand the committee," this person explained.[182] SA8000 guidelines suggest that auditors seek information about worker representation from local NGOs, but in China, this has sometimes led auditors to "just go to the local government

---

[176] Chan 2009:16.

[177] This seems to have reflected not only the ACFTU's interest in monopolizing the political space of worker rights, but also in controlling the purse strings of union activity. One underlying tension in the project was about the division of resources within the trade union structure, with Reebok pushing for more money to go to the factory-level union and ACFTU officials resisting this (interview with researcher, Beijing, 3/12/14).

[178] Interview with researcher, Beijing, 12/9/10.

[179] In some parts of Guangdong province, the ACFTU has allowed elections to occur, in line with new laws on "collective consultation" and "democratic management of enterprises".

[180] Interview with researcher, Beijing, 3/12/14. See also Friedman (2013) on the limits of participatory reforms after the Honda strike.

[181] Notes from International Center for Joint Labor Research conference, Guangzhou, 10/18/10.

[182] Interview with certification initiative representative, Shenzhen, 11/12/10.

department and trade union office near the factory"—the very structures that committees were intended to bypass.[183]

In one outerwear factory in Guangdong province that supplied Timberland—the Chai Da factory (later called Ying Xie)—SAI staff invested heavily in building an elected worker committee and touted it publicly once it was formed. Factory managers had a history of falsifying records for Timberland's auditors, and even as improvements occurred in safety and working hours, there were still high rates of turnover and payment below the minimum wage.[184] Timberland nominated the factory for a training program being developed by SAI in 2003. The next year, representatives of SAI joined with mainland labor NGOs to conduct training sessions for the factory's entire workforce, helping them to identify gaps between factory conditions and legal and international standards.[185] This training also began the process of forming an elected worker committee. After overcoming initial reluctance by factory management, the training team organized an election of twelve representatives—one for each of the factory's production groups—insisting on production workers, not supervisors, being representatives.[186] This established "China's first independent workers' committee in the garment industry."[187] SAI and its NGO partners supported the committee's work for the first year, seeking to promote "long-term dialogue and cooperation" rather than merely focusing on short-term demands regarding "quotidian issues such as food quality, bathroom cleanliness, and the abundance of drinking water."[188]

Within several years, the committee had organized another election, and follow-up visits had found lower levels of worker turnover, higher rates of worker satisfaction with management, and even a small raise, after the committee helped to document workers' rising costs of living.[189] Managers improved the food and housing at the committee's request, though they refused the committee's request to open up their business records.[190] The factory manager claimed that reforms had increased costs by 30 percent but expressed confidence that "we've been doing this long enough that we can survive."[191] SAI touted the factory as evidence of the business case for social responsibility—showing that "in a rapidly developing Chinese economy a company does not have to choose between being profitable and socially responsible."[192] Alexandra Harney's popular book, *The China Price*, profiled both the factory's visionary manager and two migrant workers who had found

---

[183] Ibid.   [184] Harney 2008; Ma 2009.
[185] This included the Institute for Contemporary Observation, a mainland labor NGO based in Shenzhen, which was becoming involved in a number of CSR initiatives.
[186] Interview with researchers, Guangzhou, 10/20/10.   [187] Ma 2009:17.
[188] Ibid.:17.   [189] Ma 2009.   [190] Interview with researchers, Guangzhou, 10/20/10.
[191] Quoted in Harney 2008; Xin 2009.   [192] Ma 2009:6.

their voices through the committee's work.[193] Chinese scholars highlighted the factory as an example of improved labor rights and corporate social responsibility.[194]

But the project was short-lived. In 2008, the factory lost its orders from Timberland—perhaps in the midst of restructuring after Timberland's sportswear operations were taken over by PVH (Phillips-Van Heusen).[195] The state of the factory after that point is unclear. When a Chinese researcher who had previously studied the factory attempted to follow up in 2010 (at my request), he reported that the manager who had sponsored the reforms had left and thus the researcher no longer had access to the company.[196] The factory manager had previously discussed the need to move inland where wages were lower, so it is possible that the factory moved or was reorganized.[197] In any case, just a few years after this highly touted experiment, the advocates and scholars who had invested so much in the factory were unsure of its status.[198]

SAI is not the only initiative that has promoted worker committees, but few committees have gone as far as Chai Da's. Some factories have worker representatives on health and safety committees, and others have canteen committees, since "management is always trying to figure out why workers don't like the food," but these kinds of groups rarely exceed their narrow bounds.[199] In one factory, worker representatives helped to align the canteen's offerings with workers' diverse tastes, but their influence on wages was limited to *explaining to other workers* how wage-setting in a team-based production system worked, not to actually influencing wage-setting.[200] Like the worker welfare committees at Yue Yuen, committees often have narrow agendas that do not include wages, the work process, or respect for rights. Even rudimentary committees can be difficult to sustain given the pressures of production. High turnover makes it difficult to sustain effective groups, while high production quotas or piecerates make workers reluctant to volunteer—and managers difficult to convince not to penalize workers for taking time for committee work.[201]

---

[193] Harney 2008.   [194] Huang 2008; Huang and Guo 2006.

[195] The Ying Xie factory is disclosed in Timberland's list of suppliers in 2008 but not in 2009, but the circumstances behind this are not clear.

[196] Email correspondence, 11/5/10.

[197] Interview with researchers, Guangzhou, 10/20/10.

[198] Although SAI had sponsored the project, the Chai Da/Ying Xie factory had never actually gotten SA8000 certified.

[199] Interview with CSR consultant, Guangzhou, 10/26/10.

[200] Interview with supplier companies' staff, Guangzhou, 11/25/10.

[201] Interview with NGO representative, Beijing, 12/6/10; interview with compliance staff members, Guangzhou, 11/10/10; interview with CSR consultant, Beijing, 7/21/10. For a litany of reasons why committees in Chinese factories have struggled, as explained by an SAI board member, see Congressional-Executive Commission on China 2003.

Outside the factory, rapidly churning labor markets and the lack of protection for shop floor leaders have hindered committees and other "alternative" vehicles of worker representation, in spite of occasional support from brands and NGOs. As one practitioner put it, "SAI can do something artificially, if you pump money and time into it. Reebok too. But the larger atmosphere doesn't support this."[202] A scholar who had supported both the Reebok and SAI projects concurred: "The moment you withdraw, it fails."[203]

The weakness and fragility of worker committees casts doubt on the ability of private initiatives to transcend domestic constraints. Reebok and SAI developed ambitious projects that seemed to work in the short term, but they soon imploded or faded away. As we will see, what has taken hold to a much greater extent are less ambitious managerial approaches that substitute *communication* for representation.

Managerialism and the Constructed Meaning of Compliance

It should be clear that full compliance with the most demanding private rules is nearly impossible for apparel and footwear factories in China. And yet many factories are being certified or otherwise deemed compliant. How does this occur?

One part of the answer is that management systems are being substituted for performance outcomes. Auditors can more easily assess whether factories have elaborate procedures for managing health and safety, hiring, and grievances than they can assess whether workplaces are actually safe, non-discriminatory, and respectful. In one audit that I witnessed, auditors had concerns about whether hazardous chemicals were accurately labeled, but they did not have the capacity to actually test the chemicals—only to ask factory management to improve its disclosure.[204] In addition, if factories are valued for business reasons but struggle to meet the letter of the standard, auditors and compliance offices can refocus their attention on whether there is a *system* in place that could lead to eventual improvement.[205] As one compliance official put it, "I'm not here to drop factories. I need factories. I just need to know why you're not able to do what we're asking. So I'm pushing to have a system in place... When I come back, I'm verifying the process, not particular violations anymore."[206] These examples suggest that the substitution of process for performance is especially likely when

---

[202] Interview with CSR consultant, Guangzhou, 12/18/10.
[203] Notes from International Center for Joint Labor Research conference, Guangzhou, 10/18/10.
[204] Audit notes, Shenzhen, 12/18/10.   [205] Audit notes, Dongguan, 11/4/10.
[206] Interview with compliance manager, Shanghai, 7/13/11.

performance outcomes are difficult to measure or when performance is routinely below compliance.

In the best case, management systems can educate managers and focus their attention. As one practitioner put it, "Once you certify, the HR and compliance people are more knowledgeable. You have to at least do paperwork and set up systems...At least it makes the people in charge knowledgeable. Whether they're performing well is hard to say."[207] But the rise of management systems can also mean little more than the "institutionalization of paperwork", as factory managers produce flimsy policy statements and numerous records (accurate or not)—of hours worked, trainings conducted, and incidents logged.[208]

Management systems are being applied not only to working conditions but to workers' rights. The difficulty of implementing freedom of association principles in China has led standards about workers' rights to be translated into the promotion of better worker-management *communication*. This is a highly managerialist way of operationalizing collective labor rights. This managerial translation of workers' rights can be seen in the work of the Fair Labor Association in China and in further analyses of the survey data from factories in Guangdong province, both of which are described below.

Substituting communication for representation: an analysis of FLA monitoring

The Fair Labor Association's accredited independent monitors assessed 352 factories in China between 2002 and 2011. The factories produced for FLA member companies (e.g., Nike, H&M, PVH) and were selected for monitoring by the FLA staff. To examine how the FLA's independent monitoring program dealt with the problem of worker representation, I selected a random sample of 116 publicly disclosed "tracking charts" (⅓ of the total), which describe the monitor's findings and remediation plans.[209]

To begin, we can see an evolution in how the FLA and its monitors dealt with the contradiction between freedom of association principles and the Chinese context. In the early years, they essentially ignored it. Two-thirds of the tracking charts in 2002–3 left the section on Freedom of Association and Collective Bargaining completely blank. Starting in 2004, the tracking charts began to include a boilerplate comment: "[T]he Trade Union Act prevents the establishment of trade unions independent of the sole official trade

---

[207] Interview with auditor, Shenzhen, 11/12/10.   [208] Sum and Pun 2005.

[209] This period captures the vast majority of FLA monitoring in China, since 2002 was the first year of auditing and audits became less frequent after 2011 as the FLA put greater emphasis on capacity-building. I took a simple random sample of ⅓ of all 352 unique reports. A sampled factory in Hong Kong was excluded from coding, leaving me with a sample of 116 reports.

union—the All-China Federation of Trade Unions (ACFTU).... As a consequence, all factories in China fall short of the ILO standards on the right to organize and bargain collectively."[210] Often the boilerplate was included without any further information on worker representation in the factory (43 percent of the time between 2004 and 2007). Over time, substantive comments and findings of various sorts began to appear. Between 2006 and 2011, 81 percent of the reports included at least some discussion of worker representation, compared to just 31 percent from 2002 to 2005.

These reports reveal several practices standing in as assurances of worker representation. First, some factory managers were just asked to create a policy stating that freedom of association is respected—in effect ignoring the forces outside the factory that made this impossible. For instance, at a Nordstrom supplier, monitors merely requested and received a "written factory policy regarding labor unions and independent worker representation."[211] At an Eddie Bauer supplier, the plan was that "the factory will issue the memo to let all workers know that they can freely set up a trade union and workers representative in the factory."[212]

Second, FLA members and monitors sometimes accepted ACFTU-affiliated unions as legitimate vehicles of worker representation. For instance, the monitors of one Nordstrom supplier cited the number of workers who had joined the ACFTU-affiliated union as evidence of compliance with the FLA's freedom of association provisions.[213]

Third, some FLA member companies promoted worker committees, like those found at Yue Yuen and Chai Da/Ying Xie. At a PVH supplier, monitors noted approvingly that "factory management has taken the initiative and has formed two independent groups; one is for all workers and one is primarily for the youth in the factory, even though formal unions are not recognized in China."[214] Illustrating the challenges of committees, though, a practitioner who worked with the FLA in China noted that few committees have actually formed, since "management doesn't want workers to be stronger... [and] brands don't pay a lot of attention to this, due to legal restrictions."[215]

---

[210] The comment also expressed some optimism that recent Chinese laws would facilitate greater consultation between workers, union officials, and management.

[211] Tracking chart, factory 08001547D, 2005.

[212] Tracking chart, factory 020015128B, 2003.

[213] Tracking chart, factory 08001542D, 2005. In a few cases, the reports reveal factory managers promising that elections of ACFTU union representatives will be held, only to show these promises fading away in follow-up visits.

[214] Tracking chart, factory 10011551A, 2001.

[215] Interview with compliance consultant, Guangzhou, 12/20/10. This person also explained that "corrective action plans on this [worker representation] usually involve training workers to tell them they have freedom of association rights to build a union or workers' committee without interference from management and local government.... [But] I'm not sure the workers' own union could actualize in China at this point."

Table 5.1. Navigating freedom of association in China: Approaches in FLA monitoring, 2002–11

Approach to dealing with worker representation	% of reports
None (no substantive discussion of the issue)	26.7%
One or more of the approaches below	73.3%
Internal grievance procedure	33.6%
Worker committee	31.0%
ACFTU union	30.2%
Policy stating support for freedom of association	20.7%

Most commonly, FLA members and monitors took a highly procedural and managerial approach to the problem of worker representation. (See Table 5.1.) Specifically, in nearly 34 percent of reports, they told factories to create internal grievance procedures, which could improve worker-management communication and potentially stave off strikes and other disruptions. The report on a factory used by Nike and Patagonia noted that the companies' "shared objective is to strengthen contract manufacturers' internal grievance systems, so that direct involvement by Nike and Patagonia in employee grievances should be considered a last resort."[216] At a factory producing collegiate-licensed floor mats and seat covers, auditors endorsed managers' plan to install a suggestion box, which "fits best with local culture and allows the employees to communicate without fear of punishment or prejudice."[217] Among FLA members, Nike and Nordstrom were especially active in promoting internal grievance mechanisms in China, while H&M took something of an "all of the above" approach, calling for free association policies, committees, and grievance mechanisms.

Internal grievance mechanisms were one part of a larger project to strengthen Chinese suppliers' human resource management (HRM) systems. Although HRM emerged in China with the labor law of 1994 and expanded with the labor contract law of 2007, in many factories HR departments are "just the person who deals with payroll—and maybe is checking basic compliance by checking IDs and watching for child labor," according to one auditor.[218] The FLA and its members have worked to create more elaborate HRM systems. One factory owner described how the FLA sent experts to help him improve his system. This included a formal grievance mechanism, which the FLA insisted on, against the owner's preference to have workers give him feedback directly by phone or text message.[219]

---

[216] Tracking chart, factory 07021541D, 2005.

[217] Tracking chart, factory 240015120B, 2003.

[218] Interview with CSR consultant, Guangzhou, 10/26/10; interview with researcher, Beijing, 7/24/11.

[219] Interview with supplier company CEO, Shanghai, 12/13/10.

Given the wide gulf between migrant workers and factory managers, opening up communication could help managers better understand the problems faced by individual workers. But grievance procedures are weak substitutes for worker representation; they provide no collective voice or bargaining power and leave workers subject to management dictates. It is ironic that the FLA's guarantee of associational and collective bargaining rights led in practice to the promotion of narrow channels for smoother workplace communication. And yet the FLA's approach was, in essence, a way of redefining labor rights to make them compatible with the Chinese context—as well as the interests of FLA member companies sourcing there.

How certified factories are different: the discourse of HRM and CSR

The FLA is not alone in spreading HRM as an assurance of compliance. Returning to the data on factories in Guangdong province, we can see similar patterns for SA8000 certification. In each factory, the researchers surveyed not only workers but also several managers, drawn from the production, marketing, finance, and human resource departments.[220] Among other questions, managers were asked to rate the importance of the human resources office/ department relative to other offices/departments on a scale from 1 (it does not matter) to 5 (it is very important). Taking the average rating as a measure of the perceived importance of HRM, managers in SA8000-certified factories attached greater importance to HRM than those in uncertified factories. The raw difference in means—a rating of 4.38 in certified factories versus 4.16 in uncertified factories—is not huge, but it is statistically discernible at the 0.10 level.[221] As shown in Figure 5.3, this difference remains when controlling for several other relevant characteristics of factories, such as their size.[222]

A difference can also be seen in the number of staff working in the HR department/office. Although the raw difference in means is not statistically discernible ($p<0.65$), the regression analyses show that when other variables are held at their means—such as factory size, product, and export-orientation— there is a clear and discernible difference between SA8000-certified and uncertified factories. As shown in Figure 5.3, the estimates suggest that

[220] In the vast majority of factories, three or (most commonly) four managers were surveyed. In a handful of factories, only one or two managers were surveyed, and in one large factory, sixteen managers were surveyed. Missing data in the management survey reduces the sample size somewhat, to as few as sixty-eight factories for the analysis of HR staff size. While this of course warrants some caution, note that the mixed-methods evidence in this chapter points in similar directions with regard to the links between private regulation and HRM.

[221] This is based on a simple t-test ($p<0.094$), supplemented with the regression models reported below.

[222] A simpler model, controlling only for factory size, shows an even clearer link between SA8000 certification and the stated importance of HRM ($p<0.032$), although the difference is not substantively huge (with a predicted value of 4.43 versus 4.14).

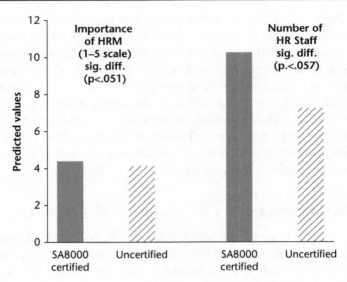

Figure 5.3. Human Resource Management: Predicted values of managers' HRM perceptions and staff in certified and uncertified factories in Guangdong province

certified factories had nearly three more HR staff members on average than did similar uncertified factories. Again, this does not necessarily mean that certification causes increased attention to HRM, but it does mean that this is one of the few areas in which certified factories are distinctive.

Managers were also asked to rate (on a scale from 1 to 7) the extent to which the factory uses specific HRM practices—such as formal performance evaluations, regular job training, and written job requirements. Regression analyses show that these are not consistently related to SA8000 certification, suggesting that perhaps certified factories are more varied in their practices than in their discourses and structures. Indeed, although there initially appear to be links between SA8000 certification and some specific HRM practices (as shown in the Appendix), these are actually attributable to buyer-imposed labor standards in general, not SA8000 in particular. Figure 5.4 illustrates that in factories where most buyers ask for compliance with labor standards of some sort, managers tend to report more substantial use of these specific HRM practices. This relationship exists controlling for size, export-orientation, and several other factors.[223]

Returning to the survey responses of workers, we can ask whether working in certified and/or scrutinized factories, with their formalized management

---

[223] Taken together, these findings suggest that SA8000 is more clearly linked to the discourse and staffing of HRM, while some degree of scrutiny from buyers, regardless of the specific standard used, may be sufficient to increase the formalization of employment practices.

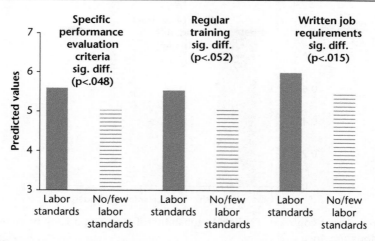

Figure 5.4. Human Resource Management: Predicted values of managers' reported use of specific practices in factories in Guangdong province

systems, is associated with particular kinds of knowledge. For instance, private rules may educate workers about their legal rights, whether directly through formal trainings or indirectly by simply drawing attention to problematic conditions, as suggested in the epigraph to this chapter. At the least, factories that are privately regulated may attract or retain workers with a higher degree of "rights consciousness", while less sophisticated workers are relegated to more marginal factories. Private rules and formalized workplaces may also help workers "use the law as a weapon" in other ways, such as by ensuring that workers get copies of their contracts, which are needed to document the employment relationship in court.

The findings from workers in factories in Guangdong province paint a mixed picture in this regard. On one hand, workers are somewhat more likely to receive a copy of their contract when they work in a factory where most buyers ask for compliance with labor standards. This pattern is discernible as a simple bivariate association and in the multivariate model (as illustrated in Figure 5.5), which controls for workers' time on the job, factory size, and SA8000 certification. Certification initially seems to matter, though not above and beyond this more general measure of standards.

On the other hand when one looks at workers' self-reported knowledge of important labor laws, there is less evidence of private regulation playing an empowering role. The survey asked workers if they were familiar with several labor laws, including the 2007 Labor Contract Law and the 2008 Labor Dispute Mediation and Arbitration Law. Although the survey did not attempt to gauge the depth of workers' understanding, it provides a chance to ask whether basic knowledge of these laws is higher in certified and/or scrutinized factories.

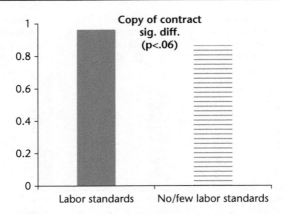

Figure 5.5. Labor contracts: Predicted probability of receiving a copy in factories in Guangdong province

The Labor Contract Law gave employees greater rights to appeal illegal dismissals and inadequate severance payments. Scholars have shown that this law greatly contributed to the "rights consciousness" of Chinese workers, while also noting that workers vary greatly in their ability to use the law effectively.[224] As shown in Figure 5.6, knowledge of this law does not depend on whether one works in an SA8000-certified factory; it is fairly high across the board.[225] Nor is knowledge of this law related to the more general measure of buyer-imposed labor standards.

The Labor Dispute Mediation and Arbitration Law was perhaps just as important as the Labor Contract Law, in that it opened up new channels for workers to press their grievances and was accompanied by a surge in registered labor disputes.[226] Yet only 52 percent of the workers in this sample claimed any knowledge of this law, and only 11 percent said they had more than a rudimentary familiarity with it. If private regulation is shaping workers' legal knowledge, we would expect to see higher rates of familiarity in certified factories. One can find a difference in the baseline rate of familiarity in SA8000 certified and uncertified factories (56 percent versus 50 percent), but this diminishes once one considers other differences in these workers and factories—especially related to industry and factory size.[227] As illustrated in

---

[224] Gallagher 2005; Lee 2007a; Michelson 2007; Ho 2009; Gallagher, Giles, Park, and Wang 2015.

[225] A series of supplemental models found no evidence of a link between SA8000 and knowledge of the labor contract law, whether in a simple bivariate association or in various specifications of the multi-level models in the Appendix.

[226] Gallagher, Giles, Park, and Wang 2015.

[227] Familiarity tends to be higher in the footwear/sporting goods industry and lower in larger factories. When SA8000 certification is the only covariate in an ordinal logistic multi-level regression model, the coefficient approaches statistical significance (p<0.11), but the effect

Figure 5.6, there is not a discernible net difference in workers' knowledge of this law in SA8000-certified and uncertified factories. Nor is knowledge of this law linked to the more general measure of labor standards imposed by buyers.[228]

In stark contrast, a different type of knowledge—more managerial than legal—is clearly linked to factory certification. The survey asked workers if they were familiar with the concept of "corporate social responsibility" (CSR). In SA8000-certified factories, only 18.7 percent of workers said they did *not* know the term CSR, compared to 26.6 percent in uncertified factories. If we control for other individual and factory-level differences, knowledge of CSR remains clearly linked to SA8000 certification, as illustrated in Figure 5.6.[229] This finding is especially notable in light of the small and/or non-significant differences between certified and uncertified factories found for most other measures. Put differently, although SA8000-certified factories appear to be similar to their peers in many ways, they are systematically different in the extent to which workers know the discourse of CSR.

Taken together, these findings about SA8000, the FLA, and buyers' codes of conduct suggest that private regulation is helping to diffuse managerialism to Chinese factories. In fact, this may be the clearest consequence of brands' attempts to "push" labor standards onto their suppliers in China. For factory managers, the diffusion of managerialism can be seen in an emphasis on formal human resource management practices, as well as a reliance on record-keeping and management systems as assurances of decent conditions. For workers, managerialism means enhanced knowledge of CSR and access to internal grievance procedures, but mostly *not* greater representation or ability to pursue legal rights. Although the survey data includes only rudimentary measures of workers' knowledge and no measure of their actions, the analyses in this chapter suggest that private regulation has been more oriented toward channeling workers' grievances inward, and perhaps muting them, than amplifying their voices outward.

---

becomes harder to discern as one incorporates measures of individual education and position, as well as factory size and industry.

[228] In a series of supplemental regression models, no statistically significant relationship with the more general measure of labor standards can be found. In addition, a simple comparison shows similar rates of knowledge in factories that are and are not subject to labor standards from most of their buyers (51% versus 52%).

[229] Figure 5.6 uses a simplified dichotomous version of the measure, comparing workers who claim no and some knowledge of CSR. The analyses in the Appendix use a trichotomous version (those with no knowledge of the concept, those who have heard of it but are only vaguely familiar, and those who know the concept), in which the links to certification are equally clear (p<0.003). Beyond certification, other kinds of standards are not significantly associated with workers' knowledge of CSR. At the individual level, supervisors and workers with urban *hukou* (that is, non-migrants) had greater knowledge of CSR, as one might expect.

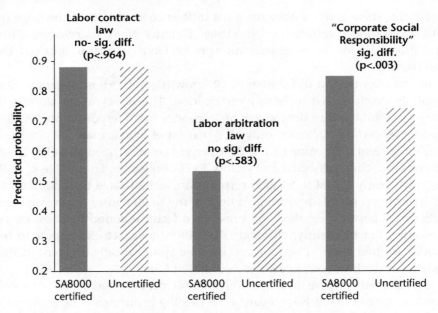

Figure 5.6. Workers' knowledge: Predicted probabilities in certified and uncertified factories in Guangdong province

Conclusion

In roughly a decade, CSR went "from heresy to dogma" in China.[230] Once seen as a western protectionist threat, CSR was soon incorporated into the Chinese Community Party's attempt to promote a harmonious society. Perhaps sensing that their buyers would accept minimally credible assurances, many factory managers became adept at falsifying records, coaching workers, and generating the paperwork necessary to gain or retain orders; some simply bribed auditors to receive a passing grade. After all, few factories could meet buyers' stated expectations for working hours, let alone the stricter standards in Chinese labor law. Still, heightened scrutiny did foster some changes. When committed brands worked closely over time with key suppliers—like Yue Yuen—recalcitrance could evolve into reform. More generally, supply-chain scrutiny helped to clean up factories and soften the hardest edges of the dormitory labor regime.

CSR could move into the mainstream in China in part *because* its implications for workers' rights were dampened. Had brands, auditors, and certifiers strictly enforced standards for worker representation, it is hard to imagine how

---

[230] See Hoffman (1997) for the initial use of this phrase in describing corporate sustainability.

they could have continued to make China a prime sourcing location. The apparent contradiction between codes trumpeting "freedom of association" and the tight controls on association among Chinese workers had contributed to early fears that the rise of CSR would interfere with the rise of China. But these fears proved unfounded, since the contradiction was typically side-stepped or ignored. Occasionally, the contradiction was prodded (as in the Reebok experiment) or navigated (as in the promotion of worker committees as a parallel means of representation), but with few lasting results. It was often smoothed over with a turn to HR management systems, grievance procedures, and a substitution of communication for representation. Initiatives like the FLA and SAI portray themselves as protectors of labor rights, but in China they are more like promoters of management systems.

Managerialism is on one hand a welcome step away from the despotic factory regime that structured the rise of export-oriented production in the 1990s—or from the "management by terror and browbeating" that facilitated Yue Yuen's rise.[231] And yet, if one treats labor standards as primarily a management issue, to be addressed within the factory walls, one ignores both the forces that have been most powerful in marginalizing migrant workers and the forces that have been most effective in improving their circumstances. China has become a global "epicenter of labor unrest," and a rising tide of strikes has produced something akin to what Eric Hobsbawm (1952) called "collective bargaining by riot."[232] In a few cases, labor unrest has contributed to sizable wage increases, as workers demanded a greater share of productivity gains. More broadly, as migrant workers have become more likely to strike and more capable of using the legal system to enforce their contracts, wages in the coastal manufacturing regions have increased. Indeed, a rising tide of strikes, combined with changes in law and labor markets, have by some accounts put Chinese workers in a new, powerful offensive position.[233] The managerialist approach to labor standards promoted by private regulatory efforts in China at best brackets these dynamics—and in many ways is designed to tame them.[234]

Of course, it is possible that labor militancy can grow even with the formalization of management systems, as it did at Yue Yuen. In a sense, this would be a failure for the proponents of CSR and private regulation, even though it could be a pathway toward greater bargaining power for Chinese workers. It is also possible, though, that the rules being pushed by brands and CSR initiatives could contribute to the demobilization of workers, as transnational

---

[231] Lee 1998.　　[232] Silver and Zhang 2009.

[233] Elfstrom and Kuruvilla 2016.

[234] While one could imagine that private regulatory efforts have indirectly facilitated labor militancy, there is strikingly little evidence to suggest this. Workers' legal consciousness appears to have little to do with CSR, and apart from Yue Yuen, the most influential strikes have *not* occurred in the industries where private regulatory efforts have been focused.

corporations, their suppliers, and the Chinese state rein in the power of workers. In either case, there is little doubt that the smoothed edges of responsible production in China belie a deeper set of tensions—about technocratic solutions to deeply social problems and about the collective power of migrant workers in the evolving Chinese economy.

Table 5.2. Monthly wages in apparel/accessories, footwear/sporting goods, or electronics/appliances factories in Guangdong province, multi-level regression models

VARIABLES	(1)	(2)	(3)	(4)
Sex (1=woman)	−139.5281***	−126.4520***	−115.0896***	−98.1076***
	(0.000)	(0.001)	(0.000)	(0.005)
Years on the job	26.9818***	30.3152***		
	(0.000)	(0.000)		
Non-working days	10.7436	14.6430		
	(0.271)	(0.172)		
Hukou (1=urban)	84.8372*	105.8407**	61.8052	72.6062
	(0.080)	(0.046)	(0.152)	(0.129)
Years since migration	27.3025***	21.2651***	34.3378***	31.8597***
	(0.000)	(0.000)	(0.000)	(0.000)
Educ: Junior high	59.6113	30.0677	22.2300	−7.8211
	(0.680)	(0.850)	(0.862)	(0.957)
Educ: High school	205.4862	159.7461	162.1184	134.1751
	(0.161)	(0.324)	(0.211)	(0.360)
Educ: Junior college	324.1472**	278.0517	268.9702*	244.9256
	(0.037)	(0.105)	(0.051)	(0.115)
Position: Supervisor	512.8036***	499.3379***	574.2794***	578.6624***
	(0.000)	(0.000)	(0.000)	(0.000)
Position: Other	123.5664***	116.3649**	169.7178***	175.3094***
	(0.004)	(0.017)	(0.000)	(0.000)
Factory size (log emps.)	78.6139***	99.4385***	71.0754***	94.1539***
	(0.005)	(0.003)	(0.007)	(0.002)
Ind: Apparel/Accessories	−14.9104	87.4159	13.7465	79.7946
	(0.864)	(0.390)	(0.865)	(0.386)
Ind: Footwear/Sports	−101.4450	−39.2546	−57.1310	−15.7788
	(0.282)	(0.691)	(0.506)	(0.860)
Majority for export	−160.6799*	−174.3644*		
	(0.091)	(0.092)		
Foreign owned	186.8199**	134.3916		
	(0.039)	(0.182)		
SA8000 certified	−41.1987	−70.1447	−49.4271	−87.6020
	(0.604)	(0.422)	(0.504)	(0.271)
Most clients want lab. st.		−103.3770		−101.0835
		(0.204)		(0.168)
Constant	907.8656***	903.9790***	1047.4957***	978.8695***
	(0.000)	(0.002)	(0.000)	(0.000)
Observations	911	755	1114	926
Number of groups	81	67	85	70

p-values in parentheses *** p<0.01, ** p<0.05, * p<0.1 (two-tailed tests)

Table 5.3. Delayed wages in apparel/accessories, footwear/sporting goods, or electronics/appliances factories in Guangdong province, multi-level logistic regression models

VARIABLES	(1)	(2)	(3)	(4)
Sex (1=woman)	−0.1653	−0.0263	−0.2083	−0.0725
	(0.346)	(0.893)	(0.232)	(0.709)
Years on the job	−0.0340	−0.0344	−0.0332	−0.0325
	(0.327)	(0.373)	(0.339)	(0.398)
Hukou (1=urban)	−0.2048	−0.2291	−0.1701	−0.1887
	(0.395)	(0.388)	(0.477)	(0.473)
Years since migration	−0.0179	−0.0278	−0.0188	−0.0296
	(0.438)	(0.299)	(0.415)	(0.265)
Educ: Junior high	1.0871	0.8311	1.0434	0.7990
	(0.194)	(0.354)	(0.211)	(0.371)
Educ: High school	1.1459	0.8794	1.1241	0.8618
	(0.176)	(0.335)	(0.183)	(0.342)
Educ: Junior college	1.0251	0.7753	1.0102	0.7500
	(0.247)	(0.417)	(0.252)	(0.429)
Position: Supervisor	−0.4652	−0.1829	−0.4190	−0.1349
	(0.162)	(0.611)	(0.202)	(0.703)
Position: Other	0.0114	0.0893	0.0043	0.0875
	(0.958)	(0.721)	(0.984)	(0.725)
Factory size (log emps.)	−0.3055**	−0.2080		
	(0.040)	(0.273)		
Ind: Apparel/Accessories	−0.7951*	−0.6673		
	(0.098)	(0.260)		
Ind: Footwear/Sports	0.2632	0.3312		
	(0.597)	(0.542)		
Majority for export	−0.4186	−0.5433	−0.3497	−0.5489
	(0.397)	(0.334)	(0.489)	(0.323)
Foreign owned	−0.5450	−0.3734	−0.5459	−0.4258
	(0.243)	(0.488)	(0.256)	(0.431)
SA8000 certified	−0.1939	0.1702	−0.0368	0.2388
	(0.648)	(0.725)	(0.930)	(0.604)
Most clients want lab. st.		−0.8500*		−0.8784**
		(0.057)		(0.041)
Constant	0.8253	0.5776	−1.4562	−0.8380
	(0.551)	(0.718)	(0.116)	(0.404)
Observations	1,179	980	1,195	996
Number of groups	81	67	82	68

Table 5.4. Verbal abuse (experienced or witnessed) in apparel/accessories, footwear/ sporting goods, or electronics/appliances factories in Guangdong province, multi-level logistic regression models

VARIABLES	(1)	(2)	(3)	(4)
Sex (1=woman)	0.2333	0.2024	0.2447	0.1933
	(0.141)	(0.251)	(0.122)	(0.270)
Years on the job	0.0226	0.0192	0.0276	0.0267
	(0.473)	(0.572)	(0.382)	(0.433)
Hukou (1=urban)	−0.2912	−0.1113	−0.3109	−0.1286
	(0.200)	(0.645)	(0.171)	(0.593)
Years since migration	−0.0366*	−0.0376	−0.0408*	−0.0441*
	(0.086)	(0.123)	(0.054)	(0.068)
Educ: Junior high	−0.4406	−0.5097	−0.4070	−0.4143
	(0.522)	(0.514)	(0.554)	(0.596)
Educ: High school	−0.1081	−0.1689	−0.0394	−0.0210
	(0.876)	(0.831)	(0.955)	(0.979)
Educ: Junior college	−0.5417	−0.6656	−0.5240	−0.5587
	(0.458)	(0.422)	(0.472)	(0.499)
Position: Supervisor	−0.2935	−0.3163	−0.3452	−0.3739
	(0.323)	(0.341)	(0.241)	(0.254)
Position: Other	−0.0759	−0.0861	−0.1096	−0.1336
	(0.696)	(0.694)	(0.573)	(0.539)
Factory size (log emps.)	0.2204**	0.2270*		
	(0.017)	(0.055)		
Ind: Apparel/Accessories	−0.2101	−0.4641		
	(0.460)	(0.199)		
Ind: Footwear/Sports	0.6601**	0.4780		
	(0.018)	(0.126)		
Majority for export	0.1402	0.3866	0.3059	0.5919
	(0.647)	(0.272)	(0.345)	(0.109)
Foreign owned	−0.2863	−0.3324	−0.2625	−0.3497
	(0.320)	(0.325)	(0.394)	(0.327)
SA8000 certified	−0.1681	−0.1629	−0.2354	−0.2521
	(0.496)	(0.570)	(0.358)	(0.386)
Most clients want lab. st.		−0.1422	−0.6762	−0.0996
		(0.596)	(0.359)	(0.714)
Constant	−2.1661**	−2.1086*	−0.6762	−0.7185
	(0.027)	(0.065)	(0.359)	(0.392)
Observations	1,124	941	1,139	956
Number of groups	81	67	82	68

p-values in parentheses *** p<0.01, ** p<0.05, * p<0.1 (two-tailed tests)

Table 5.5. Human Resource Management discourse and staffing in apparel/accessories, footwear/sporting goods, or electronics/appliances factories in Guangdong province, regression models based on management survey

VARIABLES	(1)	(2)	(3)	(4)
	HR importance	HR importance	HR staff	HR staff
Factory size (log emps.)	0.0833*	0.0544	2.8214***	3.4859***
	(0.095)	(0.401)	(0.000)	(0.000)
Ind: Apparel/Accessories	−0.1602	−0.1925	−4.0593**	−2.9299
	(0.306)	(0.326)	(0.027)	(0.217)
Ind: Footwear/Sports	−0.0251	−0.0246	−3.0278*	−3.1389
	(0.889)	(0.901)	(0.097)	(0.123)
Majority for export	0.1571	0.1193	−6.3538***	−7.9449***
	(0.355)	(0.551)	(0.001)	(0.000)
Foreign owned	−0.0403	−0.0128	2.3924	1.5919
	(0.803)	(0.947)	(0.170)	(0.445)
SA8000 certified	0.2787*	0.3031*	3.0165*	3.2292*
	(0.051)	(0.074)	(0.057)	(0.072)
Most clients want lab. st.		0.0357		0.3688
		(0.825)		(0.827)
Constant	3.4983***	3.6916***	−8.3412*	−11.2386**
	(0.000)	(0.000)	(0.058)	(0.034)
Observations	76	63	68	56
R-squared	0.126	0.126	0.414	0.478

p-values in parentheses *** p<0.01, ** p<0.05, * p<0.1 (two-tailed tests)

Table 5.6. Human Resource Management practices in apparel/accessories, footwear/sporting goods, or electronics/appliances factories in Guangdong province, regression models based on management survey

VARIABLES	(1)	(2)	(3)	(4)	(5)	(6)
	Perf. eval.	Perf. eval.	Training	Training	Job reqs	Job reqs
Factory size (log emps.)	0.1722*	0.1469	0.1252	0.1136	0.1598*	0.0489
	(0.090)	(0.193)	(0.161)	(0.242)	(0.071)	(0.560)
Ind: Apparel/Accessories	−0.1442	−0.2447	−0.0501	−0.3344	−0.0774	−0.5529**
	(0.650)	(0.471)	(0.858)	(0.255)	(0.780)	(0.032)
Ind: Footwear/Sports	0.2144	0.3843	−0.0722	0.0497	−0.3837	−0.3010
	(0.535)	(0.250)	(0.812)	(0.862)	(0.204)	(0.228)
Majority for export	−0.0285	0.0802	0.1425	0.2492	0.2730	0.5612**
	(0.934)	(0.817)	(0.640)	(0.405)	(0.366)	(0.034)
Foreign owned	−0.2881	−0.5436	0.0372	−0.2664	0.0402	−0.2028
	(0.383)	(0.111)	(0.898)	(0.361)	(0.888)	(0.423)
SA8000 certified	0.1747	−0.0580	0.4173*	0.0556	0.4868*	0.0953
	(0.539)	(0.840)	(0.098)	(0.823)	(0.052)	(0.659)
Most clients want lab. st.		0.5513**		0.4658*		0.5086**
		(0.048)		(0.052)		(0.015)
Constant	4.2319***	4.3628***	4.1481***	4.3361***	4.2561***	5.0212***
	(0.000)	(0.000)	(0.000)	(0.000)	(0.000)	(0.000)
Observations	81	67	81	67	81	67
R-squared	0.073	0.181	0.064	0.163	0.102	0.258

p-values in parentheses *** p<0.01, ** p<0.05, * p<0.1 (two-tailed tests)

Table 5.7. Receipt of labor contract copy in apparel/accessories, footwear/sporting goods, or electronics/appliances factories in Guangdong province, multi-level logistic regression models

VARIABLES	(1)	(2)
Sex (1=woman)	0.5656**	0.3183
	(0.018)	(0.254)
Years on the job	0.1925***	0.1942***
	(0.001)	(0.002)
Hukou (1=urban)	−0.3675	−0.3108
	(0.248)	(0.406)
Years since migration	−0.0121	−0.0516
	(0.696)	(0.154)
Educ: Junior high	1.4034	1.5045*
	(0.112)	(0.099)
Educ: High school	1.3637	1.0323
	(0.127)	(0.260)
Educ: Junior college	1.3486	0.9058
	(0.161)	(0.365)
Position: Supervisor	0.1788	−0.1509
	(0.680)	(0.763)
Position: Other	−0.1800	−0.3370
	(0.564)	(0.365)
Factory size (log of employees)	0.4737*	0.9382***
	(0.050)	(0.002)
Ind: Apparel/Accessories	−0.1736	0.4132
	(0.807)	(0.622)
Ind: Footwear/Sports	1.4965	1.1257
	(0.104)	(0.220)
Majority for export	1.3451*	0.6390
	(0.062)	(0.400)
Foreign owned	0.2088	−0.1976
	(0.767)	(0.793)
SA8000 certified	1.4785**	0.8699
	(0.047)	(0.257)
Most clients want labor standards		1.2414*
		(0.060)
Constant	−4.0478**	−6.1714***
	(0.043)	(0.008)
Observations	1,076	895
Number of groups	81	67

Table 5.8. Workers' knowledge in apparel/accessories, footwear/sporting goods, or electronics/appliances factories in Guangdong province, multi-level ordinal logistic regression models

VARIABLES	(1)	(2)	(1)	(4)	(1)	(5)
	Labor contract law	Labor contract law	Arbitration law	Arbitration law	CSR	CSR
Sex (1=woman)	−0.0955	−0.1366	−0.3203**	−0.2603*	−0.2013	−0.2520*
	(0.471)	(0.350)	(0.016)	(0.077)	(0.108)	(0.070)
Years on the job	−0.0192	−0.0098	0.0139	0.0373	0.0132	0.0196
	(0.453)	(0.720)	(0.591)	(0.182)	(0.590)	(0.463)
Hukou (1=urban)	0.2528	0.2060	0.3109*	0.2760	0.2992*	0.2421
	(0.166)	(0.305)	(0.080)	(0.157)	(0.085)	(0.204)
Years since migration	0.0152	0.0103	0.0010	−0.0171	0.0173	0.0119
	(0.359)	(0.579)	(0.953)	(0.380)	(0.281)	(0.513)
Educ: Junior high	−0.2391	−0.4208	−0.9862*	−1.2196**	0.2481	0.3486
	(0.664)	(0.481)	(0.087)	(0.044)	(0.652)	(0.572)
Educ: High school	−0.1736	−0.4087	−0.8150	−1.1247*	0.6020	0.5752
	(0.756)	(0.501)	(0.164)	(0.068)	(0.281)	(0.360)
Educ: Junior college	−0.0995	−0.3582	−0.3202	−0.6041	0.8858	0.7994
	(0.866)	(0.577)	(0.601)	(0.350)	(0.132)	(0.227)
Position: Supervisor	0.6446***	0.6277**	0.6109***	0.5780**	0.6215***	0.5908**
	(0.006)	(0.016)	(0.009)	(0.029)	(0.006)	(0.021)
Position: Other	0.3252**	0.3214*	0.1603	0.0897	0.2129	0.2209
	(0.043)	(0.075)	(0.328)	(0.626)	(0.161)	(0.199)
Factory size (log emps.)	−0.0071	−0.0271	−0.0746	−0.1728*	0.0159	0.0078
	(0.908)	(0.722)	(0.288)	(0.053)	(0.800)	(0.924)
Ind: Apparel/ Accessories	−0.3488*	−0.4482*	−0.1688	−0.4190	−0.5095***	−0.5596**
	(0.071)	(0.053)	(0.442)	(0.120)	(0.009)	(0.021)
Ind: Footwear/ Sports	0.1692	0.0613	0.2173	0.2856	0.0200	0.0029
	(0.410)	(0.774)	(0.349)	(0.253)	(0.923)	(0.990)
Majority for export	0.2205	0.2541	0.2813	0.1740	0.1067	0.1240
	(0.300)	(0.273)	(0.243)	(0.518)	(0.618)	(0.608)
Foreign owned	−0.2384	−0.1984	−0.1129	0.0432	−0.2743	−0.2419
	(0.245)	(0.384)	(0.624)	(0.869)	(0.182)	(0.309)
SA8000 certified	0.1004	0.1088	0.1641	0.2371	0.5197***	0.4410**
	(0.564)	(0.576)	(0.405)	(0.294)	(0.003)	(0.031)
Most clients want lab. st.		0.1559		0.1566		0.0299
		(0.390)		(0.456)		(0.876)
Constant (cut 1)	−2.0158***	−2.2969***	−1.1625	−2.0746**	−0.5094	−0.5567
	(0.005)	(0.004)	(0.133)	(0.016)	(0.485)	(0.509)
Constant (cut 2)	1.0714	0.7798	1.1515	0.3000	1.8277**	1.7937**
	(0.136)	(0.328)	(0.137)	(0.727)	(0.012)	(0.033)
Observations	1,123	935	1097	914	1,145	951
Number of groups	81	67	81	67	81	67

p-values in parentheses *** $p<0.01$, ** $p<0.05$, * $p<0.1$ (two-tailed tests)

6

Contentious Codes

The Contested Implications of Labor Standards in Indonesia

> *"If I tried to do in China or Vietnam what I do here, I would be deported—at best."*
>
> American labor activist Jim Keady, after helping to push
> a Nike supplier in Indonesia to compensate workers
> for years of forced, unpaid overtime[1]

> *"There is no guarantee from any brand today. You cannot say we demand you to do long term employment but not commit to long term contracts. . . . We haven't reaped the reward yet for making progress in the right direction. [Orders] keep moving to China and Vietnam. . . . We should be rewarded now."*
>
> Interview with factory manager and
> trade association representative[2]

General Suharto rose to the Indonesian Presidency through the brutal murder of hundreds of thousands of alleged communists. In the decades that followed, Suharto's government promoted industrialization and "harmonious" labor relations through a mix of repression and the *Pancasila* civil religion, which portrayed "workers, capital, and the state [as] parts of one big family, with the latter playing the role of benevolent father."[3] A state-backed union—Serikat Pekerja Seluruh Indonesia (SPSI)—was given the exclusive right to balance capital-labor relations.[4] Military power was available to protect employers and maintain order if necessary, and often the line between military and management was blurry. As one NGO noted in 1991, "there is at least one

---

[1] Quoted in Alford 2012.   [2] 7/8/08.   [3] Hadiz 1998:113.
[4] SPSI, created in 1985, was a revised and more centralized version of the previous state-sponsored union, Federasi Buruh Seluruh Indonesia (FBSI), created in 1973 (Athreya 1998b).

former officer working as a personnel manager" in all of Nike's contract factories in Indonesia.[5]

The export of apparel and footwear took off in the 1980s, after the government welcomed foreign investors to bolster the entrepreneurship of Indonesian factory owners. The industry capitalized on millions of young women from rural areas, where agriculture had become increasingly mechanized.[6] Migrant women in Indonesia received some of the lowest wages in Southeast Asia at the time—lower than in the Philippines, Malaysia, Taiwan, or South Korea—and factory managers routinely bribed government officials to ignore minimum wage laws.[7] By the mid-1990s, Indonesia was among the largest exporters of apparel and footwear to the US and Europe.[8]

When underground labor activism erupted in the early 1990s, American and European brands were thrust into the spotlight. From 1990 to 1993, workers waged wildcat strikes at five different Nike supplier factories, including the massive Nikomas Gemiling footwear factory (owned by the same parent company as the Yue Yuen factories described in the previous chapter).[9] Some activism was met with violent repression, generating martyrs such as Marsinah, a young woman who was brutally murdered in 1993 by security guards from the watch factory where she was organizing her fellow employees.[10] Other leaders faced prison time after organizing "alternative unions", including Muchtar Pakpahan and Dita Sari, who was arrested after leading a strike at a Reebok and Adidas supplier.[11] Labor NGOs with middle-class benefactors faced less repression and were allowed to become important centers of legal aid and pro-labor intellectualism, "as long as they did not seek to assume the industrial functions of trade unions or challenge the one-union policy and the state ideology."[12] Containment, it seems, was motivated not only by the government's desire to attract investors but also by the military's paranoid fear of "the return of the communists". Meanwhile, ethnically Chinese business leaders argued that the "uncontrollable Indonesian masses" would target them first. "Yes, we underpay the workers," said one such businessman in 1993. "We must keep the workers weak. If they become too strong, . . . it is we who will be destroyed."[13]

Then, in 1998, the Suharto regime fell. The 1997 Asian financial crisis had destabilized the rupiah, fueling skyrocketing prices, student protests, riots, and ethno-religious violence. Labor activists were late-joiners to the student protests, but they became some of the first beneficiaries of the era of *Reformasi*

---

[5] Quoted in Wolf 1992:42.   [6] Thee 2009; Wolf 1992; Vickers 2005.
[7] Wolf 1992:40–1; 119–22.   [8] Dicken and Hassler 2000.
[9] Ballinger 2000.   [10] Vickers 2005.   [11] Cockburn 2002; La Botz 2001.
[12] Ford 2009:63. Legislation introduced in 1985 would have facilitated shut-downs of "any NGO that undertook activities which threatened national security, received overseas aid without government clearance or assisted foreign parties to the detriment of the national interest" (Ford 2009:12). But the legislation was never fully implemented.
[13] Quoted in Athreya 1998b:37.

that followed. Almost immediately after Suharto's resignation, B.J. Habibie's transitional government ratified ILO Convention 87 on freedom of association, revised domestic regulations, and invited newly released dissident Muchtar Pakpahan's union to register with the government.[14]

De facto labor repression did not fall away quickly. When strikers from a textile factory came to Jakarta to appeal to the ILO in 1998, they were beaten by security forces.[15] Although Nike eventually convinced Nikomas to stop having military personnel stationed at the factory, factory managers called in the *Brimob* (mobile police brigade) to put down a strike in 1999 and threatened violence against at least one labor organizer.[16]

Still, because of the legacy of pre-Suharto-era labor law, a tendency toward repression coexisted with what one scholar has called "perhaps the most progressive set of labor legislation in Asia."[17] A new Trade Union Act eased requirements for union formation and penalized employer retaliation, and a ministerial decree mandated high severance payments when workers are dismissed.[18] The first years of *Reformasi* saw a burgeoning of trade unions. Some splintered from the SPSI, a few grew out of labor NGOs, and many arose from the ground up in particular factories. Just over two years after freedom of association was legalized, there were twenty-four national trade union organizations and more than 10,000 enterprise-level unions registered with the government.[19] Still, because the Trade Union Act set a low threshold for a union to be recognized—requiring just ten members—the labor movement was extremely fragmented, and SPSI "legacy unions" held onto power in many places.[20] Labor law enforcement was left to a weak, decentralized system of labor bureaus (*Dinas Tenaga Kerja* or *DISNAKER*) and dispute resolution bodies, though the latter began to be reformed in 2006.[21]

With independent unions permitted, strong labor law on the books, and both domestic and international scrutiny, Indonesia in the 2000s might have been a promising site for the rise of "responsible" factories and meaningful implementation of codes of conduct. Domestic labor law was poorly enforced but highly compatible with private rules, such as the SA8000 factory

---

[14] Aspinall 2005; Hadiz 1998.   [15] Hadiz 1998.

[16] Connor 2002. He reports: "Factory managers had taken him into an office, and in the presence of an Indonesian soldier he was shouted at and told that if he did not stop organizing workers, he would be attacked by hired thugs. Subsequently, he was repeatedly approached in the street by strangers and warned that his life was in danger if he did not resign from the factory" (p. 11–12).

[17] Caraway 2004:34. Among other things, Indonesian labor law provides for three months of paid maternity leave, increasing premiums for overtime hours (50% for the first hour, then 100%), and severance pay that amounts to one to two month's pay for each year of service and potentially much more for experienced workers.

[18] Caraway 2004.

[19] Ford 2009:161. By 2008, there were ninety federations and roughly 11,000 enterprise unions (Juliawan 2011).

[20] Caraway 2006.   [21] Caraway 2011; International Labour Organization 2013.

certification standard. There was a robust civil society and free press, has been found to boost compliance with codes of conduct.[22] Wages remained low, as workers suffered and foreign investors profited from the decline of the rupiah. But low labor costs allowed Indonesian factories to stay afloat in the highly competitive global apparel and footwear industries. Improving working conditions while remaining competitive would not be easy, but some observers were hopeful that Indonesia could provide a democratic, union-friendly alternative to production in China and Vietnam.[23]

Yet progress through private regulation proved elusive. As we will see, SA8000 never developed a strong presence in Indonesia, even as the number of certified factories in China, Vietnam, and Pakistan grew rapidly. Unions and NGOs built several "bottom up" initiatives to monitor codes of conduct, and insurgent unionization campaigns made progress in a few factories, only to see their gains—and often the factories—disappear. Both bottom-up monitoring and top-down auditing spurred some improvements in factories, but the limited degree of change is striking. A 2011–12 survey of workers in export-oriented garment factories, most of which had been subject to codes of conduct for several years, found "alarmingly high" rates of worker concern about sexual harassment (with 85 percent expressing concern), verbal and physical abuse (79 percent and 87 percent, respectively), and workplace accidents (73 percent), as well as low wages, late payment, and broken punch-clocks—a possible indication of unpaid working hours.[24]

This chapter addresses two puzzles of private regulation. First, why has there been so little SA8000 certification in Indonesia, where the social and political context would appear to make a number of factories certifiable? To be sure, most factories in Indonesia would need improvement to reach the SA8000 standard. But some barriers to compliance—such as restrictions on unions and a culture of excessive working hours—were far more subdued in Indonesia than in competing countries (most notably, China). As we will see, explaining the underdevelopment of high-bar factory certification in Indonesia reveals something perverse about the practical logic of SA8000—namely, that brands' sourcing priorities determine what can be certified, rather than the other way around.

The second puzzle revolves around brands' own codes of conduct, which were a more common expression of private rules. Using a quantitative analysis

---

[22] Distelhorst, Locke, Pal, and Samel 2015; Toffel, Short, and Ouellet 2015.

[23] See Barenberg 2008; The Asia Health and Safety Training Project 2003.

[24] Better Work Indonesia 2012a. Some of the factories in this project were relatively new, but most should have had at least a few years of experience with their buyers' codes of conduct. Of the twenty factories in the first Better Work Indonesia compliance report in 2012, more than half were at least three years old. (Ten were listed in the 2009 Directory of Manufacturing Industries, and one (PT Kukdong) was a factory that I visited in 2008.).

of survey data, I will show that factories governed by codes were different in some respects from their less-scrutinized peers. Furthermore, drawing on interviews, I will show how unions used a "Code of Conduct Network" to promote bottom-up monitoring. On the other hand, workplaces governed by codes were no more legally compliant or less precarious than others; and insurgent unions' attempts to leverage codes into bargaining power largely failed. Why did codes of conduct bring such paltry gains, even with bottom-up pressure and spotlighted brands? The answer, I will argue, lies both in the political economy of an industry built on precarity and in a profound mismatch between the logic of private regulation, which focuses solely on what happens within the factory walls, and the locus of Indonesian unions' power, which has been much greater *outside* the factory.

The Puzzle of Certification: The Underdevelopment of SA8000 in Indonesia

When SA8000 certification was first getting off the ground, it appeared that factories in Indonesia would be promising candidates. Anti-sweatshop activists had put suppliers for Nike, Reebok, and Adidas in the spotlight, helping to spur wage increases in apparel, textile, and footwear-manufacturing regions in the mid-1990s, although they remained low compared to other manufacturing industries.[25] After Suharto's fall, the space for independent unions and labor NGOs increased dramatically. Meanwhile, brands in North America and Europe were looking for ways to lend credibility to their CSR claims, and many saw factory certification as an important component of this.[26] Social Accountability International, which created the SA8000 standard, was partnering with leaders of an international union, the International Textile, Garment, and Leather Workers Federation, to make SA8000 a tool for workers in countries where independent unions were legal but struggling, including Indonesia.[27]

Several factories in Indonesia were in the first wave of SA8000 certifications. Three were certified as of early 2001, accounting for roughly 5 percent of the fifty-nine SA8000-certified facilities worldwide—more than in any single country except for China and Italy at this point.[28] As the number of SA8000 certificates worldwide increased, though, only a handful of Indonesian factories

---

[25] Harrison and Scorse 2010. They show that anti-sweatshop pressure raised apparel, textile, and footwear wages from a comparatively low starting point. Based on more recent surveys of Indonesia workers in different sectors, Robertson et al. (2009) found that workers in manufacturing industries earn higher wages and are more satisfied than those in the agro-food sector, but workers in textile, leather, and apparel industries earned slightly less and were less satisfied than workers in other manufacturing industries.

[26] Leipziger 2001; O'Rourke 2003.   [27] Kearney and Gearhart 2004.

[28] SA8000 Certified Facilities as of January 2001.

were among them. In 2003, there were eight certified factories in Indonesia, making up just 2.5 percent of the global total.[29] By 2010, there were ten SA8000-certified facilities in Indonesia, but this amounted to less than 0.5 percent of the 2,258 worldwide.[30] This share fell to less than 0.2 percent by 2014, when there were only six SA8000-certified facilities in Indonesia.[31]

Several countries with more repressive labor laws had far more SA8000-certified facilities. There were 440 in China, 59 in Vietnam, and 166 in Pakistan in 2011. As Table 6.1 shows, even if one adjusts for the value of exports from these countries or the size of their workforces, Indonesia lagged far behind.[32] China had roughly six SA8000-certified facilities per billion dollars of apparel, footwear, and textile exports to the "ethically sensitive" markets of the US and EU; Vietnam had eighteen, but Indonesia had only 2.5 at its peak. Pakistan's worldwide apparel exports were roughly $2 billion less than Indonesia's, but it had 156 more SA8000-certified facilities.[33]

If the goal of SA8000's backers was to show that labor-intensive production and trade union rights could go hand in hand, then Indonesia should have been a promising location.[34] In addition, standard industry practices in Indonesia were in some respects not so distant from SA8000 requirements, at least in comparison to China.[35] To be sure, verbal abuse, low wages, forced overtime, and long hours were routine in Indonesian factories. As one auditor explained, "especially at the end of the year in the peak period, a lot of

Table 6.1. SA8000 in Indonesia in comparative perspective

	Indonesia	China	Vietnam	Pakistan
SA8000-certified facilities (in 2010 or 2011)	10	440	59	166
... per billion dollars of exports of finished clothing, textiles, or footwear to US or EU-15	2.5	6	13	–
Employees in SA8000-certified facilities per 10,000 in the workforce	1.6	3	11	8

[29] SA8000 Certified Facilities as of October 31, 2003.
[30] SA8000 Certified Facilities as of June 30, 2010.
[31] SA8000 Certified Facilities as of June 30, 2014.
[32] Using the WTO-OECD Trade in Value Added (TiVA) data, I divided the number of SA8000-certified facilities by the value of exports of finished clothing, textiles, or footwear to the US and EU-15 countries, where demand for labor standards has been strongest. For estimates relative to the size of the workforce, I used World Bank data as of 2009. The data on employment in SA8000 certified facilities is from 2009, which is the most recent data with employee counts.
[33] Comparable data on Pakistan's finished apparel exports to the US and EU is not available, but we do know that Pakistan's total clothing exports were worth roughly 2 billion dollars less than Indonesia's in the 2010–11 period (WTO merchandise trade data).
[34] See Kearney and Gearhart 2004.
[35] In addition, Indonesian building codes limit factories to two floors to facilitate evacuation in case of fire (Bradsher 2013), in contrast to the dangerous high-rise factory complexes of Bangladesh and Pakistan.

factories work every day with overtime, [even though] it's against the law. They'll have no record of production for Sunday ... but there will be a broken needle ... and this gets recorded."[36]

But while falsified records are widespread in China (as described in Chapter 5), in Indonesia it "exists [here] too but isn't rampant," as one practitioner put it.[37] In fact, one can find some factories in Indonesia where working hours are close to SA8000's limit of fifty-two to fifty-four hours per week with at least one day off. When NGOs investigated six export-oriented garment factories in Jakarta and Tangerang in 2004, for instance, they found that nearly all workers had Sundays off and only two factories were operating for more than sixty hours per week.[38] When industry consultants examined five export-oriented footwear factories in Surabaya in 2007, they found that overtime rarely exceeded two hours per day.[39] Perhaps this is because Indonesian labor law calls for anything past one hour of overtime per day to be paid at double the normal rate, a larger premium than in China, Vietnam, or Bangladesh.

The organization of work and family has also kept working hours—and the need for falsification—in check. As described in the previous chapter, the Chinese "dormitory labor regime" created a workforce that was separated from family, unable to live independently in the city, and available to work essentially around the clock. Factories in Indonesia also rely on migrant workers from rural areas, but these workers have been more likely to live outside the factory complex, sometimes with spouses and children. Factory dormitory living has been the exception rather than the rule, both in the 1990s and more recently.[40] In 2001, more than a quarter of the workers in Nike's contract factories in Indonesia were parents, and estimates suggest that nearly half of them lived with their children, as opposed to leaving them with relatives in the village.[41] There was a degree of "work-life balance"—though

---

[36] Interview with auditor, Jakarta, 6/30/09.

[37] Ibid.; interview with brand representative, Jakarta, 7/10/08.

[38] Sudwind and UCM Jakarta 2004. A few workers from each factory were interviewed. In only one factory did their average reported working time exceed sixty hours per week, although in four of the six factories, at least one worker reported working more than sixty hours per week (61–66).

[39] Clark and SENADA 2007.

[40] Pangestu and Hendytio 1997; Wolf 1992; Athreya 1998b; Better Work Indonesia 2012a. A 1995 survey of women workers in textile, garment, and footwear factories in Jakarta and West Java found that most were migrants from rural areas but only 6% lived in a dormitory. Around half rented their own room, while others lived with family members (Pangestu and Hendytio 1997). Renting a room in a boarding house or apartment could be a financial strain, and some single workers traded the free rent of dormitories for the ability to work extra hours, but these were a minority of migrant workers (Athreya 1998b; Wolf 1992). More recently, a survey of over 900 workers in forty-two export-oriented garment factories in Indonesia in 2011–12 found only 3.5% living in a dormitory (Better Work Indonesia 2012a).

[41] Global Alliance for Workers and Communities 2001; Connor 2002:23. More recent research on migrant workers in Tangerang found that most were young women without children but "married couples with infants were not uncommon" (Warouw 2008:106). A recent survey of

an impoverished balance to be sure—among Indonesian migrant workers that is rare in China. Moreover, the culture of overwork may be less prevalent in Indonesia because the young Javanese women who went out to work in factories have faced less severe expectations from their families. Wolf (1992) argues that Javanese parents expected less—and often received less—from their "factory daughters" than one would imagine based on the literature on East Asian patriarchy.

The tenuous market for standards

Why, then, were there not more SA8000-certified factories in Indonesia? Part of the answer is simply that Indonesia was not a prime sourcing destination for the brands and retailers that were promoting SA8000. The Gap's support for SA8000 led to the certification of the PT Fit-U factory in Bandung in 2005, where managers reported that the requirements for certification were similar in most ways to what they were already doing.[42] German apparel retailer Olymp's expectations led to the certification of PT Metro Garmin in Bandung in 2008.[43]

But many corporate supporters of SA8000 had tenuous ties to factories in Indonesia.[44] For instance, the Dutch company WE Fashion was an early supporter of Social Accountability International and even got its corporate headquarters SA8000-certified. The brand promised to have all of its suppliers certified by 2004, and it arranged pre-audits at suppliers in Indonesia, Hong Kong, India, and the Philippines.[45] But over time the brand both shifted away from Indonesia and watered down its commitment to certification. As of 2009 and 2010, the brand was no longer sourcing from Indonesia, though a few orders returned briefly in 2011–12.[46] It went as far as having 11 percent of its suppliers worldwide SA8000-certified in 2011, but this slipped to 7 percent the following year.[47] Likewise, the Finnish retailer Kesko promoted SA8000 certification in its supply chain, but it relied far more on factories in China, India, Turkey, and Vietnam than in Indonesia.[48]

workers in export-oriented garment industries found that at least 39% (and possibly more) were parents (Better Work Indonesia 2012a). (38% reported having a son and 39% reported having a daughter. The researchers did not report the percentage of parents who had *either* a son or daughter, but by definition it must be at least 39% and is likely much higher.).

[42] Clark and SENADA 2007:10. Factory managers reported that since SA8000 standards were similar to those already set by the buyers, certification was not especially onerous, although it did cost $11,000 for auditing and require challenging work to monitor subcontractors.

[43] OLYMP 2014.

[44] Timberland, which promoted SA8000 in China, had only one supplier in Indonesia as of 2008.

[45] Schipper 2004.

[46] WE Fashion 2009; WE Fashion 2010; WE Fashion 2012; WE Fashion 2013.

[47] WE Fashion 2012.

[48] Kesko 2014. The value of Kesko's imports from Indonesia in 2014 amounted to only 1/50 of its imports from China, 1/6 of its imports from Vietnam, and 1/3 of its imports from Bangladesh.

Some factories that did get certified reported having little luck in attracting new orders. PT Fit-U reportedly "tried to attract new buyers with its SA8000 certificate, but most buyers, especially in America, had not heard of the standard."[49] The factory went out of business four years after its certification, citing declining orders and rising production costs.[50] Part of the challenge was that, as one practitioner put it, "garment factories here are primarily US-oriented, while SAI is used primarily by European clients. If I [as a factory owner] have SA8000, who will use it?"[51] Indeed, as illustrated in Figure 6.1, the American market became more important than the European market over time, likely contributing to the limited growth of SA8000 in Indonesian apparel and footwear factories.

A few American brands have promoted SA8000 certification, but most have used other methods to enforce labor standards for their suppliers. Some have focused on their own codes of conduct and compliance divisions, with support from the Fair Labor Association. This includes several brands that have been important buyers from Indonesian factories, such as Nike, PVH, and Liz Claiborne. Some European brands with suppliers in Indonesia, including Adidas and H&M, have taken a similar approach.

Other American brands have put their weight behind the WRAP certification system, which originated with the American Apparel and Footwear Manufacturers' Association. VF (owners of Lee and Wrangler jeans, Nautica,

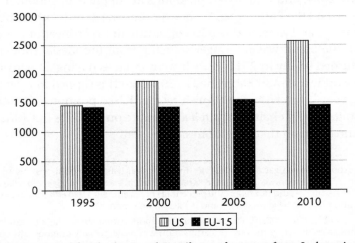

Figure 6.1. Exports of finished apparel, textiles, or footwear from Indonesia to the US and Europe (in millions of USD)

---

[49] Quoted in Clark and SENADA 2007:10.   [50] Indotextiles 2009.
[51] Interview with auditor, Jakarta, 6/30/09.

and the North Face), Hanesbrands, and Wal-Mart have at various points promoted WRAP certification, as have some British firms, including Tesco and Marks & Spencer.[52] While SA8000 was foundering in Indonesia, the number of WRAP-certified facilities grew from twenty-one in 2006 to fifty in 2009—outpacing growth in Vietnam.[53]

By all accounts, WRAP certification is less stringent than SA8000 and easier for factories to obtain.[54] Unlike SA8000, the WRAP standard does not explicitly restrict the use of short-term contract workers or ask whether the legal minimum wage amounts to a "living wage". In practice, according to one auditor, "we've found a lot of factories [that are also] audited by WRAP—but our findings conflict—some [in ways that are] critical, like falsified records or double-books."[55] While SA8000 requires significant preparation, it took only three months for a supplier for Tommy Hilfiger and Polo Ralph Lauren to get WRAP-certified, and just one month for a factory supplying Marks & Spencer and Lane Bryant.[56] Noting that few drastic changes are typically needed, one industry advisor simply noted that "if they want to have certification, they can get it."[57] Tellingly, in a promotional conference in Jakarta that I attended, a WRAP representative noted that auditors are trained to differentiate "everyday griping and complaining [from] issues that are systematic." Another presenter glossed over the Freedom of Association section of the standard in just a few seconds.[58]

The problem of contentious labor rights

In reality, though, "freedom of association" could be messy and contentious, and SA8000's certifiers often struggled to recognize or address this. In the case of the PT Teodore Garmindo factory, tensions between an upstart union and recalcitrant factory management proved more than certifiers and buyers could resolve. In 2003, an independent union, led by a woman, began to challenge the factory's "legacy union".[59] Despite allegations that managers were

---

[52] Notes from WRAP Foundations Seminar, Jakarta, 7/2/09.
[53] Clark and SENADA 2007; https://web.archive.org/web/20091101000000*/http://www.wrapcompliance.org/certified-facilities as of 2009. These counts are based on publicly disclosed WRAP facilities. Certified facilities are not required to disclose their status publicly, but since most companies view certification as a marketing tool, it is unlikely that many keep it a secret. WRAP's growth in Indonesia slowed, but as of 2015, the ratio of certified facilities in Indonesia to those in China was four times higher for WRAP than for SA8000.
[54] For instance, the WRAP standard does not explicitly restrict the use of short-term contract workers or ask whether the legal minimum wage amounts to a "living wage".
[55] Interview with auditor, Jakarta, 6/30/09.
[56] Clark and SENADA 2007. Each paid $2,100 for the initial certification audit, plus between $890 and 2,100 for surveillance audits.
[57] Interview with industry consultant, Jakarta, 6/29/09.
[58] Notes from WRAP Foundations Seminar, Jakarta, 7/2/09.
[59] Interview with NGO representatives, Bogor, 6/29/08.

intimidating union leaders, a certifier (SGS) granted the factory SA8000 certification in 2005. Reebok, one of the factory's buyers, had been investigating
and was soon joined by a team from Social Accountability Accreditation
Services, the organization responsible for SA8000 oversight.[60]

The investigation revealed that managers were forcing permanent workers
to resign, and then hiring them back as short-term contract workers.
"Worker interviews confirmed that practice had been for managers to dictate
a resignation letter to employees, who felt threatened and did not feel free to
refuse to write it," the investigators concluded. "Within days, the workers
submit similarly worded applications for the jobs from which they had just
resigned."[61] The certifier demanded corrective action, but management was
recalcitrant, refusing to rehire workers unless they returned their severance
payments. The SA8000 certificate was canceled in 2006, and factory managers reportedly decided that it no longer made sense to work with Reebok.[62]
In this case, oversight allowed SA8000 to retain some credibility, but it
provided little support for the independent union, contrary to the hopes
of some SA8000 backers.[63]

In the case of the PT Kasrie Towel factory (a supplier to Karstadt-Quelle among
others), SA8000 certification was retained, despite clear evidence of anti-union
retaliation.[64] The case stretched back to events in 1999, when managers laid off
nineteen workers in the midst of union organizing and a strike. This began a
lengthy series of proceedings on the legality of this action.[65] Yet this conflict
was apparently ignored when SGS awarded the SA8000 certification in 2001. As
a critic later noted, it is "incredible that trade unionists were fired and a new
trade union structure was raised close to management, and SGS said there was
no problem."[66] After a complaint was lodged, the oversight body concluded
that "the certification should not have been granted while a court case was
pending."[67] As a corrective action, the auditors requested that the factory hold
an open union election. By the time the factory agreed to comply, roughly
eighteen months after the initial complaint, the independent union seems to
have been in disarray. The displaced workers had not effectively navigated the
legal system, and the complaint to SAI was closed, a move the complainant
called "formally correct but deeply unjust."[68] Having effectively derailed the

---

[60] Connor and Dent 2006.   [61] Social Accountability Accreditation Services 2006:2.
[62] Social Accountability Accreditation Services 2006; Connor and Dent 2006.
[63] For example, Kearney and Gearhart 2004.
[64] See Kampagne für Saubere Kleidung 2003 for the link to Karstadt-Quelle.
[65] Serikat Pekerja Nasional, Summary of Chronology, no date.
[66] Interview with NGO representative, Bonn, 7/17/09.
[67] Social Accountability Accreditation Services 2005:2.
[68] Letter from Ingeborg Wick to Social Accountability International.

independent union, the factory was recertified in 2004, since auditors found no *current* violation.[69]

Two larger insights can be gleaned from these events. First, laws facilitating freedom of association, as well as other supportive aspects of the socio-political environment, were insufficient to allow a high-bar form of certification to take hold. Although brands were willing to push rules onto their suppliers, they did not gravitate toward factories or locations that would support the implementation of those rules. Put differently, certifiability has little to do with actual rates of certification. Second, even when high-bar certification did occur, it did not guarantee respect for union rights or provide leverage for independent unions.[70] SA8000 could have been used to promote factories with independent unions in a newly democratic country with comparatively pro-worker labor laws. But it was not. SA8000 followed business priorities rather than shaping them, and it struggled with union rights.

The Uneven Significance of Corporate Codes of Conduct

During one of my first interviews with Indonesian labor-rights advocates, I mentioned the well-known case of the Kukdong factory in Mexico, a Nike supplier where in 2001 an insurgent independent union waged a successful campaign to gain recognition and bargaining rights.[71] Although the Indonesian activists were not familiar with the case, they recognized the name Kukdong—a Korean firm that also had a factory in Indonesia. Within hours, I was meeting with union leaders at the PT Kukdong factory in Bekasi, an industrial suburb of Jakarta. The two men were proud of having kept factory managers from shifting to short-term contract workers. They had sometimes called on Reebok's compliance staff to help them resolve grievances, and they had been visited by a representative of the US-based Worker Rights Consortium. But they were worried that appealing to Nike or Adidas, which had recently acquired Reebok, could lead to a loss of orders for the factory; and

---

[69] Social Accountability Accreditation Services 2005. Factory managers were asked to state that "if in the future, there would be sufficient interest in forming another labor union, they will allow this to happen." (Social Accountability Accreditation Services 2005). Union officials noted that "the factory was not paying [has not paid] what they owe the workers who were fired in 1999 for forming an SPN union" (interview with union representatives, Jakarta, 9/24/10).

[70] Events at the Metro Garmin factory also show how SA8000 was intertwined with contentious labor relations. Not long after receiving SA8000 certification in 2008, the factory's 15,000 workers were kept out of the factory and told that layoffs would be occurring, leading to massive protests. The company was in the midst of a bitter ownership dispute, and the conflict ultimately shut down the factory for four days, delayed its shipments, and generated a great deal of uncertainty until the ownership struggle was resolved by a court in early 2009 Suwarni 2009; Pikiran Raykat 2008.

[71] See Rodríguez-Garavito 2005; Ross 2006.

in any case, they feared that the factory might move to a part of the country with a lower minimum wage.[72]

When the meeting ended, I walked outside into a sea of workers in light blue uniforms—nearly all women—who were leaving the factory at the end of their shift. Corporate codes of conduct were not irrelevant to this workplace, but their implications were mediated by a number of factors—the threat of relocation, the fragility of transnational activist networks, the gender mismatch in union leadership and membership, and the evolving landscape of apparel and footwear brands, to name just a few.

Similarly, sitting in living rooms in Tangerang, another industrial suburb of Jakarta, packed with workers producing for H&M and Nike, hopes of responsible companies and empowered unions were difficult to sustain. When asked about their main goals, union leaders and members in the H&M supplier did sanot even mention wage increases. "This is so unrealistic that we did not even think of that," one explained.[73] Instead, their pay clung to the minimum wage, with tiny bonuses (roughly 0.15 percent) for seniority.[74]

In the absence of robust factory certification, private regulation of labor standards in Indonesia has mainly occurred through the codes of conduct and ethical sourcing policies of particular brands, such as H&M, Nike, Adidas, Jones Apparel, S. Oliver, C&A, and Wal-Mart. Codes vary in their content, but most ask the supplier to comply with domestic labor law, limit working hours, avoid forced labor and child labor, respect workers' freedom of association, and ensure health and safety protections.

What do these rules mean on the factory floor? Are conditions different in factories that are subject to codes of conduct and factories that produce for markets or brands that do not impose these types of rules? Because most studies of code compliance use data supplied by brands and auditing organizations, researchers have rarely been able to compare factories that are subject to brands' scrutiny to those that are not. Like the data in the previous chapter, a 2009 survey of unionized factories in twenty major industrial cities in Indonesia allows for such comparisons. If there are clear differences, this would not prove that codes *caused* them, but it would provide valuable evidence that factories governed by codes of conduct are distinctive.

The survey was conducted by an Indonesian research firm (JRI Research) on behalf of the Jakarta office of the AFL-CIO's American Center for International Labor Solidarity. The researchers surveyed factory-level union leaders, asking them a variety of questions about workplace characteristics and union

---

[72] Interview with workers, Bekasi, 6/24/08.

[73] Interviews with worker group, Tangerang, 9/30/10.

[74] Workers reported an incentive of 1,500 rupiah per month (less than $0.20 or around 0.15% of the monthly minimum wage of roughly 1 million rupiah) for those with up to fifteen years of experience.

activities as well as whether there is "a code of conduct [or kode etik] in your company that has been required by one or more foreign brands that buy your products to be sold abroad." My focus is on the 120 apparel, textile, or footwear factories captured in the survey, which were located in the greater Jakarta area (44.2 percent), Bandung area (23.3 percent), or other cities (32.5 percent), and had a mean size of 1,356 workers (ranging from less than fifty to over 13,000). Since the survey focuses on unionized, relatively large, formal-sector firms, where conditions are better than average, it "probably underestimates labor-rights violations in Indonesia" and overlooks the factories that receive the least scrutiny.[75] Nevertheless, the survey data provides a valuable opportunity to compare the factories that were covered by codes of conduct (48 percent of the sample) and those that were not.[76] In addition, the unions in these factories are not necessarily powerful; some do not even have collective bargaining agreements in place.

In many respects, factories governed by codes of conduct are not especially different from others—that is, from factories that produce primarily for the domestic market or for foreign buyers that do not impose codes of conduct. A simple comparison reveals, for instance, that approximately 24 percent of factories subject to codes and 26 percent of others had some workers making less than the minimum wage. In other words, it is not uncommon for both code-governed and non-code-governed factories to have at least some employees making less than the minimum wage. In some instances, factory managers can receive a waiver from the government that allows them to pay less than the legal minimum in order to stay afloat. One code of conduct auditor called these waivers "bullshit", noting that "you can buy it" from the government, but he acknowledged that many brands accept them uncritically.[77]

As in the previous chapter, to properly assess the distinctiveness of factories subject to private regulation, it is important to move to regression analyses that control for other potentially relevant characteristics of these factories. The analyses in this chapter control for factory size (the logged number of workers), the product (footwear vs. apparel/textiles), factory ownership (foreign or domestic), the sex composition of the workforce, the factory's relative use of non-permanent workers, the existence of a collective bargaining agreement, and whether a government labor inspector has visited (in the past two years). The figures will show predicted probabilities or predicted values from these analyses, and the full results are available in the Appendix.

---

[75] Caraway, 2010:11.

[76] The 120 factories in this sample were those for which I could triangulate evidence (e.g., export destinations) to substantiate the union leader's response about the code of conduct. I excluded seventeen factories where triangulation produced ambiguity.

[77] Interview with auditor, Jakarta, 6/30/09.

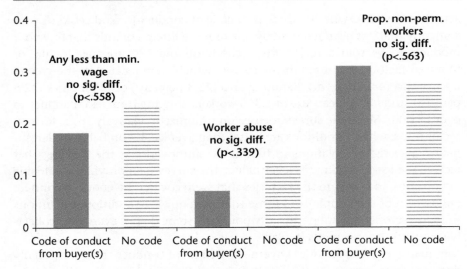

Figure 6.2. Sub-standard and contingent employment: Predicted probabilities and values in factories subject to a buyer's code of conduct in Indonesia

Figure 6.2 shows that across several measures of sub-standard and precarious employment, there are not discernible net differences between code-governed and non-code-governed factories. One might note slight differences in the probability of having workers below the minimum wage and of reported worker abuse (most commonly, being insulted by managers), but these are not statistically discernible.[78] Indeed, across a number of supplemental model specifications—from simple bivariate tests to the use of various combinations of control variables—no relationship can be found between codes of conduct and these measures of sub-standard working conditions. This does not mean that no patterns are apparent, though. As can be seen in the tables in the Appendix, these conditions are clearly less common in factories governed by union collective bargaining agreements.

Since nearly all codes of conduct call for legal compliance, one might also expect factories governed by codes to be less reliant on non-permanent workers—that is, short-term contract workers or workers hired through temporary employment agencies. Indonesian law sets strict limits the circumstances in which these types of workers can be used, such as prohibiting their use for routine work. But as seen in the figure, there is no significant

---

[78] Nor are there statistically discernible raw differences in the incidence of below-minimum wage workers (24% vs. 26%), reported abuse (14% vs. 16%), or the average proportion of non-permanent workers (32% vs. 27%). Note that the slight but non-significant net difference for worker abuse is similar to the finding from China in the previous chapter.

difference here either. Roughly 30 percent of workers are non-permanent on average in both types of factories.[79]

In the factories that utilized short-term contract workers (74 percent of the sample), the union leaders were asked whether the factory engaged in five different practices, all of which are illegal under Indonesian law, such as using contract workers for routine or permanent jobs, not just in exceptional circumstances.[80] The vast majority of factories engaged in at least one of these practices, and 56 percent of factories engaged in at least three. This is a high rate of apparent non-compliance with the 2003 Manpower Act. Nearly all codes of conduct demand legal compliance, and some brands, like Nike and Adidas, have "beyond compliance" rules about the use of contract workers.[81] As shown in Figure 6.3, though, there is no relationship between codes of conduct and illegal uses of contract workers.[82] Out of five measured types of illegal situations in the use of contract workers, the factories in this sample averaged around 2.5, regardless of whether they were subject to codes of conduct or not.

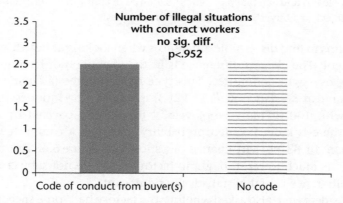

Figure 6.3. Legal non-compliance: Predicted value of illegal uses of contract workers in factories subject to a buyer's code of conduct in Indonesia

---

[79] The raw estimates are 27% vs. 32%, and the difference is not statistically discernible. This average is consistent with practitioner reports that 30–40% of employees were contract workers in the garment factories participating in one upgrading project, but lower than reports from an H&M factory, where workers said that roughly 70% of the employees were contract workers (interview with industry consultant, Jakarta, 6/29/09; interview with worker group, Tangerang, 9/30/09).

[80] The five practices were using contract workers for routine/permanent work, hiring them for longer than three years, extending the contract multiple times, transferring them to related companies, and dismissing and then rehiring contract workers.

[81] Nike limits temporary or short-term contract workers to 15% of all production workers. Adidas sets rules for how and when contract workers can be used (e.g., if contract workers are later hired as permanent workers, their time as a contract worker must count toward seniority).

[82] This result is based on a Poisson regression analysis that is appropriate for count variables and easily produces predicted values. The results are substantively identical when using negative binomial regression modeling, which is more appropriate when there is overdispersion in the outcome variable—a situation that is not present here due to this measure's upper limit of five.

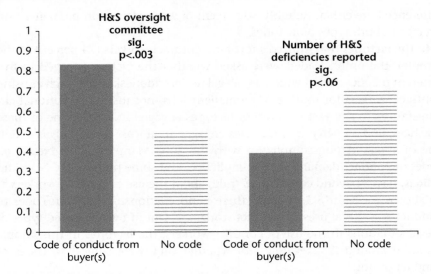

Figure 6.4. Health and Safety: Predicted probabilities of committees and deficiencies in factories subject to a buyer's code of conduct in Indonesia

One begins to find discernible differences when looking at health and safety management. The clearest difference is in the likelihood of having a health and safety oversight committee. This type of committee (a *Panitia Pembina Keselamatan dan Kesehatan Kerja* or P2K3) is required by Indonesian law for factories with 100 or more employees.[83] In factories covered by codes of conduct, there is indeed a high probability that such a committee exists—greater than an 83 percent chance—as shown in Figure 6.4. The predicted probability is much lower, though, in factories that are not subject to codes, and this difference is highly statistically significant.[84]

Union leaders were also asked whether the factory had some specific health and safety measures—namely, a comfortable temperature in the workplace, sufficient ventilation, sufficient lighting, personal safety equipment, general safety equipment, and sufficient fire exits. Summing up the number of items *not* provided, we can see that health and safety deficiencies are lower in factories that are subject to codes of conduct. Code-governed factories had nearly half as many problems on average as non-code-governed factories, although even these factories were not especially problematic by this measure.[85]

---

[83] Ministry of Manpower Decree 4, 1987, PER-04/MEN/1987.

[84] The raw difference in the chances of having such a committee, before controlling for other factors is, 83% vs. 42%.

[85] There were an baseline average of 0.94 problems in non-code and 0.41 in code-governed factories. This difference shrinks somewhat in the regression analyses, but remains statistically discernible at the 0.10 level. I have used negative binomial regression for this set of models, since there is overdispersion in the number of deficiencies despite its ceiling. Poisson and OLS regression

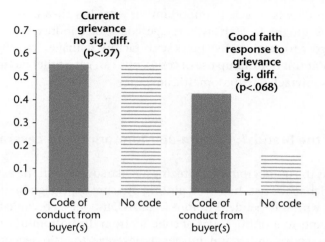

Figure 6.5. Union grievances: Predicted probabilities of grievances and responses from management in factories subject to a buyer's code of conduct in Indonesia

Finally, since these are all unionized factories, one might ask whether unions benefit from codes of conduct. The findings here are mixed, as illustrated in Figure 6.5.[86] On one hand, there is no discernible relationship between codes and the existence of a current major grievance with management, whether measured in raw percentage chances or through the predicted probabilities shown in the figure.[87] As we will see in the following section, unions raised numerous complaints about employment practices and working conditions in factories governed by codes, some of which turned into larger campaigns. On the other hand, there is suggestive evidence that if unions raised grievances, they were more likely to get a good faith response when factories were covered by codes.[88] Analyzing only the sixty-six factories in which a grievance was raised, the net difference in response is notable and fairly statistically discernible ($p<0.068$).[89] It may be that scrutiny from buyers makes factory managers more responsive to workers' complaints, at least when workers are organized.

models produce substantively identical results, with lower p-values for the code coefficient ($p<0.03$).

[86] In previous work using this data, I have found that factories governed by codes are somewhat more likely than others to have collective bargaining agreements that union leaders rate as good, although they are no more likely to have their collective bargaining agreements respected by management (Bartley and Egels-Zandén 2016). In analyses that include electronics factories, though, these differences become less discernible (Bartley and Egels-Zandén 2015).

[87] The raw percentages are 59% vs. 51%, but this difference is not statistically significant.

[88] In the survey, this means the union representative said there was a grievance, and that "the company has responded and it appears that they will address the problem in good faith."

[89] Given the smaller sample size and greater baseline comparability of cases, since a grievance has already been lodged, the full model here only includes controls for factory size, product, foreign ownership, and the proportions of women and non-permanent workers.

This last finding is especially important for what lies ahead. As we will see, some unions sought to actively leverage codes of conduct and appeal to brands in order to resolve grievances with factory management. By looking more closely at this bottom-up use of codes, one can get a fuller picture of how private rules interacted with domestic advocacy.

"Going to the Brands": Bottom-up Monitoring and Leveraging

As far back as the underground organizing at Nike suppliers in the early 1990s, Indonesian labor activists had been putting pressure on foreign brands. In the early 2000s, with independent unions legalized, Indonesia became the site of several attempts to monitor codes of conduct from the bottom-up, and sometimes to use codes and brand images as leverage to gain recognition for insurgent unions. Shaping government policy remained crucial, but "going to the brands" became an important part of some unions' repertoires. Perhaps brands' stated commitments to "freedom of association" and legal compliance could be turned into support for—or at least tolerance of—empowered unions in their suppliers' factories. "Factories are more afraid of the buyers than of the Indonesian government," explained one union leader.[90] A trade association representative essentially agreed, arguing that factory managers can easily pay off local officials, but buyers tend to look more closely.[91] Moreover, many workers saw top-down auditing of codes as either a ritualistic farce or a burden. "Monitors just put more burden on the workers," said one former garment worker. "You have to act properly when they come—put the mask on. Workers already have enough burdens."[92]

Unions and NGOs first began to strategize about codes of conduct in meetings and trainings in 1999 and 2000. As one union leader explained, "Most of us at the time didn't know that codes or CSR could be used as a weapon or tool in our struggles. Up to that time...workers assumed [CSR] was only for the community [i.e., community charity] and excluded the workers.... [Soon], we started to talk about using international labor standards, codes of conduct, as alternative tools—besides using the local and national labor law."[93] In 2002, the German social-democratic foundation, the Friedrich Ebert Stiftung (FES), began to convene Indonesian unions and labor NGOs for workshops and

---

[90] Interview with union leader, Jakarta, 9/26/10.

[91] Interview with industry association leader, Jakarta, 9/20/10. A leader in another trade association, who is also a factory manager, made a similar comment: "The brands are enforcing labor law more than the government is" (interview with factory manager and industry association representative, Jakarta, 7/8/08).

[92] Interview with union staff member, Jakarta, 6/25/08.

[93] Interview with union leader, Jakarta, 6/25/08.

trainings, focusing on factories that supplied German firms, such as Adidas, Karstadt-Quelle, and Otto Versand.[94]

Over time, these meetings evolved into an organized "Code of Conduct Network", intended to serve as a bottom-up alternative to the top-down auditing of code compliance. "If there are any violations, hopefully the workers will file a complaint to the network first," explained one organizer. "We can do advocacy work and if it doesn't work, file a complaint to the international community."[95] In a series of seminars in the Jakarta and Bandung areas, union representatives were introduced to the various players in global supply chains and the potential "moral sanction" behind codes of conduct—namely, that "the brand/buyer is humiliated" by an international campaign.[96] Network leaders hoped that trainings would help workers to monitor code compliance and help unions to strengthen their collective bargaining agreements.[97] More generally, labor-rights activists hoped that they could use codes of conduct as leverage to push for improvements in factory conditions and respect for independent unions.[98]

The Code of Conduct Network was occasionally hobbled by internal conflicts.[99] But in tandem with campaigns waged by Oxfam-Australia and investigations by the Worker Rights Consortium, labor activists generated new channels for factory scrutiny and brand accountability. "13–15 years ago, no worker would even know about the CoC, but now they at least know it exists," said one labor activist.[100] Several unions became especially active in leveraging codes of conduct. GSBI (Gabungan Serikat Buruh Indonesia), an activist-oriented union founded by an Indonesian labor NGO, organized insurgent workers in factories producing for Adidas, Nike, Tommy Hilfiger, and others.[101] SPN (Serikat Pekerja Nasional), a larger union founded by reformers who had exited the state-sponsored SPSI, used codes to push for improvements in several factories in the apparel and footwear industry. Similarly, FSPTSK unions (Federasi Serikat Pekerja Tekstil Sandang dan Kulit, which was previously joined with SPN) appealed to Liz Claiborne, Adidas, and other brands to request help in resolving grievances with factory management.

---

[94] FES report, "Code of Conducts to enforce core labour standards as subject of the national Trade Union Education Activities of FES in Indonesia," no date, FES records.

[95] Interview with NGO representative, Jakarta, 6/30/09.

[96] Notes on CoC Network seminar in Bandung, October 2005, FES records.

[97] Interview with NGO representative, Jakarta, 7/9/08 and 10/1/10.

[98] See Rodríguez-Garavito 2005.

[99] Interview with union representative, Jakarta, 9/30/10; interview with NGO representative, Jakarta, 10/1/10; interview with NGO representative, Jakarta, 6/30/09; interview with NGO representative, Jakarta, 9/23/10.

[100] Interview with NGO representative, Jakarta, 7/7/08.

[101] Mizuno, Tjandraningsih, and Herawati 2007.

Table 6.2. "Going to the Brands": Forms of leveraging by Indonesian unions

Type of Leveraging	Freq.	Illustrative Cases
Whistleblowing: *Contacting brands (or threatening to do so) to resolve a particular grievance*	12 cases found	PT Merindo PT Dong One PT SM Global PT Nikomas
Brand boomerang campaign: *Insurgent union seeking recognition*	10 cases found	PT Kolon Langgeng PT Dae Joo Leports PT Mulia Knitting PT Panarub

What forms did this bottom-up scrutiny take, and how powerful was it? Interviews with representatives of unions and NGOs in the greater Jakarta and Bandung areas revealed several types of leveraging activities and a number of specific cases in which they were used. The two most common types of leveraging are shown in Table 6.2. First, some unions engaged in a kind of "whistleblowing"—that is, making contact with brands' compliance staff to ask for help in resolving grievances with factory management. Because these contacts happened behind the scenes and usually without publicity, this type of leveraging has rarely been studied. As we will see, this activity often spurred improvements, though nearly always only modest ones. Second and more visibly, unions and their allies sometimes waged "brand boomerang campaigns" to build support for insurgent unions. Adapting the "boomerang" model of appealing to international audiences when local opportunities are blocked, labor activists in a number of locations have turned to pressuring well-known brands to appeal for support for their local struggles.[102] Several such "brand boomerang" campaigns in Indonesia appeared to work. As we will see, though, their gains were often erased by factory closures and declining union power.

Overall, this section will show how bottom-up enforcement of codes of conduct produced meaningful but modest improvements, while more ambitious attempts to alter the balance of power essentially failed. After documenting this pattern, I will explore why leveraging was so limited in influence and how leveraging strategies have evolved over time.

Blowing the whistle: leveraging codes for modest improvements

Without waging international campaigns, unions could sometimes reach out to the compliance staff of brands to get assistance in resolving particular

---

[102] For the original formulation of the boomerang model of transnational advocacy, see Keck and Sikkink 1998. For its shift from a focus on governments and inter-governmental organizations to the "brand boomerang", see especially Armbruster-Sandoval 2005.

grievances. These were usually related to treatment by factory managers, social security and health insurance, bonus payments, and job classifications (e.g., the use of short-term contract workers). Especially when brands had in-country compliance staff, unions could make routine contact without having to surmount the language barriers of contacting an office in Germany, the UK, or the US.[103] As one international activist working in Indonesia put it, "unions actually now have the cellphone numbers of compliance staff."[104]

For instance, at the PT Merindo apparel factory, the union (an affiliate of FSPTSK) sought to get the factory to make its legally required contributions to the *Jamsostek* health insurance system. When managers dragged their feet and retaliated, union leaders contacted not only local labor bureau (Disnaker) but also the factory's main buyer, Liz Claiborne, with help from a human resource manager and information from the brand's code of conduct. Factory manage-ment did begin making required insurance contributions at this point, although it is unclear what specific action Liz Claiborne took.[105]

At the PT Golden Castle factory, the same union arranged for an unannounced midnight visit by an Adidas auditor to expose excessive over-time. Appealing to Adidas also led to the firing of a manager who had sexually harassed workers and to the reinstatement of three dismissed workers. Interest-ingly, these contacts were facilitated by the Adidas auditor leaving her phone number with factory workers. The contacts were not without tension, though. The factory's HR department had instructed the union not to have further contacts with Adidas, since this might lead the brand to stop its orders.[106]

Events at SM Global, an apparel supplier for Nike, demonstrate this danger. A GSBI unionist reported to a local Nike representative that the factory was using more short-term contract workers than allowed by Nike's code of con-duct (which limits contract workers to 15 percent of all production workers). After a Nike representative promised to look into it further, the union noticed improvements. But soon but Nike soon stopped placing orders in the factory, telling the union that the factory was not improving quickly enough. Factory managers blamed the union, dismissed some workers, and forced remaining workers to sign an agreement saying that they would never again complain to the brands.[107] Yet the factory continued to produce Nike products, now as a subcontractor for one of Nike's large suppliers.[108]

---

[103] Interview (conducted by research assistant) with union leader, Jakarta, 2/8/10.
[104] Interview with NGO representative, Jakarta, 7/7/08.
[105] Interview with union representatives, Jakarta, 9/25/10.
[106] Ibid. Additional interviews with unionists, conducted by research assistants working with my collaborator, Niklas Egels-Zandén, gathered some of the details on these two cases. See Bartley and Egels-Zandén 2016. This chapter considers cases that are discussed in that article, as well as several more (e.g., PT Dae Joo Leports, PT Sinar Apparel, PT Panarub, PT Kizone, and HASI/NASA).
[107] Interview with union leaders, Jakarta, 9/23/10.
[108] Interview with worker group, Tangerang, 10/1/10.

These kinds of risks have kept workers from routinely blowing the whistle to brands. Still, codes of conduct did provide some leverage, however unreliable, for resolving grievances. In a few cases, the mere threat of contacting brands was sufficient to spur changes. At the PT Olympic garment factory, the union's threat of contacting the buyers—which included The Gap, JC Penney, Wal-Mart and J. Crew—was apparently enough to revise the plan to treat workers who went from "contract" to "permanent" status as new workers, which would have reduced their wages and bonuses.[109] The union at the PT Dong One apparel factory used a mix of actual and threatened contact with Nike's auditors and watchdogs to resolve grievances regarding severance pay, medical expenses, and an abusive manager.[110] Despite nontrivial but modest gains such as these, wages often remained close to the legal minimum in these factories, even for workers with years of experience.[111] Generally, unions could negotiate over their rights and protections, but they could rarely demand that managers increase their pay.

The one partial exception occurred in 2012 at the Nikomas Gemiling factory, where the union and its allies successfully demanded compensation for years of unpaid overtime. The Nikomas factory is one of Nike and Adidas's largest suppliers in Indonesia. It is owned by the Taiwanese footwear giant Pou Chen—the same company that owns Yue Yuen, as profiled in Chapter 5. As with Yue Yuen, Nike, Adidas, and other footwear brands pushed a series of reforms at Nikomas in the late 1990s and 2000s: The glue containing toxic toluene was phased out; excessive overtime was whittled down to a norm of sixty hours per week; and abusive managers were disciplined, though workers still reported having insults shouted at them.[112] It came to light later, though, that Nikomas had been cheating workers out of wages by using the practice of *"jam molor"* or "hour delay", in effect requiring some work off the clock.[113]

This forced, unpaid overtime at Nikomas was revealed in 2011 in discussions between SPN leaders at the factory and a US-based watchdog of Nike, Jim

---

[109] Interview with union leaders, Jakarta, 9/28/10.

[110] After initial complaints led to a connection with US-based anti-Nike activist Jim Keady, the union chairman reported that factory management was more inclined to accommodate their demands. Over time, the union began to refer to the code of conduct in internal negotiations, without actually going to Nike (interviews with union leaders, Jakarta, 9/26/10).

[111] Interview with union representative, Jakarta, 9/26/10.

[112] Connor 2002; Bernstein 2000.

[113] Note that this was not reported by the independent monitors assigned by the Fair Labor Association (FLA tracking chart 07003355B, 2003). Talking to workers, it is clear that the practice is not unique to Nikomas. Workers at SM Global, a Nike subcontractor, reported that it is common in their factory as well, although the union had managed to reduce the length of unpaid time substantially (interview with worker group, Tangerang, 10/1/10). A worker at PT Ing, which makes apparel for Wal-Mart, Aeropostale, and others, similarly noted unpaid overtime in some months (interview with worker, Bandung, 9/18/10). Workers at an H&M supplier noted that unpaid overtime is most common when new products are introduced and workers cannot meet the production target in the allotted time (interview with worker group, Tangerang, 9/30/10).

Keady, who had been focused on Nike in Indonesia for more than a decade. Keady's one-man organization, Team Sweat (previously Educating for Justice) blew the whistle to Nike and publicly pressured the company to respond. Ultimately, Nike and SPN cooperated in sending two sets of observers, one undercover, and in documenting unpaid overtime.[114] In early 2012, Nikomas management and the union reached an agreement for the company to pay approximately $1 million in back wages, to be distributed to nearly 4,500 workers. An SPN national chairman remarked that the agreement "has the potential to send shockwaves through the Indonesian labor movement."[115] Whether such achievements can be repeated in other factories, though, remains to be seen.

Brand boomerangs and the limits of "freedom of association" assurances

While both Indonesian law and brands' codes of conduct support freedom of association, union organizers are nevertheless vulnerable to dismissal from their jobs or harassment by managers, "legacy union" representatives, police, or local "strongmen". In several cases, insurgent unions sought to gain support or protection by spotlighting brands. Here, brands' claims to respect freedom of association would face their greatest test.

One notable case comes from the PT Kolon Langgeng factory, which produced apparel for Nike and other brands. When the Worker Rights Consortium investigated the factory in 2002, it found a variety of code of conduct violations, including forced overtime, verbal abuse, arbitrary firings, as well as an essentially defunct SPSI management union.[116] At the WRC's urging, factory management said it would negotiate with legitimate worker representatives, but when a group of workers registered as affiliates of the activist-oriented GSBI, managers backtracked and sought to promote a new company union. In response, the WRC convened a meeting with representatives of factory management and Nike. This led factory managers to move forward with a new union election, and the WRC reported that "intervention by Nike and its broker, particularly during [this] meeting..., played a central role in achieving this result."[117] In addition to pressure from Nike, an alliance of unions in the export processing zone reportedly told factory managers that they would come with "an army of workers" unless a meeting with the GSBI-affiliated organizers was held.[118]

---

[114] Jim Keady, Team Sweat Report "Victory at Nike's PT Nikomas factory", email of October 20, 2011.

[115] Bambang Wirahyoso, quoted in "Indonesian Nike Workers Win $1m in Unpaid Overtime," *Jakarta Globe* January 11, 2012.

[116] Worker Rights Consortium 2003b.   [117] Worker Rights Consortium 2003b:10.

[118] Interview with union representative, Jakarta, 9/26/10.

Although internal conflict threatened to derail the GSBI affiliates, they ultimately succeeded in gaining recognition from factory management and enough support from workers to begin preparing for collective bargaining negotiations.[119] The WRC reported that the factory "has made important progress on several fronts" and listed it among a handful of candidates for its new Designated Suppliers Program in 2005.[120]

Around this time, though, the factory lost its direct orders from Nike and several other brands, for reasons that are hard to pinpoint. It was reorganized under new ownership and re-named PT Kwangduk Langgeng, producing for J. C. Penney, S. Oliver, Inditex (Zara), and as a subcontractor to a Nike supplier.[121] In 2009, as the company was struggling, it turned against unionists, seeking to blacklist activists to prevent their employment throughout the export processing zone. By 2010, the factory had closed. The WRC described this as a case in which "a factory, for several years, made good faith efforts to comply with university and buyer codes of conduct, yet experienced a continuing loss of orders from buyers."[122] Another company, PT BTS, re-opened the factory with new management and new workers in 2010—essentially erasing the remaining traces of GSBI's work.[123] In this case, a "brand boomerang" process created a window of opportunity for an insurgent union, but the window was quickly shut as the union began to gain power.

A similar story occurred at PT Dae Joo Leports, which produced backpacks for Adidas and VF. After an investigation by the WRC and scrutiny from the brands, factory managers agreed to sign a collective bargaining agreement with existing union (an SPTSK affiliate) and to recognize a new independent union that was forming in the factory.[124] But soon thereafter, the parent company announced that the factory would be shutting down and production would shift to one of its factories in China.[125] Adidas and VF pushed back, asking Dae Joo Leports to reconsider or provide a legitimate business reason for the closure, but the company held fast in its decision. Although the brands pushed for displaced workers to receive higher than usual severance pay, the rising power of unions at this factory had effectively been quashed by the move to China. As Oxfam argued, this case illustrates the limits of brands' nudges in support of labor rights: "If Adidas and VF had a policy to prioritise retention of orders in factories with democratic unions then they would have likely had greater success in persuading Daejoo to stay in Indonesia."[126] Adidas severed ties with the factory's parent company, but the damage in

---

[119] Interview with NGO representatives, Jakarta, 10/1/10.
[120] Worker Rights Consortium 2003b:35; Worker Rights Consortium 2006a.
[121] Worker Rights Consortium 2011.   [122] Worker Rights Consortium 2011:5.
[123] Interview (conducted by research assistant) with former worker, Jakarta, 12/11/10.
[124] Worker Rights Consortium 2003a.   [125] Worker Rights Consortium 2004b.
[126] Connor and Dent 2006:42.

Indonesia had been done, and the factory in China continued to produce for VF as well as Timberland, REI, Decathlon, and others.[127]

In another case, when a union formed at the PT Sinar Apparel factory in 2005, management retaliated by filing not only a labor dispute but also a criminal case against a union leader, utilizing Indonesia's notoriously vague charge of "unpleasant conduct toward others". The union reached out through international trade union structures to call on the factory's main buyer, Jones Apparel, to enforce its assurance of freedom of association, and the brand quickly responded and convinced factory managers to drop the criminal charge.[128] But within two years, Jones Apparel had stopped buying from this factory, fearing it had financial problems.[129] In 2008, the factory shut down and the owner fled the country, leaving workers without their legally required severance pay.[130]

While factory closings undermined unions in these three cases, the campaign at the PT Mulia Knitting factory fell short for different reasons. In 2007, a group of workers affiliated with GSBI delivered papers to management to register a new union to challenge the SPSI legacy union. As described later by the WRC, "over the course of the following ten days, each of the workers listed on the documents was dismissed, suspended, or transferred to a far-away location, or resigned from the union under pressure from management."[131] GSBI complained to factory management but received no reply. "So we thought about international pressure," one unionist said. "We always try to negotiate first... It was three months before we decided to go to the WRC and CCC [Clean Clothes Campaign] to get their support and to talk with the brands."[132]

The union and its international allies appealed to three of the factory's buyers—Polo Ralph Lauren, Phillips-Van Heusen (PVH), and Tommy Hilfiger. Polo Ralph Lauren did not respond. PVH, a veteran of anti-sweatshop struggles, quickly conveyed its concerns to PT Mulia management, but was reportedly told to "just leave" the factory, since its orders there were small.[133] Tommy Hilfiger sent its sourcing agent to investigate and concluded that there was no problem, spurring to protests by Clean Clothes Campaign activists at Tommy Hilfiger headquarters in Amsterdam.[134] The company's response changed after it was acquired by PVH in 2010. Ultimately, Tommy

---

[127] Qingdao Dae Joo Leports Co., Ltd, "About Us", http://daejoo.en.china.cn/About-Us/ accessed July 31, 2015; Timberland 2009.

[128] ICFTU 2006; interview with NGO leaders, Jakarta, 10/1/10.

[129] Email correspondence with brand representative, November 9, 2010.

[130] US State Department 2008.   [131] Worker Rights Consortium 2008:6.

[132] Interview with union representative, Jakarta, 9/23/10.

[133] Interview with union leader, Jakarta, 9/23/10. See Armbruster-Sandoval 2005 on PVH's history.

[134] Worker Rights Consortium 2008; Clean Clothes Campaign 2010a.

Hilfiger representatives helped to broker a deal in which factory management paid compensation to five of the dismissed union leaders and signed an agreement with GSBI stating its respect for freedom of association.[135] The Clean Clothes Campaign and GSBI declared victory. But while the union had won outside the factory, inside the factory, its numbers had dwindled over time. It had only around twenty-five members out of 1,200 workers by the end of 2010, and leaders reported that further organizing was difficult due to the company's attempts to coopt dissent.[136] As of early 2011, several workers interviewed at the factory knew of the GSBI union, but said it was no longer active due to the leaders' dismissal.[137] In this case, local activists successfully worked with international allies to pressure brands to intervene but failed in their attempts to build a local base of power.

THE LONG STRUGGLE AT PT PANARUB

The most contentious and complex case occurred at PT Panarub, a large footwear supplier for Adidas. Here, there was a long struggle between two competing unions, factory management, and Adidas. On one hand, this case illustrates "the ability of Asian manufacturers to resist networked pressure from local trade unions, international NGOs and even MNC customers" as Tim Connor and Fiona Haines (2013) put it.[138] On the other hand, there are indications that the long struggle had some positive consequences, which were pre-empted in faster-moving cases with more mobile factories.[139]

In the fall of 2000, an insurgent union, Perbupas—a GSBI affiliate that had been among the first unions in Indonesia to elect rank-and-file leaders—waged a strike.[140] After a woman involved in the strikes was arrested under the notoriously vague charge of "unpleasant conduct toward others", GSBI and Oxfam-Australia pressured Adidas to take a stand.[141] In what looked like an initial victory, Adidas lobbied for the union leader to be released, and after her acquittal, pushed for her to be reinstated.[142]

In 2004, as the company moved to dismiss a group of workers, the Perbupas union "used this moment to organize them."[143] This meant challenging the existing SPN union in the factory, which Perbupas argued had gotten preferential treatment. The Worker Rights Consortium, which had been contacted by GSBI, found evidence of discrimination against Perbupas members, as well as weak safety procedures, noncompliance with labor law, and verbal

---

[135] Clean Clothes Campaign 2010b.   [136] Interview with union leader, Jakarta, 9/23/10.
[137] Interview (conducted by research assistant) with workers, Tangerang, 1/17/11.
[138] P. 207.
[139] This speaks to the role of time in allowing for contention to generate improvement, as seen in Chapter 2 on Indonesian forestry and the case of Perum Perhutani.
[140] Ballinger 2000.   [141] Jakarta Post 2001.   [142] Connor and Dent 2006.
[143] Interview with union representative, Jakarta, 9/23/10.

abuse.[144] Although some reforms followed, including office space for Perbupas, the conflict between the two unions remained intense. Roughly 15 percent of workers were Perbupas members, and around 55 percent were SPN members, but Perbupas charged that many had been improperly channeled into SPN membership.[145] Adidas endorsed the WRC's suggestion to hold a new verification of union memberships, but the two unions could not agree on how the process should work, and neither Adidas nor Panarub management was willing to push the process forward. An Adidas compliance manager described the situation as "a big headache for me.... We have tried just about everything in our power to ease the tension...It's just that the competition is very fierce."[146] Indeed, a study of union conflict in several factories in Indonesia found that Panarub had "the most intense levels of conflict.... Both unions are treated harshly by management, but each believes that the other receives favourable treatment."[147]

Questions about Adidas's responsibility resurfaced in 2005, when thirty-three Perbupas members were dismissed after a one day strike to increase holiday bonuses. Although different government agencies disagreed over whether the firings were legal, Adidas eventually supported the unionists' claim that they should be reinstated. On the other hand, Adidas announced that it would be reducing its orders from PT Panarub, due to "overall business performance, not just the union matters."[148] With factory management resistant to rehiring the unionists, Adidas helped a few get jobs at its other suppliers, although some workers worried they were being blacklisted.[149]

On the whole, even those pressuring Adidas recognize that the brands' actions went further than most. "[Adidas] did pressure management to issue a public statement that they supported freedom of association. This is pretty significant."[150] Yet the brand would not agree to guarantee orders from PT Panarub if and only if freedom of association was respected. Doing so might have strengthened the unions' responsiveness and bargaining power and lent greater weight to the brand's code of conduct. In most respects, the case of PT Panarub must be seen as an example of the limited power of the brand boomerang, as Connor and Haines (2013) argue.

And yet, in the midst of the union dispute, the WRC found that there had been "major improvements in working conditions", including changes to occupational health and safety, physical conditions in the factory, working hours, and health insurance.[151] Over time, a Perbupas union re-formed at PT

---

[144] Worker Rights Consortium 2004a.   [145] Rokhani 2008.
[146] Interview with brand representative, Jakarta, 7/10/08.   [147] Rokhani 2008:7.
[148] Interview with brand representative, Jakarta, 7/10/08.
[149] Oxfam-Australia Letter to Frank Henke and William Anderson of Adidas, September 10, 2008.
[150] Interview with NGO representative, Jakarta, 7/10/08.
[151] Worker Rights Consortium 2006d:1; Worker Rights Consortium 2006b.

Panarub, and continued to mount small-scale strikes. In 2010, Perbupas and SPN even cooperated to a degree when workers spontaneously protested against the late payment of a holiday bonus.[152] Some advocates see PT Panarub as being well above average in labor conditions, at least since the wake-up call of international pressure.[153] The factory, though smaller than in the past, has continued to be a core supplier for Adidas.[154]

The limits of leveraging

As these cases show, bottom-up monitoring and leveraging generated some improvements but usually of a very modest or fleeting sort. Indonesian factories did not become models of respect for labor rights, and Indonesian unions struggled to demand even small improvements from factory managers. Of course, the strategy of "going to the brands" is itself limited to particular segments of an industry. It is unlikely to occur in factories that produce solely for the domestic market, those that produce for brands with little investment in their images, or in non-unionized factories. Based on interviews and a review of secondary materials, it appears that there were fewer than thirty factories in the Jakarta and Bandung areas in which unions appealed to brands in some fashion between 2002 and 2012. While there were likely others that did not come to light, the total in any case would be a small fraction of the more than 400 export-oriented apparel or footwear factories located in these areas, many of which were unionized.[155]

Even when local activists sought to mobilize international networks, their efforts sometimes fell short. For instance, when the owner of PT Mutiara Mitra, which produced apparel for Talbots, S. Oliver, and other brands, shut down the factory and fled the country in 2009, workers occupied the factory and began a campaign to demand their legally entitled

---

[152] Interview with union representative, Jakarta, 9/24/10.

[153] Interview with NGO representative, Jakarta, 7/9/08; interview with NGO representative, Jakarta, 6/25/09. In 2012, a large strike occurred at another factory owned by the same parent company, PT Panarub Dwikarya Benoa. This resulted in dismissals and another round of pressure on Adidas to intervene in support of union rights. In this case, Adidas pushed for the factory management and union to engage in mediation while warning that some parts of managers' initial response may be inconsistent with Adidas's code.

[154] Adidas 2015.

[155] The Indonesian government's 2011 Directory of Exporters lists more than 400 apparel and footwear factories in these areas. Although union density in formal sector employment in Indonesia is only 8–11% (Ford 2009; Caraway 2015), it is higher in the apparel and footwear industry. One survey of workers in apparel factories supplying leading American and European brands found that 65% reported belonging to a union, and 51% said they were covered by a collective bargaining agreement. I would estimate that 40–60% of the export-oriented factories in the Jakarta and Bandung areas are unionized, although the unions may vary dramatically in their goals and activities.

severance payments.[156] A few individual labor activists from the US visited the factory, and some domestic labor NGOs provided support, but no international campaign or communication with the brands occurred. One international advocate admitted that the organization "may have dropped the ball" in this case.[157] In the end, the workers auctioned the factory's machinery, but this only allowed them to receive a fraction of the severance pay to which they were legally entitled.[158]

How can we explain the limits of leveraging? As other scholars have pointed out, the voluntary character and limited scope of corporate codes clearly matter.[159] To explain the pattern in Indonesia, though, one must also attend to several aspects of the domestic context. First, as I will argue below, the unstable and precarious position of Indonesia in the global apparel industry left little time and space for meaningful improvement. Second, there appears in this case to be a mismatch between the logic of private regulation, which focuses on changes within the factory, and the locus of Indonesian unions' power, which has been much greater *outside* the factory.

RISK AND PRECARITY

Code-related improvements occur in particular factories, but particular factories were routinely cast aside in the highly competitive and mobile apparel and footwear industry. Apparel brands routinely churn through factories as they change products and search for low prices, high quality, and timely delivery. Levi Strauss, certainly not the most fast-moving company but one of the few to disclose its supply chain, had fourteen suppliers in Indonesia in 2005. Only three of these were being used in 2009, along with ten new suppliers. By 2014, Levis had only four suppliers in Indonesia, including just one from 2009 and none from 2005.

The precarity of apparel factories in Indonesia stemmed in part from intense international competition associated with the phase out of the Multi-Fiber Arrangement (MFA). This set of trade agreements, forged in the 1970s, had limited the amount of apparel and textile imports to the US, Canada, and EU countries that could come from any single country. Because the regime conflicted with the General Agreement on Tariffs and Trade and the World Trade Organization, a phase-out began in 1995, with the final set of quotas being eliminated in 2005. Many scholars and activists feared that the apparel industry

---

[156] Hukum 2010.

[157] Interview with labor-rights advocate, Jakarta, 9/29/10.

[158] Interview with union leaders, Jakarta, 9/28/10. Each worker received the equivalent of several months' salary, but the workers who had been there many years were legally entitled to far more.

[159] Seidman 2007; Esbenshade 2012.

would gravitate entirely to China once the MFA was eliminated.[160] China's apparel exports did grow in the post-MFA period, but it did not entirely take over the industry, in part because wages also began to rise in Chinese manufacturing regions.

Instead, brands in the post-MFA period shifted orders between a portfolio of Asian countries, especially China, Vietnam, Bangladesh, India, and Indonesia. Low tariff treatment made Bangladesh especially attractive for the European market, helping the value of its apparel exports to increase by 294 percent from 2000 to 2011.[161] Indonesia continued to be an attractive sourcing location for some, though its position depended largely on labor costs and unrest in China and Vietnam. Indeed, some brands that had shifted away from Indonesia began to return as costs and disruptions began to increase in China and Vietnam around 2007. This was stated bluntly by the sourcing director of the US apparel company VF, who reported in 2009 that the company would more than triple its sourcing from Indonesia in the next four years, since "labor costs and living standards are growing so fast in China and Vietnam."[162] Yet VF, like many other companies, also moved even more aggressively into Bangladesh, where wages are lower than in Indonesia.

Intense cost competition also led to the movement of factories and orders within Indonesia. In what some labor activists have called a "race to the bottom within Indonesia", factories in the traditional manufacturing regions were replaced by those in frontier locations.[163] Apparel, textile, and footwear employment in Jakarta declined by 38 percent from 2000 to 2008, but it increased by 10 percent in Central Java, where the provincial minimum wage was 50–60 percent of Jakarta's.[164] Foreign investors set up a number of new factories in West Java cities such as Subang and Sukabumi, where minimum wages are roughly 60–70 percent of those in the traditional manufacturing cities.[165]

Annual manufacturing surveys suggest that more than half of the textile, apparel, or footwear firms (with at least fifty employees) that existed in 2000 were gone by 2008.[166] Many of the failed firms were producing for the domestic market, which was flooded by Chinese imports after the MFA-phaseout.[167] But an analysis of the directories reveals that export-oriented

---

[160] Appelbaum, Bonacich, and Quan 2005; Maquila Solidarity Network 2003.
[161] Based on calculations from WTO merchandise trade data.
[162] Notes from WRAP Foundations Seminar, Jakarta, 7/2/09.
[163] Interview with NGO representative, Jakarta, 6/24/08.
[164] Using data from the Indonesian Statistics Bureau's (Badan Pusat Statistik (BPS)) Annual Manufacturing Surveys in 2000, 2004, and 2008, I calculated the number of workers in apparel, textile, and footwear factories in each province.
[165] Interview with NGO representative, Bandung, 9/29/10.
[166] This is based on the BPS Annual Manufacturing Surveys in 2000, 2004, and 2008.
[167] AKATIGA Center for Social Analysis 2007.

apparel factories were actually *more* likely than their domestic counterparts to fail during this period.[168] Failures continued with the deepening of the global financial crisis, with more than 20 percent of apparel factories (with at least 100 employees) operating in 2009 having failed by 2014.[169]

The footwear industry has lower turnover in suppliers, since factories are more capital-intensive and must have more advanced production capabilities. Here, collaborative relationships between brands and suppliers have been more important, potentially allowing greater improvements in labor conditions.[170] Nevertheless, several large footwear factories in Indonesia lost some or all of their orders from Adidas and Nike as the brands increased their sourcing from Vietnam, shed peripheral suppliers to work closely with "core" suppliers—or in the case of Adidas, consolidated the supply chain after acquiring Reebok in 2005. Restructuring supply-chain relationships meant casting aside a number of factories, including some with above-average labor conditions. For instance, Nike stopped placing orders at the PT Doson footwear factory in 2002 as the union was gaining power.[171] According to one union leader, "from the 11 factories that produce[d] for Nike, Doson was the best in working conditions."[172]

It should be clear from the Indonesian case that brands may pledge to support freedom of association, but this does not mean they will commit to unionized factories. "So many other factors are involved in sourcing decisions. We can't just choose a unionized factory," explained one footwear brand representative.[173] This riled labor activists and factory owners alike. As one owner lamented, "we [factories in Indonesia] haven't reaped the reward yet for making progress in the right direction. [Orders] keep moving to China and Vietnam."[174] In short, both footwear and apparel factories in Indonesia faced high risks of losing orders as brands shuffled and re-shuffled their portfolios, while they reaped few rewards from operating in a context that is compatible with the standards that brands supposedly demand.

THE MISMATCH

The limits of leveraging cannot be explained solely with reference to the global political economy of apparel and footwear production. Interviewing union representatives about their demands and campaigns, one begins to see

---

[168] Bartley and Kincaid 2015.

[169] This estimate comes from the BPS's Directory of Manufacturers. Out of 582 apparel firms with at least 100 employees listed in 2009, I took a random 25% sample (N=147) and tracked whether each firm was still listed five years later in the 2014 version of the Directory. Thirty-two firms were absent from the 2014 directory, leading to an estimate of a 22% failure rate in five years.

[170] Frenkel and Scott 2002; Locke, Amengual, and Mangla 2009.

[171] Connor and Dent 2006.   [172] Interview with union leader, Jakarta, 9/24/10.

[173] Interview with brand representative, Jakarta, 7/10/08.

[174] Interview with factory manager and trade association representative, Jakarta, 7/8/08.

another part of the explanation: Indonesian unions tend to be weak at the factory level, so they have had little power to take advantage of the opportunities provided by codes of conduct.

Unions may negotiate with factory managers over holiday bonuses, transportation allowances, and the use of contract workers—and they may press managers to comply with laws on dismissals and severance pay—but they rarely bargain over wages at the factory level.[175] Instead, the legal minimum wage essentially becomes the prevailing wage, and sometimes nearly the maximum wage for production workers. In addition, unionized workplaces may lack even rudimentary collective bargaining agreements. In the survey data analyzed earlier in this chapter, 38 percent of unionized apparel, textile, and footwear factories did not have a collective bargaining agreement in place, and 30 percent had an agreement that union leaders described as doing nothing more than restating rights accorded by law. Union dues are meager—perhaps just 0.5 percent of the minimum wage, the equivalent of around 40 to 50 cents per month—and few resources flow upward to the federations, potentially leaving central offices disconnected from factory-level unions.[176] Moreover, even factory-level union leaders may not be close to production workers. Most apparel and footwear workers are women, but there are few women in union leadership positions, albeit with a few prominent exceptions.[177] At the H&M supplier mentioned above, roughly ¾ of the workers were women, but seven out of ten union leaders were men.[178]

As Teri Caraway (2015) argues, the organizational weakness of Indonesian unions can be traced to the persistence of SPSI legacy unions that were accustomed to state funding, the challenge of organizing contingent workers, and several aspects of the domestic legal environment. In particular, the low threshold for union recognition has bred fragmentation and inter-union conflict rather than rising labor power in the workplace. In addition, because unions have to "jump through a series of hoops over a period of about three weeks before they can strike legally," unions rarely use strikes to bolster collective bargaining.[179] While there are laws on the books protecting unionists from retaliation, enforcement by labor inspectors, police, and courts has been lax. Caraway (2015) reports that "in the more than ten years since the

---

[175] As a result, wages in unionized and non-unionized factories are not vastly different, although unions may increase the likelihood of minimum wage compliance. In addition, unions may matter for severance payments. One worker noted that severance payments were three times more in his unionized factory than in his wife's non-union factory (interview with worker in Bandung, 9/18/10).

[176] Juliawan 2011; interview with NGO representative, Jakarta, 6/25/09. Juliawan reports that "union dues vary according to each union's statutes, but generally they are very small. In the SPN case monthly dues were just 0.5 percent of the regional minimum wage per worker" (p. 47). In that location at the time (Tangerang city in 2006), 0.5 percent of the regional minimum wage was equivalent to $0.40 in US dollars.

[177] Interview with NGO representative, Bandung, 9/29/10.

[178] Interview with worker group, Tangerang, 9/30/10.   [179] Caraway 2015:39.

passage of the Trade Union Act, only one employer has been convicted of unfair labor practices in criminal court. During the same period, dozens of union leaders have been jailed under antiquated provisions in the criminal code based on complaints files by employers."[180] As one unionist put it, "when a factory reports a worker, it gets processed by police. But when a worker complains, it goes through DISNAKER," the weak system of labor bureaus.[181]

The irony is that for all of their weakness at the factory level, Indonesian unions have proven to be powerful outside the factories. Despite organizational fragmentation and few links to political parties, the Indonesian labor movement has repeatedly pushed provincial minimum wages upward and contained the flexibilization of labor markets. In both arenas, massive street demonstrations—or *unjuk rasa* ("demonstration of feelings")—have been the Indonesian labor movement's prime source of power.

The fight over flexible labor markets began early in the *Reformasi* period, when the Minister of Manpower issued an administrative decree (Kep-150) that expanded severance pay entitlements and amounts, in effect raising the costs of hiring and firing workers. The business community had been "asleep at the wheel" when the decree was being formulated, but they soon loudly decried it as "discriminat[ing] against employers."[182] To mollify companies and foreign investors, the government introduced a revised decree in 2001, but unions responded with "large and rambunctious" protests around the country.[183] Unable to reach a compromise and wary of instability, the government let the existing decree stand.

As the business community strengthened its organization, labor began to splinter under the weight of personal rivalries and job losses. Nevertheless, unions managed to leave a strong imprint on the Manpower Act of 2003. Against the wishes of unions, the Act allowed short-term contract work, temporary/probationary work, and outsourcing. But because of unions' involvement in the negotiations, the Act also put strict limits on the use of contract and outsourced workers. For instance, only "non-core" work activities can be outsourced, fixed term contracts can only be used for up to three years, and temporary/probationary status can last for no more than three months. Labor activists have decried the slippery slope of flexibilization, and as we saw earlier, non-compliance is rampant. Nevertheless, Caraway (2004) argues that the restrictions on employer flexibility are surprisingly strict, and Marcus Mietzner (2014) calls the Manpower Act "one of the most worker-friendly pieces of legislation in the developing world."[184]

---

[180] Caraway 2015:33.   [181] Interview with union representative, Jakarta, 9/28/10.
[182] Caraway 2004:38; Hurst 2014.   [183] Caraway 2004:39.
[184] Mietzner 2014:112. The pro-worker tone of the law should not be overstated. Employers achieved a fairly narrow definition of a legal strike and some reprieve from the rules on dismissals

Under pressure from business as well as the World Bank, the Indonesian government sought to add more flexibility to the Manpower Act in 2005–6. The revisions would have allowed more outsourcing, relaxed rules on contract workers, and reigned in the top levels of severance pay. But after unions staged three months of massive public protests, including large events on May Day of 2006, the reforms were dropped.[185] "We are a democracy, maybe a too-open democracy," lamented Vice President Kalla after the administration decided to keep the peace and drop the reforms.[186] As a result, international financial institutions and neoclassical economists continue to see Indonesian labor markets as far too rigid.[187] Labor scholars have pointed out, though, that severance payments are essentially the only social safety net that Indonesian workers have. Promoting both flexibilization and "decent work", as neoliberal reformers have sought to do, may be contradictory in this setting.[188]

Unions have also overcome their fragmentation to influence minimum wage-setting processes. Since 2003, minimum wages have been set yearly at the provincial and district levels. Tripartite councils, which include union representatives, construct a cost of living index that becomes the basis of wage increases. With the dramatic depreciation of the rupiah in the late 1990s, the real value of minimum wages plummeted, and it took until around 2002 for them to reach the pre-crisis level.[189] After years of small adjustments, significant increases in minimum wages began to occur between 2008 and 2010. In Jakarta, the monthly minimum wage went from around 816,000 rupiah in 2007 (roughly $90 at the time) to around 1.1 million rupiah in 2010 (roughly $121 at the time). More dramatic increases occurred from 2011 to 2013, when Jakarta's minimum wage reached 2.2 million rupiah (roughly $210) per month.[190] Even newer manufacturing regions had significant minimum wage increases in this period, including 20–25 percent yearly increases in districts in West Java. As Edward Aspinall (2014) surmises, minimum wage increases "have produced a dramatic increase in real wages, even if labor costs are still far less than in some relevant comparison regions, such as Southern China."[191]

---

and severance payments (Caraway 2004). As mentioned above, the strict strike rules have contributed to unions' weakness at the factory level.

[185] Juliawan 2011.   [186] Quoted in Donnan 2006.
[187] Manning and Roesad 2007; World Bank 2010.   [188] See Anner and Caraway 2010.
[189] World Bank 2010:93.
[190] International Labour Organization 2014:10. The dollar amounts are based on rough exchange rates of 9,100 rupiah to the USD in 2007, 9,100 in 2010, and 10,500 in 2013.
[191] Aspinall 2014:129. Indonesia has a comparatively high ratio of the minimum wage to the average wage (Organization for Economic Cooperation and Development (OECD) 2015). In labor-intensive industries, the minimum wage often is the prevailing wage. Thus, as minimum wages have increased, so has the problem of non-compliance and requests for exceptions (see World Bank 2010; Better Work Indonesia 2012b).

To push minimum wages up, unions have taken advantage of electoral competition at the provincial and district levels and their seat at the table in the tripartite councils. Tripartite councils were created originally as a way to promote "harmonious" labor relationships during the Suharto era, but they have facilitated key moments of coordination by an otherwise fragmented labor movement.[192] To bolster negotiations, unions have staged "periodic massive actions that demonstrate the credible threat of further disruptive actions."[193] In the largest of these, a one-day general strike in 2012 disrupted hundreds of factories, as 200,000 took to the streets in Bekasi, near Jakarta, and an estimated 2 million struck in cities around the country.[194] A May Day demonstration in Jakarta the following year attracted roughly 135,000 union members.[195] Although unions are weak at the factory level and fragmented within and across industries, they have proven capable of turning out large crowds of demonstrators at key policymaking moments.

There seems, then, to be a profound mismatch between the logic of codes of conduct and the capacities of Indonesian unions. Codes of conduct, like other forms of private regulation, focus on conditions within the factory walls—where Indonesian unions are weakest. One participant suggested that this mismatch is part of what made the Code of Conduct network a "frustrating" experience and kept unions from fully engaging. "Unions have to deal with both minimum wage and employers. But they tend to rely on the minimum wage because they're so weak. It's easier to convince government and politicians than employers. But in the long run, this is not a good strategy."[196]

Scholars of labor standards have begun to search for reinforcing "complementarity" between private rules and public regulation.[197] In Indonesia, the mismatch has hindered this. The situation might be called called "complementarity without reinforcement", since the domestic labor law and transnational codes are largely consistent but with little effect. Had private regulatory fields rewarded companies for sourcing from a country where unions held some political sway—or had Indonesian unions been stronger at the factory-level—then transnational rules and domestic governance could have been far more reinforcing in practice.

Toward stronger commitments? Evolving responses to factory closures and union capacities

Over time, there have been some shifts in what unions have demanded from leading brands—and how the brands have responded. Factory closures and

---

[192] Caraway 2015.   [193] Caraway and Ford 2014:151.   [194] Associated Press 2012.
[195] Jakarta Globe 2013.   [196] Interview with NGO representative, Jakarta, 6/25/09.
[197] See Locke, Rissing, and Pal 2013; Coslovsky and Locke 2012; Amengual 2010, and more generally Trubek and Trubek 2007.

fleeing owners did not only undermine union organizing campaigns, as described above, they provoked campaigns demanding that brands take responsibility for displaced workers. Though brands have fiercely resisted any suggestion that they are legally responsible for their suppliers' employees, one can see some hints of change in the resolution of these campaigns. In addition, a recent project has sought to mobilize brand support to build the factory-level capacities of unions, which have often been lacking.

FACTORY CLOSURES AND FLEEING OWNERS

In a precarious industry where high, legally required severance payments serve as nearly the only safety net for displaced workers, it is not uncommon for factory owners to flee the country or otherwise avoid their final wage and severance obligations. Labor-rights activists have argued that brands sourcing from these factories—especially brands that make claims about social responsibility—ought to take responsibility when this occurs.

The first such case in Indonesia occurred in 2003, when the PT Victoria factory, which produced for Eddie Bauer, shut down. The union in the factory (an FSBI affiliate) worked with a domestic labor NGO (Urban Community Mission, or PMK) to publicize the issue in Europe and the US. Advocates charged that the 875 workers were owed a total of more than $1 million in severance and backwages, but the factory owner's proposal that the workers keep the equipment in the factory would yield only around $80,000.[198] Union leaders were visited by members of the works council from Karstadt Quelle (a competitor of Eddie Bauer's parent company, Spiegel) and traveled to Hong Kong to meet with one of the factory's investors.[199] United Students Against Sweatshops publicized the workers' grievances, held campus protests, and called for action by the Fair Labor Association, of which Eddie Bauer was a member. Eddie Bauer consulted with the union but refused to make monetary contributions. The Fair Labor Association argued that Eddie Bauer had no legal responsibility for severance pay and defended its decision to endorse the company's compliance program at the same time that this conflict was under-way. What mattered to the FLA was that Eddie Bauer had "a process in place that allowed complaints to be handled in a reasonable manner."[200]

The campaign for former PT Victoria workers failed, and reports on the factory diminished after 2006. The FSBI union was reportedly "traumatized" by the experience, and the leader of the factory-level union later left this

---

[198] United Students Against Sweatshops 2005.

[199] Interview with NGO representatives, Jakarta, 10/1/10.

[200] As reported in University of Michigan, Labor Standards and Human Rights Committee, minutes of January 13, 2006 meeting, https://web.archive.org/web/20120901063422/http://irlee.umich.edu/CoLSHR/Minutes/CoLSHR20060113.pdf.

federation.[201] In this case, an extraordinarily limited conception of corporate responsibility won out.

The next wave of campaigns was only slightly more successful. In 2006, the PT Spotec footwear factory shut down after Adidas pulled its orders. The Korean investors in PT Spotec and its sister company, PT Dong Joe, had left Indonesia, leaving more than 10,000 workers uncertain about their final wages and severance pay. The reason for Adidas's exit from the factory has been the topic of much debate. According to the brand, the problem was "purely financial," having to do with the factory's ability to pay its bills.[202] There is little doubt that the factories were burdened by debt and struggling to make the necessary deliveries.[203] Yet activists argued that Adidas—and Reebok before it—had imposed new costs on the factory and driven prices down to an unsustainable level.[204]

The closure prompted demonstrations by PT Spotec workers, and a call for Adidas to take responsibility. After the factory was purchased by Ching Luh, a Taiwanese transnational corporation, to once again produce for Adidas, Oxfam urged Adidas to help ex-Spotec workers secure jobs in the new factory. Adidas agreed, and Oxfam monitored the slow and sometimes contentious process. Within a year, approximately half of the 4,500 ex-Spotec workers had applied for jobs with Ching Luh and roughly 1,250 had been hired.[205] Activists perceived Ching Luh as vehemently anti-union, and noted that several union representatives were facing discrimination in hiring.[206] In this case, sustained pressure by activists (especially Oxfam-Australia) on Adidas—and Adidas on Ching Luh—did allow some displaced workers to be re-employed. Still, the vast majority of the 10,000 workers displaced by the closing of Spotec and Dong Joe did not secure jobs with Ching Luh, and it appears that none received the legally required severance pay.

Several years later, when the PT Kizone apparel factory closed in 2011 and the owner fled the country, activists demanded not that brands assist with re-employment but that they contribute directly to the roughly $3.4 million in severance pay owed to the 2,700 displaced workers.[207] The factory produced for Nike, Adidas, and the merchandising arm of the Dallas Cowboys football team (Silver Star Merchandising). United Students Against Sweatshops had successfully pushed Nike to contribute to severance pay in Honduras the

[201] Interview with NGO representatives, Jakarta, 10/1/10.
[202] Interview with brand representative, Jakarta, 7/10/08.
[203] American Embassy in Jakarta 2007.
[204] Interviews with NGO representatives, Bogor, 6/29/08.
[205] Letter from Harry Nurmansyah of Adidas to Oxfam Australia, August 20, 2008.
[206] Interview with NGO representative, Jakarta, 7/7/08; letter from Oxfam and CCC to Adidas, October 14, 2010.
[207] This was the Worker Rights Consortium's estimate of the legally required severance pay. See Worker Rights Consortium 2012.

previous year, and they led a similar campaign focused on the PT Kizone factory, along with similar events at another Indonesian supplier, PT Dong One. Nike agreed to contribute $1.2 million to a fund for the PT Kizone workers, and Silver Star made a small contribution of roughly $55,000.[208] Adidas resisted, arguing that it had left the factory before the closure. After an escalated set of student protests, which led several universities to cut their licensing contracts with Adidas, the brand agreed in 2013 to make an undisclosed but "significant" contribution.

This was a major victory for international anti-sweatshop activists, who had shifted from demanding re-employment to demanding compensation. Due to events in Indonesia and elsewhere, Nike in particular had gradually accepted the idea of making monetary contributions in the wake of factory closures. In short, one can see some evolution in both the demands being made and in brand responses. Of course, the "victory" in this case could only soften the blow of job losses, and it is unclear whether more than a handful of brands would be likely to follow. And of course, campaigns for displaced workers were not guaranteed to even get off the ground, as seen in the case of PT Mutiara Mitra earlier in this chapter.

At the same time, events in Indonesia have made brands—and even some activists—wary of allowing factory owners to use sympathy for displaced workers as cover for shoddy business practices. This occurred in the case of two Nike suppliers—PT Hardaya Aneka Shoes Industri (HASI) and PT Naga Sakti Paramashoes (NASA)—owned by Siti Hartati Murdaya, a prominent businesswoman who had been close with the Suharto family. (Her business group also owned the PT Intracawood timber concession discussed in Chapter 3.) In 2007, Nike announced that it would be leaving the HASI and NASA factories, citing mismanagement and rising production costs. This would essentially shut down the factories, displacing 14,000 unionized workers. After large protests in Jakarta's central business district and calls for Nike to be responsible for the severance pay, Nike agreed to delay the exit by a year to allow for an adjustment period.[209] But in this case, there was little international pressure on Nike to cover severance payments, since labor-rights advocates working in Indonesia had become highly suspicious of the factory owner. "It was really a problem of management," said one labor-rights advocate after reviewing documentation provided by Nike. "It's not always true that the brands are the big devils."[210] As communicated to international solidarity networks, the owner "uses the workers and the union to discredit Nike... [though the problem is] clear fraud and mismanagement of the owner."[211]

---

[208] Worker Rights Consortium 2012.   [209] Reuters 2007.
[210] Interview with NGO representative, Jakarta, 6/25/09.
[211] Letter from FES to ITGLWF, FES records.

REVISITING UNION RIGHTS: THE PLAY FAIR CAMPAIGN'S
FREEDOM OF ASSOCIATION PROTOCOL

Evolution can also be seen on the issue of unions' rights and capacities. In the lead up to the 2010 and 2012 Olympics, Nike, Adidas, New Balance, and Puma agreed to be part of a pilot project in Indonesia, led by international unions' and NGOs' "Play Fair" campaign. Representatives of these brands and several of their largest suppliers—including Nikomas, PT Panarub, and Ching Luh—met with Indonesian unions and labor NGOs to negotiate some basic terms of agreement. They found little common ground in discussions of wages and contract workers, but they agreed to move forward with a protocol on freedom of association. The brands bristled at unions' suggestion that they should "guarantee" union rights at their suppliers, and when the negotiations stalled in 2010, some unions organized a demonstration in Jakarta.[212]

By 2011, the group had forged a signed protocol on Freedom of Association, and by 2013, six brands and seventy-one of their suppliers were signatories.[213] Companies pledged to allow unions to post information, have office space, release some leaders from normal work duties, and provide for automatic deductions of union dues.[214] These are quite modest pledges, and some ideas from earlier drafts, like facilitating unions' access to non-unionized factories, were dropped. Still, union leaders see the protocol as a useful minimum standard that may help to build their organizational capacities and perhaps better navigate the legal system.[215]

It remains to be seen whether this agreement will build unions' capacities, or whether the participating factories will be stable enough to provide a strong foundation for development over time. The tumultuous history of footwear sourcing in Indonesia, and the persistence of heavy international competition, provide some reason for concern that unions will remain organizationally weak or that they will face declining orders if they grow stronger.

Conclusion: Precarity and Patience

For workers in apparel and footwear factories in Indonesia, codes of conduct have brought occasional improvements in working conditions, especially when unions have used them as leverage to press for incremental changes. Moreover, the contentious campaigns and debates about the limits of corporate responsibility have expanded the compliance efforts of some brands. One

---

[212] Minutes of multi-stakeholder workshop at LBH Jakarta on November 23–4, 2009; interview with union leader, Jakarta, 9/30/10.

[213] Green 2015. [214] Freedom of Association Protocol, 7 June, 2011.

[215] Interview with union representative, Jakarta, 9/30/10. Additional interviews conducted by Egels-Zandén's students confirmed this perception among union leaders.

practitioner noted that the Worker Rights Consortium's multi-method investigations helped to improve the factory auditing done by leading brands. "The auditors [for brands like Adidas and H&M] are now doing some auditing outside the factory. They meet with the trade unions at the regional and national levels. This hadn't happened until the WRC."[216]

Yet the potential that global labor-rights activists saw in Indonesia after the fall of Suharto—to become a responsible, rights-respecting alternative to production in China or Vietnam—was largely squandered. It certainly was not aided by SA8000, which grew more quickly in countries *without* democracy or collective labor-rights protections than in Indonesia. Nor did "responsible sourcing" more generally come to mean that brands would commit to unionized factories or to a country in which independent unions were allowed. The potential was squandered in part by Indonesia's precarious place in a fast-moving global apparel industry, where brands added and shed suppliers quickly as costs changed in one place or another. In addition, the labor movement became powerful enough to influence government policy, but its locus of power did not fit the factory-centered logic of private regulation.

A wave of deadly industrial accidents in Bangladesh from 2010 to 2013 has led some observers to highlight Indonesia as a safer, less risky destination for global brands.[217] "At first it was because of China getting too expensive, then came the Bangladesh fire tragedy.... Some buyers feel uncomfortable placing orders in Bangladesh," said a representative of the Indonesian textile trade association.[218] Indeed, with rising costs in China and increased scrutiny of unsafe factories in Bangladesh and Pakistan, the Indonesian apparel industry is unlikely to truly become a true "sunset industry" for some time.

Perhaps there are new possibilities for building an ethical niche in Indonesia. The Better Work program in Indonesia, sponsored by the International Labour Organization and International Finance Corporation, has sought to do so. The program, which began in 2011, has garnered support from a number of US brands, from Abercrombie & Fitch to Levi Strauss to Wal-Mart, and is working with more than 140 garment factories in Indonesia to improve compliance with domestic labor law and buyers' codes. Although the overall record of improvement so far is mixed, there is evidence that the program is pushing factory managers in Indonesia to at least engage with domestic labor institutions, rather than simply buying permits to pay less than the minimum wage.[219]

This chapter reveals several contradictions that may haunt this and other newer code compliance projects in Indonesia. First, the conflict between the

---

[216] Interview with labor-rights advocate, Jakarta, 6/27/08.   [217] See Bradsher 2013.
[218] Quoted in Bradsher 2013.
[219] Amengual and Chirot 2016; Alois 2016; Better Work Indonesia 2012b.

apparel industry's demand for flexibility and the *de jure* inflexibility of Indo-nesian labor markets could not be more severe. It is difficult to see how factory managers in Indonesia could both live up to brands' demand for rapid scaling up and down of production and truly comply with domestic labor law that restricts the use of non-permanent workers. To date, firms' most common response has been to flout the law or argue that apparel manufacturing is "seasonal" work, which is provided an exception under the Manpower Act.[220] Better Work and other programs may be tempted to accept creative interpret-ations of the law or to embrace legal change for the sake of competitiveness. But doing so would reject one of the central accomplishments of the Indo-nesian labor movement—that is, forestalling the flexibilization demanded by employers, investors, and international financial institutions.

A second ongoing contradiction is that rising wages or union power appear to put a factory at great risk of losing orders, even from brands with leading CSR programs. Occasionally brands clearly "cut and run" from a factory when a union strengthens, but often brands and their critics wind up in long debates about whether there were "merely business" reasons for dropping the factory. Even if brands are not directly fleeing unions, it may be that labor conflict draws attention to factories that are then deemed problematic for other reasons or that active unionism restrains managerial autonomy in ways that brands do not appreciate. Without more durable brand commitments, it is difficult to rule out this interpretation.

As I will argue in the conclusion, these contradictions might be resolved if brands embraced a slower, more stable, more patient style of sourcing. With this, respect for Indonesian labor law would at least be possible, and unions and managers might be able to gradually negotiate a productive class com-promise. Unless sourcing strategies change, though, the principles written into codes of conduct—and auxiliary projects like Better Work—will remain elusive.

---

[220] Robertson, Sitalaksmi, Ismalina, and Fitrady 2009. One garment company profiled in this World Bank report relied heavily on contract workers to manage competition and short-term orders from buyers. This "requires circumventing labor law" (Robertson et al., 2009:217). "The common practice in the industry is to claim that work is seasonal so that firms can avoid giving workers permanent status after the two-year contract and its one-year extension. Even if the worker is a good performer, the firm still discontinues the contract. Individual workers are advised to 'lapse' for some time before getting a job back at the firm" (p. 218).

Table 6.3. Sub-standard and contingent employment in unionized apparel, textile, and footwear factories in Indonesia, regression models

VARIABLES	(1)	(2)	(3)	(4)
	Any workers under min. wage (logit)	Any worker abuse (logit)	Non-perm. as prop. of workforce (OLS)	Number of illegal situations with contract workers (Poisson)
Subject to code of conduct	−0.3188 (0.558)	−0.6546 (0.339)	0.0310 (0.563)	−0.0098 (0.952)
Product: Footwear	−0.4487 (0.492)	0.6739 (0.356)	0.0683 (0.281)	−0.0303 (0.879)
Log number of workers	0.1516 (0.546)	0.4507 (0.140)	0.0320 (0.181)	−0.0429 (0.570)
Foreign owned	−0.7606 (0.186)	1.5344** (0.015)	0.1074** (0.038)	0.1350 (0.393)
Women as prop. of workforce	1.9669** (0.064)	1.4839 (0.248)	0.0383 (0.668)	0.2849 (0.313)
Non-perm. as prop. of workforce	2.1802** (0.024)	0.2398 (0.833)		0.5012** (0.091)
Collective Bargaining Agreement	−1.0641** (0.051)	−1.6032** (0.033)	−0.1415** (0.008)	−0.0063 (0.970)
Gov. labor inspection	−0.2121 (0.678)	0.2394 (0.725)	−0.0831** (0.090)	−0.2070 (0.153)
Constant	−2.1873** (0.016)	−3.4116** (0.003)	0.3004** (0.000)	0.7725** (0.003)
Observations	120	120	120	89
R-squared			0.140	

p-value in parentheses *** $p<0.01$, ** $p<0.05$, * $p<0.1$ (two-tailed tests)

Table 6.4. Occupational health and safety practices in unionized apparel, textile, and footwear factories in Indonesia, regression models

VARIABLES	(1)	(2)
	H&S oversight committee (logit)	Number of H&S deficiencies (negative binomial)
Subject to code of conduct	1.6447***	−0.5868*
	(0.003)	(0.060)
Product: Footwear	−0.1504	−0.1010
	(0.815)	(0.759)
Log number of workers	0.7593**	−0.2695*
	(0.014)	(0.071)
Foreign owned	−0.0557	0.4042
	(0.923)	(0.159)
Women as prop. of workforce	−2.2174**	0.9863*
	(0.036)	(0.070)
Non-perm. as prop. of workforce	−0.4032	0.8564*
	(0.697)	(0.081)
Collective Bargaining Agreement	1.1200**	−0.3937
	(0.027)	(0.189)
Gov. labor inspection	−0.0978	−0.4147
	(0.856)	(0.137)
Constant	−0.5677	−0.2718
	(0.486)	(0.551)
Observations	120	120

p-value in parentheses *** p<0.01, ** p<0.05, * p<0.1 (two-tailed tests)

Table 6.5. Grievances and management responses in unionized apparel, textile, and footwear factories in Indonesia, regression models

VARIABLES	(1)	(2)
	Current grievance (logit)	Good faith response to grievance (logit)
Subject to code of conduct	−0.0177	1.3440*
	(0.970)	(0.068)
Product: Footwear	−0.1402	1.1395
	(0.799)	(0.162)
Log number of workers	0.2293	−0.2770
	(0.278)	(0.383)
Foreign owned	0.3245	0.9495
	(0.479)	(0.140)
Women as prop. of workforce	1.5256**	−0.2218
	(0.050)	(0.857)
Non-perm. as prop. of workforce	−1.1050	−1.2968
	(0.191)	(0.303)
Collective Bargaining Agreement	−0.9231*	
	(0.055)	
Gov. labor inspection	−0.3235	
	(0.456)	
Constant	−0.0558	−1.0409
	(0.936)	(0.246)
Observations	120	66

p-value in parentheses *** p<0.01, ** p<0.05, * p<0.1 (two-tailed tests)

7

Re-centering the State

Toward Place-conscious Transnational Governance?

Private regulation brought reforms to forests and factories in Indonesia and China, but rarely of an empowering and transformative kind. As we saw, under scrutiny from buyers and auditors, managers softened their relationships with workers and local residents, altered some practices on the shop floor or forest canopy, and formalized their management systems. The rules that flowed through global production networks—and the assurances of compliance that were sent in return—were profoundly shaped by their intersection with the state, civil society, and pre-existing cultures of production. As such, some rules proved virtually impossible to implement, while assurances of compliance reflected the surrounding context nearly as much as the activities occurring within the factory walls or forest boundaries.

More generally, the evidence presented in this book suggests that transnational private regulation has failed to resolve pressing concerns about land and labor in the global economy. Sites of production that have been certified to the highest multi-stakeholder standards remain highly conflictual and exploitative, and in some instances they are not especially different from their uncertified peers. Private rules have routinely fostered improvements in management systems and processes, but improvements in performance have been much rarer. As rules flowed through complex and rapidly changing global production networks, their power often dissipated, sometimes to the point of irrelevance. The collective rights of workers and villagers have proven especially challenging terrain for private regulation, generating fragile agreements, weak committees, and momentary respect at best—and endorsing the *denial* of rights at worst.

Note that my case studies have paid particular attention to the most challenging private rules and projects—including multi-stakeholder certification systems such as the Forest Stewardship Council and Social Accountability

International, as well as the expectations of brands with leading CSR and corporate sustainability programs, such as Ikea, The Home Depot, Stora Enso, Nike, Adidas, and The Gap. Many private rules for land and labor come with weaker commitments and less oversight.

Why has transnational private regulation had such modest impacts, and how might transnational governance of land and labor be revised to improve its performance? This chapter will answer these questions in the course of developing some overarching diagnoses and normative implications of the research in this book. I will call for re-centering the state and shifting toward "place conscious" transnational governance. Rather than merely calling for this sort of reform, though, I will examine a case in which it has already occurred—namely, in the emergence of a groundbreaking transnational timber legality regime. This new regime has the potential to improve upon private sustainability certification in some important respects. It may even provide a provocative model for new initiatives focused on labor standards, which have not gone as far beyond voluntarism and private authority. Legality is a multivalent but powerful concept, I will argue, which might be better harnessed to improve labor conditions in global production networks.

Rethinking Corporate Responsibility

The shortcomings of private regulation are tied in part to particular fields, initiatives, companies, and rules, as described in the preceding chapters. But a general diagnosis is also in order. First, transnational private regulation of land and labor has clearly been inhibited by countervailing forces that have simply left little room for significant improvement in forests and factories. In particular, pressures for low prices and rapid changes in the character and location of production have greatly inhibited the practical implications of private rules. This is perhaps clearest in the apparel industry, where brands' and retailers' quest for low-cost and rapidly adaptable supply chains has fostered commoditized, low-quality factory auditing, evasion and falsification by factory managers, disregard for compliance problems, and shifts away from locations where improvements—and sometimes gains by independent unions—are being made. This diagnosis is also relevant in the forest products industry, where price premiums for certification have been uncertain, and the same retailers that have pushed FSC certification have often pushed suppliers for lower prices at the same time. While some producers of high-value timber and wood products could reap rewards for improving forest management, in other parts of the timber trade, cheap illegal timber flowed freely, sometimes through the complex supply chains of companies touting their green images.

Second is the problem of voluntarism. In particular, the voluntary character of brands' and retailers' engagement with transnational private regulation reduced its impact in at least two key ways. For one, because brands and retailers are not required to push standards through their supply chains, their incentives for rigorous enforcement have been mixed at best. Remember that it is brands and retailers that are ultimately in the position of enforcing private rules for their suppliers—by rewarding compliance or withdrawing orders from recalcitrant suppliers, for instance. They have incentives to send credible assurances of compliance or progress to the various audiences that are demanding them—such as socially responsible investors, activist watchdogs, and conscientious consumers. But these incentives are balanced against interests in expanding markets, pleasing shareholders, and maximizing autonomy. In essence, this is why we have seen brands and retailers backslide on their voluntary CSR and sustainability commitments, half-heartedly enforce rules, and choose sites of production where the rules are quite difficult to enforce. Many other actors could also be blamed for the weaknesses of transnational private regulation—including the supplier company managers that have strategically evaded scrutiny, the auditors who have accepted questionable evidence, the designers of initiatives that protect corporate reputations without requiring significant reforms, and the government leaders who have directly or indirectly suppressed the rights of workers and residents. But the powerful role of large brands and retailers as de facto enforcers of private rules means that the weakness of their commitments has been especially consequential.

In addition, the voluntary nature of brands' and retailers' participation leaves even the most credible private regulatory initiatives structurally dependent on transnational corporations. Multi-stakeholder certification initiatives, as we have seen, depend on large retailers to agree to push these standards through their supply chains—and sometimes to subsidize the costs of certification as well. Private regulatory initiatives may also depend on corporations to become and remain members. In either case, although private regulatory initiatives will clearly take meaningful steps to build their credibility, they also risk losing relevance if they are so stringent as to alienate their corporate supporters. The desire by many initiatives to expand their scopes, rather than restricting themselves to niches, fuels their dependence on large corporations. To be sure, initiatives in which non-industry actors are powerful can have high standards, vigorous oversight, and can reject affiliations with the most controversial corporations. But they cannot afford to say "no" to entire markets or insist on stringent definitions of compliance with especially challenging rules. The same holds for certification and auditing bodies, who must establish their credibility without alienating their potential clients. In part, this explains why private regulators tend to define compliance in ways that are in tune with domestic governance and existing cultures of production, even if this means watering down the rules as written or substituting process for performance.

The problems of voluntarism and countervailing pressures are well known to scholars of transnational private regulation, although they are more often invoked for labor than environmental standards. This book's critique goes one step further in arguing that the *privateness* of transnational private regulation has also limited its influence. Even when brands and retailers vigorously push high standards and auditors rigorously scrutinize practices on the ground, private regulation has little influence over forms of domestic governance that profoundly shape land and labor. As I have argued, domestic governance largely wins out when it clashes with private rules, especially when these rules pertain to territory or rights. Thus, the land rights of villagers remain fragile even as auditors help negotiate agreements between companies and community leaders; and the rights of workers to unionize remain repressed even as companies claim to implement freedom of association rules.

The "hope of transcendence" is not only mythical; it is counterproductive. Animated by the hope of pulling forests and factories out of their local contexts and up to global best practices, practitioners of private regulation have avoided the messy engagements with domestic governance that would be necessary to expand land and labor rights. The basic model of transnational private regulation facilitates this, by bracketing what lies beyond the factory walls or forest boundaries. Put differently, private regulation's sphere of influence is limited to conditions within a particular site of production. It has little bearing on the surrounding labor markets, commodity trading systems, legal norms, or industry-wide cultures of production. As seen in all four of this book's case studies, these contextual factors greatly influence baseline conditions and possibilities for improvement within particular sites of production. In addition, as seen in the case of the Indonesian labor movement, domestic social movements may have more power in the socio-political context than they do within particular sites of production. This kind of mismatch must be addressed if one wants transnational governance to support domestic reformers.

Implications for the practice of private regulation

The complex and evolving world of corporate responsibility and sustainability is rife with assurances of impartiality and credibility, from multiple levels of accreditation to multi-stakeholder representational structures to various forms of transparency. And yet there is very little honesty about what is likely and unlikely to be accomplished on the ground in different contexts. Practitioners of private regulation should acknowledge that some rules will be nearly impossible to effectively implement in some locations. This does not mean that NGOs, private regulators, and other reformers should abandon those locations, but it does mean they should stop purporting to uphold a truly global standard. In China, for instance, private regulatory initiatives have at best extremely limited capacities to protect workers' freedom of association or to respect residents' land rights in the face of state-sponsored land grabs. In Indonesia, respecting indigenous communities' customary rights to forest land is extremely difficult unless there is a change in the state's practice of granting timber concessions without reference to customary claims on the land.[1]

In addition, since bypassing domestic governance is nearly impossible, practitioners of transnational private regulation should look for opportunities to connect with local reformers who are seeking stronger enforcement of the law on the books or political changes that expand the relevant rights and protections. Although the assumption of empty spaces obscures it, the law on the books often includes provisions that are congruent with transnational rules, including minimum wage and maximum hour requirements, restrictions on child labor and forced labor, requirements for land management and access, and bans on certain toxic chemicals and destructive harvesting methods. Domestic laws of course vary, and they rarely align perfectly with international norms, but stronger enforcement of existing law would clearly improve labor and environmental conditions in global industries.[2] Focusing on compliance with domestic law is one way in which transnational governance could re-center the state, as described further below.

This is not a call for an entirely state-centered approach to regulating the global economy. The scrutiny that has traveled through global production networks has been highly imperfect, but it is not meaningless. Global production networks have been turned into infrastructures for transnational governance, and they should continue to play this role. If large brands and retailers had stronger incentives to vigorously push standards—and demand rigorous evidence of compliance—then these infrastructures might be used more effectively. Doing so will require policy changes that move past voluntarism. In particular, policies that require companies in large consumer markets to ensure compliance in their supply chains—and hold them legally responsible when lapses occur—would provide an alternative to the current state of half-hearted enforcement for the purpose of managing reputational risks. This is another important way of re-centering the state, which I will argue is not as improbable as it may initially seem.

Finally, expectations for corporate responsibility and sustainability in both the public and private sectors should be revised to take greater account of the

---

[1] The Indonesian Constitutional Court's 2013 decision suggests that changes are possible here. See Chapter 3 for details.

[2] See Coslovsky and Locke 2012; Amengual 2016; Piore and Schrank 2008; McDermott, Cashore, and Kanowski 2010; Hirakuri 2003.

spatial and temporal dimensions of decent work and sustainable development. As it stands, the arbiters of corporate responsibility and sustainability—such as responsible investment raters and funds—evaluate companies largely based on the policies they have adopted and their use of best practices for certification, auditing, and/or reporting.[3] But they pay little attention to *where* a transnational corporation's suppliers are located, even though this clearly shapes the baseline conditions of production and the possibilities for improvement. Nor do they attend to *how quickly* companies move their orders from one place to another, even though this can undermine hard-fought and gradual improvement. Instead, they seem to assume that transnational corporations can create responsible and sustainable conditions wherever their suppliers are located and no matter how frequently they shift them.

If judgments of responsibility and sustainability instead incentivized transnational corporations to prioritize locations where compliance is more feasible and to be patient—that is, to keep orders there as struggles and reforms occur—the impact of private regulation could increase. This could be especially important in slowing down rapidly mobile industries such as apparel. This is not a proposal for returning labor-intensive manufacturing jobs to affluent countries. Instead, it is a call for apparel brands and retailers that want to be regarded as responsible to prioritize those poor and middle-income countries that have comparatively strong enforcement of labor law, safe working environments, and autonomous labor movements and civil society—and to stay put when improvements occur. "Patient capital" was a crucial ingredient in constructing relatively egalitarian forms of capitalism in the twentieth century. "Patient sourcing" may be a necessary ingredient for meaningful reforms in the global economy of the twenty-first century.

These proposals may seem unrealistic in light of transnational corporations' vested interest in using global production networks to minimize costs and maximize flexibility. And yet, transnational governance of land and labor *has* evolved in new directions, partly in recognition that private regulatory approaches were failing. Several new initiatives move past the false hope of transcendence and re-center the state in various ways. Most striking is the emerging transnational timber legality regime.

The Transnational Timber Legality Regime

Illegal logging, fueled in part by the tumultuous experience of democratization and decentralization in Indonesia and the voracious demand for timber in China, clearly undermined the project to promote sustainable forestry.

---

[3] Delmas, Etzion, and Nairn-Birch 2013.

As we saw in Chapters 3 and 4, cheap, legally ambiguous timber undercut more costly legal and certified timber, and sustainability standards had little ability to reach illegal loggers, whether these were individual "counter-appropriators", "timber mafias", or companies that exceeded their concessions. While sustainable forestry standards sought to improve the practices of official and legally permitted operations, unofficial and illegal operations boomed.

Progress toward a global response mounted in the late 1990s and 2000s. As researchers and environmental NGOs exposed illegal logging networks in Cambodia, Burma, Russia, Indonesia, Brazil, and elsewhere, illegal logging came onto the agenda of the Group of Eight (G8) nations and then occupied a central role at the 2002 UN World Summit on Sustainable Development in Johannesburg.[4] The World Bank began convening meetings on Forest Law Enforcement and Governance in 2001, which the European Union soon extended into a Forest Law Enforcement, Governance, and Trade (FLEGT) action plan. Importantly, this EU initiative forged Voluntary Partnership Agreements with particular countries (Ghana, Indonesia, Cameroon, Republic of Congo, and Central African Republic) to create new timber legality assurance systems that would guarantee access to the European market.

By 2010, both US and the EU had passed laws that prohibit the sale of wood harvested illegally anywhere in the world—and that impose penalties on the *seller* of the final consumer product, not just the exporting company or government. A 2008 amendment to the century-old Lacey Act in the US subjects companies to confiscation, fines, or even prison sentences for selling wood and paper products that can be traced to illegal timber. The 2010 EU Timber Regulation similarly prohibits companies from putting items made from illegal timber on the market, although the specific penalties are left up to EU member states. Both laws also require companies to exercise due diligence or "due care" of their supply chains to reduce the risk of illegality, although having such a system does not necessarily shield companies from prosecution if evidence of illegality arises, especially in the US system.

This is a remarkable and path-breaking turn for transnational governance. The transnational timber legality regime promises forms of rule enforcement that are usually dismissed as practically or politically impossible in this era of complex global production networks and neoliberal trade rules. It provides a sort of "transnational hard law", in which a company can be penalized for actions in its supply chain—that is, beyond its formal boundaries. It also provides something like "extra-territorial enforcement of territorial law", since the relevant standards lie with *domestic law*, even as enforcement may occur continents away. It replaces the hope of transcendence with a faith in

---

[4] Tacconi 2007; Global Witness 2007; Lawson and MacFaul 2010.

the law on the books, or at least in the capacity of domestic stakeholders to productively negotiate the meanings of law. That faith has its own perils, but on the whole, the timber legality regime represents a promising form of binding and "place conscious" transnational governance.

In the most significant enforcement action to date, the US-based company Lumber Liquidators was prosecuted in 2015 under the revised Lacey Act because it was selling flooring that originated with illegal logging in Russia. Activists from the Environmental Investigation Agency, a US-based NGO, had conducted an undercover investigation of a flooring manufacturer in north-eastern China, where managers admitted multiple links to illegal timber harvesting in the Russian Far East and named Lumber Liquidators as their biggest customer.[5] The US Department of Justice used this information, plus its own investigation, to press charges. Six months later, Lumber Liquidators accepted a plea bargain that included $13 million in fines and forfeiture penalties, as well as a compliance plan that, if violated, allows the Department of Justice to halt shipments.[6] This is a striking form of enforcement, which combines a market access regulation in the US, forest law in Russia, and the investigative capacities of an international NGO.[7]

Separately, Timber Legality Assurance Systems, created through exporting countries' Voluntary Partnership Agreements with the EU, have begun to operate. Once a country's system is approved by the EU, its timber has a "green lane" into the European market, meaning that it is considered legal for the purposes of enforcing the EU Timber Regulation. In 2016, Indonesia's new system, SVLK (Sistem Verifikasi Legalitas Kayu) became the first to be approved. Under this system, essentially all timber harvesting operations in the country are being assessed by private auditors overseen by the national accreditation body. In forests and plantations, auditors check whether a valid license is held, harvesting plans are in accord with relevant laws, and an environmental impact assessment has been performed. In timber processing factories, they check for the necessary licenses and the traceability of timber back to the forest.[8] Audit summaries are posted on the Ministry of Forestry's

---

[5] Environmental Investigation Agency 2013.

[6] United States of America v. Lumber Liquidators, Inc. Plea agreement, https://www.sec.gov/Archives/edgar/data/1396033/000114420415058462/v421764_ex10-1.htm, accessed December 5, 2016; "Lumber Liquidators Announces Settlement Related To Lacey Act Investigation," http://investors.lumberliquidators.com/2015-10-07-Lumber-Liquidators-Announces-Settlement-Related-To-Lacey-Act-Investigation, accessed December 5, 2016.

[7] A similar process occurred in the seizure of items from Gibson Guitars in 2009 and 2011, which included ebony and rosewood that had been illegally imported from Madagascar and India, respectively. In that case, the federal prosecution was dropped after Gibson agreed to pay a $300,000 fine and improve its compliance program (US Department of Justice, 2012).

[8] Republic of Indonesia 2009. The accredited auditors include three that were also accredited certifiers for the Lembaga Ekolabel Indonesia program—PT Sucofindo, PT Mutuagung Lestari, and PT TUV International Indonesia.

website, and "independent monitors" from civil society are given access to additional information and can appeal auditors' decisions.

Given the "900 Indonesian laws, regulations and decrees related to forests and the production of forest products," developing an operational definition of legality for this system was a daunting task.[9] As part of a 2003 Memorandum of Understanding with the UK government, a team led by The Nature Conservancy and the usually insular Indonesian Ministry of Forestry drafted an auditable legality standard and consulted with various stakeholders, with parts of the process hosted by the homegrown forest certification initiative, Lembaga Ekolabel Indonesia.[10] Later, with guidance from the EU, the task of "defining legality" was given to a multi-stakeholder team that included key Indonesian environmental and indigenous rights NGOs (e.g., Telapak, Forest Watch, WALHI, and AMAN).

The NGOs pressed for a broad definition of legality, which would include attention to customary land rights, consultations with communities, and compliance with labor laws. These were included in early drafts but later dropped from the basic legality standard.[11] Some such requirements appeared in the government's related sustainability standard (Pengelolaan Hutan Produksi Lestari, PHPL), which itself became mandatory for large, established forestry operations. Despite their defeat in attempting to set a high baseline for legality, many domestic NGOs have been hopeful that the new system will open the forestry sector to much greater scrutiny and draw attention to ambiguous forest boundaries.[12] They have pointed out a number of serious loopholes and a concerning degree of laxity in the audits.[13] But they have also invested in the independent monitoring provisions. Indeed, several independent monitoring networks (JPIK, Jaringan Pemantau Independen Kehutanan, and APIKS, Aliansi Pemantau Independen Kehutanan Sumatera) organized by environmental and indigenous rights NGOs have begun to oversee and appeal legality designations. While assessments of SVLK's potential vary, one forestry consultant called it "the best thing to happen to Indonesia—concessions can't hide anymore."[14] As part of the EU's FLEGT program, similar timber legality assurance systems are awaiting approval in Ghana, Cameroon, Republic of Congo, and the Central African Republic, and systems are forthcoming in ten other countries.

---

[9] Colchester 2004b:7.

[10] The UK government's involvement was driven in part by a 2003 in which Greenpeace showed that the wood being used to build a new UK Home Ministry building came from illegal sources in Indonesia (interview with forestry consultant, Jakarta, 7/3/09).

[11] Tim Kecil 2007.

[12] Interview with NGO representative, Jakarta, 9/24/10; phone interview with NGO representative, 6/18/09.

[13] Independent Forestry Monitoring Network (JPIK) 2016; Anti Forest-Mafia Coalition 2014.

[14] Interview with forestry consultants, Jakarta, 9/22/10.

The rise of timber legality regulations

How did this transnational timber legality regime emerge? How could a system with hard penalties, extra-territorial reach, and multiple forms of local oversight come into existence, when prior efforts to govern forests transnationally had yielded only private and voluntary certification systems? To some degree, the challenge of implementing sustainable forestry standards seems to have served as an object lesson on the need to address illegal logging.[15] In addition, the growth of forest certification deepened discussions among foresters, environmentalists, and community rights advocates, helping to solidify a community of advocates for a timber legality regime.[16] But the key factors lie largely beyond forest certification, in the mobilization of new coalitions and discourses.

One key was that companies in the US and Europe joined coalitions in support of stringent market controls. The Lacey Act amendment owes its passage to a classic "Baptist-bootlegger" coalition—that is, a coalition between groups with mission-driven and material interests in reducing the supply of illegal timber. The 2008 amendment added trees to the list of plants and animals covered by the Lacey Act, a law that was originally passed in 1900 to prevent the sale of endangered wildlife and later extended to certain plants and marine species.[17] This extension was proposed by environmental NGOs, including Greenpeace and the Environmental Investigation Agency.[18] But it garnered support from domestic timber companies and their industry association, the American Forest and Paper Association. The association had estimated that imported Chinese plywood, often made from illegal or suspicious timber, was depressing plywood prices by somewhere between 7 percent and 16 percent, so its support of the Lacey Act amendment was tied up with its hopes of raising prices and regaining market share.[19]

There were of course also companies and associations on the other side. The International Wood Products Association, whose members were more reliant on imported tropical timber, led the opposition. But it found itself on the defensive, and it focused its efforts on an "innocent owner" clause that ultimately failed.[20] Retailers with risky supply chains appear to have been late to mobilize; or they may have decided, as it appears Wal-Mart did, that earlier scandals had taught them how to manage the risks of illegality in their supply chains.[21] In any case, the Lacey Act amendment received bipartisan

---

[15] Cashore and Stone 2012.   [16] Overdevest and Zeitlin 2014a.

[17] United States Department of Agriculture, Amendments to the Lacey Act from H.R.2419, Sec. 8204, www.aphis.usda.gov/plant_health/lacey_act/downloads/background–redlinedLaceyamndmnt–forests–may08.pdf, accessed December 5, 2016.

[18] Environmental Investigation Agency 2009.

[19] American Forest & Paper Association 2004; Cashore and Stone 2014.

[20] Leipold and Winkel 2016.   [21] Khatchadouria 2008.

support and, as part of a larger farm bill, overcame a Presidential veto to become law in 2008.[22]

In Europe, a different set of companies ended up supporting the EU Timber Regulation. Large retailers and timber importers, including Carrefour, B&Q, Ikea, and companies in the European Timber Trade Federation, supported the law, apparently in hopes that a focus on legality would improve their reputations and lower expectations for more challenging sustainability standards.[23] Since the regulation requires companies to exercise due diligence and instructs the national authorities to target enforcement to the highest risks, it is perhaps not surprising that companies that were already active in tracing their supply chains would support it.[24] This might be considered a "corporate liberal" reform bloc, composed of reputation-sensitive transnational corporations on the leading edge of voluntary sustainability efforts.[25] Their interests were aligned, to a degree at least, with the legality agendas of environmental NGOs. Chatham House (the Royal Institute of International Affairs) in the UK played an especially important role in building coalitions and convening policy dialogues, and officials within the European Commission guided the policy development process.[26] Opposition in this case came from domestic timber industries, apparently due to their risk of being caught up in illegal logging in Eastern Europe and their opposition to EU-level policymaking more generally.[27]

An initial version of the EU Timber Regulation treated due diligence systems as sufficient for compliance. But seemingly emboldened by the Lacey Act amendment, the final version went much further, prohibiting illegally harvested timber products from being placed on the market and allowing national authorities to investigate when "in possession of relevant information, including on the basis of substantiated concerns provided by third parties."[28] A version containing these elements passed the European Parliament by a sizable margin in 2009 and was approved by the European Council in 2010.[29]

---

[22] H.R. 2419 (110th), Food, Conservation, and Energy Act of 2008, www.govtrack.us/congress/bills/110/hr2419, accessed December 5, 2016.

[23] Leipold, Sotirov, Frei and Winkel 2016; http://awsassets.panda.org/downloads/industry_statement_online_amended_11115.pdf.

[24] Although there is no "safe harbor" for companies with sophisticated due diligence systems, it appears that a risk-based approach to enforcement is likely to target those with shoddy or nonexistent due diligence systems. See European Union 2010.

[25] See Kolko 1963 and Domhoff 1990 for classic accounts of corporate liberalism.

[26] Leipold, Sotirov, Frei, and Winkel 2016; Overdevest and Zeitlin 2014b.

[27] Leipold, Sotirov, Frei, and Winkel 2016.

[28] European Union 2010:29. For the earlier proposed version, see Commission of the European Communities 2008.

[29] European Parliament, 2008/0198(COD)-22/04/2009 Text adopted by Parliament, 1st reading/single reading, http://www.europarl.europa.eu/oeil/popups/summary.do?id=1075301&t=e&l=en, accessed December 5, 2016.

A second key factor in the rise of the timber legality regime was that governments in timber exporting countries came to see the illegal timber agenda as a way to enhance their domestic authority. Governments that depend on the exploitation of natural resources often resist international calls for improved environmental governance, sometimes accusing foreign environmentalists of eco-imperialism.[30] But a focus on illegality can be sovereignty-enhancing rather than sovereignty-threatening.[31] It explicitly endorses national law and can be an asset for governments seeking stronger enforcement. In particular, illegal logging often means lost tax revenue for central governments, so bringing covert operations into the open may help to increase revenues.[32] In Indonesia, the central government eventually embraced the timber legality agenda in part because it could aid enforcement of raw-log export bans, which had been passed to both hinder illegal logging and support domestic timber processing industries.[33] Moreover, the Ministry of Forestry was fighting with other branches of government to hold onto control of land during this period, and it appears that some actors within this Ministry saw the "good governance" components of the timber legality agenda as consistent with their bureaucratic and political interests.[34]

Third, the discourse of legality and illegality was potent in a variety of settings. As one activist in Indonesia put it, "legality is hard to argue with," especially since sustainability standards had failed to halt deforestation.[35] In the US, frames that emphasized criminality and corruption in the global timber industry, and that drew stark distinctions between "responsible producers" and "irresponsible importers", appear to have facilitated the Lacey Act amendments.[36]

Discourses of illegality are often compelling and mobilizing, even if the lines between legality and illegality, or legitimacy and illegitimacy, are blurry in practice.[37] Going further, there may be something about the very notion of legality that makes it uniquely compatible with "hard" governance of global production processes. Some theorists of neoliberalism have argued that criminality is the one area in which market fundamentalism is compatible with strong, restrictive state controls. With the US's high incarceration rates in the background, Bernard Harcourt (2010) argues that conceptions of markets, administration, and "natural order" evolved such that "the penal sanction is

---

[30] See Gareau 2010 for a review and Agrawal 2005 and Goldman 2005 for nuanced accounts.
[31] Cashore and Stone 2014.
[32] Tacconi, Obidzinski, and Agung 2004; Kaimowitz 2003; Casson and Obidzinski 2002.
[33] Cashore and Stone 2014.
[34] Ibid. See Gellert and Andiko 2015 on the Ministry of Forestry's political situation and maneuvers.
[35] Interview with NGO representative, Jakarta, 9/24/10.   [36] Leipold and Winkel 2016.
[37] McCann 1994; Ewick and Silbey 1998; Beckert and Dewey 2017.

marked off from the dominant logic of classical economics as the only space where order is legitimately enforced by the State."[38]

This logic seems to be taking hold in the governance of global environmental problems, where the mobilization against illegal logging is just one component of a larger ascendant focus on "environmental crime", including new attempts to halt the illegal trade in wildlife and to combat "illegal, unreported, and unregulated" fishing vessels.[39] A wide variety of actors—from the World Bank and Interpol to human rights NGOs such as Global Witness to the counter-terrorism units of think tanks and government agencies—have taken up the fight against global environmental crime. Perhaps criminality and its converse, legality, are "neoliberal exceptions"—that is, arenas in which the usual neoliberal proscriptions against state interference in markets do not apply. This would help to explain the remarkable rise of the transnational timber legality regime and perhaps also its future.

One looming question is whether any of the components of the transnational timber legality regime will be found to violate World Trade Organization rules, which limit governments' ability to restrict imports on the basis of their production processes. The designers of the EU systems explicitly sought to build a WTO-compliant system, using voluntary bilateral agreements and applying the market access regulation equally to domestic and imported timber.[40] The Lacey Act may be similarly safe from WTO challenge, since it prohibits the sale of illegally obtained timber without regard to whether this occurred domestically or in another country.[41] On the other hand, the apparent protectionist motivations of the "bootlegger" part of the Lacey Act's coalition and the possibility that reporting requirements will prove more onerous for imports than domestic products could leave some parts of the regime vulnerable, in particular to charges of discriminating against "like" products from foreign sources. Because these regulations require compliance with the exporting country's own laws, not the importing country's laws, they may still be relatively safe from challenge. But this also puts them in unchartered territory when it comes to WTO jurisprudence, since "there is no experience to date of WTO dispute cases dealing with even vaguely similar issues."[42]

If legality is truly a "neoliberal exception", then one would expect the timber legality regime to prove resilient to WTO challenges. At a minimum, we should see the backers of global market fundamentalism—in international financial institutions and expert communities—accept market access

---

[38] Harcourt 2010:77.

[39] Nellemann, Henriksen, Kreilhuber, Stewart, Kotsovou, Raxter, Mrema, and Barrat 2016; Sumaila, Alder, and Keith 2006.

[40] Overdevest and Zeitlin 2014a; Overdevest and Zeitlin 2014b.

[41] Brack 2009.   [42] Ibid.:14.

restrictions on the basis of illegality to a far greater extent than they accept binding standards for production processes based on sustainability, fairness, rights protection, or other rationales.

The promise and perils of re-centering the state

The transnational timber legality regime re-centers the state in two crucial ways. First, it includes state-imposed penalties for the sellers of consumer products, which should directly punish some companies selling illegally harvested forest products and incentivize many others to strengthen their supply-chain scrutiny. As we have seen, under voluntary approaches, retailers and brands have been able to backslide on their commitments to certification or withstand scandals with only minor damage to their sales and reputations, and many companies have avoided strong voluntary standards altogether. With a threat of product seizures and significant monetary penalties, as well as a charge to exercise due diligence or due care, more companies should invest in credible auditing and traceability services—and take their results seriously when making sourcing decisions.

Second, the timber legality regime calls for compliance with domestic law, rather than with transnational standards. The consequences are sure to be complex and may vary significantly across countries. Nevertheless, by making domestic law rather than transnational standards the focus, this approach should be more compatible with meaningful negotiation and reform efforts within timber-producing countries. In countries with Voluntary Partnership Agreements, actors from domestic civil society are required to be at the negotiating table. Additionally, they will be able to appeal to local overseers of the Timber Legality Assurance System, rather than the distant and foreign accreditors that oversee private regulatory initiatives. The combination of national legal referents, public disclosure of audit reports, and independent monitoring by civil society may even provide a platform for social justice, good governance, and anti-corruption reforms.

In Indonesia, the "collusive corruption" that characterizes relationships between timber companies and subnational governments will not be eliminated simply through increased transparency and a stronger platform for civil society; but these are nevertheless crucial components of a path to reform.[43] More broadly, even in countries without EU-approved Timber Legality Assurance Systems, national law should be far more familiar and intuitive to residents than are standards that emanate from foreign corporations and transnational certification initiatives, which typically have only a few small

---

[43] Smith, Obidzinski, Subarudi, and Suramenggala 2003.

outposts in a given country. If one wants transnational governance to resonate with the priorities of local activists and reformers, the timber legality
regime presents an appealing design.

On the other hand, this type of state re-centering could also foster repression. In particular, a "law enforcement" approach to forest governance could
target small-scale subsistence loggers and erase informal respect for community rights, while shoring up the power of state agencies and politically
connected timber companies.[44] As Paul Gellert and Andiko (2015) note
about Indonesia, "the activities of poor and indigenous people living in and
around the forest areas are much more often criminalized than activities of
companies." An apparent call for the "rule of law", then, may actually aid
"powerful political and economic actors [in] the maintenance of their authority and the reorganization of their power to extract."[45] Similar concerns have
been raised about other countries with Voluntary Partnership Agreements,
including Ghana, Cameroon, and Vietnam, among others.[46]

These concerns should not be taken lightly. The EU has sought to address
some of them with its procedures for reviewing timber legality assurance systems.[47] Still, there is little doubt that politically powerful actors will have greater
influence on the practical meaning of legality than will impoverished and
marginalized groups. If the transnational timber legality regime is to make the
global timber trade more just, not merely more orderly, it will have to be
combined with robust domestic social movements, watchdogs that expose
both repressive crackdowns and lax legality verifications, and ultimately
reforms in the various state agencies that govern land use. These factors are by
no means guaranteed, even in the most democratic and dynamic settings. But
they are at least allowed—and perhaps encouraged—by the transnational timber legality regime. Transnational *private* regulation, in contrast, at best brackets
these dynamics. At worst, it undermines contentious but important domestic
reforms, as sustainability practitioners pretend to transcend the local context
and transnational corporations look for less contentious sourcing destinations.

It is likely that the auditing done for legality verification will be no better—
and possibly much worse—than the auditing for sustainability certification,
which this book has critiqued. One critical review of the timber legality
assurance system (SVLK) in Indonesia showed that the scoring system had
been revised to allow nearly all companies to pass, that auditors had ignored

---

[44] Kaimowitz 2003.   [45] Gellert and Andiko 2015:659. See also Kaimowitz 2003.
[46] Ros-Tonen, Insaidoo, and Acheampong 2013; Buhmann and Nathan 2012; Eba'a Atyi,
Assembe-Mvondo, Lescuyer, and Cerutti 2013; McDermott, Irland, and Pacheco 2015. Yet
Wiersum and Elands (2013) argue that although negotiations in Ghana were fraught, "a new
policy assemblage emerged in which international concerns on timber legality became integrated
with international concerns on improving forest–livelihood relations" (p. 21).
[47] Overdevest and Zeitlin forthcoming.

or glossed over overlapping permits, community conflicts, and corruption in the original issuance of logging permits, and that independent monitors had insufficient access to information.[48] Some aspects of SVLK were subsequently strengthened in order to gain EU approval, particularly with regard to independent monitoring and appeals.[49] Most likely, SVLK audits will continue to be quite circumscribed, but independent monitoring networks will have significant opportunities to expose cursory auditing and appeal controversial decisions.

Finally, it is possible that legality verification in its various forms may crowd out the higher bar of sustainability certification. Although some have argued that legality will provide a baseline for the expansion of FSC certification, it is quite possible that retailers, brands, and forest managers will gravitate toward less costly and more achievable assurances of legality.[50] This would be a blow for private sustainability certification, although for the reasons discussed above, it would not an entirely bad thing for the trajectories of forest governance and transnational governance more broadly. Simply put, acknowledging and grappling with domestic governance should be a more productive route than trying to transcend it. Ideally, though, the transnational timber legality regime will improve the average level of forest governance while other projects, including high-bar sustainability standards, promote truly "beyond compliance" protections for ecosystems and livelihoods.

This hope dovetails in some respects with recent accounts of experimentalist governance in global forest management, which have celebrated the multi-level and interactive character of the emerging global forestry regime complex.[51] Yet while these scholars emphasize the potential for meaningful discovery and alteration of firms' preferences, this book paints a far more critical portrait of entrenched interests and compromised rules in the global forest products industry. In this light, it is the timber legality regime's *transnationally binding penalties* and the potential for *domestic contention* led by robust social movements that will most profoundly reshape the global governance of forests.

Toward Place-conscious Transnational Governance of Labor Standards?

Transnational governance of labor standards has also evolved, with several notable efforts seeking to get beyond the pitfalls of private regulation. For

---

[48] Anti Forest-Mafia Coalition 2014. Interestingly, given the discussion of observability in Chapter 2, this report used GIS and photo evidence to document problematic logging concessions. See also Human Rights Watch 2013.
[49] Overdevest and Zeitlin forthcoming.
[50] See Bartley 2014; Cashore and Stone 2012; Overdevest and Zeitlin 2014a.
[51] See Overdevest and Zeitlin 2014a; Overdevest and Zeitlin 2014b; Overdevest and Zeitlin forthcoming.

some, this means getting brands to sign binding agreements to improve factory conditions, rather than relying on voluntary commitments. For others, it means combining private code and labor law compliance efforts. These are promising developments, which move toward "place-conscious" transnational governance in some ways. But as we will see, none go as far as the timber legality regime in both re-centering the state and requiring accountability beyond the boundaries of the firm.

Building safety in Bangladesh: from voluntary to binding agreements

In April of 2013, the Rana Plaza complex of factories near Dhaka, Bangladesh, collapsed, killing more than 1,100 workers. Despite visible and worsening cracks in the building and an evacuation the previous afternoon, thousands of garment workers were pushed back inside on the morning of the collapse. The worst industrial accident in the history of the garment industry occurred in spite of the codes of conduct of Primark, Benetton, The Children's Place, and other companies that were sourcing there, and in spite of audits conducted under the auspices of the Business Social Compliance Initiative, which later tried to explain that "audits do not include building construction or integrity."[52] A factory producing for Inditex (the owner of Zara) in the same industrial district had collapsed eight years earlier, leading the company to re-think its approach to compliance and assistance but clearly not altering the larger landscape of building safety in Bangladesh.[53] The Rana Plaza collapse also followed on the heels of a series of deadly factory fires in Bangladesh from 2010 to 2012, and the death of nearly 300 workers in a fire in a factory in Pakistan that had just been approved for SA8000 certification.[54]

The Rana Plaza collapse generated a moment of crisis for corporate responsibility and private regulatory initiatives. In the midst of trials, protests, and promises of reform within Bangladesh, two new compliance initiatives emerged. A group of American brands, including The Gap, Wal-Mart, Target, and VF organized the Alliance for Bangladesh Worker Safety, which coordinates private inspections and remediation plans for factories used by its corporate members. This initiative largely accepts the voluntary and private auditing model already used by brands and initiatives, but it focuses intensively on building safety and supports remediation processes in various ways.

A second new initiative rejects the voluntary character of existing compliance initiatives, asking instead for brands and retailers to sign a binding agreement to improve building safety in Bangladesh. This initiative, the Bangladesh Accord on Fire and Building Safety, was developed by international

---

[52] Business Social Compliance Initiative 2013.   [53] Miller 2012.
[54] Theuws, Huijstee, Overeem, Seters, and Pauli 2013; Walsh and Greenhouse 2012.

union federations and labor-rights groups—especially the IndustriALL Global Union, the Worker Rights Consortium, and the Clean Clothes Campaign—as an extension of an agreement forged with PVH after an earlier factory fire. Over 200 companies, mostly European brands and retailers (e.g., H&M, Primark, Carrefour) as well as a few major American firms (e.g., PVH, Abercrombie and Fitch), signed onto the Accord in the eighteen months after Rana Plaza.[55] Signatories commit, for a five-year period (2013–18), to fund a new safety inspection and remediation program headed by international experts, demand that their suppliers cooperate with inspections and remediation plans, and negotiate contract terms that allow suppliers to take the necessary corrective actions.[56] The Accord also gives Bangladeshi labor unions a seat at the table and promotes workers' right to refuse unsafe work.

The Accord rejects voluntary commitments, and this is largely why brands formed the Alliance as an alternative. But even the binding Accord accepts a fundamentally private sort of regulation that seeks to bypass the state. As one profile describes it, "the Accord has become almost a shadow, parallel Ministry of Labor alongside the Bangladeshi government."[57] To the extent the Accord—and perhaps also the Alliance—can prevent orders from being shifted to unmonitored subcontractors and get brands to stay with their suppliers as conditions improve and prices most likely increase, the average safety level of Bangladesh's garment industry should improve significantly. And yet, because the Accord sets up a parallel private safety inspectorate, it is unlikely to push the Bangladeshi government to enforce its own labor laws. Nor is it likely to build state capacities that could outlast this transnational project and the spotlight now on Bangladesh.

The desire to bypass the Bangladeshi state is not difficult to understand. The current ruling party is closely allied with factory owners, and the main competing party is little different in the domain of economic and industrial policy.[58] Nevertheless, the Accord's attempt to produce binding accountability without the (Bangladeshi) state means that its supporters are left to lament that "on paper, labor law goes much further, but the laws are unenforced," without considering whether transnational governance could support stronger labor law enforcement.[59]

Better Work: integrating labor law and private regulation

Concerns that private regulation was failing throughout the global apparel industry inspired another new initiative, Better Work, sponsored by the

---

[55] Accord on Fire and Building Safety in Bangladesh 2014.
[56] See http://www.bangladeshaccord.org.   [57] Ross 2015.
[58] Ahmed, Greenleaf, and Sacks 2014.   [59] Ross 2015:78.

International Labour Organization and International Finance Corporation. This initiative re-centers the state by emphasizing compliance with domestic labor law, but for the most part it relies on the voluntary participation of brands and their suppliers.

In country-level programs in Cambodia, Jordan, Lesotho, Indonesia, Vietnam, and Nicaragua, Better Work trains its own monitoring teams to assess factories' compliance with national labor law as well as internationally recognized labor rights (e.g., absence of forced labor, freedom of association). The results are shared with factory managers and worker representatives within the factory, and government representatives are incorporated into larger industry-level reviews and dialogues.[60] Brands and retailers participate by purchasing access to the monitoring reports, or in a more committed role, allow Better Work to essentially take over their auditing and remediation activities with participating suppliers.[61] In most countries, the incentive for supplier factories to participate comes from the requests of their buyers. In general, this hybrid form of governance promises to improve the quality of factory oversight, improve interactions between public and private regulators, and help factories improve their productivity in tandem with their compliance.[62]

The origins of Better Work lie in the ILO's Better Factories program in Cambodia, which began in 2001, backed by a trade agreement giving the Cambodian garment industry preferential access to the US market in return for improving labor conditions.[63] Interestingly, as the agreement was being negotiated, the ILO's initial plan was to help strengthen the ability of Cambodian government labor inspectors to enforce national labor law. But after the US government, along with American labor unions, argued that the results would not be credible or cover the necessary international labor rights, a new plan emerged: The ILO would become a factory monitor, and its core labor standards would be used as a supplement to Cambodian labor law.[64]

Initially, the Cambodian government mandated that garment factories had to at least participate in the program to receive export licenses, but when the trade agreement expired in 2004, the initiative shifted to become a voluntary program. The interest of brands such as The Gap, Levi Strauss, and H&M was to become the main incentive for suppliers to participate. A growing number of buyers—more than twenty by 2007—were looking to the Better Factories initiative for credible assurances about factories in Cambodia, but their participation was voluntary, and it did not require major changes to their

---

[60] Bair 2017.
[61] Better Work Global. "Buyer Partners." http://betterwork.org/global/?page_id=361, accessed December 8, 2016.
[62] Brown, Dehejia, and Robertson 2013; Rossi, Luinstra, and Pickles 2014; Oka 2012.
[63] Polaski 2006.   [64] Kolben 2004.

sourcing practices.[65] Still, evidence from the program suggests that improvements in labor law compliance continued after the program's shift, and that factories' level of compliance was related to the number of participating buyers the factories supplied.[66] On the other hand, the program has had an awkward relationship with Cambodian unions. The ILO was reluctant to get embroiled in competition between independent unions and those with close ties to management or the state, and the Better Factories program initially said almost nothing about the killing of Chea Vichea, an independent union leader in the garment industry, in 2004.[67]

Links to trade agreements or export licenses did not exist as Better Factories Cambodia expanded into Better Work programs in Vietnam, Indonesia, Lesotho, and Nicaragua.[68] Therefore, although Better Work integrates private pressures for compliance with national labor law to a far greater extent than do private regulatory initiatives, it remains subject to the challenges of voluntarism. In Nicaragua, many exporters have hesitated to participate in the program, uncertain about whether buyers will truly demand it.[69] In Indonesia, factories' rate of non-compliance with laws about overtime, employment contracts, social security and benefits, termination, and several other issues have remained high (78 percent, 73 percent, 78 percent, and 58 percent respectively as of the fifth compliance report in 2015), and yet participating suppliers and buyers have been able to continue with no real penalties.[70] There is compelling evidence that Better Work Indonesia has fostered new interactions between employers and the state. But substantively, this means that employers have had to go through a more formal process to get waivers to pay below the legal minimum wage.[71]

This version of "place conscious" transnational governance is certainly an improvement on the hope of transcendence that animates many private regulatory initiatives. In addition, it has finally ratcheted up the quality of factory auditing, since visits are unannounced.[72] But Better Work programs to not appear to have the power to provide strong enforcement of labor law. Indeed, doing so would risk alienating the roughly thirty participating brands and retailers that the initiative depends upon.

These are of course not the only examples of evolution in the field of labor and human rights. The UN's Guiding Principles on Business and Human Rights—the so-called Ruggie Principles, after their chief architect—have

---

[65] Better Factories Cambodia 2007; Community Legal Education Centre and Clean Clothes Campaign 2012.

[66] Brown, Dehejia, and Robertson 2013; Oka 2010a.   [67] Hughes 2007; Kolben 2004.

[68] The Better Work programs in Jordan and Haiti are exceptions, which are linked to some degree to trade agreements with the US.

[69] Bair 2017.   [70] Better Work Indonesia 2015.

[71] Amengual and Chirot 2016.   [72] Rossi, Luinstra, and Pickles 2014.

spawned a series of National Action Plans to be developed by governments. These may be useful in generating new dialogues and national policies to promote corporate social responsibility, but they remain "soft" goal-setting exercises with a light touch on issues of enforcement.[73] The California Transparency in Supply Chains Act of 2010 and the UK Modern Slavery Act of 2015 both require companies to report on the steps they are taking to prevent forced labor and human trafficking in their supply chains, but they demand only reporting, not particular standards of performance. In fact, a variety of new regulations in affluent countries are requiring companies to exercise due diligence and/or report on their private compliance activities pertaining to forced labor, but none of these include penalties for selling items made with forced labor.[74] If one views enforcement, not rule-making, as the problem with current governance architectures for global production networks, these new policies are insufficient.

Toward a transnational labor legality regime?

A transnational legality regime is being implemented in the global forest products industry but has not even been included in discussions of apparel and other labor-intensive manufacturing industries. This is perhaps a testament to the stark divisions in the study of land and labor and the practical barriers this creates. Although the industries, products, and fields are not identical, as theorized in Chapter 2, the timber legality regime provides an intriguing model for improving transnational governance of labor standards. While the Bangladesh Accord represents a move toward binding agreements, and Better Work is forging a closer engagement with the state, there are no transnational labor standards initiatives that both enforce domestic labor law and penalize lead firms for violations in their supply chains. Labor-rights advocates might see this as practically impossible, but my earlier review of the timber legality regime suggests several possibilities.

The cornerstone of a transnational labor legality regime would be laws in large markets, such as the US and EU, prohibiting the sale of items made in violation of labor law in the country of origin, with penalties for the seller of the items. Some import bans currently exist in these markets, such as section 307 of the Tariff Act of 1930 in the US, which prohibits the import of items made using forced labor. But enforcement depends on the US Customs and Border Patrol barring items from entering the market. In 2016, the Obama

[73] UN Working Group on Business and Human Rights 2016.

[74] Nieuwenkamp, Roel. 2016. "Game Changing Trade Regulations in US Shake Up Corporate Supply Chain Responsibility." OECD Insights blog, http://oecdinsights.org/2016/05/31/game-changing-trade-regulations-in-us-shake-up-corporate-supply-chain-responsibility/, accessed December 10, 2016.

administration increased the agency's authority to exclude, and several specific food and chemical items made by companies in China using prison labor were subsequently blocked.[75] But in other circumstances, the agency has been reluctant to enforce section 307, even when evidence of forced labor is clear. The agency failed to prohibit the import of cotton from Uzbekistan, for instance, despite evidence that essentially all cotton from that country was made through a state-sponsored system of forced labor.[76]

Rather than relying on initial exclusion at the border, enforcement could be more robust if retailers and brands faced fines and confiscations for products that had already entered the market, as they do under the Lacey Act. If violations of labor law in their supply chains carried the risk of direct and significant penalties, one would also expect retailers and brands to be much more rigorous in choosing and monitoring their suppliers. This would combine public and private enforcement of labor standards in a new way at the global level. Within the US, the Department of Labor has at some points used "hot goods" provisions to seize products made in violation of domestic labor law, and in the mid-1990s it used this approach to promote private monitoring of contractors in domestic garment districts.[77] A transnational labor legality regime would require authority to seize products within a major market regardless of where the labor law violation occurred. Penalties would apply to both imports and domestically made products, whether this meant apparel from Pakistan or produce from North Carolina.

Market access regulations might be supplemented with voluntary partnership agreements between major importing countries and willing exporting countries, perhaps building on existing Better Work programs. These could mandate multi-stakeholder dialogues to operationally define legality in each country—a task that it seems Better Work programs have already begun to do on their own.[78] The agreements could also create new systems for verifying the legality of labor conditions, again perhaps building on Better Work programs. Once these systems were fully vetted, imports from that country might be offered guaranteed access into the regulated market, much as the EU's does with approved timber legality assurance systems.

By making domestic labor law the relevant standard, a transnational labor legality regime would resonate with the rising "rights consciousness" of workers in export-oriented industries around the world. In China, migrant workers have become much more aware of their legal rights since the implementation

[75] Baker & McKenzie 2016.

[76] Gottwald, Eric. "Tariff Act Strengthened, But Will Enforcement Follow?" International Labor Rights Forum blog post, http://www.laborrights.org/blog/201602/tariff-act-strengthened-will-enforcement-follow, accessed December 10, 2016.

[77] See Bartley 2005; Fine and Gordon 2010; Weil 2014.

[78] Amengual and Chirot 2016; Bair 2017.

of the 2007 Labor Contract Law and more likely to "use the law as a weapon."[79] In Indonesia, as we saw, unions have mobilized millions for massive demonstrations over minimum wages and laws on labor market flexibility, and Indonesian workers are quite attuned to their "normative rights"—that is, their basic legal rights.[80] Indeed, labor law has been at the center of labor movements and employment conflicts all over the world.[81] The language of global standards, and even fundamental international labor rights, appears to be several steps more removed.

It would be naïve to have too much faith in labor law. After all, it can be repressive, inaccessible to marginalized workers, or manipulated by governments. I will address these problems to some degree below. What is crucial to note at this point, though, is that despite its central position in domestic struggles over rights and dignity, labor law has played at best a background role in most transnational governance agendas to date. This must be rectified if one is to seriously address labor standards in the global economy.

A transnational labor legality regime could be constructed to cover not only manufacturing industries, but also agricultural and extractive industries, where labor exploitation is often severe and geographically dispersed. Recall from Chapters 2 and 4 that labor rights are included in FSC certification but rarely taken seriously. A labor legality regime that included forest products could improve private scrutiny of wage payment and labor contracts in both forests and factories manufacturing forest products. Similarly, although it is beyond the scope of this book's purview, there is evidence that fair trade and sustainable agriculture standards have done a poor job of protecting the rights of hired farm laborers, not to mention forced laborers in fishing operations.[82] A multi-product transnational labor legality regime could improve the chances for decent work in agro-food supply chains.

To be sure, it would take an unusual confluence of factors to make a transnational labor legality regime politically viable. The story of the timber legality regime suggests several facilitating conditions. First, some segment of politically powerful companies in countries with large consumer markets would need to join coalitions in favor of laws that penalize the sale of illegally produced goods. The corporate members of a "Baptist-bootlegger" coalition might be domestic producers—perhaps companies with factories in parts of Eastern or Southern Europe where labor-intensive manufacturing remains

---

[79] Lee 2007a; Gallagher 2005; Friedman 2013. But see Perry 2008 for a different sort of "rules without rights".

[80] Ford and Sirait 2016; Caraway 2015.

[81] See Caraway, Cook, and Crowley 2015.

[82] See Jaffee 2007; Barrientos et al. 2003. For somewhat more optimistic accounts of how evolving forms of private regulation can improve harsh labor conditions in agricultural sectors, see Coslovsky and Locke 2012, Raynolds 2017, and Tampe forthcoming.

viable—who felt undercut by labor law violations elsewhere. Or perhaps a "corporate liberal" reform group could emerge out of the transnational corporations that have invested the most in their compliance programs but are struggling to differentiate themselves from competitors. Although transnational corporations would almost surely balk at binding penalties, some might endorse a system that included a clear lane into the regulated market for properly verified legal products.

Although some degree of corporate support or acquiescence would likely be necessary, the pressure for a transnational labor legality regime would of course need to come from labor-rights advocates. Many labor and human rights NGOs have already called for binding rules rather than voluntary norms.[83] Unions in affluent countries might also find their interests supported by a labor legality regime, in that they could use information from global watchdogs to gain leverage over the target of an organizing campaign, such as a retailer.[84]

Second, if exporting governments are to help formulate new systems for verifying labor legality, they would need to see this as an opportunity to enhance their own authority. Some might see a chance to recoup tax revenues that are being lost to unregistered informal factories or to fraudulent reporting of revenues. Governments might also commit to a transnational labor legality regime as a way to quell internal labor unrest, cope with workers' rising expectations, or solidify projects to professionalize domestic labor law enforcement. To be sure, many governments prefer a *lack* of labor law enforcement, at least to the extent that it attracts investment, greases the wheels of commerce, and allows selective enforcement to be used for political purposes. For a transnational labor legality regime to be viable, some critical mass of governments would need instead to see labor law as a viable path to a high road development strategy.[85]

Third, the timber legality example suggests that discourse is powerful, such that robust coalitions and policy change would depend on violations of labor law being firmly linked to discourses of illegality and law enforcement. There are some notable moves in this direction. Human trafficking has, for better or worse, been theorized and popularized as a matter of security and law enforcement. This has facilitated broad attention and policy-making, although it has also made for a sensationalistic, gendered, and sexually panicked discourse of victimhood.[86] Whether this discourse can be revised

---

[83] See the Joint Civil Society Statement on the draft Guiding Principles on Business and Human Rights, https://www.fidh.org/IMG/pdf/Joint_CSO_Statement_on_GPs.pdf, accessed May 22, 2017.

[84] I thank Marion Crain for this point.

[85] See Piore and Schrank 2008 for evidence of some selected moves in this direction.

[86] Parreñas, Hwang, and Lee 2012.

to carry a more empowering, respectful, and labor-centered frame is the subject of important debate.[87] The language of "wage theft" has gained increasing use in campaigns focused on low-wage workers in the US, and has been central to some international exposés as well.[88] Apart from that, though, mundane violations of labor law are rarely theorized as matters of law enforcement. An overarching discourse of "employment crime" that would be analogous to "environmental crime" does not yet exist, but it may be possible. "Legality" is a multivalent concept, and there are both challenges and opportunities in applying it to domains, like labor, where the law on the books has developed in complex and contradictory ways over different historical periods.

The idea of a labor legality regime would no doubt face resistance, perhaps including charges that it violates WTO rules. An emphasis on enforcement of laws that governments have already approved and the hypothesized "neoliberal exception" would perhaps lighten the charges. Still, a labor legality regime might also need to rest on the GATT/WTO's exceptions for regulations that are necessary to protect human health or safety and "public morals".[89] Moreover, as discussed in Chapter 2, framings of labor standards as a global public good have at best weak backing in elite policy communities. Strengthening this would be crucial for allowing a transnational labor legality regime to attract broad coalitions and withstand inevitable challenges. Under current conditions, it is difficult to see a transnational labor legality regime as feasible. Nevertheless, pushing reforms down this path makes sense, given the essential link between labor law and decent work and the positive example in the timber case.

To be sure, a transnational labor legality regime would not address all of the problems of exploitation in global industries. Depending on national law, it might not deal with gender discrimination or sexual harassment or live up to international norms about freedom of association and collective bargaining rights. The meaning of compliance would of course vary across countries—perhaps even more than it already does—following differences in laws about child labor, minimum wages, maximum working hours, and safety hazards. Supplemental approaches would clearly be needed, including transnational advocacy networks focused on gender and employment rights,

---

[87] See, for instance, Kempadoo, Sanghera, and Pattanaik 2016.

[88] See Milkman, González, and Narro 2010 and Weil 2014 on the US setting. See Worker Rights Consortium 2013 and Clean Clothes Campaign 2012 for "wage theft" language in international campaigns.

[89] General Agreement on Tariffs and Trade (GATT), Agreement on Technical Barriers to Trade; GATT Article XX. The human health clause is often interpreted as applying to consumers and product safety standards, but perhaps it could be applied to workers' health and safety as well.

wage-harmonization projects at the industry or regional level, and the reforms to CSR fields discussed earlier in this chapter.[90]

There are also dangers that labor law enforcement could be used to further repress labor activism, or that countries would weaken their laws to enhance their competitiveness. These are serious risks, and it would largely be up to domestic labor movements to confront them directly. But reformed transnational governance arrangements could help—by adding additional layers of watchdogs and support scaffolding focused on the implementation of domestic legal norms rather than the setting of global standards. Rather than hoping to transcend the local context or fill in empty spaces, the practice of transnational governance would then mean grappling with contested meanings of law, supporting local enforcement, and bolstering the power of domestic advocates.

---

[90] See Miller 2013 and Evans 2016 for some promising new approaches.

Bibliography

Abbott, Kenneth, and Duncan Snidal. 2009a. "The Governance Triangle: Regulatory Standards Institutions and the Shadow of the State." Pp. 44–88 in *The Politics of Global Regulation*, edited by Walter Mattli and Ngaire Woods. Princeton and Oxford: Princeton University Press.

Abbott, Kenneth, and Duncan Snidal. 2009b. "Strengthening International Regulation through Transnational New Governance: Overcoming the Orchestration Deficit." *Vanderbilt Journal of Transnational Law* 42(501–78).

Abbott, Kenneth, and Duncan Snidal. 2013. "Taking Responsive Regulation Transnational: Strategies for International Organizations." *Regulation & Governance* 7(1):95–113.

Abbott, Kenneth W., Philipp Genschel, Duncan Snidal, and Bernhard Zangl. 2015. *International Organizations as Orchestrators*. New York: Cambridge University Press.

Abbott, Kenneth W., David Levi-Faur, and Duncan Snidal. 2017. "Theorizing Regulatory Intermediaries: The RIT Model." *The ANNALS of the American Academy of Political and Social Science* 670(1):93–111.

Abubakar, Datuk H. 2009. "The Guguk Indigenous Community Jambi: Protecting Customary Forests with Local Regulation." Pp. 63–99 in *Forests for the Future: Indigenous Forest Management in a Changing World*, edited by Emilianus Ola Kleden, Liz Chidley, and Yuyun Indradi. Jakarta: AMAN and Down to Earth.

Accord on Fire and Building Safety in Bangladesh. 2014. "Annual Report." http://bangladeshaccord.org/wp-content/uploads/Annual-Report-Bangladesh-Accord-Foundation-2014.pdf, accessed December 9, 2016.

Accreditation Services International. 2014. "ASI-FSC Forest Management Assessment—China—SCS March 2014." Accreditation Services International, http://www.accreditation-services.com/resources/document-library/download-info/asi-fsc-forest-management-assessment-china-scs-march-2014, accessed June 10, 2016.

Adidas. 2015. "Global Factory List: Primary Suppliers." Adidas, January 6, 2015, http://www.adidas-group.com/media/filer_public/db/82/db8268b9-1bc6-4cad-a1f4-186a6c706fb9/jan_2015_-_primary_supplier_list.pdf, accessed May 10, 2016.

Adler, E. 2005. *Communitarian International Relations: The Epistemic Foundations of International Relations*. New York: Routledge.

Agrawal, Arun. 2005. *Environmentality: Technologies of Government and the Making of Subjects*. Durham: Duke University Press.

Agrawal, Arun, and Clark C. Gibson. 2001. *Communities and the Environment: Ethnicity, Gender, and the State in Community-Based Conservation*. New Brunswick: Rutgers University Press.

Aguilar, Francisco X., and Richard P. Vlosky. 2007. "Consumer Willingness to Pay Price Premiums for Environmentally Certified Wood Products in the US." *Forest Policy and Economics* 9(8):1100–12.

Ahmed, Faisal Z., Anne Greenleaf, and Audrey Sacks. 2014. "The Paradox of Export Growth in Areas of Weak Governance: The Case of the Ready Made Garment Sector in Bangladesh." *World Development* 56:258–71.

Ahrne, Goran, Nils Brunsson, and Christina Garsten. 2000. "Standardizing through Organization." Pp. 50–68 in *A World of Standards*, edited by Nils Brunsson and Bengt Jacobsson. Oxford: Oxford University Press.

AKATIGA Center for Social Analysis. 2007. "ATC Phase-out and Indonesian Textile and Clothing Industry: Where Do We Stand?" Bandung and Jakarta: AKATIGA Center for Social Analysis and Friedrich Ebert Stiftung.

Alford, Peter. 2012. "One-Man Crusade to End Nike Sweatshops Pays Off." *The Australian* January 21, 2012.

Alois, Paul. 2016. "Better Work and Global Governance." PhD Dissertation, Department of Political Science, City University of New York.

Amengual, Matthew. 2010. "Complementary Labor Regulation: The Uncoordinated Combination of State and Private Regulators in the Dominican Republic." *World Development* 38(3):405–14.

Amengual, Matthew. 2016. *Politicized Enforcement in Argentina: Labor and Environmental Regulation*. New York: Cambridge University Press.

Amengual, Matthew, and Laura Chirot. 2016. "Reinforcing the State: Transnational and State Labor Regulation in Indonesia." *Industrial & Labor Relations Review* 69(5): 1056–80.

American Embassy in Jakarta. 2007. "Korean Investment Dispute Highlights Labor Problems." Cable from American Embassy in Jakarta, January 4, 2007, https:// wikileaks.org/plusd/cables/07JAKARTA24_a.html, accessed May 10, 2016.

American Forest & Paper Association. 2004. "'Illegal' Logging and Global Wood Markets: The Competitive Impacts on the U.S. Wood Products Industry." Prepared for AFPA by Seneca Creek Associates and Wood Resources International, https:// www.illegal-logging.info/sites/default/files/uploads/1_AF_and_PA_summary.pdf.

Amsden, Alice H. 1989. *Asia's Next Giant: South Korea and Late Industrialization*. New York: Oxford University Press.

Anam, Khoirul. 2010. "Prospects for Green Jobs in Indonesian Forestry Sector (Trade Union Perspective)." Presentation at the Green Jobs National Conference, Jakarta, December 16–18, 2010. http://www.ilo.org/jakarta/WCMS_150056/lang–en/index. htm, accessed October 24, 2016.

Anderson, Benedict. 1983. *Imagined Communities: Reflections on the Origin and Spread of Nationalism*. London: Verso.

Anderson, Roy C., and Eric N. Hansen. 2004. "Determining Consumer Preferences for Ecolabeled Forest Products: An Experimental Approach." *Journal of Forestry* 102(4):28–32.

Anner, Mark. 2009. "Two Logics of Labor Organizing in the Global Apparel Industry." *International Studies Quarterly* 53(3):545–70.

Anner, Mark, Jennifer Bair, and Jeremy Blasi. 2013. "Towards Joint Liability in Global Supply Chains: Addressing the Root Causes of Labor Violations in International Subcontracting Networks." *Journal of Comparative Labor Law and Policy* 35:1–44.

Anner, Mark, and Teri Caraway. 2010. "International Institutions and Workers' Rights: Between Labor Standards and Market Flexibility." *Studies in Comparative International Development* 45(2):151–69.

Anti Forest-Mafia Coalition. 2014. "SVLK Flawed: An Independent Evaluation of Indonesia's Timber Legality Certification System." http://assets.worldwildlife.org/publications/775/files/original/Indonesia_timber_report_March_2014_SVLK.pdf?1426711645&_ga=1.210749725.982410419.1479789686, accessed November 22, 2016.

Appelbaum, Richard P. 2008. "Giant Transnational Contractors in East Asia: Emergent Trends in Global Supply Chains." *Competition & Change* 12(1):69–87.

Appelbaum, Richard P., Edna Bonacich, and Katie Quan. 2005. "The End of Apparel Quotas: A Faster Race to the Bottom?": Working paper, University of California-Santa Barbara, http://escholarship.org/uc/item/40f8w19g, accessed October 9, 2016.

Arjaliès, Diane-Laure. 2010. "A Social Movement Perspective on Finance: How Socially Responsible Investment Mattered." *Journal of Business Ethics* 92(1):57–78.

Armbruster-Sandoval, Ralph. 2005. *Globalization and Cross-Border Labor Solidarity in the Americas: The Anti-Sweatshop Movement and the Struggle for Social Justice.* New York: Routledge.

Armstrong, Elizabeth A. 2002. *Forging Gay Identities: Organizing Sexuality in San Francisco, 1950–1994.* Chicago: University of Chicago Press.

ASEAN Affairs. 2009. "Export Decline Triggers Mass Layoffs at Indonesian Furniture Firms." http://www.aseanaffairs.com/indonesia_news/trade/export_decline_triggers_mass_layoffs_at_indonesian_furniture_firms, accessed November 2, 2009.

Aspinall, Edward. 2005. *Opposing Suharto: Compromise, Resistance, and Regime Change in Indonesia.* Stanford, CA: Stanford University Press.

Aspinall, Edward. 2014. "Popular Agency and Interests in Indonesia's Democratic Transition and Consolidation." Pp. 117–38 in *Beyond Oligarchy: Wealth, Power, and Contemporary Indonesian Politics*, edited by Michele Ford and Thomas B. Pepinsky. Ithaca: Cornell University Press.

Associated Press. 2012. "More Than 2 Million Workers Strike in Indonesia." (October 3, 2012, http://bigstory.ap.org/article/more-2-million-workers-strike-indonesia).

Athreya, Bama. 1998a. "Codes of Conduct and Independent Monitoring: Strategies to Improve Labor Rights Enforcement." Discussion paper: International Labor Rights Fund.

Athreya, Bama. 1998b. *Economic Development and Political Change in a Workers' Community in Jakarta, Indonesia.* University of Michigan, PhD Dissertation.

Auld, Graeme. 2006. "Choosing How to Be Green: An Examination of Domtar Inc.'s Approach to Forest Certification." *Journal of Strategic Management Education* 3(1):37–92.

Auld, Graeme. 2014. *Constructing Private Governance: The Rise and Evolution of Forest, Coffee, and Fisheries Certification.* New Haven: Yale University Press.

Auld, Graeme, and Lars H. Gulbrandsen. 2010. "Transparency in Nonstate Certification: Consequences for Accountability and Legitimacy." *Global Environmental Politics* 10(3):97–119.

Auld, Graeme, Lars H. Gulbrandsen, and Constance L. McDermott. 2008. "Certification Schemes and the Impacts on Forests and Forestry." *Annual Review of Environment and Resources* 33:187–211.

Avetisyan, Emma, and Jean-Pascal Gond. 2013. "Institutional Dynamics of CSR Standardization: A Multilevel Perspective in the Field of ESG Rating." *Academy of Management Proceedings* 2013(1):15122.

Bair, Jennifer. 2017. "Contextualizing Compliance: Hybrid Governance in Global Value Chains." *New Political Economy* 22(2):169–85.

Bair, Jennifer, and Florence Palpacuer. 2012. "From Varieties of Capitalism to Varieties of Activism: The Antisweatshop Movement in Comparative Perspective." *Social Problems* 59(4):522–43.

Baker & McKenzie. 2016. "International Trade, Client Alert: Increased Enforcement of U.S. Forced Labor Prohibition Carries High Risks for U.S. Companies." http://bakerxchange.com/cv/961439f20d4e8806d11c1160a498f0732ee7de8b#7, accessed May 19, 2017.

Baker, Tom. 2009. "Bonded Import Safety Warranties." Pp. 215–32 in *Import Safety: Regulatory Governance in the Global Economy*, edited by Cary Coglianese, Adam M. Finkel, and David Zaring. Philadelphia: University of Pennsylvania Press.

Bakker, Laurens. 2008. " 'Can We Get Hak Ulayat?': Land and Community in Pasir and Nunukan, East Kalimantan." Paper presented at the UC Berkeley-UCLA Joint Conference on Southeast Asia, Ten Years After: Reformasi and New Social Movements in Indonesia, 1998–2008.

Bakker, Laurens, and Sandra Moniaga. 2010. "The Space Between: Land Claims and the Law in Indonesia." *Asian Journal of Social Science* 38(2):187–203.

Ballinger, Jeff. 2000. "Nike Chronology." University of Washington, Center for Communication & Civic Engagement, http://depts.washington.edu/ccce/polcommcampaigns/NikeChronology.htm.

Bamberger, Kenneth A., and Andrew T. Guzman. 2009. "Importers as Regulators: Product Safety in a Globalized World." Pp. 193–214 in *Import Safety: Regulatory Governance in the Global Economy*, edited by Cary Coglianese, Adam M. Finkel, and David Zaring. Philadelphia: University of Pennsylvania Press.

Banerjee, Subhabrata Bobby. 2008. "Corporate Social Responsibility: The Good, the Bad and the Ugly." *Critical Sociology* 34(1):51–79.

Barenberg, Mark. 2008. "Toward a Democratic Model of Transnational Labour Monitoring." Pp. 37–66 in *Regulating Labour in the Wake of Globalisation: New Challenges, New Institutions*, edited by Brian Bercusson and Cynthia Estlund. Portland: Hart Publishing.

Barman, Emily. 2016. *Caring Capitalism: The Meaning and Measure of Social Value*. New York: Cambridge University Press.

Barr, Christopher. 2001. "Banking on Sustainability: Structural Adjustment and Forestry Reform in Post Suharto Indonesia." Bogor, Indonesia: Center for International Forestry Research.

Barr, Christopher. 2007. "Intensively Managed Forest Plantations in Indonesia: Overview of Recent Trends and Current Plans." Penkanbaru, Indonesia: Presentation to the Forests Dialogue, http://tfd.yale.edu/sites/default/files/cbarr_english.pdf, accessed August 7, 2014.

Barr, Christopher, Ahmad Dermawan, John McCarthy, Moira Moeliono, and Ida Aju Pradnja Resosudarmo. 2006. "Decentralization and Recentralization in Indonesia's Forestry Sector: Summary and Recommendations." Pp. 121–44 in *Decentralization of Forest Administration in Indonesia*, edited by Christopher Barr, Ida Aju Pradnja Reso-sudarmo, Ahmad Dermawan, and John McCarthy. Bogor, Indonesia: Center for International Forestry Research.

Barrett, Joyce. 1994. "Baucus Wants Importers Working to Improve Human Rights in China." *WWD* May 10, 1994:23.

Barrientos, Stephanie. 2016. "Beyond Fair Trade." Pp. 213–27 in *The Economics of Chocolate*, edited by Mara P. Squicciarini and Johan Swinnen. Oxford: Oxford University Press.

Barrientos, Stephanie, Catherine Dolan, and Anne Tallontire. 2003. "A Gendered Value Chain Approach to Codes of Conduct in African Horticulture." *World Development* 31(9):1511–26.

Barrientos, Stephanie, and Sally Smith. 2007. "Do Workers Benefit from Ethical Trade? Assessing Codes of Labour Practice in Global Production Systems." *Third World Quarterly* 28(4):713–29.

Bartley, Tim. 2005. "Corporate Accountability and the Privatization of Labor Standards: Struggles over Codes of Conduct in the Apparel Industry." *Research in Political Sociology* 12:211–44.

Bartley, Tim. 2007a. "How Foundations Shape Social Movements: The Construction of an Organizational Field and the Rise of Forest Certification." *Social Problems* 54(3): 229–55.

Bartley, Tim. 2007b. "Institutional Emergence in an Era of Globalization: The Rise of Transnational Private Regulation of Labor and Environmental Conditions." *American Journal of Sociology* 113(2):297–351.

Bartley, Tim. 2014. "Transnational Governance and the Re-Centered State: Sustainability or Legality?" *Regulation & Governance* 8(1):93–109.

Bartley, Tim, and Curtis Child. 2011. "Movements, Markets and Fields: The Effects of Anti-Sweatshop Campaigns on U.S. Firms, 1993–2000." *Social Forces* 90(2): 425–51.

Bartley, Tim, and Curtis Child. 2014. "Shaming the Corporation: The Social Production of Targets and the Anti-Sweatshop Movement." *American Sociological Review* 79(4): 653–79.

Bartley, Tim, and Niklas Egels-Zandén. 2015. "Responsibility and Neglect in Global Production Networks: The Uneven Significance of Codes of Conduct in Indonesian Factories." *Global Networks* 15(s1):S21–S44.

Bartley, Tim, and Niklas Egels-Zandén. 2016. "Beyond Decoupling: Unions and the Leveraging of Corporate Social Responsibility in Indonesia." *Socio-Economic Review* 14(2):231–55.

Bartley, Tim, and Doug Kincaid. 2015. "The Mobility of Industries and the Limits of Corporate Social Responsibility: Labor Codes of Conduct in Indonesian Factories." Pp. 393–429 in *Corporate Social Responsibility in a Globalizing World: Global Dynamics and Local Practices*, edited by Kiyoteru Tsutsui and Alwyn Lim. Cambridge: Cambridge University Press.

Bartley, Tim, Sebastian Koos, Hiram Samel, Gustavo Setrini, and Nikolas Summers. 2015. *Looking Behind the Label: Global Industries and the Conscientious Consumer.* Bloomington: Indiana University Press.

Bartley, Tim, and Shawna Smith. 2010. "Communities of Practice as Cause and Consequence of Transnational Governance: The Evolution of Social and Environmental Certification." Pp. 347–74 in *Transnational Communities: Shaping Global Economic Governance*, edited by Marie-Laure Djelic and Sigrid Quack: Cambridge University Press.

Beckert, Jens, and Patrik Aspers. 2011. *The Worth of Goods: Valuation and Pricing in the Economy.* Oxford: Oxford University Press.

Beckert, Jens, and Matias Dewey (Eds.). 2017. *The Architecture of Illegal Markets.* Oxford: Oxford University Press.

Beijing Forestry Society. 2012. "Forest Certification for a Water Protection Forest at the Badaling Forest Farm." Beijing: Beijing Forestry Society, http://www.bjfs.org.cn/en/contents/103/1175.html, accessed June 10, 2016.

Beisheim, Marianne, Andrea Liese, Hannah Janetschek, and Johanna Sarre. 2014. "Transnational Partnerships: Conditions for Successful Service Provision in Areas of Limited Statehood." *Governance* 27(4):655–73.

Bellassen, Valentin, and Sebastiaan Luyssaert. 2014. "Carbon Sequestration: Managing Forests in Uncertain Times." *Nature* 506(7487):153–5.

Benoit, William L, and Bruce Dorries. 1996. "Dateline NBC's Persuasive Attack on Wal-Mart." *Communication Quarterly* 44(4):463–77.

Bernstein, Aaron. 2000. "A World of Sweatshops: Progress Is Slow in the Drive for Better Conditions" in *Business Week* November 6, 2000.

Bernstein, Steven. 2001. *The Compromise of Liberal Environmentalism.* New York: Columbia University Press.

Bernstein, Steven, and Benjamin Cashore. 2004. "Non-State Global Governance: Is Forest Certification a Legitimate Alternative to a Global Forest Convention?" Pp. 33–63 in *Hard Choices, Soft Law: Voluntary Standards in Global Trade, Environment and Social Governance*, edited by John J. Kirton and Michael J. Trebilcock. Aldershot: Ashgate.

Bernstein, Steven, and Benjamin Cashore. 2007. "Can Non-State Global Governance Be Legitimate? An Analytical Framework." *Regulation & Governance* 1(4):347–71.

Bernstein, Steven, and Erin Hannah. 2008. "Non-State Global Standard Setting and the WTO: Legitimacy and the Need for Regulatory Space." *Journal of International Economic Law* 11(3):575–608.

Better Factories Cambodia. 2007. "Newsletter, No. 9, December 2007." Phnom Penh: Better Factories Cambodia, http://betterwork.org/cambodia/wp-content/uploads/2013/05/Better-Factories-Newsletter-No.9-en.pdf, accessed December 9, 2016.

Better Work Indonesia. 2012a. "Baseline Report: Worker Perspectives from the Factory and Beyond." Geneva: International Labour Organization.

Better Work Indonesia. 2012b. "Garment Industry 1st Compliance Synthesis Report." Geneva: International Labour Office and International Finance Corporation.

Better Work Indonesia. 2015. "Garment Industry 5th Compliance Synthesis Report." Geneva: International Labor Office, International Finance Corporation.

Biermann, Frank, and Steffen Bauer. 2004. "Assessing the Effectiveness of Intergovernmental Organisations in International Environmental Politics." *Global Environmental Change* 14(2):189–93.

Black, Julia. 2001. "Decentring Regulation: Understanding the Role of Regulation and Self-Regulation in a 'Post-Regulatory' World." *Current Legal Problems* 54(1):103.

Blanton, Robert, and Shannon Lindsey Blanton. 2016. "Globalization and Collective Labor Rights." *Sociological Forum*: 31(1):181–202.

Blaser, Juergen, Alastair Sarre, Duncan Poore, and Steven Johnson. 2011. *Status of Tropical Forest Management 2011*. Yokohama, Japan: International Tropical Timber Organization, ITTO Technical Series No. 38.

Boddewyn, J.J. 1985. "Advertising Self-Regulation: Organization Structures in Belgium, Canada, France and the United Kingdom." Pp. 30–43 in *Private Interest Government: Beyond Market and State*, edited by Wolfgang Streeck and Philippe Schmitter. Beverly Hills: SAGE.

Boli, John, and George M. Thomas (Eds.). 1999a. *Constructing World Culture: International Nongovernmental Organizations since 1875*. Stanford, CA: Stanford University Press.

Boli, John, and George M. Thomas. 1999b. "Introduction." Pp. 1–12 in *Constructing World Culture: International Nongovernmental Organizations since 1875*, edited by John Boli and George M. Thomas. Stanford, CA: Stanford University Press.

Boltanski, Luc, and Laurent Thévenot. 2006. *On Justification: Economies of Worth*. Princeton, NJ: Princeton University Press.

Bonacich, Edna, and David V. Waller. 1994. "Mapping a Global Industry: Apparel Production in the Pacific Rim Triangle." Pp. 21–41 in *Global Production: The Apparel Industry in the Pacific Rim*, edited by Bonacich, Cheng, Chinchilla, Hamilton, and Ong. Philadelphia: Temple University Press.

Borromeo, Leah. 2014. "How Adidas Supported Worker Rights in China Factory Strike." *The Guardian Professional* June 12, 2014, https://www.theguardian.com/sustainable-business/sustainable-fashion-blog/adidas-worker-rights-china-factory-strike.

Borrus, Michael, and John Zysman. 1997. "Globalization with Borders: The Rise of Wintelism as the Future of Global Competition." *Industry and innovation* 4(2):141–66.

Börzel, Tanja A., and Thomas Risse. 2010. "Governance without a State: Can It Work?" *Regulation & Governance* 4(2):113–34.

Boström, Magnus. 2006. "Regulatory Credibility and Authority through Inclusiveness: Standardization Organizations in Cases of Eco-Labelling." *Organization* 13(3):345–67.

Boström, Magnus, and Kristina Tamm Hallström. 2010. "NGO Power in Global Social and Environmental Standard-Setting." *Global Environmental Politics* 10(4):36–59.

Botzem, Sebastian, and Leonhard Dobusch. 2012. "Standardization Cycles: A Process Perspective on the Formation and Diffusion of Transnational Standards." *Organization Studies* 33(5–6):737–62.

Boulan-Smit, M. Christine. 2002. "'When the Elephants Fight the Grass Suffers': Decentralisation and the Mining Industry in Indonesia." *Anthropologi Indonesia* 68:57–64.

Bourdieu, Pierre, and Lois Wacquant. 1992. *An Invitation to Reflexive Sociology*. Chicago: University of Chicago Press.

Boyle, Elizabeth Heger, Fortunata Songora, and Gail Foss. 2001. "International Discourse and Local Politics: Anti-Female-Genital-Cutting Laws in Egypt, Tanzania, and the United States." *Social Problems* 48(4):524–44.

Brack, Duncan. 2009. "Combating Illegal Logging: Interaction with WTO Rules." London: Chatham House.

Bradsher, Keith. 2013. "After Bangladesh, Seeking New Sources." *New York Times* May 15, 2013.

Braithwaite, John. 2006. "Responsive Regulation and Developing Economies." *World Development* 34(5):884–98.

Brammer, Stephen, Gregory Jackson, and Dirk Matten. 2012. "Corporate Social Responsibility and Institutional Theory: New Perspectives on Private Governance." *Socio-Economic Review* 10(1):3–28.

Broad, Robin. 1995. "The Political Economy of Natural Resources: Case Studies of the Indonesian and Philippine Forest Sectors." *Journal of Developing Areas* 29(3): 317–40.

Bromley, Patricia, and Walter W. Powell. 2012. "From Smoke and Mirrors to Walking the Talk: Decoupling in the Contemporary World." *The Academy of Management Annals* 6(1):483–530.

Brooks, Ethel C. 2007. *Unraveling the Garment Industry: Transnational Organizing and Women's Work*. Minneapolis: University of Minnesota Press.

Brown, David William. 1999. *Addicted to Rent: Corporate and Spatial Distribution of Forest Resources in Indonesia: Implications for Forest Sustainability and Government Policy*: Jakarta: Indonesia-UK Tropical Forest Management Programme, Provincial Forest Management Programme, http://www.environmentalpaper.eu/indonesia/index. php/component/phocadownload/category/1-report?download=89:addicted-to-rent-corporate-and-spatial-distribution-of-forest-resources-in-indonesia-implications-for-forest-sustainability-and-government-policy&start=80, accessed August 7, 2014.

Brown, Drusilla, Rajeev Dehejia, and Raymond Robertson. 2013. "Regulations, Monitoring, and Working Conditions: Evidence from Better Factories Cambodia and Better Work Vietnam." http://users.nber.org/~rdehejia/papers/Brown_Dehejia_Robertson_RDW.pdf.

Brown, Garrett. 2005. "Maquiladora Health & Safety Support Network Newsletter." Berkeley, CA: Vol. IX, Number 2, October 30, 2005.

Brown, Garrett. 2008. "Genuine Worker Participation – an Indispensable Key to Effective Global Ohs." Paper presented to the AIHA Academy of Industrial Hygiene professional conference, Tampa, FL. http://mhssn.igc.org/PCIH08_GBrown.pdf.

Brown, Garrett D. 2003. "China's Factory Floors: An Industrial Hygienist's View." *International Journal of Occupational and Environmental Health* 9(4):326–39.

Brundtland Commission. 1987. "Report of the World Commission on Environment and Development: Our Common Future."

Brunsson, Nils, and Bengt Jacobsson (Eds.). 2000. *A World of Standards*. Oxford: Oxford University Press.

Buckingham, Kathleen, and Paul Jepson. 2013. "Forest Certification with Chinese Characteristics: State Engagement with Non-State Market-Driven Governance." *Eurasian Geography and Economics* 54(3):280–99.

Buckingham, Kathleen, and Paul Jepson. 2015. "The Legitimacy of Bamboo Certification: Unpacking the Controversy and the Implications for a 'Treelike' Grass." *Society & Natural Resources* 28(6):575–92.

Buhmann, Karin, and Iben Nathan. 2012. "Plentiful Forest, Happy People?: The EU's FLEGT Approach and Its Impact on Human Rights and Private Forestry Sustainability Schemes." *Nordisk Miljörättslig Tidsskrift/Nordic Environmental Law Journal* 2:53–82.

Building and Wood Worker's International. 2016. "Rulita Wijayaningdyah Elected Chair of FSC Board." March 14, 2016. https://www.bwint.org/cms/sectors-in-action-55/wood-and-forestry-59/news-60/rulita-wijayaningdyah-elected-chair-of-fsc-board-140.

Bunker, Stephen G. 1990. *Underdeveloping the Amazon: Extraction, Unequal Exchange, and the Failure of the Modern State.* Chicago: University of Chicago Press.

Burawoy, Michael. 1998. "The Extended Case Method." *Sociological Theory* 16(1): 4–33.

Bureau Veritas Certification. 2012. "Initial Audit Report, Forest Management Certification: Guangxi Stora Enso Forestry Co., Ltd." Paris: Bureau Veritas.

Bush, Simon R., Ben Belton, Derek Hall, Peter Vandergeest, Francis J. Murray, Stefano Ponte, Peter Oosterveer, Mohammad S. Islam, Arthur P.J. Mol, and Maki Hatanaka. 2013. "Certify Sustainable Aquaculture?" *Science* 341(6150):1067–8.

Business Social Compliance Initiative. 2013. "Statement on the Rana Plaza Building Collapse." https://web.archive.org/web/20130818041113/https://bsci-intl.org/news-events/statement-rana-plaza-building-collapse-bangladesh, accessed June 14, 2014.

Business Week. 2006. "Secrets, Lies, and Sweatshops." *Business Week* November 27, 2006.

Büthe, Tim. 2010. "Private Regulation in the Global Economy: A (P)Review." *Business and Politics* 12(3).

Büthe, Tim, and Walter Mattli. 2011. *The New Global Rulers: The Privatization of Regulation in the World Economy.* Princeton: Princeton University Press.

Butler, Rhett A. 2013. "In Landmark Ruling, Indonesia's Indigenous People Win Right to Millions of Hectares of Forest." Mongabay, May 17, 2013, http://news.mongabay.com/2013/0517-indonesia-customary-forest.html, accessed August 7, 2014.

Buttel, Frederick H. 2000. "World Society, the Nation-State, and Environmental Protection: Comment on Frank, Hironaka, and Schofer." *American Sociological Review* 65 (1):117–21.

Cafaggi, Fabrizio. 2012. "Introduction: The Transformation of Transnational Private Regulation: Enforcement Gaps and Governance Design." Pp. 1–38 in *Enforcement of Transnational Regulation: Ensuring Compliance in a Global World*, edited by Fabrizio Cafaggi. Cheltenham, UK: Edward Elgar.

Cafaggi, Fabrizio, and Agnieszka Janczuk. 2010. "Private Regulation and Legal Integration: The European Example." *Business and Politics* 12(3).

CAFOD. 2004. "Clean up Your Computer: Working Conditions in the Electronics Sector." London: Catholic Agency for Overseas Development (CAFOD).

Cai, Yongshun. 2008. "Local Governments and the Suppression of Popular Resistance in China." *China Quarterly* 193:24–42.

Campaign for Labor Rights. 1997. "Newsletter #9." Washington, DC: Campaign for Labor Rights.

Campbell, John L. 2007. "Why Would Corporations Behave in Socially Responsible Ways? An Institutional Theory of Corporate Social Responsibility." *Academy of Management Review*: 32 (3):946–67.

Caplan, Jeremy. 2005. "Paper War: Environmentalists Take on Victoria's Secret for Mailing More Than 1 Million Catalogs a Day." *Time* December 19.

Caraway, Teri L. 2004. "Protective Repression, International Pressure, and Institutional Design: Explaining Labor Reform in Indonesia." *Studies in Comparative International Development* 39(3):28–49.

Caraway, Teri L. 2006. "Freedom of Association: Battering Ram or Trojan Horse?" *Review of International Political Economy* 13(2):210–32.

Caraway, Teri L. 2008. "Explaining the Dominance of Legacy Unions in New Democracies: Comparative Insights from Indonesia." *Comparative Political Studies* 41(10):1371–97.

Caraway, Teri L. 2009. "Labor Rights in East Asia: Progress or Regress." *Journal of East Asian Studies* 9:153–86.

Caraway, Teri L. 2010. "Core Labor Rights in Indonesia: A Survey of Violations in the Formal Sector." Jakarta: American Center for International Labor Solidarity.

Caraway, Teri L. 2011. "Final Report: Labor Courts in Indonesia." American Center for International Labor Solidarity.

Caraway, Teri L. 2015. "Strength Amid Weakness: Legacies of Labor in Post-Suharto Indonesia." Pp. 25–43 in *Working through the Past: Labor and Authoritarian Legacies in Comparative Perspective*, edited by Teri L. Caraway, Maria Lorena Cook, and Stephen Crowley. Ithaca and London: Cornell University Press.

Caraway, Teri L., Maria Lorena Cook, and Stephen Crowley (Eds.). 2015. *Working through the Past: Labor and Authoritarian Legacies in Comparative Perspective*. Ithaca and London: Cornell University Press.

Caraway, Teri L., and Michele Ford. 2014. "Labor and Politics under Oligarchy." Pp. 139–56 in *Beyond Oligarchy: Wealth, Power, and Contemporary Indonesian Politics*, edited by Michele Ford and Thomas B. Pepinsky. Ithaca: Cornell University Press.

Carey, Christine. 2008. "Tuscany Region (Italy) and the SA8000 Standard for Social Accountability." Governmental Use of Voluntary Standards Case Study 10. London: ISEAL Alliance.

Carlson, Kimberly M., Lisa M. Curran, Dessy Ratnasari, Alice M. Pittman, Britaldo S. Soares-Filho, Gregory P. Asner, Simon N. Trigg, David A. Gaveau, Deborah Lawrence, and Hermann O. Rodrigues. 2012. "Committed Carbon Emissions, Deforestation, and Community Land Conversion from Oil Palm Plantation Expansion in West Kalimantan, Indonesia." *Proceedings of the National Academy of Sciences* 109(19):7559–64.

Carlton, Jim. 2000. "Against the Grain: How Home Depot and Activists Joined to Cut Logging Abuse—If a Tree Falls in the Forest, the Small, Powerful FSC Wants to Have Its Say." *Wall Street Journal* September 26:A1.

Carruthers, Bruce G., and Terence C. Halliday. 2006. "Negotiating Globalization: Global Scripts and Intermediation in the Construction of Asian Insolvency Regimes." *Law & Social Inquiry* 31(3):521–84.

Cashore, Benjamin. 2002. "Legitimacy and the Privatization of Environmental Governance: How Non-State Market-Driven (NSMD) Governance Systems Gain Rulemaking Authority." *Governance* 15(4):503–29.

Cashore, Benjamin, Graeme Auld, and Deanna Newsom. 2004. *Governing through Markets: Forest Certification and the Emergence of Non-State Authority*. New Haven: Yale University Press.

Cashore, Benjamin, Elizabeth Egan, Graeme Auld, and Deanna Newsom. 2007. "Revising Theories of Nonstate Market-Driven (NSMD) Governance: Lessons from the Finnish Forest Certification Experience." *Global Environmental Politics* 7(1):1–44.

Cashore, Benjamin, Fred Gale, Errol Meidinger, and Deanna Newsom. 2006. "Forest Certification in Developing and Transitioning Countries." *Environment* 48(9):6–25.

Cashore, Benjamin, and Michael W. Stone. 2012. "Can Legality Verification Rescue Global Forest Governance?" *Forest Policy and Economics* 18:13–22.

Cashore, Benjamin, and Michael W. Stone. 2014. "Does California Need Delaware? Explaining Indonesian, Chinese, and United States Support for Legality Compliance of Internationally Traded Products." *Regulation & Governance* 8(1):49–73.

Casson, Anne, and Krystof Obidzinski. 2002. "From New Order to Regional Autonomy: Shifting Dynamics of 'Illegal' Logging in Kalimantan, Indonesia." *World Development* 30(12):2133–51.

Castells, Manuel. 2016. "Space of Flows, Space of Places: Materials for a Theory of Urbanism in the Information Age." Pp. 229–40 in *The City Reader*, edited by Richard T. LeGates and Frederic Stout. New York: Routledge.

Cattau, Megan E., Miriam E. Marlier, and Ruth DeFries. 2016. "Effectiveness of Roundtable on Sustainable Palm Oil (RSPO) for reducing fires on oil palm concessions in Indonesia from 2012 to 2015." *Environmental Research Letters* 11(10):105007.

Center for International Environmental Law. 2002. "Whose Resources? Whose Common Good? Towards a New Paradigm of Environmental Justice and the National Interest in Indonesia." Washington, DC: Center for International Environmental Law, with Lembaga Studi dan Advokasi Masyarakat (ELSAM) (Institute for Policy Research and Advocacy), Indonesian Center for Environmental Law (ICEL), and International Centre for Research in Agroforestry (ICRAF), http://www.ciel.org/Publications/Whose_Resources_3-27-02.pdf, accessed July 28, 2013.

Cerutti, Paolo Omar, Luca Tacconi, Robert Nasi, and Guillaume Lescuye. 2011. "Legal Vs. Certified Timber: Preliminary Impacts of Forest Certification in Cameroon." *Forest Policy and Economics* 13(3):184–90.

Chan, Anita. 1996. "Boot Camp at the Shoe Factory: Where Taiwanese Bosses Drill Chinese Workers to Make Sneakers for American Joggers." *Washington Post* November 3, 1996.

Chan, Anita. 2001. *China's Workers under Assault: The Exploitation of Labor in a Globalizing Economy*: ME Sharpe.

Chan, Anita. 2009. "Challenges and Possibilities for Democratic Grassroots Union Elections in China: A Case Study of Two Factory-Level Elections and Their Aftermath." *Labor Studies Journal* 34(3):293–317.

Chan, Anita, and Robert J.S. Ross. 2003. "Racing to the Bottom: International Trade without a Social Clause." *Third World Quarterly* 24:1011–28.

Chan, Chris King-Chi, and Elaine Sio-Ieng Hui. 2012. "The Dynamics and Dilemma of Workplace Trade Union Reform in China: The Case of the Honda Workers' Strike." *Journal of Industrial Relations* 54(5):653–68.

Chang, Joseph Y.S., Kinglun Ngok, and Wenjia Zhuang. 2010. "The Survival and Development Space for China's Labor NGOs: Informal Politics and Its Uncertainty." *Asian Survey* 50(6):1082–106.

Chang, Leslie T. 2009. *Factory Girls: From Village to City in a Changing China*. New York: Spiegel & Grau.

Chatham House. 2013. "China–Assessment Findings." Chatham House, http://indica tors.chathamhouse.org/explore-the-data/china, accessed June 10, 2016.

Chatterji, Aaron K., David I. Levine, and Michael W. Toffel. 2009. "How Well Do Social Ratings Actually Measure Corporate Social Responsibility?" *Journal of Economics & Management Strategy* 18(1):125–69.

Cheit, Ross E. 1990. *Setting Safety Standards: Regulation in the Public and Private Sectors*. Berkeley: University of California Press.

Chen, Juan, and John L. Innes. 2013. "The Implications of New Forest Tenure Reforms and Forestry Property Markets for Sustainable Forest Management and Forest Certi- fication in China." *Journal of Environmental Management* 129:206–15.

Chen, Meei-shia, and Anita Chan. 1999. "China's 'Market Economy in Command:' Footwear Workers' Health and Jeopardy." *International Journal of Health Services* 29(4):793–811.

Cheng, Joseph Y.S., Kinglun Ngok, and Wenjia Zhuang. 2010. "The Survival and Development Space for China's Labor NGOs: Informal Politics and Its Uncertainty." *Asian Survey* 50(6):1082–106.

Cheung, Jennifer. 2011. "Will China's Pepsico Workers Halt a Proposed Merger?" *Forbes* November 29, 2011.

Chibber, Vivek. 2002. "Bureaucratic Rationality and the Developmental State." *American Journal of Sociology* 107(4):951–89.

Child, Curtis. 2015. "Bulwarks against Market Pressures: Value Rationality in the For- Profit Pursuit of Social Missions." *Journal of Contemporary Ethnography* 44(4):480–509.

China Capacity Building Project: Occupational Health and Safety. 2002. "Final Report of the Project Coordinating Committee, March 2001–March 2002." http://lohp. org/wp-content/uploads/2013/10/CHINARPT.pdf.

China Daily. 2015. "China to Phase out Commercial Logging of Natural Forests by 2017." *China Daily-Europe* June 10, 2015, http://europe.chinadaily.com.cn/china/ 2015-06/10/content_20962964.htm.

China Forest Certification Council. 2012. "Forest Certification in China—Forest Man- agement." China Forest Certification Council, http://www.cfcs.org.cn/english/ zh/systemfile-view/38.action, accessed June 9, 2016.

China Forest Certification Council. 2013. "Certified Enterprise Basic Information: Muling Forestry Bureau of Heilongjiang Province." CFCC, http://www.cfcs.org.cn/ english/zh/findcompany.action?cid=11467, accessed June 10, 2016.

China Forest Certification Council. 2015. "4th Meeting of the CFCC Stakeholder Forum Held in Beijing." CFCC Information Center, November 2, 2015, http:// www.cfcs.org.cn/english/zh/news-view/115.action, accessed June 9, 2016.

China Labor News Translations. 2008. "Workers Fight to Save Their Union Activists: The Case of Ole Wolff." China Labor News Translations, http://www.clntranslations. org/file_download/67.

China Labor Watch. 2008. "Academic Research Report on Lever Style, Inc." http://www.chinalaborwatch.org/report/23.

China Labor Watch. 2009. "Corrupt Audits Damage Worker Rights: A Case Analysis of Corruption in Bureau Veritas Factory Audits" New York: China Labor Watch.

China Labor Watch. 2010. "A Case Study: Adidas and Yue Yuen." New York: China Labor Watch.

China Labor Watch. 2014. "Statement on Large Strike at the Yue Yuen Shoe Factory." New York: China Labor Watch, http://www.chinalaborwatch.org/news/new-482.html.

China Labor Watch v. Intertek Group PLC. 2011. "Complaint, Supreme Court of the State of New York." http://digitalcommons.ilr.cornell.edu/cgi/viewcontent.cgi?article=2169&context=globaldocs.

China Labour Bulletin. 2012. "China's Social Security System." Hong Kong: China Labour Bulletin, http://www.clb.org.hk/en/view-resource-centre-content/110107.

China Labour Bulletin. 2014. "Defeat Will Only Make Us Stronger: Workers Look Back at the Yue Yuen Shoe Factory Strike." Hong Kong: China Labour Bulletin, http://www.clb.org.hk/en/content/defeat-will-only-make-us-stronger-workers-look-back-yue-yuen-shoe-factory-strike.

Chinese Academy of Forestry. 2007. "Trade Flows and Distribution of Tropical Wood Products in China." Research Institute of Forestry Policy and Information, Chinese Academy of Forestry. International Tropical Timber Organization, Technical Report of ITTO Project PD 171/02 Rev.4 (M).

Chorev, Nitsan. 2012. "Changing Global Norms through Reactive Diffusion the Case of Intellectual Property Protection of AIDS Drugs." *American Sociological Review* 77 (5):831–53.

Chowdhry, Geeta, and Mark Beeman. 2001. "Challenging Child Labor: Transnational Activism and India's Carpet Industry." *The Annals of the American Academy of Political and Social Science* 575(1):158–75.

Chu, Kathy. 2013. "China Manufacturers Survive by Moving to Asian Neighbors." *Wall Street Journal* May 1, 2013.

Chuang, Julia. 2014. "China's Rural Land Politics: Bureaucratic Absorption and the Muting of Rightful Resistance." *China Quarterly* 219:649–69.

Clark, Phoebe, and SENADA. 2007. "Assessment of Social Accountability Standards: Light Manufacturing–Small and Medium-Sized Enterprises." Report prepared by DAI for USAID.

Clean Clothes Campaign. 2005. "Looking for a Quick Fix: How Weak Social Auditing Is Keeping Workers in Sweatshops." Amsterdam: Clean Clothes Campaign.

Clean Clothes Campaign. 2007. "Sportswear workers in the dominican republic need your support." Clean Clothes Campaign, http://digitalcommons.ilr.cornell.edu/globaldocs/114/.

Clean Clothes Campaign. 2010a. "Annual Report 2010." Amsterdam: Clean Clothes Campaign, https://cleanclothes.org/about/annual-reports/annual-report-2010, accessed July 15, 2015.

Clean Clothes Campaign. 2010b. "Indonesian Garment Workers Win Back Their Rights after Lengthy Campaign." https://web.archive.org/web/20120207182722/http://

www.cleanclothes.org/urgent-actions/indonesian-garment-workers-win-back-their-rights-after-lengthy-campaign, accessed August 18, 2017.

Clean Clothes Campaign. 2012. "Stop Wage Theft Campaign." https://cleanclothes.org/news/2012/03/08/stop-wage-theft-campaign, accessed May 22, 2017.

Clifford, Mark L., Hiroko Tashiro, and Anand Natarajan. 2003. "The Race to Save a Rainforest; Can an Experiment in Indonesia Prove the Merits of Sustainable Logging to Big Timber?" *Business Week* November 24, 2003:125–6.

Clifford, Stephanie, and Steven Greenhouse. 2013. "Fast and Flawed Inspections of Factories Abroad." *New York Times* September 1, 2013.

Cockburn, Alexander. 2002. "Dita Sari to Reebok Award: No Thanks." *Albion Monitor* February 6, 2002.

Cody, Edward. 2005. "Chinese Police Bring Villagers to Heel after Latest Uprising." *Washington Post* December 21, 2005.

Coe, Neil M., Peter Dicken, and Martin Hess. 2008. "Global Production Networks: Realizing the Potential." *Journal of Economic Geography* 8(3):271–95.

Cohen, M.L. 2006. "Pou Chen." in *International Directory of Company Histories, Vol. 81*, edited by Jay P. Pederson: Gale.

Colchester, Marcus. 2004a. "Forest Certification in Indonesia," in *Annex 4 to Certification in Complex Socio-Political Settings: Looking Forward to the Next Decade*, edited by Michael Richards. Washington, DC: Forest Trends, http://www.forest-trends.org/documents/files/doc_365.pdf, accessed August 7, 2014.

Colchester, Marcus. 2004b. "Strengthening the Social Component of a Standard for Legality of Wood Origin and Production in Indonesia." Forest People's Programme.

Colchester, Marcus, and Maurizio Farhan Ferrari. 2007. "Making FPIC–Free, Prior and Informed Consent–Work: Challenges and Prospects for Indigenous Peoples." Moreton-in-Marsh, UK: Forest Peoples Programme, http://www.forestpeoples.org/sites/fpp/files/publication/2010/08/fpicsynthesisjun07eng.pdf, accessed July 28, 2013.

Colchester, Marcus, Martua Sirait, and Boedhi Wijardjo. 2003. "The Application of FSC Principles 2 and 3 in Indonesia: Obstacles and Possibilities." Jakarta: WALHI and AMAN.

Collier, Robert. 2000. "Labor Rights and Wrongs: Some U.S. Firms Work to Cut Abuses in Chinese Factories." *San Francisco Chronicle* May 17, 2000.

Collingsworth, Terry, J. William Goold, and Pharis Harvey. 1994. "Time for a Global New Deal." *Foreign Affairs* 48(1):8–13.

Commission of the European Communities. 2008. "Proposal for a Regulation of the European Parliament and of the Council Laying Down the Obligations of Operators Who Place Timber and Timber Products on the Market." http://ec.europa.eu/environment/forests/pdf/proposal_illegal_logging.pdf, accessed December 5, 2016.

Committee for a Workers' International. 2014. "Massive Strike by Footwear Workers in Dongguan." http://chinaworker.info/en/2014/04/17/6769/.

Community Legal Education Centre and Clean Clothes Campaign. 2012. "Ten Years of the Better Factories Cambodia Project: A Critical Evaluation." Amsterdam: Clean Clothes Campaign, https://cleanclothes.org/resources/publications/ccc-clec-betterfactories-29-8.pdf, accessed December 9, 2016.

Compa, Lance. 2008. "Corporate Social Responsibility and Workers' Rights." *Comparative Labor Law & Policy Journal* 30:1–11.

Congressional-Executive Commission on China. 2003. "Roundtable: Freedom of Association for Chinese Workers." House Hearing, 108th Congress. Washington, DC: Government Printing Office. http://www.gpo.gov/fdsys/pkg/CHRG-108hhrg89103/html/CHRG-108hhrg89103.htm.

Connor, Tim, and Kelly Dent. 2006. "Offside! Labour Rights and Sportswear Production in Asia." Oxfam.

Connor, Tim, and Fiona Haines. 2013. "Networked Regulation as a Solution to Human Rights Abuse in Global Supply Chains? The Case of Trade Union Rights Violations by Indonesian Sports Shoe Manufacturers." *Theoretical Criminology* 17(2):197–214.

Connor, Timothy. 2002. "We Are Not Machines." Victoria, Australia, Oxfam Community Aid Abroad, http://www.cleanclothes.org/resources/publications/we-are-not-machines.pdf, accessed June 14, 2012.

Conroy, Michael E. 2007. *Branded!: How the Certification Revolution Is Transforming Global Corporations*. Gabriola Island, BC, Canada: New Society Publishers.

Control Union Certifications. 2011. "Main Evaluation Report 2010: PT. Suka Jaya Makmur." Zwolle, Netherlands: Control Union Certifications.

Corporate Register. 2012. "SA8000 Passes 1.8 Million Mark." http://www.corporateregister.com/news/item/?n=219.

Coslovsky, Salo, and Richard Locke. 2012. "Parallel Paths to Enforcement: Private Compliance, Public Regulation, and Labor Standards in the Brazilian Sugar Sector." *Politics & Society* 41(4):496–525.

Coslovsky, Salo V. 2011. "Relational Regulation in the Brazilian Ministério Publico: The Organizational Basis of Regulatory Responsiveness." *Regulation & Governance* 5(1):70–89.

Cronon, William. 1996. "The Trouble with Wilderness: Or, Getting Back to the Wrong Nature." *Environmental History* 1(1):7–28.

Cui, Ernan, Ran Tao, Travis J. Warner, and Dali L. Yang. 2015. "How Do Land Takings Affect Political Trust in Rural China?" *Political Studies* 63:91–109.

Cutler, A. Claire, Virginia Haufler, and Tony Porter (Eds.). 1999. *Private Authority and International Affairs*: SUNY Press.

Dai, Limin, Yue Wang, Dongkai Su, Li Zhou, Dapao Yu, Bernard J Lewis, and Lin Qi. 2011. "Major Forest Types and the Evolution of Sustainable Forestry in China." *Environmental Management* 48(6):1066–78.

Daly, Herman E., and John B. Cobb. 1994. *For the Common Good*. Boston: Beacon Press.

Dauvergne, Peter. 1997. *Shadows in the Forest: Japan and the Politics of Timber in Southeast Asia*. Cambridge: MIT Press.

Dauvergne, Peter. 1998. "The Political Economy of Indonesia's 1997 Forest Fires." *Australian Journal of International Affairs* 52(1):13–17.

Dauvergne, Peter. 2017. "Is the Power of Brand-Focused Activism Rising? The Case of Tropical Deforestation." *Journal of Environment & Development* 26(2):135–55.

Dauvergne, Peter, and Jane Lister. 2011. *Timber*. Malden, MA: Polity Press.

Dauvergne, Peter, and Jane Lister. 2012. "Big Brand Sustainability: Governance Prospects and Environmental Limits." *Global Environmental Change* 22(1):36–45.

Bibliography

Davis, Gerald F. 2009. *Managed by the Markets: How Finance Re-Shaped America*. Oxford: Oxford University Press.

Davis, Gerald F., Doug McAdam, W. Richard Scott, and Mayer N. Zald (Eds.). 2005. *Social Movements and Organization Theory*. New York: Cambridge University Press.

Dean, Robin, and Tobias Damm-Luhr. 2010. "A Current Review of Chinese Land-Use Law and Policy: A 'Breakthrough' in Rural Reform?" *Pacific Rim Law & Policy Journal* 19(1):121–59.

Deddy, Ketut. 2006. "Community Mapping, Tenurial Rights and Conflict Resolution in Kalimantan." Pp. 89–110 in *State, Communities and Forests in Contemporary Borneo*, edited by Fadzilah Majid Cooke. Canberra: Australian National University Press.

Delmas, Magali A., Dror Etzion, and Nicholas Nairn-Birch. 2013. "Triangulating Environmental Performance: What Do Corporate Social Responsibility Ratings Really Capture?" *The Academy of Management Perspectives* 27(3):255–67.

Deng, Yanhua, and Kevin J. O'Brien. 2013. "Relational Repression in China: Using Social Ties to Demobilize Protesters." *China Quarterly* 215:533–52.

DeSombre, Elizabeth R., and J. Samuel Barkin. 2002. "Turtles and Trade: The WTO's Acceptance of Environmental Trade Restrictions." *Global Environmental Politics* 2(1):12–18.

Dezalay, Yves, and Bryant Garth. 2010a. "Marketing and Selling Transnational 'Judges' and Global 'Experts': Building the Credibility of (Quasi)Judicial Regulation." *Socio-Economic Review* 8:113–30.

Dezalay, Yves, and Bryant G Garth. 2010b. *Asian Legal Revivals: Lawyers in the Shadow of Empire*. Chicago: University of Chicago Press.

Dezalay, Yves, and Bryant G. Garth. 1996. *Dealing in Virtue: International Commercial Arbitration and the Construction of a Transnational Legal Order*. Chicago: University of Chicago Press.

Dicken, Peter, and Markus Hassler. 2000. "Organizing the Indonesian Clothing Industry in the Global Economy: The Role of Business Networks." *Environment and Planning A* 32:263–80.

Dingwerth, Klaus, and Philipp Pattberg. 2009. "World Politics and Organizational Fields: The Case of Transnational Sustainability Governance." *European Journal of International Relations*: 15(4):707–43.

Distelhorst, Greg, Richard Locke, Timea Pal, and Hiram Samel. 2015. "Production Goes Global, Compliance Stays Local: Private Regulation in the Global Electronics Industry." *Regulation & Governance* 9(3):224–42.

Djama, Marcel, Eve Fouilleux, and Isabelle Vagneron. 2011. "Standard-Setting, Certifying and Benchmarking: A Governmentality Approach to Sustainability Standards in the Agro-Food Sector." Pp. 184–209 in *Governing through Standards: Origins, Drivers and Limitations*, edited by Stefano Ponte, Peter Gibbon, and Jakob Vestergaard. New York: Palgrave.

Djelic, Marie-Laure, and Sigrid Quack. 2010. *Transnational Communities: Shaping Global Economic Governance*. Cambridge: Cambridge University Press.

Djelic, Marie-Laure, and Kerstin Sahlin-Andersson. 2006a. "Institutional Dynamics in a Re-Ordering World," in *Transnational Governance: Institutional Dynamics of Regulation*, edited by Marie-Laure Djelic and Kerstin Sahlin-Andersson. New York: Cambridge University Press.

Djelic, Marie-Laure, and Kerstin Sahlin-Andersson. 2006b. "Introduction: A World of Governance: The Rise of Transnational Regulation." Pp. 1–28 in *Transnational Governance: Institutional Dynamics of Regulation*, edited by Marie-Laure Djelic and Kerstin Sahlin-Andersson. New York: Cambridge University Press.

DLH. 2011. "Guide to Certification and Verification." http://www.dlh.com/csr/downloads/publications.aspx.

Domhoff, G. William. 1990. *The Power Elite and the State*. New York: Aldine de Gruyter.

Donnan, Shawn. 2006. "Indonesia Drops Plan for Labour Reform." *Financial Times* September 12, 2006.

Donovan, Richard. 2001. "A Perspective on the Perum Perhutani Certification Suspension." Rainforest Alliance, https://web.archive.org/web/20080229100928/http://www.rainforest-alliance.org/news/2001/perhutani-perspective.html.

Donovan, Richard Z. 2010. "Status of April's FSC Controlled Wood Certificate & Monitoring of High Conservation Value Forests." Memo of April 15, 2010. Rainforest Alliance.

Dove, Michael R. 2011. *The Banana Tree at the Gate: A History of Marginal Peoples and Global Markets in Borneo*. New Haven: Yale University Press.

Dove, Michael R., and Daniel M. Kammen. 2001. "Vernacular Models of Development: An Analysis of Indonesia under the 'New Order'." *World Development* 29 (4):619–39.

Dowell, Glenn, Anand Swaminathan, and Jim Wade. 2002. "Pretty Pictures and Ugly Scenes: Political and Technological Maneuvers in High Definition Television." *Advances in Strategic Management* 19:97–134.

Down to Earth. 2001. "Certification and Indonesia." *Down to Earth Briefing.* http://www.downtoearth-indonesia.org/story/certification-and-indonesia, accessed March 15, 2017.

Down to Earth. 2006. "A Portrait of Indigenous Forest Management in Sungai Utik." *Down to Earth* newsletter 70 (August).

Down to Earth. 2013. "A turning point for Indonesia's indigenous peoples." *Down to Earth* update (June 7, 2013). http://www.downtoearth-indonesia.org/story/turning-point-indonesia-s-indigenous-peoples, accessed June 14, 2017.

Drahozal, Christopher R. 2009. "Private Ordering and International Commercial Arbitration." *Penn State Law Review* 113(4).

Drezner, Daniel W. 2007. *All Politics Is Global: Explaining International Regulatory Regimes*. Princeton, NJ: Princeton University Press.

Du, Yang, and Weiguang Pan. 2009. "Minimum Wage Regulation in China and Its Applications to Migrant Workers in the Urban Labor Market." *China and World Economy* 17(2):79–93.

Dudley, Nigel, Jean-Paul Jeanrenaud, and Francis Sullivan. 1995. *Bad Harvest? The Timber Trade and the Degradation of the World's Forests*. London: Earthscan.

Dupuy, Kendra, James Ron, and Aseem Prakash. 2016. "Hands Off My Regime! Governments' Restrictions on Foreign Aid to Non-Governmental Organizations in Poor and Middle-Income Countries." *World Development* 84:299–311.

Durst, Patrick D., and Thomas Enters. 2001. "Illegal Logging and the Adoption of Reduced Impact Logging." Denspasar, Indonesia: Paper presented at the Forest Law Enforcement and Governance: East Asia Regional Ministerial Conference, September 11–13, 2001, http://siteresources.worldbank.org/INTINDONESIA/FLEG/20171714/Patrick_Durst.pdf

Dyck, I.J., Karl V. Lins, Lukas Roth, and Hannes F. Wagner. 2015. "Do Institutional Investors Drive Corporate Social Responsibility? International Evidence." Rotman School of Management Working Paper No. 2708589, http://ssrn.com/abstract=2708589.

Eba'a Atyi, Richard, Samuel Assembe-Mvondo, Guillaume Lescuyer, and Paolo Cerutti. 2013. "Impacts of International Timber Procurement Policies on Central Africa's Forestry Sector: The Case of Cameroon." *Forest Policy and Economics* 32:40–8.

Eberlein, Burkard, Kenneth W. Abbott, Julia Black, Errol Meidinger, and Stepan Wood. 2014. "Transnational Business Governance Interactions: Conceptualization and Framework for Analysis." *Regulation & Governance* 8(1):1–21.

Ecological Trading Company. 1990. "Letter of July 1990." Personal archives of a member of the Certification Working Group.

The Economist. 2016. "For Peat's Sake: Despite tough talk, Indonesia's government is struggling to stem deforestation." *The Economist* (November 26, 2016), http://www.economist.com/news/asia/21710844-weather-helping-little-despite-tough-talk-indonesias-government-struggling-stem, accessed June 14, 2017.

Economy, Elizabeth C. 2010. *The River Runs Black: The Environmental Challenge to China's Future*. Ithaca and London: Cornell University Press.

Edelman, Lauren B., Christopher Uggen, and Howard Erlanger. 1999. "The Endogeneity of Legal Regulation: Grievance Procedures as Rational Myth." *American Journal of Sociology* 105:406–54.

Edwards, David P., Trond H. Larsen, Teegan D. S. Docherty, Felicity A. Ansell, Wayne W. Hsu, Mia A. Derhé, Keith C. Hamer, and David S. Wilcove. 2011. "Degraded Lands Worth Protecting: The Biological Importance of Southeast Asia's Repeatedly Logged Forests." *Proceedings of the Royal Society B: Biological Sciences* 278(1702):82–90.

Edwards, Richard C. 1979. *Contested Terrain: The Transformation of the Workplace in the Twentieth Century*. New York: Basic Books.

Egels-Zandén, Niklas, and Jeroen Merk. 2014. "Private Regulation and Trade Union Rights: Why Codes of Conduct Have Limited Impact on Trade Union Rights." *Journal of Business Ethics* 123(3):461–73.

Ekawati, Arti. 2009. "New Rule to Add Indonesian Timber Revenues to Government Coffers." *Jakarta Globe* (July 28, 2009).

Elfstrom, Manfred and Sarosh Kuruvilla. 2016. "The Changing Nature of Labor Unrest in China." *Industrial and Labor Relations Review* 67(2):453–80.

Elliott, Chris. 2000. *Forest Certification from a Policy Network Perspective*. Jakarta: Center for International Forestry Research (CIFOR).

Elson, Dominic. 2011. "An Economic Case for Tenure Reform in Indonesia's Forests." Washington, DC: Rights and Resources Initiative.

Environmental Investigation Agency. 2007. "Attention Wal-Mart Shoppers: How Wal-Mart's Sourcing Practices Encourage Illegal Logging and Threaten Endangered

Species." Washington, DC: Environmental Investigation Agency, https://eia-global.org/reports/attention-wal-mart-shoppers-how-wal-marts-sourcing-practices-encourage-ille, accessed June 9, 2016.

Environmental Investigation Agency. 2009. "The U.S. Lacey Act: Frequently Asked Questions About the World's First Ban on Trade in Illegal Wood." EIA, https://eia-global.org/reports/lacey-act-faq.

Environmental Investigation Agency. 2013. "Liquidating the Forests: Hardwood Flooring, Organized Crime, and the World's Last Siberian Tigers." Washington, DC: Environmental Investigation Agency.

Environmental Panorama International. 2009. "Certified Chinese Forest Reaches Million Hectares." Beijing: Environmental Panorama International, http://www.pick-upau.org.br/site_english/environmental_panorama/2009/2009.01.09/certifield_chinese_forest.htm, accessed June 10, 2016.

Esbenshade, Jill. 2004. *Monitoring Sweatshops: Workers, Consumers, and the Global Apparel Industry*. Philadelphia: Temple University Press.

Esbenshade, Jill. 2012. A Review of Private Regulation: Codes and Monitoring in the Apparel Industry. *Sociology Compass* 6(7):541–56.

Espach, Ralph. 2006. "When Is Sustainable Forestry Sustainable? The Forest Stewardship Council in Argentina and Brazil." *Global Environmental Politics* 6:55–84.

Espach, Ralph H. 2009. *Private Environmental Regimes in Developing Countries: Globally Sown, Locally Grown*. New York: Palgrave Macmillan.

Espeland, Wendy Nelson, and Michael Sauder. 2006. "Rankings and Reactivity: How Public Measures Recreate Social Worlds." *American Journal of Sociology* 113:1–40.

Espeland, Wendy Nelson, and Berit Irene Vannebo. 2007. "Accountability, Quantification, and Law." *Annual Review of Law and Social Science* 3:21–43.

European Timber Trade Federation. 2011. "2011 Statistics—EU Totals: Timber Trade Monitoring in Support of Effective, Efficient and Equitable Operation of the EU Timber Regulation (EUTR)." European Timber Trade Federation, http://www.ettf.info/sites/default/files/ettf_2011-statistics_eu-totals.pdf.

European Union. 2010. "Regulation No. 995/2010 of the European Parliament and of the Council of 20 October 2010, Laying Down the Obligations of Operators Who Place Timber and Timber Products on the Market." http://eur-lex.europa.eu/legal-content/EN/TXT/PDF/?uri=CELEX:32010R0995&from=EN, accessed December 5, 2016.

Evans, Alice. 2016. "Thinking and Working Politically in the Global Garment Industry: Strengthening Trade Unions, Tackling Gender Ideologies, and Reforming International Trade." Working paper, University of Cambridge.

Evans, Peter. 1995. *Embedded Autonomy: States and Industrial Transformation*. Princeton: Princeton University Press.

Evans, Peter. 2010. "Is It Labor's Turn to Globalize? Twenty-First Century Opportunities and Strategic Responses." *Global Labour Journal* 1(3):352–79.

Evans, Rhonda, and Tamara Kay. 2008. "How Environmentalists Greened Trade Policy: Strategic Action and the Architecture of Field Overlap." *American Sociological Review* 73:970–91.

Ewick, P., and S.S. Silbey. 1998. *The Common Place of Law: Stories from Everyday Life*: University of Chicago Press.

Eyes on the Forest. 2011. "Natural Forest Clearance by PT Citra Sumber Sejahtera, Affiliated to April, Becomes Evidence of the Group's Broken Promise for Its Commitment to Forest Protection." http://www.eyesontheforest.or.id/attach/ EoF_Inv_Report_PT_CSS_APRIL_Aug2010_March2011.pdf.

Fair Labor Association. 2004. "Year Two Annual Public Report." Washington, DC: Fair Labor Association.

Fair Labor Association. 2012. "2011 Annual Report." Washington, DC: Fair Labor Association.

Fauzi, Noer. 2003. "The New Sundanese Peasants' Union: Peasant Movements, Changes in Land Control, and Agrarian Questions in Garut, West Java": Paper presented at "Crossing Borders" Workshop: New and Resurgent Agrarian Questions in Indonesia and South Africa, Center for Southeast Asia Studies and Center for African Studies University California at Berkeley.

Favotto, Alvise, Kelly Kollman, and Patrick Bernhagen. 2016. "Engaging Firms: The Global Organisational Field for Corporate Social Responsibility and National Varieties of Capitalism." *Policy and Society* 35(1):13–27.

Fewsmith, Joseph. 2008. "Tackling the Land Issue—Carefully." *China Leadership Monitor* 27:1–8.

Fields, Gary S. 2003. "International Labor Standards and Decent Work: Perspectives from the Developing World." Pp. 61–80 in *International Labor Standards: Globalization, Trade, and Public Policy*, edited by R.J. Flanagan and W.B. Gould IV. Stanford: Stanford University Press.

Fine, Janice and Jennifer Gordon. 2010. "Strengthening Labor Standards Enforcement through Partnerships with Workers' Organizations." *Politics & Society* 38(4): 552–85.

Fiorino, Daniel J. 2009. "Green Clubs: A New Tool for Government?" Pp. 209–30 in *Voluntary Programs: A Club Theory Perspective*, edited by Matthew Potoski and Aseem Prakash. Cambridge, MA: MIT Press.

Fitrani, Fitria, Bert Hofman, and Kai Kaiser. 2005. "Unity in Diversity? The Creation of New Local Governments in a Decentralising Indonesia." *Bulletin of Indonesian Economic Studies* 41(1):57–79.

Fitzpatrick, Daniel. 1997. "Disputes and Pluralism in Modern Indonesian Land Law." *Yale Journal of International Law* 22(1):171–212.

Fitzsimons, Gráinne M, Tanya L. Chartrand, and Gavan J. Fitzsimons. 2008. "Automatic Effects of Brand Exposure on Motivated Behavior: How Apple Makes You 'Think Different'." *Journal of Consumer Research* 35(1):21–35.

Fligstein, Neil. 2001. *The Architecture of Markets: An Economic Sociology of Twenty-First Century Capitalist Societies*. Princeton: Princeton University Press.

Fligstein, Neil, and Doug McAdam. 2012. *A Theory of Fields*. Oxford: Oxford University Press.

Food and Agriculture Organization (FAO). 2006. "Global Forest Resources Assessment 2005."

Food and Agriculture Organization (FAO). 2010. "Global Forest Resources Assessment 2010." Rome: Food and Agriculture Organization of the United Nations.

Food and Agriculture Organization (FAO). 2012. "The Russian Federation Forest Sector: Outlook Study to 2030." Rome: Food and Agriculture Organization of the United Nations.

Ford, Michele. 2009. *Workers and Intellectuals: NGOs, Trade Unions and the Indonesian Labour Movement*. Honolulu: University of Hawaii Press.

Ford, Michele, and George M. Sirait. 2016. "The State, Democratic Transition and Employment Relations in Indonesia." *Journal of Industrial Relations* 58(2):229–42.

Forest Stewardship Council. 2000. "List of FSC Members." FSC Doc. 5.2.2, October 30, 2000.

Forest Stewardship Council. 2002. "FSC Principles and Criteria for Forest Stewardship." Bonn, Germany: Forest Stewardship Council, FSC-STD-01-001(Version 4-0) EN, https://ic.fsc.org/preview.fsc-std-01-001-v4-0-fsc-principles-and-criteria-for-forest-stewardship.a-315.pdf.

Forest Stewardship Council. 2010. "Market Potential of FSC Products Coming from Smallholder Forestry Operations in Europe (Exhibit 6)." Bonn: Forest Stewardship Council.

Forest Stewardship Council. 2013a. "ASI Suspends SCS Global Services for FSC Certification Activities in Pr China." Forest Stewardship Council, Newsroom, September 27, 2013, https://ic.fsc.org/en/news/id/524, accessed June 10, 2016.

Forest Stewardship Council. 2013b. "Forest Stewardship Council Disassociates from the Danzer Group." https://ic.fsc.org/en/news/id/386, accessed October 25, 2016.

Forest Stewardship Council. 2013c. "FSC Market Info." Bonn: Forest Stewardship Council, https://ca.fsc.org/preview.market-info-pack-2013.a-723.pdf, accessed June 9, 2016.

Forest Stewardship Council. 2015a. "China Adopts New Forest Certification Regulation: FSC Operations Will Continue." Forest Stewardship Council news release, Friday, July 17, 2015, https://ic.fsc.org/en/news/id/1199, accessed June 9, 2016.

Forest Stewardship Council. 2015b. "Market Info Pack 2015." Bonn: Forest Stewardship Council, https://ic.fsc.org/preview.2015-fsc-market-info-pack.a-5067.pdf, accessed June 9, 2016.

Forest Stewardship Council-China. 2014. "FSC Commitment to Sustainable Forest Management." FSC China, March 20, 2014.

Forests Monitor. 2001. "Sold Down the River: The Need to Control Transnational Forestry Corporations: A European Case Study." Cambridge: Forests Monitor Ltd.

Fortin, Elizabeth. 2013. "Transnational Multi-Stakeholder Sustainability Standards and Biofuels: Understanding Standards Processes." *Journal of Peasant Studies* 40(3):563–87.

Fourcade, Marion, and Kieran Healy. 2007. "Moral Views of Market Society." *Annual Review of Sociology* 33:285–311.

Frank, Dana. 2003. "Where Are the Workers in Consumer-Worker Alliances? Class Dynamics and the History of Consumer-Labor Campaigns." *Politics & Society* 31 (3):363–79.

Frank, David John, Ann Hironaka, and Evan Schofer. 2000. "The Nation-State and the Natural Environment over the Twentieth Century." *American Sociological Review* 65:96–116.

Frank, T.A. 2008. "Confessions of a Sweatshop Inspector." *Washington Monthly* April.

Fransen, Luc. 2011. "Why Do Private Governance Organizations Not Converge? A Political–Institutional Analysis of Transnational Labor Standards Regulation." *Governance* 24(2):359–87.

Fransen, Luc. 2012. "Multi-Stakeholder Governance and Voluntary Programme Interactions: Legitimation Politics in the Institutional Design of Corporate Social Responsibility." *Socio-Economic Review* 10(1):163–92.

Fransen, Luc, and Brian Burgoon. 2011. "A Market for Worker Rights: Explaining Business Support for International Private Labour Regulation." *Review of International Political Economy* 19(2):236–66.

Fransen, Luc, and Brian Burgoon. 2015. "Global Labour-Standards Advocacy by European Civil Society Organizations: Trends and Developments." *British Journal of Industrial Relations* 53(2):204–30.

Fransen, Luc, and Thomas Conzelmann. 2015. "Fragmented or Cohesive Transnational Private Regulation of Sustainability Standards? A Comparative Study." *Regulation and Governance* 9(3):259–75.

Fransen, Luc, Jelmer Schalk, and Graeme Auld. 2016. "Work Ties Beget Community? Assessing Interactions among Transnational Private Governance Organizations in Sustainable Agriculture." *Global Networks* 16(1):45–67.

Freeman, Richard B. 2005. "What Do Unions Do?—the 2004 M-Brane Stringtwister Edition." *Journal of Labor Research* 26(4):641–68.

Frenkel, Stephen J., and Duncan Scott. 2002. "Compliance, Collaboration, and Codes of Labor Practice: The Adidas Connection." *California Management Review* 45(1):29–49.

Friedman, Eli. 2013. "Insurgency and Institutionalization: The Polanyian Countermovement and Chinese Labor Politics." *Theory and Society* 42(3):295–327.

Frost, Stephen, and Margaret Burnett. 2007. "Case Study: The Apple Ipod in China." *Corporate Social Responsibility and Environmental Management* 14(2):103–13.

FSC Watch. 2014. "FSC's Re-Association with Danzer: Surely Some Mistake?" https://fsc-watch.com/2014/10/07/fscs-re-association-with-danzer-surely-some-mistake/, accessed October 25, 2016.

Fuchs, Doris, and Agni Kalfagianni. 2010. "The Causes and Consequences of Private Food Governance." *Business and Politics* 12(3).

Fung, Archon, Dara O'Rourke, Charles Sabel, Joshua Cohen, and Rogers. 2001. *Can We Put an End to Sweatshops?* Boston, MA: Beacon Press.

Gale, Fred. 2006. "The Political Economy of Sustainable Development in the Asia-Pacific: Lessons from the Forest Stewardship Council Experience." Paper presented to the Second Oceanic Conference on International Studies.

Gale, Fred P. 1998. *The Tropical Timber Trade Regime.* New York: St. Martin's Press.

Gallagher, Mary E. 2004. "'Time Is Money, Efficiency Is Life': The Transformation of Labor Relations in China." *Studies in Comparative International Development* 39(2):11–44.

Gallagher, Mary E. 2005. *Contagious Capitalism: Globalization and the Politics of Labor in China.* Princeton: Princeton University Press.

Gallagher, Mary E., and Baohua Dong. 2011. "Legislating Harmony: Labor Law Reform in Contemporary China." Pp. 33–60 in *From Iron Rice Bowl to Informalization: Markets, Workers, and the State in a Changing China*, edited by Sarosh Kuruvilla, Ching Kwan Lee, and Mary E. Gallagher. Ithaca, NY: ILR Press/Cornell University Press.

Gallagher, Mary E., John Giles, Albert Park, and Meiyan Wang. 2015. "China's 2008 Labor Contract Law: Implementation and Implications for China's Workers." Human Relations 68(2):197–235.

Gareau, Brian J. 2010. "Ecological Imperialism." Pp.125–7 in *Green Politics: An A-to-Z Guide*, edited by Dustin Mulvane and Paul Robbins. Thousand Oaks, CA: Sage.

Gaventa, John. 1982. *Power and Powerlessness: Quiescence and Rebellion in an Appalachian Valley*. Urbana-Champagne: University of Illinois Press.

Gellert, Paul. 2005. "The Shifting Natures of 'Development': Growth, Crisis, and Recovery in Indonesia's Forests." *World Development* 33(8):1345–64.

Gellert, Paul K., and Andiko. 2015. "The Quest for Legal Certainty and the Reorganization of Power: Struggles over Forest Law, Permits, and Rights in Indonesia." *Journal of Asian Studies* 74(3):639–66.

Gereffi, Gary. 1999. "International Trade and Industrial Upgrading in the Apparel Commodity Chain." *Journal of International Economics* 48:37–70.

Gereffi, Gary, John Humphrey, and Timothy Sturgeon. 2005. "The Governance of Global Value Chains." *Review of International Political Economy* 12(1):78–104.

Gereffi, Gary, and Miguel Korzeniewicz (Eds.). 1994. *Commodity Chains and Global Capitalism*. Westport, CT: Praeger.

Gibbon, P., J. Bair, and S. Ponte. 2008. "Governing Global Value Chains: An Introduction." *Economy and Society* 37(3):315–38.

Gille, Zsuzsa. 2016. *Paprika, Foie Gras, and Red Mud: The Politics of Materiality in the European Union*. Bloomington: Indiana University Press.

Ginting, Longgena, and Simon Counsell. 2001. "Complaint Concerning Certification of PT Diamond Raya." Letter to SGS, available at https://web.archive.org/web/20101130224153/ http://www.rainforestfoundationuk.org/files/PTDR_complaint_2001.pdf.

Global Alliance for Workers and Communities. 2001. "Workers' Voices: An Interim Report on Workers' Needs and Aspirations in Indonesia." Global Alliance for Workers and Communities, in partnership with Atma Jaya Catholic University and Nike Inc., http://web1.calbaptist.edu/dskubik/nike_rpt.pdf.

Global Witness. 2007. "Cambodia's Family Trees: Illegal Logging and the Stripping of Public Assets": https://www.globalwitness.org/en/reports/cambodias-family-trees/.

Global Witness. 2009. "A Disharmonious Trade: China and the Continued Destruction of Burma's Northern Frontier Forests." London: Global Witness.

Global Witness. 2010. "Bankrolling Brutality: Why European Timber Company DLH Should Be Held to Account for Profiting from Liberian Conflict Timber." London: Global Witness Limited.

Global Wood. 2014. "China Wood Products Prices." Global Wood, http://www.globalwood.org/market/timber_prices_2013/aaw20140101d.htm, accessed June 10, 2016.

Goldman, Michael. 2005. *Imperial Nature: The World Bank and Struggles for Social Justice in the Age of Globalization*. New Haven: Yale University Press.

Goodland, Robert, and Herman Daly. 1996. "If Tropical Log Export Bans Are So Perverse, Why Are There So Many?" *Ecological Economics* 18(3):189–96.

Goodman, Peter S., and Peter Finn. 2007. "Corruption Stains Timber Trade: Forests Destroyed in China's Race to Feed Global Wood-Processing Industry." *Washington Post* April 1, 2007.

Graz, Jean-Christophe, and Andreas Nölke. 2007. *Transnational Private Governance and Its Limits*: Routledge.

Green, Duncan. 2015. "The Indonesian Labor Rights Project." Oxfam Active Citizenship Case Studies, Oxfam International.

Green, Jessica F. 2013. *Rethinking Private Authority: Agents and Entrepreneurs in Global Environmental Governance*. Princeton, NJ: Princeton University Press.

Greenhill, Brian, Layna Mosley, and Aseem Prakash. 2009. "Trade-Based Diffusion of Labor Rights: A Panel Study." *American Political Science Review* 103(4):169–90.

Greenpeace. 2003. "Partners in Crime: A Greenpeace Investigation of the Links between the UK and Indonesia's Timber Barons." London: Greenpeace.

Greenpeace. 2007. "Merbau's Last Stand: How Industrial Logging Is Driving the Destruction of the Paradise Forests of Asia Pacific." Greenpeace, http://www.greenpeace.org/seasia/ph/Global/seasia/report/2007/4/merbau-s-last-stand-how-indus.pdf, accessed June 9, 2016.

Greenpeace. 2014a. "FSC at Risk: FSC in Russia—Certifying the Destruction of Intact Landscapes." Amsterdam: Greenpeace International, http://www.greenpeace.org/international/Global/international/publications/forests/2014/FSC-Case-Studies/454-6-FSC-in-Russia.pdf, accessed October 27, 2016.

Greenpeace. 2014b. "Weaker Certification Schemes: Other Forest Industry Driven Certification Schemes Fail to Meet Basic Performance Indicators." Greenpeace, March 3, 2014, http://www.greenpeace.org/international/en/campaigns/forests/solutions/alternatives-to-forest-destruc/Weaker-Certification-Schemes/, accessed June 10, 2016.

Grigg, Angus, and Lisa Murray. 2013. "Qantas Named as Forced Labour in Chinese Prisons Exposed." *Australian Financial Review* (June 26, 2013).

Gulbrandsen, Lars H. 2005. "Explaining Different Approaches to Voluntary Standards: A Study of Forest Certification Choices in Norway and Sweden." *Journal of Environmental Policy and Planning* 7(1):43–59.

Gulbrandsen, Lars H. 2006. "Creating Markets for Eco-Labelling: Are Consumers Insignificant?" *International Journal of Consumer Studies* 30(5):477–89.

Gulbrandsen, Lars H. 2010. *Transnational Environmental Governance: The Emergence and Effects of the Certification of Forests and Fisheries*. Northampton, MA: Edward Elgar.

Gullison, R.E. 2003. "Does Forest Certification Conserve Biodiversity?" *Oryx* 37(2):153–65.

Gunningham, Neil, and Peter Grabosky. 1998. *Smart Regulation: Designing Environmental Policy*. Oxford: Clarendon Press.

Gunther, Mark. 2008. "At Ikea, Green Is Gold: The Swedish Furniture Chain Aims to Save Money While Protecting the Planet." *Fortune* November 26: http://archive.fortune.com/2008/11/25/news/companies/gunther_ikea.fortune/index.htm.

Guthman, Julie. 2004. *Agrarian Dreams: The Paradox of Organic Farming in California*. Berkeley: University of California Press.

Guthman, Julie. 2007. "The Polanyian Way? Voluntary Food Labels as Neoliberal Governance." *Antipode* 39(3):456–78.

Hadiz, Vedi R. 1998. "Reformasi Total? Labor after Suharto." *Indonesia* 66:109–25.

Hadiz, Vedi R. 2010. *Localising Power in Post-Authoritarian Indonesia: A Southeast Asia Perspective*. Stanford: Stanford University Press.

Hafner-Burton, Emilie M. 2009. *Forced to Be Good: Why Trade Agreements Boost Human Rights*. Ithaca: Cornell University Press.

Hainmueller, Jens, Michael Hiscox, and Sandra Sequeira. 2015. "Consumer Demand for Fair Trade: Evidence from a Multistore Field Experiment." *Review of Economics and Statistics* 97(2):242–56.

Hall, Derek. 2013. *Land*. Cambridge: Polity Press.

Hall, Rodney Bruce, and Thomas J. Biersteker (Eds.). 2002. *The Emergence of Private Authority in Global Governance*. New York: Cambridge University Press.

Halliday, Terence C., and Bruce G. Carruthers. 2009. *Bankrupt: Global Lawmaking and Systemic Financial Crisis*. Stanford: Stanford University Press.

Harcourt, Bernard E. 2010. "Neoliberal Penality a Brief Genealogy." *Theoretical Criminology* 14(1):74–92.

Hardin, Garrett. 1968. "The Tragedy of the Commons." *Science* 162:1243–8.

Harney, Alexandra. 2008. *The China Price: The True Cost of Chinese Competitive Advantage*. New York: Penguin.

Harney, Alexandra, and John Ruwitch. 2014. "In China, Managers Are the New Labor Activists." *Reuters* June 1, 2014, http://www.reuters.com/article/2014/06/01/china-labor-strikes-idUSL3N0O929U20140601.

Harrison, Ann, and Jason Scorse. 2010. "Multinationals and Anti-Sweatshop Activism." *American Economic Review* 100(1):247–73.

Hatanaka, Maki, Carmen Bain, and Lawrence Busch. 2005. "Third-party certification in the global agrifood system." *Food Policy* 30(3):354–69.

Havinga, Tetty. 2006. "Private Regulation of Food Safety by Supermarkets." *Law & Policy* 28(4):515–33.

Hawkins, Keith. 1984. *Environment and Enforcement: Regulation and the Social Definition of Pollution*. Oxford: Clarendon Press.

He, Baogang, and Mark E. Warren. 2011. "Authoritarian Deliberation: The Deliberative Turn in Chinese Political Development." *Perspectives on Politics* 9(02):269–89.

Heilmayr, Robert, and Eric F. Lambin. 2016. "Impacts of Nonstate, Market-Driven Governance on Chilean Forests." *Proceedings of the National Academy of Sciences* 113(11):2910–15.

Henderson, Jeffrey, Peter Dicken, Martin Hess, Neil Coe, and Henry Wai-Chung Yeung. 2002. "Global Production Networks and the Analysis of Economic Development." *Review of International Political Economy* 9(3):436–64.

Herbert, Bob. 1997. "Brutality in Vietnam." *New York Times* March 28, 1997.

Hilson, Gavin, and Natalia Yakovleva. 2007. "Strained Relations: A Critical Analysis of the Mining Conflict in Prestea, Ghana." *Political Geography* 26(1):98–119.

Hinrichs, Alexander, and Agung Prasetyo. 2007. "Forest Certification Credibility Assessment in Indonesia." http://assets.panda.org/downloads/certification_assessement_in_indonesia.pdf.

Hirakuri, Sofia R. 2003. *Can Law Save the Forest?: Lessons from Finland and Brazil*. Bogor, Indonesia: Center for International Forestry Research.

Hironaka, Ann. 2014. *Greening the Globe: World Society and Environmental Change*. New York: Cambridge University Press.

Hiscox, Michael J., and Nicholas F. B. Smyth. 2007. "Is There Consumer Demand for Improved Labor Standards? Evidence from Field Experiments in Social Labeling." Working paper, Dept. of Government, Harvard University.

Ho, Peter. 2001. "Who Owns China's Land? Policies, Property Rights and Deliberate Institutional Ambiguity." *China Quarterly* 166:394–421.

Ho, Peter. 2006. "Credibility of Institutions: Forestry, Social Conflict, and Titling in China." *Land Use Policy* 23(4):588–603.

Ho, Virginia E Harper. 2009. "From Contracts to Compliance: An Early Look at Implementation under China's New Labor Legislation." *Columbia Journal of Asian Law* 23(1):33–107.

Hobsbawm, Eric J. 1952. "The Machine Breakers." *Past & Present* 1:57–70.

Hoffman, Andrew J. 1997. *From Heresy to Dogma: An Institutional History of Corporate Environmentalism*. San Francisco: The New Lexington Press.

Hoffman, Andy, and Mark MacKinnon. 2011. "The Roots of the Sino-Forest Mystery." *Globe and Mail* September 3, 2011. http://www.theglobeandmail.com/globe-investor/the-roots-of-the-sino-forest-mystery/article594111/?page=all, accessed June 9, 2016.

Holzer, Boris. 2007. "Framing the Corporation: Royal Dutch/Shell and Human Rights Woes in Nigeria." *Journal of Consumer Policy* 30:281–301.

Hopkins, Terence K., and Immanuel Wallerstein. 1986. "Commodity Chains in the World-Economy Prior to 1800." *Review (Braudel Center)* 10(1):157–70.

Horner, Rory. 2015. "Responding to the Rising Power 'Threat:' Pharmaceutical Mnes and the Intellectual Property 'Institutional Void'." *Critical Perspectives on International Business* 11(3/4):285–300.

Howse, R., and D. Regan. 2000. "The Product/Process Distinction—an Illusory Basis for Disciplining 'Unilateralism' in Trade Policy." *European Journal of International Law* 11(2):249–89.

Huang, Yan. 2008. "Labor Solidarity in Contract Manufacturing: The Staff Committee Experiment in Xinda Company as an Example." *Chinese Journal of Sociology* 28(4):20–33.

Huang, Yan, and Weiqing Guo. 2006. "The Transnational Network and Labor Rights in China." *China Rights Forum* 3:57–62.

Hughes, Caroline. 2007. "Transnational Networks, International Organizations and Political Participation in Cambodia: Human Rights, Labour Rights and Common Rights." *Democratization* 14(5):834–52.

Huising, Ruthanne, and Susan S. Silbey. 2011. "Governing the Gap: Forging Safe Science through Relational Regulation." *Regulation & Governance* 5(1):14–42.

Hukum. 2010. "Pengusaha Kabur, Ratusan Buruh Tuntut Hak Ke Phi." *Hukum* January 16, 2010, http://www.hukumonline.com/berita/baca/lt4b5167d767c46/pengusaha-kabur-ratusan-buruh-tuntut-hak-ke-phi, accessed July 25, 2015.

Human Rights Watch. 2006. "Too High a Price: The Human Rights Cost of the Indonesian Military's Economic Activities." New York: Human Rights Watch.

Human Rights Watch. 2009. "'Wild Money:' The Human Rights Consequences of Illegal Logging and Corruption in Indonesia's Forestry Sector." New York: Human Rights Watch.

Human Rights Watch. 2010. "Unkept Promise: Failure to End Military Business Activity in Indonesia." New York: Human Rights Watch.

Human Rights Watch. 2013. "The Dark Side of Green Growth: Human Rights Impacts of Weak Governance in Indonesia's Forestry Sector." New York: Human Rights Watch.

Hung, Ho-fung (Ed.). 2009. *China and the Transformation of Global Capitalism*. Baltimore: Johns Hopkins University Press.

Hurst, William. 2014. "Nascent Protections in Emerging Giants: Struggles to Judicialize Labor Rights in China and Indonesia." Pp. 270–87 in *Law and Development of Middle-Income Countries: Avoiding the Middle-Income Trap*, edited by Randall Peerenboom and Tom Ginsburg. New York: Cambridge University Press.

ICFTU. 2006. "Indonesia: Annual Survey of Violations of Trade Union Rights."

Impactt Ltd. 2005. "Changing over Time: Tackling Supply Chain Labour Issues through Business Practice." London: Impactt Ltd.

Independent Forestry Monitoring Network (JPIK). 2016. "Enforcement of FLEGT License Must Become a Landmark for Sustainability in Improving Forest Governance." http://jpik.or.id/info/wp-content/uploads/2016/09/JPIK-Statement_FLEGT-Licence_EN.pdf, accessed November 22, 2016.

Indonesia Today. 2010. "President's Sister-in-Law Dragged into Sumalindo Illegal Logging Case." *Indonesia Today*, October 18, 2010.

Indonesia Today. 2011. "Amir Sunarko Released from Corruption Charges." *Indonesia Today*, April 18, 2011.

Indotextiles. 2009. "PT Fit-U Dismissed 1.400 Workers." Accessed via indotextiles.com on September 13, 2010.

Institute for Marketecology. 2009. "Public Evaluation Report: Kaihua Forest Farm." Weinfelden, Switzerland: Institute for Marketecology.

Institute for Marketecology. 2010. "Public Evaluation Report: Joinhands (Huazhou) Enterprises Co., Ltd." Weinfelden, Switzerland: Institute for Marketecology.

International Labour Organization. 2010. "Labour Conditions in Forestry in Indonesia." Jakarta: ILO. http://www.ilo.org/wcmsp5/groups/public/@asia/@ro-bangkok/@ilo-jakarta/documents/publication/wcms_126142.pdf, accessed October 24, 2016.

International Labour Organization. 2013. "Labour and Social Trends in Indonesiar." Jakarta: ILO.

International Labour Organization. 2014. "General Survey of the Reports on the Minimum Wage Fixing Convention, 1970 (No. 131), and the Minimum Wage Fixing Recommendation, 1970 (No. 135)." Geneva: ILO.

International Labour Organization. 2014. "Wages in Asia and the Pacific: Dynamic but Uneven Progress." Bangkok: ILO.

International Labour Organization. 2015. "World Employment Social Outlook: The Changing Nature of Jobs." Geneva: ILO.

Ivarsson, Inge, and Claes Göran Alvstam. 2010. "Supplier Upgrading in the Home-Furnishing Value Chain: An Empirical Study of Ikea's Sourcing in China and South East Asia." *World Development* 38(11):1575–87.

Jacobs, Andrew. 2011. "Village Revolts over Inequities of Chinese Life." *New York Times* December 14, 2011.

Jacobs, B.A. 1992. "China Continues to Be Risky Business: The Debate over the Future of China's Most-Favored-Nation (MFN) Status Drags On. But U.S. Companies Doing Business with China Can Do Much to Protect Themselves During This Troubled Period." Pp. 84–5 in *Bobbin*, February 1992.

Jacoby, Stanford M. 1997. *Modern Manors: Welfare Capitalism since the New Deal*. Princeton, NJ: Princeton University Press.

Jaffee, Daniel. 2007. *Brewing Justice: Fair Trade Coffee, Sustainability, and Survival*. Berkeley: University of California Press.

Jaffee, Daniel. 2012. "Weak Coffee: Certification and Co-Optation in the Fair Trade Movement." *Social Problems* 59(1):94–116.

Jakarta Globe. 2013. "May Day Protests Shut Down Central Jakarta." *Jakarta Globe* (May 1, 2013, http://jakartaglobe.beritasatu.com/news/may-day-protests-shut-down-central-jakarta/).

Jakarta Post. 2001. "Union Vows to Take Adidas' Case to ILO." *Jakarta Post* May 11, 2001.

Jarvie, James, Ramzy Kanaan, Michael Malley, Trifin Roule, and Jamie Thomson. 2007. "Conflict Timber: Dimensions of the Problem in Asia and Africa, Vol. Ii." Burlington, VT: ARD, Inc., Final Report Submitted to the United States Agency for International Development.

Jauhiainen, Jyrki, Suwido Limin, Hanna Silvennoinen, and Harri Vasander. 2008. "Carbon Dioxide and Methane Fluxes in Drained Tropical Peat before and after Hydrological Restoration." *Ecology* 89(12):3503–14.

Jenkins, Michael B., and Emily T. Smith. 1999. *The Business of Sustainable Forestry*. Washington, DC: Island Press.

Jepson, Paul, James K. Jarvie, Kathy MacKinnon, and Kathryn A. Monk. 2001. "The End for Indonesia's Lowland Forests?" *Science* 292(5518):859–61.

Jessop, B. 1997. "Capitalism and Its Future: Remarks on Regulation, Government and Governance." *Review of International Political Economy* 4(3):561–81.

Jiang, Steven. 2013. "Chinese Labor Camp Inmate Tells of True Horror of Halloween 'Sos'." *CNN* (November 7, 2013, http://www.cnn.com/2013/11/06/world/asia/china-labor-camp-halloween-sos/).

Jin, Zhang. 2004. "SA8000 Requires Positive Attitude." *China Daily* (July 6, 2004):11.

Johnson, Nels, and Bruce Cabarle. 1993. *Surviving the Cut: Natural Forest Management in the Humid Tropics*. Washington, DC: World Resources Institute.

Johnson, Thomas R. 2016. "Regulatory Dynamism of Environmental Mobilization in Urban China." *Regulation & Governance* 10(1):14–28.

Juliawan, Benny Hari. 2011. "Street-Level Politics: Labour Protests in Post-Authoritarian Indonesia." *Journal of Contemporary Asia* 41(3):349–70.

Jurgens, Emile. 2006. "Learning Lessons to Promote Certification and Combat Illegal Logging in Indonesia." Bogor, Indonesia: Center for International Forestry Research.

Kaimowitz, David. 2003. "Forest Law Enforcement and Rural Livelihoods." *International Forestry Review* 5(3):199–210.

Kampagne für Saubere Kleidung. 2003. "Beschwerde Bei Social Accountability International Erfolgreich." Wuppertal, Germany: Vereinte Evangelische Mission Wuppertal, http://www.sauberekleidung.de/2011_alte-ccc-d-website/downloads/archiv_ccc-rundbriefe/RB_2003-1-2-CCC.pdf.

Kaplinsky, Raphael, Anne Terheggen, and Julia Tijaja. 2011. "China as a Final Market: The Gabon Timber and Thai Cassava Value Chains." *World Development* 39 (7):1177–90.

Karmann, Marion, and Alan Smith. 2009. "FSC Reflected in Scientific and Professional Literature: Literature Study on the Outcomes and Impacts of FSC Certification." Forest Stewardship Council, FSC Policy Series No. 2009-P001.

Kato, Tsuyoshi. 1989. "Different Fields, Similar Locusts: Adat Communities and the Village Law of 1979 in Indonesia." *Indonesia* (47):89–114.

Katz, Donald R. 1994. *Just Do It: The Nike Spirit in the Corporate World*. New York: Random House.

Kaup, Brent Z. 2015. "Markets, Nature, and Society Embedding Economic & Environmental Sociology." *Sociological Theory* 33(3):280–96.

Kearney, Neil, and Judy Gearhart. 2004. "Workplace Codes as Tools for Workers." *Development in Practice* 14(1–2):216–23.

Keck, Margaret, and Kathryn Sikkink. 1998. *Activists Beyond Borders: Trans-National Advocacy Networks in International Politics*. Ithaca: Cornell University Press.

Kelly, Annie. 2012. "Ikea to Go 'Forest Positive' - but Serious Challenges Lie Ahead." *The Guardian*, http://www.theguardian.com/sustainable-business/ikea-sustainability-forest-positive-karelia, accessed June 8, 2016.

Kempadoo, Kamala, Jyoti Sanghera, and Bandana Pattanaik (Eds.). 2016. *Trafficking and Prostitution Reconsidered: New Perspectives on Migration, Sex Work, and Human Rights*, 2nd edition. Abingdon: Routledge.

Kesko. 2014. "Responsibility in Figures: Human Rights." http://kesko2014.kesko.fi/en/responsibility-in-figures/performance-indicators/social-impacts/human-rights.

Khatchadouria, Raffi. 2008. "The Stolen Forests." *New Yorker* (October 6, 2008):64–73.

Kim, Jee Young. 2013. "The Politics of Code Enforcement and Implementation in Vietnam's Apparel and Footwear Factories." *World Development* 45:286–95.

Kinderman, Daniel. 2012. " 'Free Us up So We Can Be Responsible!' the Co-Evolution of Corporate Social Responsibility and Neo-Liberalism in the UK, 1977–2010." *Socio-Economic Review* 10(1):29–57.

Kinderman, Daniel. 2016. "Time for a Reality Check: Is Business Willing to Support a Smart Mix of Complementary Regulation in Private Governance?" *Policy and Society* 35(1):29–42.

King, Brayden G., and Nicholas A. Pearce. 2010. "The Contentiousness of Markets: Politics, Social Movements, and Institutional Change in Markets." *Annual Review of Sociology* 36(1):249–67.

King, Brayden G., and Sarah A. Soule. 2007. "Social Movements as Extra-Institutional Entrepreneurs: The Effect of Protest on Stock Price Returns." *Administrative Science Quarterly* 52:413–42.

Kipnis, Andrew B. 2008. "Audit Cultures: Neoliberal Governmentality, Socialist Legacy, or Technologies of Governing?" *American Ethnologist* 35(2):275–89.

Kishor, Nalin, and Guillaume Lescuyer. 2012. "Controlling Illegal Logging in Domestic and International Markets by Harnessing Multi-Level Governance Opportunities." *International Journal of the Commons* 6(2):255–70.

Klein, Helmut, Christoph Thies, László Maráz, and Mike Brune. 2004. "Formal Dispute Regarding SGS Certification of PT Diamond Raya." Letter to FSC-International, available at https://web.archive.org/web/20101130224345/ http://www.rainforestfoundationuk.org/files/formal%20complaint.pdf.

Klein, Naomi. 1999. *No Logo: Taking Aim at the Brand Bullies*. New York: Picador.

Klooster, Dan. 2010. "Standardizing Sustainable Development? The Forest Stewardship Council's Plantation Policy Review Process as Neoliberal Environmental Governance." *Geoforum* 41(1):117–29.

Kobrin, Stephen J. 2008. "Globalization, Transnational Corporations, and the Future of Global Governance." Pp. 249–72 in *Handbook of Research on Global Corporate Citizenship*, edited by Andreas Georg Scherer and Guido Palazzo. Northampton, MA: Edward Elgar.

Koh, Lian Pin, and David S. Wilcove. 2007. "Cashing in Palm Oil for Conservation." *Nature* 448(7157):993–4.

Koh, Lian Pin, and David S. Wilcove. 2008. "Is Oil Palm Agriculture Really Destroying Tropical Biodiversity?" *Conservation Letters* 1(2):60–4.

Kolben, Kevin. 2004. "Trade, Monitoring, and the ILO: Working to Improve Conditions in Cambodia's Garment Factories." *Yale Human Rights and Development Law Journal* 7:79.

Kolko, Gabriel. 1963. *The Triumph of Conservatism*. Glencoe, IL: The Free Press.

Kollert, Walter, and Lucia Cherubini. 2012. "Teak Resources and Market Assessment 2010." Rome: Food and Agriculture Organization of the United Nations, Working Paper FP/47/E.

Koskinen, Mika. 2012. "Red Forest Hotel." Finland: Luxian productions.

Kram, Megan, Charles Bedford, Matthew Durnin, Yongmei Luo, Karlis Rokpelnis, Benjamin Roth, Nancy Smith, Yue Wang, Guangzhi Yu, Qian Yu, and Xingmin Zhao. 2012. "Protecting China's Biodiversity: A Guide to Land Use, Land Tenure, and Land Protection Tools." Arlington, VA: The Nature Conservancy.

Kristof, Nicholas D., and Sheryl WuDunn. 2000. "Two Cheers for Sweatshops." *New York Times Magazine* (September 24, 2000).

Kröger, Markus. 2012. "The Expansion of Industrial Tree Plantations and Dispossession in Brazil." *Development and Change* 43(4):947–73.

Krugman, Paul. 1997. "In Praise of Cheap Labor." *Slate* March 20, 1997.

Krupat, Kitty. 1997. "From War Zone to Free Trade Zone: A History of the National Labor Committee." Pp. 51–77 in *No Sweat: Fashion, Free Trade and the Rights of Garment Workers*, edited by Andrew Ross. New York: Verso.

Kysar, Douglas A. 2004. "Preferences for Processes: The Process/Product Distinction and the Regulation of Consumer Choice." *Harvard Law Review* 118(2):525–642.

La Botz, Dan. 2001. *Made in Indonesia: Indonesian Workers since Suharto*. Cambridge, MA: South End Press.

Lai, Catherine. 2016. "Guangdong labour activist Meng Han sentenced to 1 year, 9 months." *Hong Kong Free Press* (November 3, 2016), https://www.hongkongfp.com/2016/11/03/guangdong-labour-activist-meng-han-sentenced-1-year-9-months/, accessed April 3, 2017.

Larson, Anne M., and Jesse C. Ribot. 2007. "The Poverty of Forestry Policy: Double Standards on an Uneven Playing Field." *Sustainability Science* 2(2):189–204.

Larson, Anne M., and Jesse C. Ribot. 2009. "Lessons from Forestry Decentralisation." Pp. 175–87 in *Realising Redd+: National Strategy and Policy Options*, edited by Arild Angelsen. Bogor, Indonesia: Center for International Forestry Research.

Lau, Mimi. 2014. "Guangdong Collective Bargaining Proposal Seen as Bellwether for China." *South China Morning Post* July 6, 2014.

Lawrence, Jessica, Noriko Toyoda, and Helvi Lystiani. 2003. "Importing Destruction: How U.S. Imports of Indonesia's Tropical Hardwoods Are Devastating Indigenous Communities and Ancient Forests." San Francisco: Rainforest Action Network.

Lawson, Sam, and Larry MacFaul. 2010. "Illegal Logging and Related Trade." Chatham House, London.

Lee, Ching Kwan. 1998. *Gender and the South China Miracle: Two Worlds of Factory Women*: Univ of California Press.

Lee, Ching Kwan. 2007a. *Against the Law: Labor Protests in China's Rustbelt and Sunbelt*. Berkeley: University of California Press.

Lee, Ching Kwan, and Yuan Shen. 2011. "The Anti-Solidarity Machine? Labor Nongovernmental Organizations in China." Pp. 173–87 in *From Iron Rice Bowl to Informalization: Markets, Workers, and the State in a Changing China*, edited by Sarosh Kuruvilla, Ching Kwan Lee, and Mary E. Gallagher. Ithaca: ILR Press/Cornell University Press.

Lee, Ching Kwan, and Yonghong Zhang. 2013. "The Power of Instability: Unraveling the Microfoundations of Bargained Authoritarianism in China." *American Journal of Sociology* 118(6):1475–508.

Lee, Peter. 2007b. "Reebok's Chinese Trade Union Experiment: Five Years On." China Labor News Translations, http://www.clntranslations.org/file_download/19.

Leipold, Sina, Metodi Sotirov, Theresa Frei, and Georg Winkel. 2016. "Protecting 'First World' Markets and 'Third World' Nature: The Politics of Illegal Logging in Australia, the European Union and the United States." *Global Environmental Change* 39:294–304.

Leipold, Sina, and Georg Winkel. 2016. "Divide and Conquer—Discursive Agency in the Politics of Illegal Logging in the United States." *Global Environmental Change* 36:35–45.

Leipziger, Deborah. 2001. *SA8000: The Definitive Guide to the New Social Standard*. London: Financial Times/Prentice Hall.

Levi-Faur, David, and Jacint Jordana. 2005. "Globalizing Regulatory Capitalism." *The Annals of the American Academy of Political and Social Science* 598:6–9.

Levien, Michael. 2013. "The Politics of Dispossession Theorizing India's 'Land Wars'." *Politics & Society* 41(3):351–94.

Li, Jing. 2010a. "Paper Plant Project Sparks Protests." *China Daily* July 12, 2010.

Li, Ping, and Robin Nielsen. 2010. "A Case Study on Large-Scale Forestland Acquisition in China: The Stora Enso Plantation Project in Hepu County, Guangxi Province." Washington, DC: Rights and Resources Initiative.

Li, Ping, and Xiaobei Wang. 2014. "Forest Land Acquisition by Stora Enso in South China: Status, Issues, and Recommendations." Washington, DC: Rights and Resources Initiative.

Li, Ping, and Keliang Zhu. 2007. "A Legal Review and Analysis of China's Forest Tenure System with an Emphasis on Collective Forestland." Rural Development Institute and Rights and Resources International, http://www.rightsandresources.org/en/publication/a-legal-review-and-analysis-of-chinas-forest-tenure-system-with-an-emphasis-on-collective-forestland-2/#.VumfeeIrLX4, accessed June 9, 2016.

Li, Tania Murray. 2001. "Masyarakat Adat, Difference, and the Limits of Recognition in Indonesia's Forest Zone." *Modern Asian Studies* 35(3):645–76.

Li, Tania Murray. 2010. "Indigeneity, Capitalism, and the Management of Dispossession." *Current Anthropology* 51(3):385–414.

Liddle, R. William, and Saiful Mujani. 2013. "Indonesian Democracy: From Transition to Consolidation." Pp. 24–50 in *Democracy and Islam in Indonesia*, edited by Mirjam Künkler and Alfred Stepan. New York: Columbia University Press.

Lieberthal, Kenneth, and David M. Lampton (Eds.). 1992. *Bureaucracy, Politics, and Decision Making in Post-Mao China*. Berkeley: University of California Press.

Lim, Alwyn, and Kiyoteru Tsutsui. 2012. "Globalization and Commitment in Corporate Social Responsibility." *American Sociological Review* 77(1):69–98.

Lim, Suk-Jun, and Joe Phillips. 2008. "Embedding CSR Values: The Global Footwear Industry's Evolving Governance Structure." *Journal of Business Ethics* 81(1): 143–56.

Lin, Li-Wen. 2010. "Corporate Social Responsibility in China: Window Dressing or Structural Change?" *Berkeley Journal of International Law* 28(1):64–100.

Lindemann, January 2009. "The Financial Value of Brands." Pp. 26–44 in *Brands and Branding*, edited by Rita Clifton. New York: Bloomberg Press.

Liu, Jie. 2009. "Tetra Pak Supports Chinese, Swedish Tree Farms." *China Daily* November 9, 2009.

Liu, Mingwei. 2010. "Union Organizing in China: Still a Monolithic Labor Movement?" *Industrial and Labor Relations Review* 64(1):30–52.

Liu, Mingwei. 2011. "'Where There Are Workers, There Should Be Trade Unions:' Union Organizing in the Era of Growing Informal Employment." Pp. 157–72 in *Iron Rice Bowl to Informalization: Markets, Workers, and the State in a Changing China*, edited by Sarosh Kuruvilla, Ching Kwan Lee, and Mary E. Gallagher. Ithaca, NY: ILR Press/Cornell University Press.

Locke, Richard, Fei Qin, and Alberto Brause. 2007. "Does Monitoring Improve Labor Standards? Lessons from Nike." *Industrial & Labor Relations Review* 61(1):3–31.

Locke, Richard M. 2013. *The Promise and Limits of Private Power: Promoting Labor Standards in a Global Economy*. New York: Cambridge University Press.

Locke, Richard M., Matthew Amengual, and Akshay Mangla. 2009. "Virtue out of Necessity?: Compliance, Commitment and the Improvement of Labor Conditions in Global Supply Chains." *Politics & Society* 37:319–51.

Locke, Richard M., Ben A. Rissing, and Timea Pal. 2013. "Complements or Substitutes? Private Codes, State Regulation and the Enforcement of Labour Standards in Global Supply Chains." *British Journal of Industrial Relations* 51(3):519–52.

Loconto, Allison, and Eve Fouilleux. 2014. "Politics of Private Regulation: Iseal and the Shaping of Transnational Sustainability Governance." *Regulation & Governance* 8(2):166–85.

Long, Yan. 2013. "Constructing Transnational Actorhood: The Emergence and Transformation of the AIDS Movement in China, 1989-2012." Dissertation, University of Michigan Department of Sociology.

Longhofer, Wesley, and Evan Schofer. 2010. "National and Global Origins of Environmental Association." *American Sociological Review* 75(4):505–33.

Lounsbury, Michael, Marc J. Ventresca, and Paul M. Hirsch. 2003. "Social Movements, Field Frames and Industry Emergence: A Cultural-Political Perspective on U.S. Recycling." *Socio-Economic Review* 1(1):71–104.

Loya, Thomas A., and John Boli. 1999. "Standardization in the World Polity: Technical Rationality over Power." Pp. 169–97 in *Constructing World Culture: International Nongovernmental Organizations since 1875*, edited by John Boli and George M. Thomas. Stanford, CA: Stanford University Press.

Lu, Vanessa. 2014. "Sino-Forest Executives Deny Any Fraud at OSC Hearing." *Star (Toronto)* September 2, 2014, https://www.thestar.com/business/2014/09/02/sinoforest_executives_deny_any_fraud_at_osc_hearing.html, accessed June 9, 2016.

Lucas, Anton, and Carol Warren. 2003. "The State, the People, and Their Mediators: The Struggle over Agrarian Law Reform in Post-New Order Indonesia." *Indonesia* (76):87–126.

Lund-Thomsen, Peter, and Adam Lindgreen. 2014. "Corporate Social Responsibility in Global Value Chains: Where Are We Now and Where Are We Going?" *Journal of Business Ethics* 123(1):11–22.

Lyon, Sarah, and Mark Moberg (Eds.). 2010. *Fair Trade and Social Justice: Global Ethnographies*. New York: NYU Press.

Lytton, Timothy. 2014. "Competitive Third-Party Regulation: How Private Certification Can Overcome Constraints That Frustrate Government Regulation." *Theoretical Inquiries in Law* 15(2):539–72.

Lytton, Timothy D. 2013. *Kosher: Private Regulation in the Age of Industrial Food*. Cambridge: Harvard University Press.

Ma, Martin. 2009. "The Story of Ying Xie: Democratic Workers' Representation in China as a Tool for Better Business." Pp. 6–22 in *From Words to Action: A Business Case for Implementing Workplace Standards*. Center for International Private Enterprise and Social Accountability International, http://www.cipe.org/sites/default/files/publication-docs/SAI.pdf.

MacKinnon, Mark. 2011. "The Empire Sino-Forest Built and the Farmers Who Paid the Price." *The Globe and Mail*, October 15, 2011.

Macqueen, D. 2010. "Building Profitable and Sustainable Community Forest Enterprises: Enabling Conditions." Edinburgh: International Institute for Environment and Development.

Malaysian Timber Council. 2011. "Malaysia: Forestry & Environment." Kuala Lumpur: Malaysian Timber Council.

Malets, Olga. 2013. "The Translation of Transnational Voluntary Standards into Practices: Civil Society and the Forest Stewardship Council in Russia." *Journal of Civil Society* 9(3):300–24.

Malets, Olga. 2015. "When Transnational Standards Hit the Ground: Domestic Regulations, Compliance Assessment and Forest Certification in Russia." *Journal of Environmental Policy & Planning* 17(3):332–59.

Manning, Chris, and Kurnya Roesad. 2007. "The Manpower Law of 2003 and Its Implementing Regulations: Genesis, Key Articles and Potential Impact." *Bulletin of Indonesian Economic Studies* 43(1):59–86.

Maquila Solidarity Network. 2003. "Codes Memo Number 15, September 2003." http://en.archive.maquilasolidarity.org/sites/maquilasolidarity.org/files/codesmemo15.pdf, accessed October 9, 2016.

Marquis, Christopher, Jianjun Zhang, and Yanhua Zhou. 2011. "Regulatory Uncertainty and Corporate Responses to Environmental Protection in China." *California Management Review* 54(1):39–63.

Marx, Axel, and Dieter Cuypers. 2010. "Forest Certification as a Global Environmental Governance Tool: What Is the Macro-Effectiveness of the Forest Stewardship Council?" *Regulation & Governance* 4(4):408–34.

Maryudi, Ahmad. 2009. "Forest Certification for Community-Based Forest Management in Indonesia: Does LEI Provide a Credible Option?" Kamiyamaguchi, Japan: Institute for Global Environmental Strategies.

Maryudi, Ahmad. 2012. "Restoring State Control over Forest Resources through Administrative Procedures: Evidence from a Community Forestry Programme in Central Java, Indonesia." *Austrian Journal of South-East Asian Studies* 5(2):229–42.

Matten, Dirk, and Jeremy Moon. 2008. "'Implicit' and 'Explicit' CSR: A Conceptual Framework for a Comparative Understanding of Corporate Social Responsibility." *Academy of Management Review* 33(2):404–24.

Mattli, Walter, and Tim Büthe. 2003. "Setting International Standards: Technological Rationality or Primacy of Power?" *World Politics* 56(1):1–42.

Mayer, Frederick, and Gary Gereffi. 2010. "Regulation and Economic Globalization: Prospects and Limits of Private Governance." *Business and Politics* 12(3).

Mayers, James, and Sonja Vermeulen. 2002. "Company-Community Forestry Partnerships: From Raw Deals to Mutual Gains?" London: International Institute for Environment and Development.

McAdam, Doug, and W. Richard Scott. 2005. "Organizations and Social Movements." Pp. 4–40 in *Social Movements and Organization Theory*, edited by Gerald F. Davis, Doug McAdam, W. Richard Scott, and Mayer N. Zald. New York: Cambridge University Press.

McAllister, Lesley. 2008. *Making Law Matter: Environmental Protection and Legal Institutions in Brazil*: Stanford University Press.

McCann, Michael W. 1994. *Rights at Work: Pay Equity Reform and the Politics of Legal Mobilization*. Chicago: University of Chicago Press.

McCarthy, John F. 2004. "Changing to Gray: Decentralization and the Emergence of Volatile Socio-Legal Configurations in Central Kalimantan, Indonesia." *World Development* 32(7):1199–223.

McCarthy, John F. 2009. "Where Is Justice? Resource Entitlements, Agrarian Transformations and Regional Autonomy in Jambi, Sumatra." Pp. 167–94 in *Community, Environment, and Local Governance in Indonesia*, edited by Carol Warren and John F. McCarthy. London and New York: Routledge.

McCarthy, John F. 2012. "Certifying in Contested Spaces: Private Regulation in Indonesian Forestry and Palm Oil." *Third World Quarterly* 33(10):1871–88.

McCarthy, John F., and R.A. Cramb. 2009. "Policy Narratives, Landholder Engagement, and Oil Palm Expansion on the Malaysian and Indonesian Frontiers." *Geographical Journal* 175(2):112–23.

McCarthy, John F., and Carol Warren. 2009. "Communities, Environments and Local Governance in Reform Era Indonesia." Pp. 1–26 in *Environmental and Local Governance in Indonesia: Locating the Commonweal*, edited by Carol Warren and John F. McCarthy. London and New York: Routledge.

McCarthy, John F., Piers Gillespie, and Zahari Zen. 2012. "Swimming Upstream: Local Indonesian Production Networks in 'Globalized' Palm Oil Production." *World Development* 40(3):555–69.

McDermott, Constance, Benjamin Cashore, and Peter Kanowski. 2010. *Global Environmental Forest Policies: An International Comparison*. London: Earthscan.

McDermott, Constance L. 2012. "Trust, Legitimacy and Power in Forest Certification: A Case Study of the FSC in British Columbia." *Geoforum* 43(3):634–44.

McDermott, Constance L, Lloyd C Irland, and Pablo Pacheco. 2015. "Forest Certification and Legality Initiatives in the Brazilian Amazon: Lessons for Effective and Equitable Forest Governance." *Forest Policy and Economics* 50:134–42.

McDermott, John. 2011. "Sino-Forest: The Case for the Defence." FTAlphaville, June 7, 2011. https://ftalphaville.ft.com/2011/06/07/587181/sino-forest-the-case-for-the-defence/, accessed June 9, 2016.

McGuire, William. 2014. "The Effect of ISO 14001 on Environmental Regulatory Compliance in China." *Ecological Economics* 105:254–64.

McNichol, Jason. 2003. "The Forest Stewardship Council as a New Para-Regulatory Social Form." Pp. 249–64 in *The Social and Political Dimensions of Forest Certification*, edited by Errol Meidinger, Chris Elliott, and Gerhard Oesten. Remagen-Oberwinter, Germany: Forstbuch.

McNichol, Jason. 2006. "Transnational NGO Certification Programs as New Regulatory Forms: Lessons from the Forestry Sector," in *Transnational Governance: Institutional Dynamics of Regulation*, edited by Marie-Laure Djelic and Kerstin Sahlin-Andersson. New York: Cambridge University Press.

Meidinger, Errol E. 2003. "Forest Certification as a Global Civil Society Regulatory Institution." Pp. 265–89 in *The Social and Political Dimensions of Forest Certification*, edited by Errol Meidinger, Chris Elliott, and Gerhard Oesten. Remagen-Oberwinter, Germany: Forstbuch.

Meidinger, Errol E. 2009. "Private Import Safety Regulation and Transnational New Governance." Pp. 233–53 in *Import Safety: Regulatory Governance in the Global Economy*, edited by Cary Coglianese, Adam Finkel, and David Zaring. Philadelphia: University of Pennsylvania Press.

Meng, Xin, and Chris Manning (Eds.). 2010. *The Great Migration: Rural–Urban Migration in China and Indonesia*. Cheltenham: Edward Elgar.

Merk, Jeroen. 2008. "Restructuring and Conflict in the Global Athletic Footwear Industry: Nike, Yue Yue and Labour Codes of Conduct." Pp. 79–97 in *Global Economy Contested: Power and Conflict across the International Division of Labour*, edited by Marcus Taylor. Abingdon: Routledge.

Merry, Sally Engle. 2006. *Human Rights and Gender Violence: Translating International Law into Local Justice*. Chicago: University of Chicago Press.

Mertha, Andrew. 2009. " 'Fragmented Authoritarianism 2.0': Political Pluralization in the Chinese Policy Process." *The China Quarterly* 200:995–1012.

Meyer, John M., John Boli, George M. Thomas, and Francisco O. Ramirez. 1997. "World Society and the Nation State." *American Journal of Sociology* 103:144–81.

Meyer, John W., Shawn M. Pope, and Andrew Isaacson. 2015. "Legitimating the Transnational Corporation in a Stateless World Society." Pp. 27–72 in *Corporate Social Responsibility in a Globalizing World*, edited by Kiyoteru Tsutsui and Alwyn Lim. Cambridge: Cambridge University Press.

Miao, Guangping, and R.A. West. 2004. "Chinese Collective Forestlands: Contributions and Constraints." *International Forestry Review* 6(3–4):282–98.

Michelson, Ethan. 2007. "Climbing the Dispute Pagoda: Grievances and Appeals to the Official Justice System in Rural China." *American Sociological Review* 72(3): 459–85.

Michelson, Ethan. 2012. "Public Goods and State-Society Relations: An Impact Study of China's Rural Stimulus." Pp. 131–57 in *The Global Recession and China's Political Economy*, edited by Dali L. Yang. New York: Palgrave Macmillan.

Mietzner, Marcus. 2014. "Oligarchs, Politicians, and Activists: Contesting Party Politics in Post-Suharto Indonesia." Pp. 99–116 in *Beyond Oligarchy: Wealth, Power, and Contemporary Indonesian Politics*, edited by Michele Ford and Thomas B. Pepinsky. Ithaca: Cornell University Press.

Milkman, Ruth, Ana Luz González, and Victor Narro. 2010. *Wage Theft and Workplace Violations in Los Angeles: The Failure of Employment and Labor Law for Low-wage Workers*. UCLA Institute for Research on Labor and Employment. https://escholar-ship.org/uc/item/5jt7n9gx, accessed May 22, 2017.

Miller, Doug. 2012. *Last Nightshift in Savar: The Story of Spectrum Sweater Factory Collapse*. Carmarthen: McNidder and Grace.

Miller, Doug. 2013. "Towards Sustainable Labour Costing in UK Fashion Retail": Capturing the Gains working paper 14.

Miraftab, Faranak. 2015. *Global Heartland: Displaced Labor, Transnational Lives, and Local Placemaking*: Indiana University Press.

Mitchell, Tom. 2016. "Xi's China: Smothering Dissent." *Financial Times* July 27, 2016.

Mitchell, Tom, and Charles Clover. 2014. "IBM Workers Strike in China over Terms of Lenovo Takeover." *Financial Times* March 6, 2014.

Miteva, Daniela A., Colby J. Loucks, and Subhrendu K. Pattanayak. 2015. "Social and Environmental Impacts of Forest Management Certification in Indonesia." *PLoS ONE* 10(7):e0129675.

Mizuno, Kosuke, Indrasari Tjandraningsih, and Rina Herawati. 2007. *Directory of Trade Unions in Indonesia* Bandung and Kyoto: AKATIGA Center for Social Analysis and Center for Southeast Asian Studies Kyoto University.

Mol, Arthur P.J., and Gert Spaargaren. 2006. "Towards a Sociology of Environmental Flows: A New Agenda for Twenty-First-Century Environmental Sociology." Pp. 39–82 in *Governing Environmental Flows: Global Challenges to Social Theory*, edited by Gert Spaargaren, Arthur P.J. Mol, and Frederick H. Buttel. Cambridge: MIT Press.

Monument, Alistair. 2008. "FSC in China and the Global Paper Market." Presentation at the Developing Certified Forests, Forest Products and Markets International Conference, Beijing, April 2–3, 2008.

Moon, Jeremy. 2004. "Government as a Driver of Corporate Social Responsibility." Nottingham University, International Centre for Corporate Social Responsibility Research Paper Series, ISSN 1479-5124

Morris, Mike, and Nikki Dunne. 2004. "Driving Environmental Certification: Its Impact on the Furniture and Timber Products Value Chain in South Africa." *Geoforum* 35(2):251–66.

Morris, Mike, Leonhard Plank, and Cornelia Staritz. 2015. "Regionalism, End Markets and Ownership Matter: Shifting Dynamics in the Apparel Export Industry in Sub Saharan Africa." *Environment and Planning A* 48(7):1244–65.

Mosley, Layna. 2011. *Labor Rights and Multinational Production*. New York: Cambridge University Press.

Muddy Waters. 2011. "Sino-Forest Corporation (TRE.TO, OTC: SNOFF) Report." June 2, 2011, http://d.muddywatersresearch.com/wp-content/uploads/2011/06/MW_TRE_060211.pdf, accessed June 9, 2016.

Mügge, Daniel, and Bart Stellinga. 2015. "The Unstable Core of Global Finance: Contingent Valuation and Governance of International Accounting Standards." *Regulation & Governance* 9(1):47–62.

Muhtaman, Dwi Rahmad, and Ferdinandus Agung Prasetyo. 2006. "Forest Certification in Indonesia." Pp. 33–68 in *Confronting Sustainability: Forest Certification in Developing and Transitioning Countries*, edited by Benjamin Cashore, Fred Gale, Errol Meidinger, and Deanna Newsom. New Haven: Yale School of Forestry & Environmental Studies.

Mujani, Saiful, and R. William Liddle. 2004. "Politics, Islam, and Public Opinion." *Journal of Democracy* 15(1):109–23.

Mullan, Katrina, Pauline Grosjean, and Andreas Kontoleon. 2011. "Land Tenure Arrangements and Rural-Urban Migration in China." *World Development* 39(1): 123–33.

Mundlak, Guy, and Issi Rosen-Zvi. 2011. "Signaling Virtue? A Comparison of Corporate Codes in the Fields of Labor and Environment." *Theoretical Inquiries in Law* 12(2):603–63.

Murphy, Craig N., and JoAnne Yates. 2009. *The International Organization for Standardization (ISO): Global Governance through Voluntary Consensus*. New York Routledge.

Murphy, Hannah. 2014. "The World Bank and Core Labour Standards: Between Flexibility and Regulation." *Review of International Political Economy* 21(2):399–431.

Mutersbaugh, T. 2005. "Fighting Standards with Standards: Harmonization, Rents, and Social Accountability in Certified Agrofood Networks." *Environment and Planning A* 37(11):2033–51.

Nadvi, Khalid, and Gale Raj-Reichert. 2015. "Governing Health and Safety at Lower Tiers of the Computer Industry Global Value Chain." *Regulation & Governance* 9(3):243–58.

Natahadibrata, Nadya. 2013. "Government Recognizes Customary Forests." *Jakarta Post* (May 18, 2013).

Nathan, Andrew J. 2003. "Authoritarian Resilience." *Journal of Democracy* 14(1):6–17.

National Labor Committee. 2010. "China's Youth Meet Microsoft." New York: National Labor Committee.

Nebel, Gustav, Lincoln Quevedo, Jette Bredahl Jacobsen, and Finn Helles. 2005. "Development and Economic Significance of Forest Certification: The Case of FSC in Bolivia." *Forest Policy and Economics* 7:175–86.

Nellemann, Christian, Rune Henriksen, Arnold Kreilhuber, Davyth Stewart, Maria Kotsovou, Patricia Raxter, Elizabeth Mrema, and Sam Barrat. 2016. "The Rise of Environmental Crime: A Growing Threat to Natural Resources Peace, Development and Security." Nairobi: United Nations Environment Programme and RHIPTO Rapid Response–Norwegian Center for Global Analyses.

Neumayer, Eric. 2004. "The WTO and the Environment: Its Past Record Is Better Than Critics Believe, but the Future Outlook Is Bleak." *Global Environmental Politics* 4(3):1–8.

Newsom, Deanna, Volker Bahn, and Benjamin Cashore. 2006. "Does Forest Certification Matter? An Analysis of Operation-Level Changes Required During the Smartwood Certification Process in the United States." *Forest Policy and Economics* 9(3):197–208.

Newsom, Deanna, and Daphne Hewitt. 2005. "The Global Impacts of Smartwood Certification." Rainforest Alliance report.

Nomura, Ko. 2008. "The Politics of Participation in Forest Management : A Case from Democratizing Indonesia." *Journal of Environment and Development* 17(2):166–91.

Nussbaum, Ruth, and Markku Simula. 2004. "Forest Certification: A Review of Impacts and Assessment Frameworks." New Haven: The Forests Dialogue, Yale University School of Forestry & Environmental Studies, research.yale.edu/gisf/assets/pdf/tfd/TFD%20Certification%20Impacts%20and%20Assessment%20Paper.pdf, accessed July 28, 2013.

O'Brien, Kevin J., and Lianjiang Li. 2006. *Rightful Resistance in Rural China*. Cambridge: Cambridge University Press.

O'Rourke, Dara. 1997. "Smoke from a Hired Gun: A Critique of Nike's Labor and Environmental Auditing in Vietnam as Performed by Ernst & Young." Transnational Resource and Action Center (http://nature.berkeley.edu/orourke/PDF/smoke.pdf).

O'Rourke, Dara. 2003. "Outsourcing Regulation: Analyzing Non-Governmental Systems of Labor Standards and Monitoring." *Policy Studies Journal* 31:1–29.

Oka, Chikako. 2010a. "Accounting for the Gaps in Labour Standard Compliance: The Role of Reputation-Conscious Buyers in the Cambodian Garment Industry." *European Journal of Development Research* 22(1):59–78.

Oka, Chikako. 2010b. "Channels of Buyer Influence and Labor Standard Compliance: The Case of Cambodia's Garment Sector." *Advances in Industrial and Labor Relations* 17:153–83.

Oka, Chikako. 2012. "Does Better Labour Standard Compliance Pay? Linking Labour Standard Compliance and Supplier Competitiveness." Better Work Discussion Paper Series: No. 5. Geneva: International Labour Organization.

OLYMP. 2014. "Olymp: Silver Anniversary with the Indonesian Tiger." https://company.olymp.com/en/news/artikel/2014-10-20/1/olymp-silver-anniversary-with-the-indonesian-tiger.html, accessed October 9, 2016.

Organization for Economic Cooperation and Development (OECD). 2015. "Economic Survey of Indonesia 2015." Paris: OECD, http://www.oecd.org/eco/surveys/economic-survey-indonesia.htm, accessed October 9, 2016.

Ostrom, Elinor. 1990. *Governing the Commons: The Evolution of Institutions for Collective Action.* New York: Cambridge University Press.

Overdevest, Christine. 2010. "Comparing Forest Certification Schemes: The Case of Ratcheting Standards in the Forest Sector." *Socio-Economic Review* 8 (1):47–76.

Overdevest, Christine, and Jonathan Zeitlin. 2014a. "Assembling an Experimentalist Regime: Transnational Governance Interactions in the Forest Sector." *Regulation & Governance* 8(1):22–48.

Overdevest, Christine, and Jonathan Zeitlin. 2014b. "Constructing a Transnational Timber Legality Assurance Regime: Architecture, Accomplishments, Challenges." *Forest Policy and Economics* 48:6–15.

Overdevest, Christine, and Jonathan Zeitlin. Forthcoming. "Experimentalism in Transnational Forest Governance: Implementing EU Forest Law Enforcement Governance and Trade (FLEGT) Voluntary Partnership Agreements in Indonesia and Ghana." *Regulation & Governance.*

Owari, Toshiaki, and Yoshihide Sawanobori. 2007. "Analysis of the Certified Forest Products Market in Japan." *Holz als Roh- und Werkstoff* 65(2):113–20.

Pan, Philip P. 2002. "Poisoned Back into Poverty: As China Embraces Capitalism, Hazards to Workers Rise." *Washington Post* Aug. 4, 2002:A1.

Pangestu, Mari, and Medelina K. Hendytio. 1997. "Survey Responses from Women Workers in Indonesia's Textile, Garment, and Footwear Industries." *World Bank Policy Research Working Paper* (1755).

Parreñas, Rhacel Salazar, Maria Cecilia Hwang, Heather Ruth Lee. 2012. "What Is Human Trafficking? A Review Essay." *Signs* 37(4):1015–29.

PEFC. 2012. "PEFC Annual Review 2012." Geneva: Programme for the Endorsement of Forest Certification, http://pefc.org/images/documents/PEFC_Annual_Review_2012_WEB_2013_08_19.pdf.

PEFC. 2014. "China's National Forest Certification System Achieves PEFC Endorsement." Geneva: Programme for the Endorsement of Forest Certification, http://pefc.org/news-a-media/general-sfm-news/1459-china-s-national-forest-certification-system-achieves-pefc-endorsement, accessed June 10, 2016.

PEFC-China. 2008. "PEFC China Initiative in Action." Beijing: Programme for the Endorsement of Forest Certification China Initiative.

PEFC and SFI. 2015. "Press Release: PEFC Week Brings International Partners Together to Address Sustainable Forestry." Program for the Endorsement of Forest

Certification (PEFC) and Sustainable Forestry Initiative (SFI), December 14, 2015, http://www.sfiprogram.org/media-resources/news/pefc-week-brings-international-partners-together-to-address-sustainable-forestry/, accessed June 10, 2016.

Peluso, Nancy Lee. 1992. *Rich Forests, Poor People: Resource Control and Resistance in Java*. Berkeley: University of California Press.

Peluso, Nancy Lee. 2005. "Seeing Property in Land Use: Local Territorializations in West Kalimantan, Indonesia." *Geografisk Tidsskrift-Danish Journal of Geography* 105(1): 1–15.

Peluso, Nancy Lee, Suraya Afiff, and Noer Fauzi Rachman. 2008. "Claiming the Grounds for Reform: Agrarian and Environmental Movements in Indonesia." *Journal of Agrarian Change* 8(2–3):377–407.

Peluso, Nancy Lee, and Mark Poffenberger. 1989. "Social Forestry in Java: Reorienting Management Systems." *Human Organization* 48(4):333–44.

Peluso, Nancy Lee, and Peter Vandergeest. 2001. "Genealogies of the Political Forest and Customary Rights in Indonesia, Malaysia, and Thailand." *Journal of Asian Studies* 60(3):761–812.

Peña, Alejandro Milcíades. forthcoming. "The Politics of Resonance: Transnational Sustainability Governance in Argentina." *Regulation & Governance*.

People's Republic of China. 1994. "Labour Act." China Daily, July 6, 1994. https://www.ilo.org/dyn/natlex/docs/WEBTEXT/37357/64926/E94CHN01.htm.

People's Republic of China State Council. 1995. "The Regulations of the State Council on the Hours of Work of Employees, Revised, March 25, 1995." http://www.ilo.org/dyn/travail/docs/369/The%20Regulations%20of%20the%20State%20Council%20on%20the%20Hours%20of%20Work%20of%20Employees.pdf.

Perez-Aleman, Paola. 2013. "Regulation in the Process of Building Capabilities: Strengthening Competitiveness While Improving Food Safety and Environmental Sustainability in Nicaragua." *Politics & Society* 41(4):589–620.

Perry, Elizabeth J. 2008. "A New Rights Consciousness?" *Journal of Democracy* 20(3): 17–20.

Perry, Elizabeth J., and Sebastian Heilmann (Eds.). 2011. *Mao's Invisible Hand: The Political Foundations of Adaptive Governance in China*. Cambridge, MA: Harvard University Asia Center.

Pikiran Raykat. 2008. "Kericuhan Di Metro Garmin Hambat Ekspor." *Pikiran Raykat* October 21, 2008.

Pils, Eva. 2005. "Land Disputes, Rights Assertion, and Social Unrest in China: A Case from Sichuan." *Columbia Journal of Asian Law* 19(1):235–92.

Piore, Michael, and Andrew Schrank. 2008. "Toward Managed Flexibility: The Revival of Labour Inspection in the Latin World." *International Labour Review* 147:1–23.

Pires, Roberto R.C. 2013. "The Organizational Basis of Rewarding Regulation Contingency, Flexibility, and Accountability in the Brazilian Labor Inspectorate." *Politics & Society* 41(4):621–46.

Polanyi, Karl. 1944. *The Great Transformation*. Boston: Beacon Press.

Polaski, Sandra. 2006. "Combining Global and Local Forces: The Case of Labor Rights in Cambodia." *World Development* 34(5):919–32.

Ponte, Stefano. 2008. "Greener Than Thou: The Political Economy of Fish Ecolabeling and Its Local Manifestations in South Africa." *World Development* 36(1):159–75.

Ponte, Stefano. 2012. "The Marine Stewardship Council (MSC) and the Making of a Market for 'Sustainable Fish'." *Journal of Agrarian Change* 12(2-3):300–15.

Ponte, Stefano. 2014. " 'Roundtabling' sustainability: Lessons from the Biofuel Industry." *Geoforum* 54:261–71.

Porter, Tony. 2014. "Technical Systems and the Architecture of Transnational Business Governance Interactions." *Regulation & Governance* 8(1):110–25.

Posner, Michael, and Justine Nolan. 2003. "Can Codes of Conduct Play a Role in Promoting Workers' Rights," in *International Labor Standards: Globalization, Trade and Public Policy*. Stanford, CA: Stanford University Press.

Posthuma, Anne Caroline. 2004. "Taking a Seat in the Global Marketplace: Opportunities for 'High Road' Upgrading in the Indonesian Wood Furniture Sector?" *Research in the Sociology of Work* 13(3):175–94.

Posthuma, Anne Caroline. 2008. "Seeking the High Road to Jepara: Challenges for Economic and Social Upgrading in Indonesian Wood Furniture Clusters." Pp. 23–44 in *Upgrading Clusters and Small Enterprises in Developing Countries: Environmental, Labor, Innovation and Social Issues*, edited by Jose Puppim de Oliveira. Hampshire, UK: Ashgate Publishing.

Potoski, Matthew, and Aseem Prakash (Eds.). 2009. *Voluntary Programs: A Club Theory Approach*. Cambridge, MA: MIT Press.

Potoski, Matthew, and Aseem Prakash. 2013. "Do Voluntary Programs Reduce Pollution? Examining ISO 14001's Effectiveness across Countries." *Policy Studies Journal* 41(2):273–94.

Power, Michael. 1997. *The Audit Society: Rituals of Verification*. Oxford: Oxford University Press.

Poynton, Scott. 2013. "Chain of Custordy Nonsense from FSC & PEFC: Protecting Income Streams Rather Than the World's Forests." Mongabay, https://news.mongabay.com/2013/07/chain-of-custody-nonsense-from-fsc-pefc-protecting-income-streams-rather-than-the-worlds-forests/, accessed June 10, 2016.

Prakash, Aseem, and Matthew Potoski. 2006a. "Racing to the Bottom? Trade, Environmental Governance, and ISO 14001." *American Journal of Political Science* 50(2):350–64.

Prakash, Aseem, and Matthew Potoski. 2006b. *The Voluntary Environmentalists: Green Clubs, ISO 140001, and Voluntary Environmental Regulations*. New York: Cambridge University Press.

Prakash, Aseem, and Matthew Potoski. 2014. "Global Private Regimes, Domestic Public Law ISO 14001 and Pollution Reduction." *Comparative Political Studies* 47(3):369–94.

Prasetyo, Agung, James Hewitt, and Chen Hin Keong. 2012. "Indonesia: Scoping Baseline Information for Forest Law Enforcement, Governance and Trade." Kuala Lumpur: EU Forest Law Enforcement, Governance and Trade (FLEGT) Facility, https://www.illegal-logging.info/sites/files/chlogging/uploads/baselinestudyindonesiafinal.pdf, accessed August 7, 2014.

Prudham, Scott. 2007. "Sustaining Sustained Yield: Class, Politics, and Post-War Forest Regulation in British Columbia." *Environment and Planning D: Society and Space* 25(2):258.

Pun, Ngai. 2005a. "Global Production, Company Codes of Conduct, and Labor Conditions in China: A Case Study of Two Factories." *The China Journal* 54:101–13.

Pun, Ngai. 2005b. *Made in China: Women Factory Workers in a Global Workplace.* Durham, NC: Duke University Press.

Putz, Francis E, Geoffrey M. Blate, Kent H. Redford, Robert Fimbel, and John Robinson. 2001. "Tropical Forest Management and Conservation of Biodiversity: An Overview." *Conservation Biology* 15(1):7–20.

Qin, Liu. 2014. "China Tests Outright Logging Ban in State Forests." *Guardian* (October 17, 2014, https://www.theguardian.com/environment/2014/oct/17/china-tests-outright-logging-ban-in-state-forests, accessed June 10, 2016).

Quack, Sigrid. 2007. "Legal Professionals and Transnational Law-making: A Case of Distributed Agency." *Organization* 14(5):643–66.

Quack, Sigrid. 2010. "Law, Expertise and Legitimacy in Transnational Economic Governance: An Introduction." *Socio-Economic Review* 8(1):3–16.

Quark, Amy A. 2013. *Global Rivalries: Standards Wars and the Transnational Cotton Trade.* Chicago: University of Chicago Press.

Rainforest Foundation, The. 2002. *Trading in Credibility: The Myth and Reality of the Forest Stewardship Council.* London: Rainforest Foundation.

Raitzer, David A. 2008. "Assessing the Impact of CIFOR's Influence on Policy and Practice in the Indonesian Pulp and Paper Sector." Bogor, Indonesia: Center for International Forestry Research.

Raj-Reichert, Gale. 2011. "The Electronic Industry Code of Conduct: Private Governance in a Competitive and Contested Global Production Network." *Competition & Change* 15(3):221–38.

Rao, Hayagreeva, Calvin Morrill, and Mayer N. Zald. 2000. "Power Plays: How Social Movements and Collective Action Create New Organizational Forms." *Research in Organizational Behavior* 22:237–81.

Raynolds, Laura T. 2009. "Mainstreaming Fair Trade Coffee: From Partnership to Traceability." *World Development* 37(6):1083–93.

Raynolds, Laura T. 2014. "Fairtrade, Certification, and Labor: Global and Local Tensions in Improving Conditions for Agricultural Workers." *Agriculture and Human Values* 31(3):499–511.

Raynolds, Laura T. 2017. "Fairtrade Labour Certification: The Contested Incorporation of Plantations and Workers." *Third World Quarterly* 38(7):1473–92.

Rees, Joseph V. 1994. *Hostages of Each Other: The Transformation of Nuclear Safety since Three Mile Island.* Chicago: University of Chicago Press.

Renckens, Stefan. 2015. "The Basel Convention, US Politics, and the Emergence of Non-State E-Waste Recycling Certification." *International Environmental Agreements: Politics, Law and Economics* 15(2):141–58.

Republic of Indonesia. 2009. "The Republic of Indonesia Forestry Minister's Regulation No P.38/Menhut-Ii/2009 Concerning Standard and Guidelines on Assessment of

Performance of Sustainable Production Forest Management and Verification of Timber Legality for License Holders or in Private Forests."

RESOLVE. 2012. "Toward Sustainability: The Roles and Limits of Certification." Steering Committee of the State-of-Knowledge Assessment of Standards and Certification. Washington, DC: RESOLVE.

Resosudarmo, Ida Aju Pradnja, Stibniati Atmadja, Andini Desita Ekaputri, Dian Y. Intarini, Yayan Indriatmoko, and Pangestuti Astri. 2014. "Does Tenure Security Lead to REDD+ Project Effectiveness? Reflections from Five Emerging Sites in Indonesia." *World Development* 55:68–83.

Reuters. 2007. "Nike Offers to Extend Contracts at Indonesia Firms." *Reuters* July 30, 2007:http://mobile.reuters.com/article/idUSJAK28178120070731.

Riles, Annelise. 2009. *Collateral Knowledge: Legal Reason in the Global Markets*. Chicago: University of Chicago Press.

Rinaldo, Rachel. 2013. *Mobilizing Piety: Islam and Feminism in Indonesia*. New York: Oxford University Press.

Risse, Thomas. 2013. *Governance without a State?: Policies and Politics in Areas of Limited Statehood*: Columbia University Press.

Robbins, Alicia. 2011. "China's Forest Sector: Essays on Production Efficiency, Foreign Investment, and Trade and Illegal Logging." Dissertation, School of Forest Resources, University of Washington.

Robbins, Alicia S.T., and Stevan Harrell. 2014. "Paradoxes and Challenges for China's Forests in the Reform Era." *China Quarterly* 218:381–403.

Robertson, Raymond, Sari Sitalaksmi, Poppy Ismalina, and Ardyanto Fitrady. 2009. "Globalization and Working Conditions: Evidence from Indonesia." Pp. 203–36 in *Globalization, Wages, and the Quality of Jobs: Five Country Studies*, edited by Raymond Robertson, Drusilla Brown, Gaëlle Pierre, and María Laura Sanchez-Puerta. Washington, DC: The World Bank.

Robson, Karen and David Pevalin. 2015. *Multilevel Modeling in Plain Language*. Thousand Oaks, CA: SAGE.

Rodríguez-Garavito, César A. 2005. "Global Governance and Labor Rights: Codes of Conduct and Anti-Sweatshop Struggles in Global Apparel Factories in Mexico and Guatemala." *Politics and Society* 33(2):203–33.

Rodríguez-Garavito, César A., and Boaventura de Sousa Santos. 2005. *Law and Globalization from Below: Towards a Cosmopolitan Legality*. New York: Cambridge University Press.

Rodrik, Dani. 2007. *One Economics, Many Recipes: Globalization, Institutions, and Economic Growth*. Princeton: Princeton University Press.

Rodrik, Dani. 2011. *The Globalization Paradox*. New York: W.W. Norton.

Rokhani, Endang. 2008. "Inter-Union Conflict in Three Indonesian Factories." *Labour and Management in Development* 9:1–10.

Rolnick, Alan L. 1997. "Muzzling the Offshore Watchdogs." *Bobbin* February, pp. 72–3.

Ros-Tonen, Mirjam A. F., Thomas F. G. Insaidoo, and Emmanuel Acheampong. 2013. "Promising Start, Bleak Outlook: The Role of Ghana's Modified Taungya System as a Social Safeguard in Timber Legality Processes." *Forest Policy and Economics* 32:57–67.

Rosen, Ellen Israel. 2002. *Making Sweatshops: The Globalization of the U.S. Apparel Industry*. Berkeley: University of California Press.

Ross, Robert J.S. 2004. *Slaves to Fashion: Poverty and Abuse in the New Sweatshops*. Ann Arbor: University of Michigan Press.

Ross, Robert J.S. 2006. "A Tale of Two Factories: Successful Resistance to Sweatshops and the Limits of Firefighting." *Labor Studies Journal* 30(4):65–85.

Ross, Robert J.S. 2015. "Bringing Labor Rights Back to Bangladesh." *The American Prospect* Summer 2015:74–9.

Rosser, Andrew. 2007. "Escaping the Resource Curse: The Case of Indonesia." *Journal of Contemporary Asia* 37(1):38–58.

Rossi, Arianna, Amy Luinstra, and John Pickles. 2014. *Towards Better Work: Understanding Labour in Apparel Global Value Chains*. London: Palgrave MacMillan.

Ruslandi, Oscar Venter, and Francis E. Putz. 2011. "Overestimating Conservation Costs in Southeast Asia." *Frontiers in Ecology and the Environment* 9(10):542–4.

Rysman, Marc, and Timothy Simcoe. 2008. "Patents and the Performance of Voluntary Standard-Setting Organizations." *Management Science* 54(11):1920–34.

Sabel, Charles. 2007. "Rolling Rule Labor Standards: Why Their Time Has Come, and Why We Should Be Glad of It." Pp. 257–73 in *Protecting Labour Rights as Human Rights: Present and Future of International Supervision (Conference Proceedings)*, edited by George P. Politakis. Geneva: ILO.

Sabel, Charles, Dara O'Rourke, and Archon Fung. 2000. "Ratcheting Labor Standards: Regulation for Continuous Improvement in the Global Workplace." KSG Working Paper No. 00-010, ssrn.com/abstract=253833.

Salzinger, Leslie. 2003. *Genders in Production: Making Workers in Mexico's Global Factories*. Berkeley: University of California Press.

Samford, Steven. 2015. "Innovation and Public Space: The Developmental Possibilities of Regulation in the Global South." *Regulation & Governance* 9(3):294–308.

Sassen, Saskia. 2006. *Territory, Authority, Rights: From Medieval to Global Assemblages*. Princeton and Oxford: Princeton University Press.

Sasser, Erika N., Aseem Prakash, Benjamin Cashore, and Graeme Auld. 2006. "Direct Targeting as an NGO Political Strategy: Examining Private Authority Regimes in the Forestry Sector." *Business and Politics* 8(3):1–32.

Saturi, Sapariah, Ridzki Sigit, Indra Nugraha, and Philip Jacobson. 2015. "Indonesia extends moratorium on partial forest clearing." *The Guardian* (May 14, 2015).

Schiller, Jim, and Achmad Uzair Fauzan. 2009. "Local Resource Politics in Reform Era Indonesia." Pp. 27–56 in *Community, Environment, and Local Governance in Indonesia*, edited by Carol Warren and John F. McCarthy. London and New York: Routledge.

Schimel, David, Britton B Stephens, and Joshua B Fisher. 2015. "Effect of Increasing Co2 on the Terrestrial Carbon Cycle." *Proceedings of the National Academy of Sciences* 112(2):436–41.

Schipper, Irene. 2004. "WE Europe: A Report on CSR Policy and SA8000." Amsterdam: SOMO.

Schleifer, Philip. 2013. "Orchestrating Sustainability: The Case of European Union Biofuel Governance." *Regulation & Governance* 7(4):533–46.

Schneck, Joshua. 2009. "Assessing the Viability of HTR—Indonesia's Community Based Forest Plantation Program." Master's Thesis, Nicholas School of the Environment. Durham, NC: Duke University.

Schofer, Evan, and Ann Hironaka. 2005. "The Effects of World Society on Environmental Protection Outcomes." *Social Forces* 84(1):25–47.

Schofer, Evan, and Wesley Longhofer. 2011. "The Structural Sources of Association." *American Journal of Sociology* 117(2):539–85.

Schofer, Evan, and John W. Meyer. 2005. "The Worldwide Expansion of Higher Education in the Twentieth Century." *American Sociological Review* 70(6):898–920.

Schouten, Greetje, and Pieter Glasbergen. 2011. "Creating Legitimacy in Global Private Governance: The Case of the Roundtable on Sustainable Palm Oil." *Ecological Economics* 70(11):1891–9.

Schrank, Andrew. 2004. "Ready-to-Wear Development? Foreign Investment, Technology Transfer, and Learning by Watching in the Apparel Trade." *Social Forces* 83 (1):123–56.

Schrank, Andrew. 2009. "Professionalization and Probity in a Patrimonial State: Labor Inspectors in the Dominican Republic." *Latin American Politics and Society* 51(2): 91–115.

Schurman, Rachel. 2004. "Fighting 'Frankenfoods': Industry Opportunity Structures and the Efficacy of the Anti-Biotech Movement in Western Europe." *Social Problems* 51:243–68.

Schurman, Rachel, and William Munro. 2009. "Targeting Capital: A Cultural Economy Approach to Understanding the Efficacy of Two Anti-Genetic Engineering Movements." *American Journal of Sociology* 115(1):155–202.

Scott, Allen J. 2006. "The Changing Global Geography of Low-Technology, Labor-Intensive Industry: Clothing, Footwear, and Furniture." *World Development* 34(9): 1517–36.

Scott, Colin. 2012. "Non-Judicial Enforcement of Transnational Private Regulation." Pp. 147–64 in *Enforcement of Transnational Regulation: Ensuring Compliance in a Global World*, edited by Fabrizio Cafaggi. Cheltenham, UK: Edward Elgar.

Scott, James C. 1998. *Seeing Like a State: How Certain Schemes to Improve the Human Condition Have Failed*. New Haven: Yale University Press.

Sedjo, Roger, and Brent Sohngen. 2012. "Carbon Sequestration in Forests and Soils." *Annual Review of Resource Economics* 4(1):127–44.

Seidman, Gay. 2007. *Beyond the Boycott: Labor Rights, Human Rights and Transnational Activism*. New York: Russell Sage Foundation/ASA Rose Series.

Sellnow, Timothy, and Jeffrey Brand. 2001. "Establishing the Structure of Reality for an Industry: Model and Anti-Model Arguments as Advocacy in Nike's Crisis Communication." *Journal of Applied Communication Research* 29(3):278–95.

Sevastopulo, Demetri. 2014a. "China Charges Labour Activist after Yue Yuen Shoe Factory Strike." *Financial Times* April 29, 2014.

Sevastopulo, Demetri. 2014b. "China Wakes up to Growing Pension Problem." *Financial Times* May 5, 2014.

Sevastopulo, Demetri. 2014c. "Chinese Factory Told to Reimburse Striking Workers." *Financial Times* April 24, 2014.

SGS QUALIFOR Programme. 2000. "FM Main Assessment Report: PT Diamond Raya Timber." Oxford, UK: SGS QUALIFOR Programme.

SGS QUALIFOR Programme. 2003. "Forest Management Surveillance Report for PT Diamond Raya Timber." SGS QUALIFOR Programme.

SGS QUALIFOR Programme. 2005. "Forest Management Certification Report: PT-DRT." Southdale, South Africa: SGS QUALIFOR Programme.

SGS QUALIFOR Programme. 2008. "Forest Management Certification Report: Fujian Yong'an Forestry." Southdale, South Africa: SGS South Africa (Qualifor Programme).

SGS QUALIFOR Programme. 2009. "Forest Management Certification Report: PT-DRT." Southdale, South Africa: SGS QUALIFOR.

SGS QUALIFOR Programme. 2012. "Forest Management Certification Report: The Communities Have a Legally Binding Agreement." Southdale, South Africa: SGS Qualifor Programme.

Shaffer, Gregory. 2001. "The World Trade Organization under Challenge: Democracy and the Law and Politics of the WTO's Treatment of Trade and Environment Matters." *Harvard Environmental Law Review* 25:1–93.

Shaffer, Gregory. 2015. "How the World Trade Organization Shapes Regulatory Governance." *Regulation & Governance* 9(1):1–15.

Shapiro, Judith. 2001. *Mao's War against Nature: Politics and the Environment in Revolutionary China*. Cambridge: Cambridge University Press.

Shapiro, Susan. 1987. "The Social Control of Impersonal Trust." *American Journal of Sociology* 93:623–58.

Shaw, Randy. 1999. *Reclaiming America: Nike, Clean Air, and the New National Activism*. Berkeley: University of California Press.

Siciliano, Giuseppina. 2014. "Rural-Urban Migration and Domestic Land Grabbing in China." *Population, Space and Place* 20(4):333–51.

Sikkink, Kathryn. 1986. "Codes of Conduct for Transnational Corporations: The Case of the WHO/UNICEF Code." *International Organization* 40(4):815–40.

Silva-Castañeda, Laura. 2012. "A Forest of Evidence: Third-Party Certification and Multiple Forms of Proof—a Case Study of Oil Palm Plantations in Indonesia." *Agriculture and Human Values* 29(3):361–70.

Silver, Beverly J. 2003. *Forces of Labor: Workers' Movements and Globalization Since 1870*. New York: Cambridge University Press.

Silver, Beverly J., and Lu Zhang. 2009. "China as an Emerging Epicenter of World Labor Unrest." Pp. 175–87 in *China and the Transformation of Global Capitalism*, edited by Ho-fung Hung. Baltimore: Johns Hopkins University Press.

Singer, Judith D. 1998. "Using SAS PROC MIXED to Fit Multilevel Models, Hierarchical Models, and Individual Growth Models." *Journal of Educational and Behavioral Statistics* 23(4):323–55.

Sklar, Kathryn Kish. 1998. "The Consumers' White Label Campaign of the National Consumers' League, 1898–1918." Pp. 17–36 in *Getting and Spending: European and American Consumer Societies in the Twentieth Century*, edited by McGovern Strasser, and Judt. New York: Cambridge University Press.

Slater, Dan. 2009. "Revolutions, Crackdowns, and Quiescence: Communal Elites and Democratic Mobilization in Southeast Asia." *American Journal of Sociology* 115(1): 203–54.

Slaughter, Anne-Marie. 2004. *A New World Order*. Princeton, NJ: Princeton University Press.

SmartWood. 2001a. "Forest Management Public Summary for Cepus, Kebonharjo and Mantingan Forest Management Districts, Perum Perhutani Unit I, Central Java, Indonesia." New York: Rainforest Alliance, SmartWood Program.

SmartWood. 2001b. "Forest Management Public Summary for Perhum Perhutani District of Madiun." New York: Rainforest Alliance, SmartWood Program.

SmartWood. 2005a. "Forest Management Public Summary for Pt Erna Djuliawati." New York: Rainforest Alliance, SmartWood Program.

SmartWood. 2005b. "Forest Management Public Summary for Sino-Forest Corporation/Gaoyao City JiaYao Forestry Development Company, Limited." New York: Rainforest Alliance SmartWood Program.

SmartWood. 2006a. "Forest Management 2006 CAR Verification Audit Report for PT Intracawood Manufacturing." Richmond, VT: SmartWood.

SmartWood. 2006b. "Forest Management Public Summary for Pt Sumalindo Lestari Jaya Ii." New York: Rainforest Alliance.

SmartWood. 2006c. "Smartwood Certification Assessment Report for PT Intracawood Manufacturing." Richmond, VT: SmartWood.

SmartWood. 2007a. "Forest Management 2006 CAR Verification Audit Report for PT Sumalindo Lestari Jaya." Richmond, VT: SmartWood.

SmartWood. 2007b. "Forest Management 2006 CAR Verification Audit Report for PT Xylo Indah Pratama." Richmond, VT: SmartWood.

SmartWood. 2007c. "Forest Management Certification Assessment Report for PT Sari Bumi Kusuma." Richmond, VT: SmartWood.

SmartWood. 2008a. "Corrective Action Request Verification Report (November 18): PT Intracawood Manufacturing." Richmond, VT: SmartWood.

SmartWood. 2008b. "Forest Management 2008 Annual Audit Report for PT Intracawood Manufacturing." Richmond, VT: SmartWood.

SmartWood. 2008c. "Forest Management 2008 Annual Audit Report for PT Sari Bumi Kusuma." Richmond, VT: SmartWood.

SmartWood. 2008d. "Forest Management 2008 CAR Verification Audit Report for PT Intracawood Manufacturing."

SmartWood. 2008e. "Forest Management Certification Re-Assessment Report for Sino-Forest Corporation, Jiayao Forestry Development Co. Ltd. (JFDC)." Richmond, VT: SmartWood, November 3, 2008.

SmartWood. 2009a. "Annual Audit Public Summary for Muling Forestry Bureau of Heilongjiang Province." Richmond, VT: Rainforest Alliance SmartWood Program.

SmartWood. 2009b. "Forest Management 2009 Annual Audit Report for PT Sari Bumi Kusuma." Richmond, VT: SmartWood.

SmartWood. 2009c. "Forest Management 2009 Annual Audit Report for PT Xylo Indah Pratama." Richmond, VT: SmartWood.

SmartWood. 2010a. "Forest Management 2010 Annual Audit Report for Sino-Forest Corporation/Gaoyao City Jiayao Forestry Development Co., Ltd. (JFDC)": Richmond, VT: SmartWood.

Bibliography

SmartWood. 2010b. "Forest Management Controlled Wood Surveillance Audit 2009 Report for PT Riau Andalan Pulp and Paper Forestry Division (Riaufiber)." Richmond, VT: SmartWood.

SmartWood. 2012. "Forest Management Certification Reassessment 2011 Report for PT Intracawood Manufacturing." Richmond, VT: SmartWood.

Smith, J., K. Obidzinski, Subarudi, and I. Suramenggala. 2003. "Illegal Logging, Collusive Corruption and Fragmented Governments in Kalimantan, Indonesia." *International Forestry Review* 5(3):293–302.

Snyder, Rachel Louise. 2009. *Fugitive Denim: A Moving Story of People and Pants in the Borderless World of Global Trade*. New York: W.W. Norton.

Social Accountability Accreditation Services. 2005. "Complaint #006: Certification Improper Because of Major Non-Conformance."

Social Accountability Accreditation Services. 2006. "Complaint #010: Certification Complaint PT Teodore Garmindo Indonesia."

Social Accountability Accreditation Services. 2008. "Saas Global Procedures Guideline 304." http://www.saasaccreditation.org/sites/default/files/u7/Procedure%20304% 2C%20January.2008_1.pdf, accessed October 25, 2016.

Social Accountability International. 2012. "Q & A: Ali Enterprises Fire in Karachi, Pakistan." http://www.sa-intl.org/_data/n_0001/resources/live/Q&A_AliEnterprises_8Dec2012. pdf, accessed May 13, 2016.

Soil Association. 2011. "Woodmark Forest Certification Public Report: Perum Perhutani Kph Kebonharjo." Bristol, UK: Soil Association.

Soule, Sarah A. 2009. *Contention and Corporate Social Responsibility*. New York: Cambridge University Press.

Spar, Debra L., and Lane T. LaMure. 2003. "The Power of Activism: Assessing the Impact of NGOs on Global Business." *California Management Review* 45(3):78–101.

Spires, Anthony J. 2011. "Contingent Symbiosis and Civil Society in an Authoritarian State: Understanding the Survival of China's Grassroots NGOs." *American Journal of Sociology* 117(1):1–45.

Srinivasan, T.N. 2013. "International Trade and Labor Standards." Pp. 922–56 in *The Handbook of Trade Policy for Development*, edited by Arvind Lukauskas, Robert M. Stern, and Gianni Zanini. Oxford: Oxford University Press.

Stern, Rachel E., and Kevin J. O'Brien. 2012. "Politics at the Boundary: Mixed Signals and the Chinese State." *Modern China* 38(2):174–98.

Stockmann, Daniela, and Mary E. Gallagher. 2011. "Remote Control: How the Media Sustain Authoritarian Rule in China." *Comparative Political Studies* 44(4):436–67.

Stora Enso. 2009. "Planting for Our Future: Sustainability Performance 2009." Helsinki: Stora Enso.

Stora Enso. 2012. "Rethink." Volume 3. Helsinki: Stora Enso.

Strathern, Marilyn. 2000. *Audit Cultures: Anthropological Studies in Accountability, Ethics, and the Academy*. London New York: Routledge.

Strauss, Julia C. 2009. "Forestry Reform and the Transformation of State Capacity in Fin-De-Siècle China." *Journal of Asian Studies* 68(4):1163–88.

Streeck, Wolfgang. 2009. *Re-Forming Capitalism: Institutional Change in the German Political Economy*. Oxford: Oxford University Press.

Sudwind and UCM Jakarta. 2004. "Research on Working & Living Conditions of Women in Export Processing Zones (Epz) and Sweatshops in Indonesia": http://digitalcommons. ilr.cornell.edu/cgi/viewcontent.cgi?article=2070&context=globaldocs.

Sum, Ngai-Ling, and Ngai Pun. 2005. "Globalization and Paradoxes of Ethical Transnational Production: Code of Conduct in a Chinese Workplace." *Competition and Change* 9(2):181–200.

Sumaila, Ussif Rashid, J Alder, and Heather Keith. 2006. "Global Scope and Economics of Illegal Fishing." *Marine Policy* 30(6):696–703.

Sun, Xiufang, Nian Cheng, and Kerstin Canby. 2005. "China's Forest Product Exports: An Overview of Trends by Segment and Destinations." Washington, DC: Forest Trends.

Sun, Xiufang, Liqun Wang, and Zhenbin Gu. 2004. "A Brief Overview of China's Timber Market System." *International Forestry Review* 6(3–4):221–6.

Sun, Yanfei, and Dingxin Zhao. 2008. "Environmental Campaigns." Pp. 145–62 in *Popular Protest in China*, edited by Kevin J. O'Brien. Cambridge: Harvard University Press.

Sunderlin, William, Ananda Artono, Sri Palupi, Rochyana, and Ellya Susanti. 1990. "Social Equity and Social Forestry in Java Preliminary Findings from Four Case Studies." Social Forestry Network, paper 10a, https://www.odi.org/sites/odi.org.uk/ files/odi-assets/publications-opinion-files/962.pdf, accessed July 28, 2013.

Suwarni, Yuli Tri. 2009. "Ownership Dispute: Court Ruling Saves Garment Workers." *The Jakarta Post* January 13, 2009.

Synnott, Timothy. 2005. "Some Notes on the Early Years of FSC." https://web.archive. org/web/20060822135033/ http://www.fsc.org/keepout/en/content_areas/45/2/files/ FSC_FoundingNotes.doc, accessed November 2, 2006.

Szudy, Betty, Dara O'Rourke, and Garrett Brown. 2003. "Developing an Action-Based Health and Safety Training Project in Southern China." *International Journal of Occupational and Environmental Health* 9:357–67.

Tacconi, Luca (Ed.). 2007. *Illegal Logging: Law Enforcement, Livelihoods and the Timber Trade*. London: Earthscan.

Tacconi, Luca, Krystof Obidzinski, and Ferdinandus Agung. 2004. "Learning Lessons to Promote Forest Certification and Control Illegal Logging in Indonesia." Bogor, Indonesia: Center for International Forestry Research.

Tampe, Maja. Forthcoming. "Leveraging the Vertical: The Contested Dynamics of Sustainability Standards and Labour in Global Production Networks." *British Journal of Industrial Relations*.

Tarrow, Sidney. 2005. *The New Transnational Activism*. New York: Cambridge University Press.

Taylor, J. Gary, and Patricia J. Scharlin. 2004. *Smart Alliance: How a Global Corporation and Environmental Activists Transformed a Tarnished Brand*. New Haven: Yale University Press.

Tempo. 2012. "Hartati Murdaya's Powers in the Forestry Business." *Tempo* July 24, 2012.

Thauer, Christian R. 2014. *The Managerial Sources of Corporate Social Responsibility: The Spread of Global Standards*. New York: Cambridge University Press.

The Asia Health and Safety Training Project. 2003. "Training Activists in Indonesia." Final report, http://mhssn.igc.org/Indonesia-finalreport.pdf.

The Globe and Mail. 2012. "Co-Founder Kai Kit Poon Exits Role at Sino-Forest." *The Globe and Mail* (October 10, 2012. https://www.theglobeandmail.com/globe-investor/co-founder-kai-kit-poon-exits-role-at-sino-forest/article4601010/).

Thee, Kian Wie. 2009. "The Development of Labour-Intensive Garment Manufacturing in Indonesia." *Journal of Contemporary Asia* 39(4):562–78.

Theuws, Martje, Mariette van Huijstee, Pauline Overeem, Jos van Seters, and Tessel Pauli. 2013. "Fatal Fashion: Analysis of Recent Factory Fires in Pakistan and Bangladesh: A Call to Protect and Respect Garment Workers' Lives." Amsterdam: Centre for Research on Multinational Corporations (SOMO) and Clean Clothes Campaign.

Tim Kecil. 2007. "Draft: Sistem Verifikasi Legalitas Kayu—Lampiran 6." Records of working group member.

Timberland. 2009. "Q3 2009 Factory Disclosure." https://www.yumpu.com/en/document/view/50096329/q3-2009-factory-list-formatted-timberland-responsibility, accessed July 31, 2015.

Tjandraningsih, Indrasari, and Hari Nugroho. 2008. "The Flexibility Regime and Organised Labour in Indonesia." *Labour and Management in Development* 9:1–14.

Toffel, Michael W., Jodi L. Short, and Melissa Ouellet. 2015. "Codes in Context: How States, Markets, and Civil Society Shape Adherence to Global Labor Standards." *Regulation & Governance* 9(3):205–23.

Tollefson, Chris, Fred Gale, and David Haley. 2008. *Setting the Standard: Certification, Governance, and the Forest Stewardship Council* Vancouver: University of British Columbia Press.

Trac, Christine Jane, Stevan Harrell, Thomas M. Hinckley, and Amanda C. Henck. 2007. "Reforestation Programs in Southwest China: Reported Success, Observed Failure, and the Reasons Why." *Journal of Mountain Science* 4(4):275–92.

Trubek, David M., and Louise G. Trubek. 2007. "New Governance and Legal Regulation: Complementarity, Rivalry or Transformation." *Columbia Journal of European Law* 13:539–64.

Tsing, Anna L. 2005. *Friction: An Ethnography of Global Connection.* Princeton: Princeton University Press.

Tully, Stephanie M., and Russell S. Winer. 2014. "The Role of the Beneficiary in Willingness to Pay for Socially Responsible Products: A Meta-Analysis." *Journal of Retailing* 90(2):255–74.

Tuohinen, Petteri. 2009. "Chinese Farmers Lose Land to Stora Enso Tree Plantations." *Helsingin Sanomat* April 26, 2009.

Tysiachniouk, Maria S. 2012. *Transnational Governance through Private Authority: The Case of the Forest Stewardship Council Certification in Russia.* Wageningen: Wageningen Academic Publishers.

U.S. Consulate General. 2009. "Guangxi Snapshot: Local Volunteer Association Flourishing." Cable from U.S. Consulate in Guangzhou, December 30, 2009, https://wikileaks.org/plusd/cables/09GUANGZHOU716_a.html, accessed June 10, 2016.

U.S. Department of Justice. 2012. "Gibson Guitar Corp. Agrees to Resolve Investigation into Lacey Act Violations." Press release of Aug. 6, 2012, https://www.justice.gov/opa/pr/gibson-guitar-corp-agrees-resolve-investigation-lacey-act-violations, accessed May 19, 2017.

U.S. State Department. 2008. "Human Rights Report: Indonesia."

UN Working Group on Business and Human Rights. 2016. "Guidance on National Action Plans on Business and Human Rights." Geneva: United Nations.

Underal, Arild. 2002. "One Question, Two Answers." Pp. 3–44 in *Environmental Regime Effectiveness: Confronting Theory with Evidence*, edited by Edward L. Miles, Arild Underal, Steinar Andresen, Jørgen Wettestad, Jon Birgir Skjærseth, and Elaine M. Carlin. Cambridge, MA: MIT Press.

United Nations Development Program. 2012. "Stora Enso Guangxi Forest and Industrial Project: Summary Integrated Environmental and Social Impact Analysis." New York: UNDP, http://assets.storaenso.com/se/renewablepackaging/Documents/UNDP%20ESIA%20report.pdf, accessed June 10, 2016.

United Nations Environment Programme. 2011. "Sustaining Forests: Investing in Our Common Future." Nairobi: UNEP Policy Series, Ecosystem Management, Issue 5, August 2011.

United Nations Office of the High Commissioner on Human Rights. 2011. "Guiding Principles on Business and Human Rights: Implementing the United Nations 'Protect, Respect and Remedy' Framework." New York and Geneva: United Nations.

United Students Against Sweatshops. 2005. "Action Alert on PT Victoria." April 6, 2005.

USDA Foreign Agricultural Service. 2009. "China's Forestry Resource Inventory." Washington, DC: GAIN Report Number CH9132, Global Agricultural Research Network.

Van Agtmael, Antoine 2007. *The Emerging Markets Century: How a New Breed of World-Class Companies Is Overtaking the World*. New York: Free Press.

Van Assen, Bart Willem. 2005. "Diamond Raya Timber Concession: Diamonds Are Forever?" Pp. 303–14 in *In Search of Excellence: Exemplary Forest Management in Asia and the Pacific*, edited by Patrick B. Durst, Chris Brown, Henrylito D. Tacio, and Miyuki Ishikawa. Bangkok: Food and Agriculture Organization of the United Nations (FAO).

Van der Vist, Leo, and Simche Heringa. 2010. "Impacts of the Dutch Economy on Indigenous Peoples: The Import of Soy from Brazil and Tropical Timber from Indonesia and Malaysia." Amsterdam: Netherland Centre for Indigenous Peoples, http://www.aidenvironment.org/media/uploads/documents/Impact_of_the_Dutch_Economy_on_Indigenous_Peoples.pdf.

Van Rooij, Benjamin, and Lesley K. McAllister. 2014. "Environmental Challenges in Middle-Income Countries: A Comparison of Enforcement in Brazil, China, Indonesia, and Mexico." Pp. 288–308 in *Law and Development in Middle-Income Countries*, edited by Randall Peerenboom and Tom Ginsburg. New York: Cambridge University Press.

Van Rooij, Benjamin, Rachel E Stern, and Kathinka Fürst. 2016. "The Authoritarian Logic of Regulatory Pluralism: Understanding China's New Environmental Actors." *Regulation & Governance* 10(1):3–13.

Vandenbergh, Michael P. 2007. "The New Wal-Mart Effect: The Role of Private Contracting in Global Governance." *UCLA Law Review* 54:913–70.

Vandergeest, Peter. 2007. "Certification and Communities: Alternatives for Regulating the Environmental and Social Impacts of Shrimp Farming." *World Development* 35(7):1152–71.

Varangis, Panos, Rachel Crossley, and Carlos Primo Braga. 1995. "Is There a Commercial Case for Tropical Timber Certification?" *World Bank Policy Research Working Paper* (1479).

Varley, Pamela (Ed.). 1998. *The Sweatshop Quandary: Corporate Responsibility on the Global Frontier*. Washington, DC: Investor Responsibility Research Center.

Vayda, Andrew P., and Bradley B. Walters. 1999. "Against Political Ecology." *Human Ecology* 27(1):167–79.

Verbruggen, Paul. 2013. "Gorillas in the Closet? Public and Private Actors in the Enforcement of Transnational Private Regulation." *Regulation & Governance* 7(4):512–32.

Verbruggen, Paul, and Tetty Havinga. 2016. "How Domestic State Actors Influence Transnational Private Food Safety Governance: A Case of Regulatory Enrolment." Paper presented at the workshop on Transnational Business Governance Interactions, May 2016, Toronto.

Verite. 2012. "For Workers' Benefit: Solving Overtime Problems in Chinese Factories": White Paper, February 2012. Verite.

Vickers, Adrian. 2005. *A History of Modern Indonesia*. Cambridge: Cambridge University Press.

Vietnam Labor Watch. 1997. "Nike Labor Practices in Vietnam." Vietnam Labor Watch, March 20, 1997. http://www.saigon.com/nike/reports/report1.html.

Vogel, David. 1978. *Lobbying the Corporation: Citizen Challenges to Business Authority*. New York: Basic Books.

Vogel, David. 1995. *Trading Up: Consumer and Environmental Regulation in a Global Economy*. Cambridge, MA: Harvard University Press.

Vogel, David. 2005. *The Market for Virtue: The Potential and Limits of Corporate Social Responsibility*. New York: Brookings Institution Press.

Vogel, David. 2008. "Private Global Business Regulation." *Annual Review of Political Science* 11:261–82.

Vogel, David. 2012. *The Politics of Precaution: Regulating Health, Safety, and Environmental Risks in Europe and the United States*: Princeton University Press.

Vogel, David, and Robert A. Kagan. 2004. "Dynamics of Regulatory Change: How Globalization Affects National Regulatory Policies." Berkeley: University of California Press.

Von Benda-Beckmann, Franz. 1989. "Scape-Goat and Magic Charm: Law in Development Theory and Practice." *Journal of Legal Pluralism* 21(28):129–48.

Von Benda-Beckmann, Franz, and Keebet von Benda-Beckmann. 2009. "Contested Spaces of Authority in Indonesia." Pp. 115–35 in *Spatializing Law: An Anthropological Geography of Law in Society*, edited by Franz von Benda-Beckmann, Keebet von Benda-Beckmann, and Anne Griffiths. London: Ashgate Publishing.

Wade, Robert. 1992. *Governing the Market: Economic Theory and the Role of Government in East Asian Industrialization*. Princeton, NJ: Princeton University Press.

Wagner, Owen. 2007. "China's Wood Processing Sector and Re-Exports of Imported US Wood Materials." USDA Foreign Agricultural Service, GAIN Report.

Walker, Kathy Le Mons. 2008. "From Covert to Overt: Everyday Peasant Politics in China and the Implications for Transnational Agrarian Movements." *Journal of Agrarian Change* 8(2–3):462–88.

Wall Street Journal. 2014. "Yue Yuen Strike Is Estimated to Cost $60 Million." *Wall Street Journal* April 28, 2014.

Walsh, Declan, and Steven Greenhouse. 2012. "Certified Safe, a Factory in Karachi Still Quickly Burned." *New York Times* December 7, 2012.

Wang, Xiaobei, Elisa Scalise, and Renee Giovarelli. 2012. "Ensuring That Poor Rural Women Benefit from Forestland Reforms in China: Fieldwork Findings and Policy Recommendations." Seattle: LANDESA Rural Development Institute.

Ward, Halina and Mai-Lan Ha. 2012. *Voluntary Social and Environmental Standards and Public Governance.* London and Oakland, CA: Foundation for Democracy and Sustainable Development and the Pacific Institute. http://www.fdsd.org/site/wp-content/uploads/2014/11/pacinst-standards-and-public-governance-review-nov-2012.pdf, accessed June 17, 2017.

Warouw, Nicolaas. 2008. "Industrial Workers in Transition: Women's Experiences of Factory Work in Tangerang." Pp. 105–19 in *Women and Work in Indonesia*, edited by Michele Ford and Lyn Parker. London: Routledge.

Watts, Michael. 2004. "Resource Curse? Governmentality, Oil and Power in the Niger Delta, Nigeria." *Geopolitics* 9(1):50–80.

WE Fashion. 2009. "We Care: CSR Report 2009." https://www.wefashion.nl/on/demandware.static/-/Library-Sites-WE-Default/default/dwab6fca5f/Static%20pages/corporate/csr/NL/we-care-csr-report-2009-en-nl.pdf.

WE Fashion. 2010. "We Care: CSR Report 2010." https://www.wefashion.de/on/demandware.static/-/Library-Sites-WE-Default/default/dwca88b8fb/Static%20pages/corporate/csr/DE/we-care-csr-report-2010-de-de.pdf.

WE Fashion. 2012. "We Care: CSR Update 2011–2012." https://www.wefashion.nl/on/demandware.static/-/Library-Sites-WE-Default/default/dw2e1dc127/Static%20pages/corporate/csr/NL/we-care-csr-report-2011-2012-en-nl.pdf.

WE Fashion. 2013. "We Care: CSR Update 2013." https://www.wefashion.nl/on/demandware.static/-/Library-Sites-WE-Default/default/dwb2acdd80/Static%20pages/corporate/csr/NL/we-care-csr-report-2013-en.pdf.

Weil, David. 2014. *The Fissured Workplace.* Cambridge: Harvard University Press.

Weiss, Robert S. 1995. *Learning from Strangers: The Art and Method of Qualitative Interview Studies.* New York: Free Press.

Wellesley, Laura. 2014. "Trade in Illegal Timber: The Response in China." London: Chatham House, the Royal Institute of International Affairs.

Wessells, Cathy R., Kevern Cochrane, Carolyn Deere, Paul Wallis, and Rolf Willman. 2001. "Product Certification and Ecolabelling for Fisheries Sustainability." Rome: Food & Agriculture Organization of the United Nations.

Western, Bruce. 1998. "Institutions and the Labor Market." Pp. 224–43 in *The New Institutionalism in Sociology*, edited by Mary C. Brinton and Victor Nee. Stanford: Stanford University Press.

White, Andy, Xiufang Sun, Kerstin Canby, Jintao Xu, Christopher Barr, Eugenia Katsigris, Gary Bull, Christian Cossalter, and Sten Nilsson. 2006. "China and the Global Market for Forest Products: Transforming Trade to Benefit Forests and Livelihoods." Washington, DC: Forest Trends.

White, Ben, Saturnino M Borras Jr, Ruth Hall, Ian Scoones, and Wendy Wolford. 2012. "The New Enclosures: Critical Perspectives on Corporate Land Deals." *Journal of Peasant Studies* 39(3–4):619–47.

Wiersum, K. Freerk, and Birgit H.M. Elands. 2013. "Opinions on Legality Principles Considered in the FLEGT/VPA Policy in Ghana and Indonesia." *Forest Policy and Economics* 32:14–22.

Williams, R.A. 2015. "Mitigating Biodiversity Concerns in Eucalyptus Plantations Located in South China." *Journal of Biosciences and Medicines* 3:1–8.

Wolf, Diane Lauren. 1992. *Factory Daughers: Gender, Household Dynamics, and Rural Industrialization in Java*. Berkeley: University of California Press.

Wolfe, Allis Rosenberg. 1975. "Women, Consumerism, and the National Consumers' League in the Progressive Era, 1900–1923." *Labor History* 16(3):378–92.

Wong, Chun Han. 2015. "China Detains Labor Activists as Authorities Sweep Industrial Hub." *The Wall Street Journal* (December 7, 2015).

Wong, Edward. 2011. "Canny Villagers Grasp Keys to Loosen China's Muzzle." *New York Times* (December 22, 2011).

Wood, Stepan, Kenneth W. Abbott, Julia Black, Burkard Eberlein, and Errol Meidinger. 2015. "The Interactive Dynamics of Transnational Business Governance: A Challenge for Transnational Legal Theory." *Transnational Legal Theory* 6(2): 333–69.

Worker Rights Consortium. 2003a. "Assessment Re PT Dae Joo Leports (Indonesia)." Worker Rights Consortium, Washington, DC.

Worker Rights Consortium. 2003b. "Assessment Re PT Kolon Langgeng (Indonesia)." Worker Rights Consortium, Washington, DC.

Worker Rights Consortium. 2004a. "Assessment Re PT Panarub (Indonesia)." Washington, DC: Worker Rights Consortium.

Worker Rights Consortium. 2004b. "Update on PT Dae Joo Leports."

Worker Rights Consortium. 2006a. "Case Summary: Gina Form Bra (Thailand)." Washington, DC: Worker Rights Consortium, http://digitalcommons.ilr.cornell. edu/cgi/viewcontent.cgi?article=1348&context=globaldocs, accessed October 27, 2016.

Worker Rights Consortium. 2006b. "The Designated Suppliers Program—Revised." Washington, DC: Worker Rights Consortium, http://digitalcommons.ilr.cornell. edu/cgi/viewcontent.cgi?article=1204&context=globaldocs.

Worker Rights Consortium. 2006c. "PT Panarub." Worker Rights Consortium, update of February 15, 2006.

Worker Rights Consortium. 2006d. "Update on Code of Conduct Violations at PT Panarub (Indonesia)." Washington, DC: Worker Rights Consortium.

Worker Rights Consortium. 2008. "Assessment Re PT Mulia Knitting (Indonesia)." Worker Rights Consortium, Washington, DC.

Worker Rights Consortium. 2011. "Factory Update: Kwangduk Langgeng (Indonesia) (Formerly, Kolon Langgeng)." WRC, March 9, 2011.

Worker Rights Consortium. 2012. "PT Kizone (Indonesia): Findings, Recommendations, and Status." Washington, DC: Worker Rights Consortium.

Worker Rights Consortium. 2013. "Stealing from the Poor: Wage Theft in the Haitian Apparel Industry." Washington, DC: Worker Rights Consortium.

World Bank. 2010. "Indonesia Jobs Report: Towards Better Jobs and Security for All." World Bank.

World Rainforest Movement. no date. "Another Death at Perhutani's Hands: Villager Shot in East Java Teak Forest." World Rainforest Movement, http://wrm.org.uy/oldsite/countries/Indonesia/Killing_Villagers.html, accessed Aug. 8, 2014.

Wright, Tom, and Jim Carlton. 2007. "FSC's 'Green' Label for Wood Products Gets Growing Pains." *Wall Street Journal* October 30, 2007.

WWD. 1996. "Reich Says Kathie Lee Joining His Campaign against Sweatshops." *WWD* May 24, pp. 1–2.

WWF-Global. 2006. "WWF Welcomes Launch of Forest Stewardship Council in China." WWF-Global, April 7, 2006, http://wwf.panda.org/wwf_news/?66040/WWF-welcomes-launch-of-Forest-Stewardship-Council-in-China, accessed June 10, 2016.

WWF-Global. 2008. "Over 1 Million Ha of FSC-Certified Forests Owned by GFTN-China Participants." WWF-Global, http://wwf.panda.org/wwf_news/?153581/Over-1-million-ha-of-FSC-Certified-Forests-Owned-by-GFTN-China-Participants, accessed June 10, 2016.

WWF-UK. 2011. "What Wood You Choose? Tracking Forest Products on Sale in the UK Back to Their Forest Source." Godalming, Surrey, UK: WWF-UK.

Xin, Xin. 2009. "The Road to Urbanization." *China Daily* April 2, 2009, http://www.chinatoday.com.cn/ctenglish/se/txt/2009-04/02/content_189242.htm.

Xinhua. 2011. "NE China Province Bans Logging in China's Largest Forest for 10 Years." *Xinxua News Service*, January 10, 2011, http://en.people.cn/90001/90776/90882/7255762.html, accessed June 10, 2016.

Xinhua. 2015. "China Bans Commercial Logging in NE Forests." Xinhua News Service, March 26, 2015. http://news.xinhuanet.com/english/2015-03/26/c_134100703.htm.

Xu, Jintao. 2013. "State Forest Reform in Northeastern China: Issues and Options." PROFOR Working Paper. Washington, DC: Program on Forests (PROFOR).

Xu, Jintao, and Xuemei Jiang. 2009. "Collective Forest Tenure Reform in China: Outcomes and Implications." Paper for the World Bank Conference on Land Governance, https://www.researchgate.net/publication/237524828_Collective_Forest_Tenure_Reform_in_China_Outcomes_and_Implications.

Yang, Dennis Tao. 1997. "China's Land Arrangements and Rural Labor Mobility." *China Economic Review* 8(2):101–15.

Yang, Dennis Tao, Vivian Weijia Chen, and Ryan Monarch. 2010. "Rising Wages: Has China Lost Its Global Labor Advantage?" *Pacific Economic Review* 15(4):482–504.

Yang, Ling. 2014. "The Politics of Transnational Labor Certification in the Chinese Export Toy Industry." *Academy of Management Proceedings* 2014(1).

Yao, Yang. 2014. "Green Timber Preferred Overseas but Not Locally." *China Daily* February 19, 2014.

Yap, S.K. 2010. "Forest Management and Stump-to-Forest Gate Chain of Custody Compliance Certification Evaluation Report for the Wuhua Eucalyptus Forest, under the Management of Wuhua County Senhui Forest Development Co., Ltd." Scientific Certification Systems, Certificate No. SCS-FM/COC-00122P, http://fsc.force.com/servlet/servlet.FileDownload?file=00P4000000KBDT2EAP, accessed June 10, 2016.

Yasmi, Y., J. Guernier, and C.J.P. Colfer. 2009. "Positive and Negative Aspects of Forestry Conflict: Lessons from a Decentralized Forest Management in Indonesia." *International Forestry Review* 11(1):98–110.

Bibliography

Yee, Wai-Hang, Carlos Wing-Hung Lo, and Shui-Yan Tang. 2013. "Assessing Ecological Modernization in China: Stakeholder Demands and Corporate Environmental Management Practices in Guangdong Province." *The China Quarterly* 213:101–29.

Yeung, Henry Wai-chung, and Neil M. Coe. 2015. "Toward a Dynamic Theory of Global Production Networks." *Economic Geography* 91(1):29–58.

Yin, Runsheng, Jintao Xu, and Zhou Li. 2003. "Building Institutions for Markets: Experiences and Lessons from China's Rural Forest Sector." *Environment, Development and Sustainability* 5(3–4):333–51.

Yong, Kwek Ping. 2013. *Due Diligence in China: Beyond the Checklists*. Singapore: Wiley.

Yu, Xiaomin. 2008a. "Impacts of Corporate Code of Conduct on Labor Standards: A Case Study of Reebok's Athletic Footwear Supplier Factory in China." *Journal of Business Ethics* 81(3):513–29.

Yu, Xiaomin. 2008b. "Workplace Democracy in China's Foreign-Funded Enterprises: A Multilevel Case Study of Employee Representation." *Economic and Industrial Democracy* 29(2):274–300.

Yue Yuen Industrial (Holdings) Limited. 2014. "2013 Annual Report." Hong Kong, http://www.yueyuen.com/index.php/en/about-us-7/investor-annos/902-2014-04-24-annual-report-2013.

Zeitlin, Jonathan. 2011. "Pragmatic Transnationalism: Governance across Borders in the Global Economy." *Socio-Economic Review* 9(1):187–206.

Zelizer, Viviana. 2013. *Economic Lives: How Culture Shapes the Economy*. Princeton: Princeton University Press.

Zhan, Shaohua, and Joel Andreas. 2015. "Beyond the Countryside: Hukou Reform and Agrarian Capitalism in China." Paper for a conference on "Land Grabbing, Conflict and Agrarian-Environmental Transformations: Perspectives from East and Southeast Asia," Chang Mai University, June 2015.

Zhang, Qian Forrest, and John A. Donaldson. 2013. "China's Agrarian Reform and the Privatization of Land: A Contrarian View." *Journal of Contemporary China* 22(80): 255–72.

Zhang, Yaoqi, and Shashi Kant. 2005. "Collective Forests and Forestland: Physical Asset Rights Versus Economic Rights." Pp. 249–69 in *Developmental Dilemmas: Land Reform and Institutional Change in China*, edited by Peter Ho. New York: Routledge.

Zhao, Jingzhu, Dongming Xie, Danyin Wang, and Hongbing Deng. 2011. "Current Status and Problems in Certification of Sustainable Forest Management in China." *Environmental Management* 48(6):1086–94.

Zhou, Chao, and Dan Banik. 2014. "Access to Justice and Social Unrest in China's Countryside: Disputes on Land Acquisition and Compensation." *Hague Journal on the Rule of Law* 6(02):254–75.

Zhou, Wen. 2012. "Transnational Paper and Pulp: The Production of Eucalyptus Plantations in China and Laos." Thesis, Master of Science in Environmental Change and Management, University of Oxford.

Zong, Yongqiang, and Xiqing Chen. 2000. "The 1998 Flood on the Yangtze, China." *Natural Hazards* 22(2):165–84.

Index

(Ch) and (In) after an entry refer to China and Indonesia, respectively. Figures and tables are indicated with an italicized page locator.

Index

Index

Index

Index